S0-AAZ-566

Ninth Edition

Contemporary American Speeches

Richard L. Johannesen
Northern Illinois University

R. R. Allen
University of Wisconsin

Wil A. Linkugel
University of Kansas

Ferald J. Bryan
Northern Illinois University

KENDALL/HUNT PUBLISHING COMPANY
4050 Westmark Drive   Dubuque, Iowa 52002

Cover image courtesy of Corel.

Copyright © 1965, 1969, 1972 by Wadsworth Publishing Company, Inc.

Copyright © 1978, 1982, 1988, 1992, 1997, 2000 by Kendall/Hunt Publishing Company

Library of Congress Catalog Card Number: 99-69740

ISBN 978-0-7872-5805-4

All rights reserved. No part of this publication may be reproduced,
stored in a retrieval system, or transmitted, in any form or by any
means, electronic, mechanical, photocopying, recording, or otherwise,
without the prior written permission of the copyright owner.

Printed in the United States of America
10 9 8 7 6 5 4 3

Contents

Alternate Topical Contents

Note: Asterisked speeches are "paired" speeches that present differing views on essentially the same general topic.

Military and Foreign Policy ◆

Economic and Social Issues ◆

Concerns of Women ◆

Concerns of Minorities ◆

The Political Process ◆

Technology and the Environment ◆

Contemporary Morals and Values ◆

CD-ROM Speeches

 # Preface

In producing a ninth edition of *Contemporary American Speeches,* we again faced the critical question of which speeches to retain and which ones to replace. As we have done with earlier editions, we approached this problem by surveying as many users of the previous editions as we could, asking them to tell us which speeches they found especially useful. We have also been guided by our own teaching experience, noting those addresses that generated student discussion and insight.

This book can serve as a core textbook in courses such as Contemporary Public Address and Contemporary Speakers and Speeches. We have continued to emphasize speech forms, but in this edition more than in previous editions, we have included speeches by well-known speakers. And always we have sought speeches that typify current public scrutiny of some of society's most pressing questions. The speech forms themselves assure coverage of the spectrum of contemporary public address. Knowledge, facts, values, problems, and policies have always been rhetoric's essence. At the same time, ceremonial address continues to be a vital form for social cohesion.

Contemporary

For our purpose, *contemporary* includes the sixties, seventies, and eighties with primary emphasis on the nineties. Nine of the speeches in this edition are from the sixties, seventies, and eighties, and thirty are from the nineties. Thirty-six percent of the speeches are new to this edition. Three speeches have continued through all nine editions: Martin Luther King's "I Have a Dream," Douglas MacArthur's "Farewell to the Cadets," and John F. Kennedy's "Inaugural Address."

Diversity

We have continued the diversity of "voices" represented in the eighth edition. Certainly the political spectra of Democrat-Republican and liberal-conservative are represented. Thirty-three percent of the speakers are women. Twenty-six percent of the speakers are African American, Chinese American, Hispanic/Latino(a) American, and Native American.

Differing Viewpoints

Again we have "paired" speeches that present differing viewpoints on essentially the same general topic: Bill Clinton and Joe Lieberman on Clinton's public deception in the Lewinsky Affair; Russell Train and Virginia Postrel on values central to the environmental movement; Diane Ravitch and Molefi Asante on multi-culturalism in education; Faye Wattleton and Jerry Falwell on legalized abortion; and Charlton Heston and Bill Bradley on gun control.

Introductory Headnotes

The introductory headnotes that precede each speech provide background information and pose questions to aid in evaluation. In these headnotes we undertake briefly our own analysis of a speech to illustrate a few of the ways in which a rhetorical critic might describe, interpret, and evaluate important dimensions of the speech.

Chapter Updates

In addition to the general criteria for assessing speeches discussed in Chapter Two, each subsequent chapter essay develops criteria useful in exploring and evaluating that particular form of public speaking. The suggestions "For Further Reading" in each chapter have been updated.

A significant addition in Chapter One is a lengthy section on diverse public speaking traditions as influenced by culture and gender. Chapter Two contains important additions on narration as a rhetorical technique and on ideological criticism as a perspective for evaluation. The language in all chapters has been changed in places to increase clarity.

CD-ROM

An exciting feature new to this edition is the inclusion of a dual platform CD-ROM with each book. The CD-ROM contains 42 notable speeches from previous editions. By making the speeches (along with introductory comments) available on CD-ROM, we have been able to update the new edition, and still provide some of the "best of the best" speeches.

Web Site

A web site provides selected current speeches along with comments from the authors. For access to this site, go to *www.kendallhunt.com* and click on College Division Catalog→Johannesen→ *Contemporary American Speeches.*

Acknowledgments

We again wish to acknowledge our indebtedness to the many people and sources who have given us permission to reprint speeches in this book. *Vital Speeches of the Day* continues to be an important source for representative speeches on current issues. We are also grateful for the recommendations that have been so thoughtfully provided by colleagues.

R. L. J.

R. R. A.

W. A. L.

F. J. B.

Chapter One

Why Study Speeches?

The primary purpose of *Contemporary American Speeches* is to present a collection of speeches for student analysis and evaluation. We hope that this chapter will stimulate your thinking about the importance of such study in your own intellectual life.

We Study Speeches to Increase Our Knowledge of Humanity

One of the purposes of a college education is to encourage students to ponder the nature of their own humanity. In most degree programs, students are encouraged to engage in liberal studies as a complement to the sequence of professional courses that leads to specialized careers. A professional person is, after all, a person: a lawyer is a person who practices law, a teacher is a person who teaches, a doctor is a person who practices medicine, a scientist is a person who studies the physical world in which we live. Through liberal studies, students are encouraged to develop insights regarding the potentialities and limitations of the human condition. Through such knowledge, a system of values should emerge that provides the basis for future decisions, both professional and personal.

Students may take varied paths in their efforts to understand what it means to be human. Each liberal study holds such promise—and rightfully so. Nothing thought or made or done by people is alien to the student in search of human understanding. Emerson said: "Raphael paints wisdom; Handel sings it; Phidias carves it; Shakespeare writes it; Wren builds it; Columbus sails it; Luther preaches it; Washington arms it; Watt mechanizes it." In each of these studies, students may find evidence of the creative struggle of human beings with their environment. And from each of these studies, students may gain insights into their own lives.

In the liberal arts tradition, speeches deserve to be studied because they are a unique form of human expression. No other artifact of social life reflects the same exact process. A painting encompasses the elements of thought and form; yet a speech is composed of language. A poem embraces thought, language, and form; yet a speech is conveyed by sound. Theatre makes use of thought, language, form, and sound; yet a speech is at once more urgent and real, more literal and spontaneous. A speech is a unique product of human creativity; it calls for special understanding as does a painting or a poem, a statue or a scroll.

Speeches have a quality that makes them especially deserving of study by students in search of human understanding. They are the product of human beings in dynamic confrontation with ideas and audiences. In speeches, students will find men and women articulating the noble ideals of our civilization and making enlightened judgments on the great social, moral, and political issues of our own and other times. In speeches, students will also find men and women degrading our common humanity and concocting themes of hatred and bigotry. In speeches, the potentialities and limitations of the human condition are clearly reflected.

We Study Speeches to Derive Standards for the Critical Appraisal of Public Discourse

Few will question the claim that the quality of our public dialogue is not what it might be. In lecture halls, we have grown accustomed to speakers who are dull, disorganized, and unclear. In chambers of social decisionmaking, we have come to accept as the norm underdeveloped ideas expressed in careless language and sloppy speech. And even at moments of public ceremony, we expect speeches that are trite and mundane when what is called for is an inspiring rearticulation of our social purpose and identity.

As members of audiences, we have come to demand too little of those who address us. Through the study of speeches, we may develop higher standards for the public dialogue. We may come to demand more of those who address us, both in terms of the merit of their ideas and their means of public expression.

The study of speeches offers a broad familiarity with the crucial issues of humanity. Our communion with the past, the freedom of our citizens, the quality of our private and public life, our hopes for the future—all of these are evident in the public dialogue. Through an awareness of the significant issues of our own and other times, students may come to reject trivial issues and petty thoughts as unworthy of public attention.

Through the study of speeches, students may also acquire insights regarding the habits of intellect through which responsible speakers examine, test, and temper ideas. Through such knowledge, they may appraise the worth of a speaker's critical processes. They may test the sufficiency of the speaker's proof. They may deny the specious inference and the faulty deduction. They may reject simplistic answers to complex social questions.

But the enlightened critic must not stop here. Public discourse does not exist in a social vacuum. It is not soliloquy, but purposive address seeking to impart to its hearers some knowledge or interpretation, some value or course of action. Public discourse always seeks to influence the hearer and to change his or her behavior—whether cognitive or overt. If ideas are to have social utility, they must be transformed from private conceptions into meaningful public statements. Speakers must so develop and project their thoughts that direction is given to those who listen. They must choose from a complex of elements those most likely to give energy and vitality to their ideas in a particular public context.

Through the study of speeches, students will come to realize that speakers can adapt ideas to audiences in meaningful and socially productive ways. While recognizing the shortcomings of the public intellect, they will know that speakers have made complex ideas clear. While recognizing that speakers have exploited public greed and ignorance in achieving personal power, they will know that other speakers have fostered social excellence. While recognizing that speeches have embodied appeals to low motives and base instincts, they will know that oratory has sometimes inspired audiences to act in accord with the noble ideas of humanity.

The dimensions of rhetorical choice are numerous. In Chapter 2, you will be introduced to thirteen questions that will guide your study of the means speakers employ in rendering their ideas clear, persuasive, and memorable. As you apply these questions to speeches, you will develop an increased appreciation for the artistry which undergirds effective public communication. As you witness speakers conveying the essence of significant thoughts with skill and integrity, you will have cause to reject other speakers whose expressions are feeble, whose appeals are base, whose strategies are unethical, and whose purposes are suspect.

We Study Speeches to Enlarge and Deepen Our Understanding of Rhetorical Theory

The student of speech, faced with a body of precepts set forth in a contemporary basic public speaking textbook, will often fail to assign importance to the ideas expressed. The text, it may seem, is too firm in its adherence to inviolate rules, too committed to the perpetuation of useless names and distinctions, and too verbose in the expression of common sense. Any body of principles divorced from the context that gave it being may seem drab and useless. But if these principles are viewed in their proper context, they tend to become meaningful and even intellectually stimulating.

Rhetorical theory was born of the attempt of people to systematize their observations of the purposive and dynamic public interactions of other people. In the fifth century B.C. the first body of rhetorical precepts emerged from Corax's observations of the attempts of his fellow citizens of Syracuse to give social order to a society newly emerged from tyranny. In the centuries that followed, countless other people recorded their observations of identifiable speech principles. While those who followed owed a great debt to those who preceded them, each generation of theorists sought to redefine and reconceptualize the art of speaking in a manner consistent with their own perceptions of public address as it occurred in their own cultures and in their own times.

Authors of modern public speaking textbooks must also acknowledge their debt to the great rhetorical tradition. Their task, however, is not the perpetuation of "the intellectual faults of eminent men." Rather, they seek to test and temper the principles of the art of public communication. They must blend with the old the particular insights of the new—insights gleaned from the scholarship of their own and related disciplines, insights gathered from their own judicious observation of public discourse. Building on the rhetorical philosophies of the past with a knowledge of the present, modern theorists seek to create not a memorial to the past but a structure consistent with the needs and realities of the present. Such work is vital and meaningful, not drab or devoid of intellectual stimulation.

Is it strange that what is bright with intellectual challenge in process often seems boring in product? Not really. The excitement of the intellectual search for precepts by one person is easily lost when relegated to a body of generalizations for the consumption of another. It is not that the theory is bad; it is just that theory alone, divorced from the world from which it was abstracted, is inadequate.

Would it not be best, then, for the student of speech to seek out his or her own precepts? Not really. The perceptive student, skilled in listening to popular instances of communication and afforded such great examples as Churchill, Roosevelt, and King could derive his or her own theory of speech. But at what expense of time? At what expense to progress? Each student would have to begin anew the quest for order and meaning, as helplessly alone as if no one else had ever walked the same path.

While the problem is not fully solved by presenting the student with the generalizations of another's mind, concisely arranged, neither is it fully solved by presenting the student with a body of speech masterpieces, past and present, with the caution to keep "an open mind and vigilant eye." The study of a public speaking textbook is, like the study of examples of public discourse, one important element in the training of the student of public speaking. Preference for one should not lead to a discarding of the other. A public speaking textbook is a body of generalizations drawn from the author's contemplation of the long tradition of rhetorical theory, the scholarship of the day, and his or her own perceptions of human communication. It exists not to inhibit but to stimulate. Intelligent students will put the precepts of a textbook to the pragmatic test of actual public life. They will realize, as did Quintilian, that "rhetoric would be a very easy and small matter, if it could be included in one short body of rules, but rules must generally be altered to suit the nature of each individual case, the time, the occasion, and the necessity itself. . . ." By testing the generalizations of a textbook in the light of real and varied instances of public discourse, students will learn to challenge, question, and compare and, ultimately, develop for themselves a theory of speech that is both comprehensive and personal.

We Study Speeches to Develop an Appreciation for Excellence in Public Address

In 1852, Chauncey Goodrich, Professor of Rhetoric at Yale College, reviewed his teaching philosophy in the preface to his work *Select British Eloquence.* He wrote:

> My object was not only to awaken in the minds of the class that love of genuine eloquence which is the surest pledge of success, but to aid them in catching the spirit of the authors read, and, by analyzing passages selected for the purpose, to initiate the pupil in those higher principles which (whether they were conscious of it or not) have always guided the great masters of the art, till he should learn the *unwritten* rules of oratory, which operate by a kind of instinct upon the mind, and are far more important than any that are found in the books.

This passage has merit today for students who would be more than followers of blueprints. It recommends that students develop an appreciation for excellence in public address, a love of eloquence, by looking beyond textbook principles to the unwritten rules of the art. It suggests the importance of developing a sense of the rightness, or the strength, or the felicity of a thought or an expression through exposure to speeches. Such an appreciation serves to inspire students to seek in their own works only the highest level of excellence.

Students who have come to acquire this appreciation for excellence will reject trivial subjects. They will understand that a concern for significant ideas has been at the heart of great oratory since ancient times. Demosthenes spoke for the freedom of a city. Churchill spoke for the survival of a nation. Roosevelt spoke for human freedom. Kennedy spoke for peace in a divided world. Rhetorical eminence presupposes worthy ideas to express, ideas that merit the attention and efforts of the speaker and the concern of the audience.

But rhetorical excellence also requires eloquence in expression. Given significant ideas, great public address demands an expression that renders the idea in a striking and compelling way, giving it life and vitality. Stephen Spender once wrote a poem called *I Think Continuously of Those Who Were Truly Great.* As public speakers, students may find great inspiration from the speeches of people who surpassed the ordinary and achieved new heights in skillful and effective communication.

The dimensions of rhetorical excellence are diverse. Some speakers are models of eminence in delivery. Jesse Jackson, Sr., to whom charisma is often attributed, is a model of both vocal and physical involvement and intensity. Barbara Jordan, who captured the spirit of the 1976 Democratic Convention, was known for her vocal precision and overall dynamism. Paul Harvey, with his distinctive oral style, has captivated generations of Americans via radio. Student speakers, finding inspiration in the delivery of able speakers, may seek in their own delivery the same sense of dynamism and involvement.

Students may also gain inspiration from those who use language in lively and memorable ways. The history of public discourse is rich with examples of language which illuminated thoughts in compelling ways: Roosevelt dispelled panic with the expression, "The only thing we have to fear is fear itself"; Churchill imparted strength with the expression, "This was their finest hour"; Kennedy inspired dedication with the expression, "Ask not what your country can do for you—ask what you can do for your country"; Martin Luther King generated hope with the expression, "I have a dream." Students who are exposed to eminence in language usage may acquire an intimate sense of the rightness, appropriateness, and artistry of language that will help them to give greater force to their own ideas.

In the study of speeches, students may also find excellence in ordering ideas, marshalling supporting materials, and enlisting the emotions of audiences. Having acquired an appreciation for eloquence, students may demand more of themselves and others at those moments when they give public expression to their ideas.

We Study Speeches to Broaden Our Understanding of Diverse Public Speaking Traditions within Our Society

The predominant tradition of rhetorical theory and public speaking practice in the United States is a heritage of the male-dominated cultures of ancient Greece and Rome and modern Europe. But there also exist in contemporary American society diverse but valuable and typically neglected public speaking traditions of various co-cultures and gender perspectives. As suggested earlier in this chapter, ideally rhetorical theory and practice should adopt and adapt the best of past major traditions, but be perceptive and flexible enough to learn lessons from, to appreciate insights of, various cultures and current contexts.

The four scholars who contributed the introduction to *Voices of Multicultural America* (pp. xi–xix), edited by Deborah Gillan Straub, sketch some of the diversity, and similarity, in public speaking traditions of the African American, Hispanic American, Asian American, and Native American co-cultures within American society. These scholars emphasize that within each of these co-cultures is further diversity of sub-cultural traditions and that statements about each co-culture must be taken as generalizations. For example, the Native American scholar cautions that "there is no such thing as 'Native American culture'." There is no "single, monolithic culture in which all 'Indians' look, act, and speak the same."

The length of a speech most preferred represents one variable in the co-cultural traditions. Within the general Native American tradition, shorter, succinct speeches are valued whereas within the Hispanic American tradition longer, elaborate speeches are valued. In the European American tradition as influenced by radio and television, the preferred length of speeches has diminished from well over one hour to the 20–30 minute range. The appropriate degree of audience participation with the speaker is another co-cultural variable. Within the Native American tradition, shouting or interruptions by the audience would not be appropriate. But in the African American public speaking tradition, it would not at all be unusual for audience members to engage in "call-response" positive reactions throughout the speech through such comments aloud as "that's right," "tell it," or "I hear you." While there is a British tradition of "heckling" speakers with negative comments during a speech, the European American tradition generally does not find audience interruptions (positive or negative) to be appropriate. The approved or disapproved role of women as public speakers represents a further co-cultural variable. The Hispanic tradition largely has excluded women from valued roles as public speakers advocating positions on public issues. But according to the Native American scholar, "women in most Native American cultures are not second-class citizens and have therefore always been the equal of men in all areas, including speechmaking." Up until recent decades, the male European American tradition trivialized, marginalized, even sometimes prohibited, women as public speakers.

In their textbook, *Public Speaking in a Diverse Society,* 2nd ed. (pp. 49–61), Patricia Kearney and Timothy Plax discuss the research on varied co-cultural styles of communication, especially as applied to public address. They do so at length for the following co-cultures: Euroamerican; African American; Latino/Latina American; Asian American; Native American; and Middle Eastern American. They, too, note that each co-culture has sub-cultures within it and caution that general summaries may not apply to particular individuals within a co-culture. Perhaps two of their summaries will illustrate their approach. ". . . Asian American speakers are likely to be restrained in both their manner and their words. They do not typically engage in assertive behavior or self-disclosure. Their style is simple and restrained, with little or no dramatic, illustrative facial expressions or gestures. They tend to be more indirect in their approach, preferring the audience to provide their own interpretations and draw their own conclusions." As a group, African American public speakers "value competition and personal distinctiveness, trust their emotions and feelings but also appreciate the power of the spoken word, and tend to be highly intense and assertive." They also "tend to use personal testimonies" to support arguments.

Kearney and Plax (pp. 362–368) also examine the "feminine" and "masculine" public speaking styles that have evolved in the European American tradition in the United States. While these styles have been associated culturally with women and men, the styles can be employed by both men and women. Public speakers in the "feminine" style emphasize maintenance of relationships and connectedness with the audience. The tone is one of equality with their audience and of inclusiveness of divergent viewpoints. Collaboration and areas of agreement are stressed over conflict. Speakers in the "feminine" style tend to use inductive or associative logic that moves from example to example. They appeal to the emotions and personal experiences of the audience. "They use personal stories and their own observations to support their position." In contrast, in the "masculine" style of public speaking the emphasis is on the speaker's control, authority, expertise, and superior show of power and independence. Speakers in the "masculine" style assume their right to advise and influence the audience. The tone is forceful, aggressive, even combative, and one of absoluteness and certainty. "Masculine speakers use objective facts, hard data, and expert testimony to support their position." In *Eloquence in an Electronic Age,* Kathleen Hall Jamieson contends that the "feminine" style of public speaking has become the most effective mode for political communication via television.

What does this discussion of diversity in public speaking traditions contribute to our understanding of reasons for studying speeches? We can study speeches to listen to the voices of co-cultures and women whose voices typically have been omitted, silenced, marginalized, or trivialized. Thus we can expand our range of insights into what it means to be human and can broaden our view of possible standards for critical appraisal of speeches. We can study speeches to understand the "masculine" and "feminine" styles of public address developed in the United States. Thus we can widen our understanding of how the public speaking practices of women can contribute to the development of rhetorical theory. We can study speeches to increase our awareness of how "eloquence" and excellence in public speaking are viewed in various co-cultural traditions and in terms of a "feminine" style. Thus we can better appreciate how standards for eloquence and excellence may differ somewhat among these various heritages.

Conclusion

The study of speeches can play an important role in the intellectual development of contemporary college students. Through such study we may expect to *increase our knowledge of humanity, to derive standards for the critical appraisal of public discourse, to enlarge and deepen our understanding of rhetorical theory, to develop an appreciation for excellence in public address, and to broaden our understanding of diverse speaking traditions within our society.*

FOR FURTHER READING

On Speech as a Humane Study

Linkugel, Wilmer A., and Johannesen, Richard L. "The Study of Masterpieces of Public Address." *Southern Speech Journal,* Summer 1960, pp. 289–97. Presents the rationale for the scrutiny of noted speeches in the classroom.

Nichols, Marie Hochmuth. *Rhetoric and Criticism.* Louisiana State University Press, 1963. Chapter 1 analyzes rhetoric and public address as a humane study—as a study of people making enlightened choices in a rhetorical context.

Wilson, John F., Arnold, Carroll C., and Wertheimer, Molly. *Public Speaking as a Liberal Art.* 6th ed. Allyn and Bacon, 1990. Chapter 1 examines speech as a liberal study showing people apprehending truths about themselves and their environment and communicating them to others.

On the Critical Analysis of Speeches

Andrews, James R., Leff, Michael C., and Terrill, Robert. *Reading Rhetorical Texts: An Introduction to Criticism.* Houghton Mifflin, 1998. Presents standards for and sample analyses of public addresses.

Campbell, Karlyn Kohrs. *The Rhetorical Act.* 2nd ed. Wadsworth, 1996. Discusses at length each of the dimensions of a rhetorical transaction that a critic might examine.

Campbell, Karlyn Kohrs, and Burkholder, Thomas R. *Critiques of Contemporary Rhetoric.* 2nd ed. Wadsworth, 1997. Chapters 1–5 consider in detail the process of rhetorical criticism.

On Rhetorical Theory

Conley, Thomas M. *Rhetoric in the European Tradition.* Longman, 1990. Traces the history of rhetorical theory from origins in ancient Greece and Rome, through development in Western Europe and England, to continuation in the United States.

Golden, James, et al., eds. *The Rhetoric of Western Thought.* 6th ed. Kendall/Hunt Publ. Co., 1997. A collection of original and reprinted essays that trace the development of theories of rhetoric from Greco-Roman times to the present.

Herrick, James A. *The History and Theory of Rhetoric: An Introduction.* Gorsuch Scarisbrick, 1997. A survey of rhetorical theories from Greco-Roman times to the present.

Kennedy, George A. *Comparative Rhetoric: A Historical and Cross-Cultural Introduction.* Oxford University Press, 1998. Compares theories of rhetoric in ancient oral cultures without writing (such as Australian and

Native American) and in ancient cultures with writing (such as the Near East, China, India, Greece, and Rome).

On Excellence in Public Address

Bryant, Donald C. *Rhetorical Dimensions in Criticism.* Louisiana State University Press, 1973. Chapter 6 explores the concept of "eloquence" in discourse.

Foss, Karen A., and Foss, Sonja A., eds. *Women Speak: The Eloquence of Women's Lives.* Waveland Press, 1991. Challenges the traditional conception of "eloquence" rooted in the white male European-American heritage.

Jamieson, Kathleen Hall. *Eloquence in an Electronic Age.* Oxford University Press, 1988. Assesses the functions, forms, and quality of contemporary American public address.

On Cultural and Gender Diversity in Public Speaking

Burke, Ronald K., ed. *American Public Discourse: A Multicultural Perspective.* University Press of America, 1992. Contains 42 speeches from past and recent United States history of male and female Native Americans, African Americans, Mexican Americans, and of white American females.

DeFrancisco, Victoria L., and Jensen, Marvin D., eds. *Women's Voices in Our Time.* Waveland Press, 1994. Contains 28 contemporary speeches by women of varied ethnic backgrounds.

Foner, Philip S., and Branham, Robert James, eds. *Lift Every Voice: African-American Oratory. 1787–1900.* University of Alabama Press, 1998.

Halliburton, Warren J., ed. *Historic Speeches of African Americans.* Franklin Watts, 1993. Covers the period from the Declaration of Independence to 1983.

Kearney, Patricia, and Plax, Timothy G. *Public Speaking in a Diverse Society.* 2nd ed. Mayfield, 1999. Chapter 3 examines the influence of culture on public speaking styles and describes distinctive styles for co-cultural groups in the United States: Euro-Americans, African Americans, Latino/Latina Americans, Asian Americans, Native Americans, and Middle Eastern Americans. Chapter 16 includes extended discussion of "masculine" and "feminine" styles of contemporary public speaking.

Straub, Deborah Gillan, ed. *Voices of Multicultural America: Notable Speeches Delivered by African, Asian, Hispanic, and Native Americans, 1790–1995.* Gale Research, 1996.

Chapter Two

The Analysis of Speeches

This book is a collection of speeches on significant current issues that exemplify the major forms of public speaking in contemporary American society. Attention now will be given to the nature of rhetoric, the forms of speeches in which the art of rhetoric commonly is practiced in our European-American culture, and some guidelines for critical analysis of speeches.

The Art of Rhetoric

Rhetoric is a term with varied and vague meanings today. Major dictionaries, reflecting the popular confusion, list numerous definitions. Among those commonly cited are the following: the speech of stereotyped politicians—empty, misleading, insincere, and high-flown; an oratorical display or exaggeration; highly figurative language, commonly called "purple patches"; the art of prose writing; and, originally, the art of oratory. *Rhetoric, oratory,* and *eloquence* all come from roots meaning *to speak.* Quintilian, the Roman schoolmaster, placed the art of rhetoric at the center of his educational system. Aristotle thought that rhetoric had the capacity to prevent the triumph of fraud and injustice, to instruct popular audiences, to help persons see both sides of an issue, and to help provide a dignified and distinctive means of self-defense.

As used in this book, *rhetoric* is the art of selecting, adapting, and communicating ideas primarily through verbal means to achieve a desired response from a specific audience. The rhetorical act involves making choices related to both the matter of communication—what subjects may be chosen, what issues they embrace, and what values they embody—and the manner of communicating perceptions in order to produce a desired effect. It is important to the welfare of a democratic society that both of these types of choices be enlightened and ethical. Interest in the effectiveness of rhetorical techniques must not outstrip concern for their ethical use. Ethical judgments about rhetorical means employed to achieve ends or judgments of the ethics of the ends cannot be escaped. Each of us must decide for ourself the ethical balance point between our own idea in its pure form and that idea modified to achieve maximum impact on the specific audience.

In seeking to define the nature of rhetoric, theorists have identified those dimensions common to all instances of public discourse. First, there is a person with an idea and a speech purpose—the *speaker.* Governed by personal, physical, intellectual, and experiential characteristics, the speaker seeks to choose, structure, and present the message so as to elicit a desired response. Next, there is the *audience,* whose members see the rhetorical context through individual lenses. They may view the speaker as expert, trustworthy, and of good will, or they may set up emotional blocks to the message because the speaker's image and reputation strike them unfavorably. They may view the speaker's thesis as interesting, wise, accurate, and of unquestionable merit, or they may erect barriers to the message because the speaker's ideas run contrary to the beliefs, attitudes, and values that their personal experiences have dictated to them. Finally, there is the *situation* in which the speech occurs: a place—a college classroom, the United States Senate, an ancient synagogue, or London's Hyde Park; a time—fourth century Athens, twentieth century Washington, before lunch or after, November 22, 1963, December 7, 1941; an occasion—a prep-school commencement, a Rotary Club meeting, a Presidential inaugural, a murder trial, a Presidential impeachment trial, a United Nations Security Council meeting, a business association luncheon, or a scientific conference.

In addition to the dimensions of speaker, audience, and situation, speech theorists have identified four variables common to the speech itself. In attempting to promote a desired response, the speaker makes choices about each of these four variables. Through the process that rhetoricians call *invention,* or the discovery and selection of the central idea and its supports, the speaker utilizes appropriate evidence, reasoning, and appeals to audience motives and values to substantiate the message. The remaining three variables relate to transmission of the idea. The speaker selects relevant patterns of *organization* to provide structure and design. Furthermore, the speaker employs impelling symbolization through *language* best suited to himself or herself, to the subject, to the audience, and to the situation. Finally, the speaker uses *delivery* to get the idea across to the audience. Whether he or she uses the impromptu, extemporaneous, manuscript, or memorized methods of delivery, the speaker employs both voice and body to reinforce the meaning and feeling embodied in the message.

Standard speech textbooks contain general principles on these dimensions and variables as they pertain to all types of speeches. By including these principles, these books seek to provide a foundation for purposive and responsible public address that you may use as a guide for your speaking behavior. We will not discuss all of these principles. Rather, we will present examples of speeches illustrating them. Additionally, the introduction to each chapter will focus on the nature of the constraints that influence the speaker's choices in adapting principles to that speech form.

The Forms of Speeches

Since ancient times, scholars have sought to classify those social contexts that give rise to public discourse. They have done so in order to understand the nature of the rhetorical act and to formulate principles by which it might be taught. In 336 B.C. Aristotle saw men in law courts trying to secure justice concerning past actions. Accordingly, he identified one class of speeches as *forensic.* In a second instance, he witnessed men deliberating about problems and the best courses of action for their solution. He saw statesmen in the political assembly giving counsel and advice about the practicality and desirability of future policies. He saw men in legislative chambers seeking to exhort or dissuade those who could decide future action. These speeches he classified as *deliberative.* Finally, he observed men at ceremonial gatherings praising the virtuous and eulogizing the noble dead. At other times he beheld men launching vitriolic attacks against others at public gatherings. These speeches of praise and blame he labeled *epideictic.*

As Aristotle profited from appraising the speeches of his day, so too may the modern scholar of rhetoric profit from an examination of contemporary speeches. As we survey twentieth century public address, we see people in public gatherings translating technical information into popular terms; we see others describing an experience or event. At other times we see people publicly probing for definitive meanings, searching for the causes of natural and social phenomena, dispelling stereotypes, and seeking out the implications of things and events. We classify such speeches as attempts to increase *understanding*. In other situations, we see lawyers seeking decisions on the guilt or innocence of their clients, politicians asking for acceptance of what they validate as facts, and citizens arguing over the "real" cause of something. These speakers are *affirming propositions of fact*. On some occasions, we witness speakers urging adoption of new standards for human behavior, and we see drama and literary critics applying criteria to art forms to establish a judgment about their quality. When people seek to formulate or change human values or to apply standards as measurements of quality, we label their efforts *affirming propositions of value*. In some instances, we observe speakers seeking to make people vitally aware of problems that hinder personal and social fulfillment. These persons are *creating concern for problems*. In still other situations, we see persons advocating programs for the solution of perplexing problems and for the ultimate betterment of society. This effort we call *affirming propositions of policy*. Finally, we see speakers on ceremonial occasions asking for a unity of spirit or for a reenergizing of effort or commitment. When a person urges increased dedication to the existing values of a group, we label that purpose *intensifying social cohesion*.

Some Guidelines for Analysis of Speeches

As a type of rhetorical criticism, the analysis of speeches is not a fool-proof, mathematically precise act of description and calculation. An act of criticism is, by its very nature, an act of persuasion and argument. As a critic you apply standards, make claims, and offer support for those claims. As a critic you argue for the reasonable probability, not absolute certainty, of your descriptions and judgments. In addition, your own beliefs and predispositions will influence your selection and application of a framework for criticism. Such influential factors would include your assumptions about the nature and sources of reality and truth, the ways in which humans derive reliable knowledge, the basis of ethics, and the capacities that mark the essence of human nature. In turn the critical framework that you employ will focus your analysis *toward* some aspects while at the same time deflecting your attention *away from* other aspects. And another critic employing a different critical perspective might reasonably describe and evaluate a particular speech differently than you.

Each of the remaining chapters in this anthology is introduced by a brief essay setting forth guidelines for analyzing the speeches which illustrate that form. At this point we will limit ourselves to suggesting some potential general dimensions and questions for use in judging speechmaking.[1]

Our suggestions are not intended as a definitive statement on speech criticism. They simply are some starting points for possible use in assessing speeches inside and outside the classroom. We do not view this set of guidelines as the only method or the "best" method of speech analysis. Other useful

---

1. Some of the following material is adapted from the contributions of Richard L. Johannesen for *Principles and Types of Speech Communication,* Seventh Edition, by Alan H. Monroe and Douglas Ehninger, pp. 245–47, 249–57, 453–63. Copyright © 1974, 1967, 1962, 1955, 1949, 1939, 1935 by Scott, Foresman and Company.

approaches for the criticism of speeches are described in some of the Sources for Further Reading at the end of this and subsequent chapters.

Obviously, in assessing a specific speech, each dimension or question would not be of equal importance. You might, for instance, consider reasonableness and ethicality more crucial than language and delivery. The criteria you use for evaluation should be those particularly appropriate for both the general speech form and the specific speech. Furthermore, consider how dimensions and questions may point to an interaction of factors. How might a listener's value system influence her or his perception of what is reasonable? Or how might a speaker's attitude toward an audience influence that speaker's credibility or perceived ethicality?

As you analyze a particular speech, you may find that some aspects of it are so prominent and worthy of note that they "invite," indeed they "demand," your critical attention. Aspects of a speech may be noteworthy, for example, because they are so frequent, so obvious, so unique, so subtle, so probably effective, so superbly handled, so poorly done, or so detrimental to effectiveness. Based on the general nature of the speech and the rhetorical aspects that invite your critical attention, you probably will select for use only some of the following dimensions or questions.

In presenting an oral or written analysis of a speech, the quality of your criticism will be improved if you discuss *both* strengths and weaknesses; criticism is not solely the making of negative judgments. In addition, quality is improved by specifying, explaining, and justifying the lines of inquiry, framework for analysis, or standards for evaluation you will utilize.

1. To what factors in the immediate occasion or more general relevant situation does the speaker seem to be responding?

Speechmaking is situationally motivated and a speaker makes choices of communicative ends and means in response to a set of circumstances and to a specific audience. Hence, it is well to begin an analysis of most speeches by discussing the societal milieu, the nature of the physical and ideological setting, and the probable causes that led up to the speech. How might factors in the occasion or prevailing ideological climate have influenced the speaker's purpose and/or methods? To what in particular does the speaker seem to be responding: To a problem, opportunity, lack of information, duty, challenge, ceremonial obligation, attack, issue, or routine invitation?

What is the nature and significance of the specific audience addressed by the speaker? Consider the relevance of such matters as size, age, sex, occupation, educational background, memberships in organizations, ethnic background, and knowledge of the subject of the speech. Is the primary audience the one physically present, or is it perhaps one to be exposed "second-hand" through the various mass media, or is it one "observing" a confrontation between a speaker and audience? Are there any secondary audiences intended for the message?

Sometimes the impact of a speech is influenced by such factors in the occasion as time of day, room acoustics and seating arrangement, preceding and following speeches, and audience customs and expectations. Clearly the expectations for a presidential inaugural address and for a political rally speech differ. Depending upon the role the audience expects a speaker to fulfill (such as leader, advisor, expert, lecturer, intruder, spokesperson for them or others), they may expect different evidence, appeals, proposals, language, and delivery. How adequately a speaker handles questions and answers in a forum period after the speech may influence audience perceptions of the speech.

The speech may play a role in some larger campaign of communication or in the activities of a particular social movement. Is the speaker a spokesperson in behalf of some group or other person and thus probably less free to voice entirely his or her own viewpoint? Is the speech a major effort to be supplemented by other modes of communication? Is it one in a planned series of addresses on the subject? Is the central communication thrust on this subject being carried out through other modes and channels with this speech as only a minor part of the total program? What influence might presentation via radio and/or television have on the impact of the speech? Would posting the speech on the Internet reach a unique audience?

2.   What seem to be the speaker's general and specific purposes?

Typical general purposes are to entertain, to present information and increase understanding, to reinforce existing beliefs and values, to change values and beliefs, and to secure overt action. Consider whether the speaker's intent seems to be identification and agreement, shock and arousal, or confrontation and alienation. What more concrete outcome does the speaker seem to want from his or her audience? What exactly does the speaker want the audience to believe, feel, or do? Does the specific purpose seem appropriate for the subject, audience, and occasion?

Given the audience and relevant circumstances, probe whether the speaker's purposes appear realistic and achievable. Remember that countermessages from other communicators, or unexpected and uncontrollable events, may work on listeners' minds to weaken the impact of the speaker's message. Remember, also, that some situations are not altered very easily through public speech. No matter what is said to some audiences, for instance, they may refuse to modify their strongly held beliefs, values, and actions. And some audiences may believe, accurately or inaccurately, that they do not possess the power, authority, skill, money, or facilities to adopt the speaker's idea.

3.   How does the speaker capture and sustain audience attention and interest?

No matter how sincere the speaker's intent, no matter how sound her or his reasoning, no matter how worthwhile the message, if the audience's attention is not aroused at the outset and maintained throughout, the speaker's efforts are doomed to failure. If no one listens, belief and action cannot be influenced as the speaker hopes. In the content, language, and delivery of the speech, are such interest-factors as conflict, suspense, familiarity, novelty, humor, action, curiosity, and concreteness capitalized on? Is interest heightened through such means as narration of a story, vivid description, analogy, contrast, hypothetical and factual examples, and extended illustrations?

4.   How does the speaker strive to insure that the audience clearly understands the message as intended?

Assess the probability that listeners will know exactly what the speaker is asking of them and concretely how to help implement that idea or proposal. Judge whether ideas are presented accurately and clearly and whether extremes of complexity and simplification are avoided. If ambiguity seems employed intentionally, what factors in the subject or occasion might account for or even justify it? How adequately does the introductory portion of the speech gain attention, challenge the audience, lead smoothly into the topic, or create good will for the speaker and topic? How adequately does the conclusion summarize basic ideas, convey a sense of completion, leave the listeners in an appropriate mood, or stimulate acceptance of the central belief or action sought? Consider what patterns of organization the speaker uses to foster unity and clarity: chronological, spatial, problem-solution, general-to-specific or vice versa, cause-effect, examination of alternatives, and so forth. If the speech lacks clear structure, is this apparently due to speaker ineptness or may there be some justification for it?

To promote understanding, how does the speaker utilize such devices as repetition, restatement, transitions, internal summaries, parallel phrasing, numerical "sign-posts," itemization, association with the familiar, examples and illustrations, questions and answers, statistics, and definitions? Some definitions are "objective" in the sense that they report widely accepted, noncontroversial meanings current with experts or with the public. Other definitions are "persuasive" in the sense that the speaker is asking the audience to accept her or his particular meaning as the correct or appropriate definition for a concept which is subject to challenge or controversy. How does the speaker employ audiovisual aids and vocal-physical delivery to increase understanding? If appropriate, how adequately does the speaker answer such standard questions as who, what, where, when, why, and how?

5. To what degree might listeners perceive the speaker's proposal (idea, belief, policy) as sound and reasonable?

Bear in mind that accepted standards of reason, logic, and soundness may vary from one audience to another, from one culture to another, or between fields of discourse (such as politics, religion, natural science, law, historiography). As a critic you may wish to apply to the message some "universal" or "traditional" tests of soundness for evidence and reasoning. But also consider whether such tests are appropriate for the specific speech situation or subject matter. Furthermore, an audience may not make a sharp distinction between so-called logical and emotional appeals. For instance, a set of statistics showing a high probability of listeners being stricken with some form of cancer during their lifetime may be perceived by them as both logical and emotional; for them it simply is a reasonable item of support.

Assess how adequately the speaker employs evidence and reasoning to demonstrate that his or her proposal actually will work, will solve the problem, will be efficient, and will not be too costly. Is the proposal feasible despite such potential limitations as minimal time, personnel, or finances? Evaluate the soundness of the factual examples, expert testimony, literal analogies, statistics, and cause-effect reasoning the speaker employs. Is the speaker's idea consistent with the relevant beliefs and attitudes of the audience? If not, is such inconsistency seemingly due to speaker ineptitude or planned to serve some persuasive function? Is there a legitimate connection between the speaker's idea or purpose and the audience's relevant needs, motives, goals, and emotions? Are listeners made to "feel" a personal stake in the outcome? Has the speaker exaggerated the connection or appealed to irrelevant needs?

What premises or fundamental beliefs are verbalized by the speaker as underpinnings for further argument? Implicitly undergirding the speaker's ideas, are there any unstated assumptions, any unspoken basic beliefs, values, premises, or stereotypes? Are such unstated assumptions probably omitted to avoid scrutiny by the audience or because the speaker and audience already share the assumption? Consider in what ways the spoken and unspoken assumptions reflect the speaker's conception of reality, truth, dependable knowledge, goodness, religion, or the essence of human nature. What might be the intended function or unintended impact of omission of an expected idea or of silence on a controversial issue?

6. To what degree do the speaker's ideas harmonize with the audience's relevant values?

A value, for our purposes, is defined as a conception of "The Good" or "The Desirable." Honesty, fairness, honor, efficiency, progress, economy, courage, safety, prudence, and patriotism all are examples of possible values for persons. In numerous speeches throughout his two terms as president,

Ronald Reagan stressed a cluster of "traditional" American values: family, neighborhood, work, patriotism, peace, and freedom. A value may function either generally, as a goal motivating our behavior, or specifically, as a standard we use to assess the acceptability of means to accomplish ends. We might, for instance, recognize that a policy or solution is efficient and economical, but reject that program for being dishonest and inhumane. Frequently dominant personal or group values are reflected in slogans or mottos: "Liberty, Equality, Fraternity"; "Duty, Honor, Country"; "Law and Order"; "Law and Order with Justice"; "Freedom Now"; "All Power to the People"; "Peace with Honor."

Values are not proved or disproved in quite the same way as "factual" matters. We measure the length of a table with a ruler to demonstrate that it is indeed one meter long. But it is difficult, if not impossible, to measure precisely degrees of beauty, courage, and honesty. And proposed measures of freedom, progress, or efficiency often themselves are controversial. As a culture or subculture develops, a given value becomes accepted as functional for that group. Naturally, the values which predominate often vary from one culture to another. One culture may hold punctuality as a basic value, for example, while another deems being on time of little importance. We develop our own individual value systems in the context of larger cultural and subcultural value systems.

Usually we *rank* the values we hold into a rough *hierarchy* so that some values to which we are committed take precedence over others. Note also that in a specific situation several audience values may come into conflict, thus forcing a choice of one value over another in making a decision. The audience may continue to believe in both values, but temporarily set one aside in favor of the other. For instance, a speaker may advocate in a given situation adherence to honesty over efficiency, patriotism over self-concern, economy over education, or humaneness over frankness.

A warning is in order. A speaker often overtly appeals to a seemingly potent value to which the audience *says* it is committed. But do not assume that the audience always will *act* in accordance with the declared value. In a particular instance the audience may perceive some other value as more important; they may not *apply* the value appealed to and to which they in general are devoted.

In assessing the various value appeals of a speaker, consider the general approach used. Is the aim to get listeners to adopt a new value to replace an outmoded one, perhaps through a redefinition of the meaning we should have for the original value-word? Is the speaker urging acceptance of her or his value judgment of something as an accurate and appropriate judgment? In what ways does the speech function to reinforce and reenergize values already held by the audience? Is the speaker creating concern for a problem by showing that relevant audience values are being threatened or violated? Is the speaker advocating adoption of a policy or solution in part because it harmonizes with or fosters relevant audience values? By exploring such questions, you can move toward an understanding of specific techniques through which a speaker attempts to link an idea or proposal to potent audience values.

7. To what degree is the speaker perceived as a credible source on the subject?

The positive or negative perceptions that listeners have of a speaker's personal qualities play a major role in determining whether they will accept his or her information, arguments, or proposal. Ancient Greek and Roman rhetorical theorists called this concept *ethos* and identified its three major elements as good sense, good character, and good will. Contemporary communication scholars use such labels as source credibility, image, and reputation to describe audience attitude toward the speaker; they have identified expertness and trustworthiness as the two most potent dimensions of speaker credibility. Listeners assess a speaker's *expertness* by making judgments about competency, experience, and knowledge of the subject. *Trustworthiness* is a quality audiences attribute to a speaker whom they perceive as honest, dependable, sincere, fair, and similar to them in values, beliefs, and background. Researchers have identified a moderately influential dimension, often called *dynamism,* rooted in how alert, energetic, firm-minded, and interesting an audience considers a speaker. And informed observation would suggest that listeners evaluate a speaker's *good will* toward them by judging her or his friendliness, likability, and concern for them.

Ethos is variable rather than static. A speaker's credibility might vary from one audience to another, from one decade to another, or from one subject to another. Different cultures or subcultures may prize different personal qualities as constituting positive *ethos,* or an audience may perceive different qualities as relevant on different topics. The *ethos* attributed to a speaker by listeners will fluctuate during presentation of the speech as the audience judges use of evidence and reasoning, motivational appeals, language, structure, and vocal-physical delivery. Sometimes speakers directly attempt to foster positive *ethos* with an audience by overtly mentioning experiences or qualifications as marks of their expertise or by quoting or indicating associations with persons whose *ethos* with the audience already is high. A speaker's *ethos* level at the conclusion of the speech is an outcome of interaction of her or his reputation (prior audience knowledge of speaker's views, accomplishments, associations, and personality) with the audience's assessment of how well the speaker performed during the speech itself.

Although high *ethos* will not guarantee speaker success, markedly low source credibility usually thwarts a communicative effort. No matter how *actually* sound and ethical are a speaker's program, information, arguments, and appeals, if the audience *perceives* the speaker as incompetent, unethical, untrustworthy, bored, overly nervous, or aloof, then her or his message probably will have little of the desired impact.

8. What attitudes toward his or her audience does the speaker seem to reveal?

A speaker's attitude toward an audience reflects his or her view of the listener's personal worth and abilities as well as an indication of the speaker's orientation or stance toward the audience. First, attempt to isolate how the speaker's attitude orientation is revealed in communicative choices, strategies, and techniques. Such reflections may be inferred from verbal and nonverbal elements such as word choice, level of abstraction, types of examples, specificity of analysis, emphasis given to items, vocal pitch and quality, facial expression, and directness of eye contact.

Second, attempt to identify the attitudinal stances characteristic of all or parts of the speech. Is the attitude that you perceive probably the one perceived by the audience, the one intended by the speaker, and a sincere index of his or her "real" view? Are any of the speaker's attitudinal stances especially ethical or unethical? Our discussion later in this chapter of question #13 on ethical standards for assessing public discourse may help you consider this issue. Your efforts may be aided by considering to what degree the speech reveals one or more of the following attitude clusters: (1) respect, equality, understanding, honesty, genuineness, concern for audience welfare and improvement, sincerity, openness to new views, trust, selflessness, empathy, helpfulness, humility; (2) prudence, moderation, indifference, aloofness, unconcern, apathy, disinterest, blandness, coldness; (3) objectivity, neutrality; (4) self-aggrandizement, ego-satisfaction, personal "showing off," pretentiousness; (5) superiority, domination, exploitation for personal gain, deception, insincerity, dogmatism, coercion, facade, judgmentalism, arrogance, contempt, condescension, possessiveness, selfishness; (6) aggressiveness, abrasiveness, hostility, nonconciliation, insult, derogation, curtness; (7) inferiority, supplication, pleading, deference; (8) defensiveness, competitiveness, fear, distrust, suspicion; (9) conciliation, consensus, cooperation, identification.

Third, explore in what ways the speaker's attitude toward the audience seems to reflect personal philosophy; beliefs about human nature, society, reality, values, and ethics are some elements of such a philosophy. Does the attitude reflect optimism or pessimism toward human capabilities and potential? Does the speaker see humans as capable of reflective self-decision or only of being coerced or dominated? An attitude might indicate a belief that reality and knowledge are perceived and attained with certainty or with much relativism and uncertainty. Attitudes of cynicism, duplicity, and domination may stem from a commitment to the end justifying the means.

Fourth, probe how the speaker's attitude toward an audience relates to her or his purposes and motives. Does the attitude revealed appear to reinforce or to thwart achievement of the speaker's intended purpose? Is there any verbal and nonverbal inconsistency between the speaker's attitude and the apparent intended meaning of the speech? Does a perceived attitude of insincerity, unconcern, or superiority contradict words proclaiming sincerity, concern, or equality?

Finally, attempt to assess the influence of the speaker's attitudinal stance on the effects or consequences of the speech. Does the attitude seem appropriate for the speaker, subject, audience, and occasion? What effects might the speaker's attitude have on the audience's beliefs, feelings, and actions? Listeners' perception of a speaker's attitude toward them may influence their estimate of expertness, trustworthiness, goodwill, and similarity to them. Attitudes of dominance, superiority, or aloofness, for example, may contribute to people's doubts about the speaker's sincere concern for their welfare.

9. In what ways does the speaker's language usage contribute to clarity, interest, and persuasiveness?

Consider whether the language is appropriate for the speaker, audience, subject, and occasion. Examine the communicative function served by stylistic resources such as repetition, restatement, rhetorical question, comparison, contrast, parallel structure, antithesis, alliteration, analogy, metaphor, imagery, personification, or narration. Do any stylistic devices seem ornamental or "added on" primarily for "showing off"? What does the speaker's language reveal about him or her personally or about the speaker's view of the audience? How do language choices compare with those the speaker reasonably might have made? What stylistic alternatives seem available to the speaker and why might the speaker have made particular choices? If the speaker's language is militant and abrasive, why might this choice have been made?

Why might the speaker rely heavily on one particular stylistic device? If use of metaphors is a major stylistic characteristic, are they largely trite and overly familiar, or are they fresh and insightful for that particular audience? Might the audience have expected to be addressed in familiar, even stereotyped, metaphorical images? If there is a dominant or thematic metaphor woven throughout the speech, what might be its significance? What functions might be served by a speaker's heavy reliance on "god terms" and "devil terms," on value-laden concepts with intense positive or negative meanings? In what ways are names, labels, and definitions employed to channel perceptions—to direct attention toward or away from both relevant and irrelevant aspects of persons and programs? Remember, also, that public tastes in rhetorical style vary from era to era and even between different audiences in the same era. For the particular speech you are analyzing, consider what might be the most appropriate standards of stylistic judgment.

10. In what noteworthy ways does the speaker's delivery of the speech contribute to clarity, interest, and persuasiveness?

Do nonverbal elements of speech presentation reinforce or conflict with the speaker's verbal meaning? Does the speaker's vocal and physical delivery convey one meaning while his or her words convey another? If so, which would the audience probably believe and why? Does the manner of delivery seem appropriate for the speaker, subject, audience, and occasion? Examine the roles of loudness, vocal pitch, vocal quality, pauses, and rapidity in the presentation. How do the speaker's posture, gestures, facial expression, and eye contact help or hinder effectiveness? Are there any distracting mannerisms of vocal or bodily delivery that hinder audience attentiveness or comprehension? Explore also the communicative functions of various nonverbal cues accompanying the speech. Examine the possible intended and unintended implications of music, flags, banners, salutes, emblems, lapel pins, mode of dress, and pictures of family or revered persons.

11. What rhetorical strategies seem noteworthy because of their frequent use, apparent function in the speech, or probable effectiveness?

This line of inquiry obviously builds upon insights and questions from previously suggested guidelines for analysis. But such a scrutiny of concrete strategies will aid you as practitioner and critic of public discourse to see more clearly how others have approached different audiences and situations. The strategies briefly explained here are not offered as an exhaustive list but only as some possibilities. Strategies typical of discourse about values, problems, and solutions are discussed briefly in later chapters which focus on that type of speechmaking.

In the *this-or-nothing* strategy the speaker evaluates leading alternative solutions to a problem, shows in turn why each is unworkable or inappropriate, and finally presents his or her policy as the only sound remaining choice. *Visualization* involves painting a vivid word picture of the positive consequences of adopting or negative results of rejecting a proposal. Sometimes speakers use the *scapegoat* technique wherein they shift all responsibility or blame for problems or faults afflicting their own group onto the shoulders of some other person or group depicted as the embodiment of evil. As a variation of scapegoating, a *conspiracy* appeal claims that the cause of problems facing the group resides in a powerful, widespread, organized, secret effort of some other person or group.

The strategy of *persuasive definition* finds a speaker offering the audience her or his particular meaning as the correct or appropriate definition for a concept which actually is open to challenge or controversy. A speaker might employ *association* to emphasize values, beliefs, experiences mutually held with the audience and/or with persons and programs esteemed by the audience. *Disassociation* involves the speaker's repudiation of relationships with or favorable views toward undesirable people, ideas, or policies. In a strategy of *differentiation,* the speaker avoids guilt or responsibility by arguing the rationale that the action or belief under attack is different or unique from some other state of affairs which may be open to condemnation. Finally, there is a strategy of *transcendence* in which speaker and audience, or opposing groups, are to submerge, at least temporarily, differences of opinion or policy in the name of some commonly agreed upon higher value or goal: national security, political party unity, victory, humanitarianism, or national honor.

Does the speaker rely heavily on *narration*—on the telling of several lengthy stories or of a number of brief anecdotes? Are the stories fictional ones (perhaps created by the speaker or taken from literature or some other source) told to illustrate a point? Are the stories factual ones that recount the speaker's or someone else's personal experiences? Does a particular story function as a kind of proof for a speaker's argument? In his book, *Human Communication as Narration* (pp. 47–48, 108–109), Walter R. Fisher suggests lines of inquiry to aid the critic in evaluating the reasonableness of stories according to a "narrative rationality." Here we will paraphrase or adapt only some of his suggested questions. Do the elements of the story (chronology, plot, characters, scene, motives, values) "hang together" as internally consistent or are there contradictions? Is the known ethical character of the speaker telling the story consistent with the lesson or point of the story? In comparison to stories told on the same subject in other discourses, are important facts omitted, counter arguments ignored, or pertinent issues overlooked? Are factual aspects of the story truly factual or are there omissions, distortions, or misrepresentations that weaken factuality? If the story is offered as representative of numerous other similar stories, is it truly representative? Are the explicit or implied values reflected in the story relevant to the point being made or issue being decided? If you actually were to accept the values being advocated by the story, what would be the impact on your self-concept, on your relationships with others, and on your conduct as a citizen? Are the values advocated by the story confirmed by your own personal experience, by other persons you respect, or by the best audience you could imagine? Even if the story seems reasonable at the moment, are the story's values ones that should be an ideal basis for human behavior?

12. As best you can determine, what are some of the effects or consequences of the speech?

Often it is very difficult to determine exact and certain causal connections between a specific speech and later outcomes. And an effect may be the result of a number of rhetorical and nonrhetorical events. Remember, too, that a speech may have consequences never intended by a speaker; these, also, can be scrutinized. You may attempt to assess the effects of a speech by noting the impact on the immediate audience, the long-term impact on the policies and ideology of society-at-large, the impact on persons in positions of public opinion leadership, the influence on experts, and the reactions of news media reporters. You might also explore whether the speaker's aim has been achieved, whether the speaker's ideas have been verified by later historical events, or whether the audience's expectations have been met. Sometimes virtually nondetectible shifts in audience attitudes and beliefs may occur, such as from a favorable to a strongly favorable position. Finally, you may want to consider the influence of the speech on the *speaker.* Did it enhance or lower the speaker's reputation? How did the speech affect the speaker's subsequent rhetoric and actions? Did the speaker in any way become trapped by his or her own rhetoric? When speakers publicly become "locked in" to a position, later modification may be difficult.

13. What ethical judgments seem appropriate regarding the speaker's purposes, arguments, appeals, and strategies?

Ethical judgments focus on degrees of rightness and wrongness in human behavior. A speech is designed by one person (sometimes with the aid of a speechwriter or speechwriting team) to influence the lives of other persons. And a speaker makes conscious choices concerning specific ends and communicative techniques to achieve those ends. Potential ethical issues regarding means and ends seem inherent in any act of speechmaking. But how those issues are to be faced and resolved (by speaker, listener, and critic) is not clear-cut.

Traditional American textbook discussions of the ethics of public speaking, argumentation, and persuasion often include lists of standards to be applied in assessing the ethicality of an instance of discourse. What follows is Johannesen's synthesis and adaptation of a half-dozen or so typical traditional lists of ethical criteria for public discourse.[2] Such ethical criteria usually are rooted in a commitment to values deemed essential to the health and growth of our political-governmental system of representative democracy. Obviously other cultures and other governmental systems may embrace basic values that lead to quite different standards for public discourse.

Even within our own society, the following criteria are not necessarily the only or best ones possible; they are suggested as general guidelines rather than inflexible rules, and they may stimulate discussion on the complexity of judging the ethics of communication. Consider, for example, under what circumstances there may be justifiable exceptions to some of these criteria. Also bear in mind that one difficulty in applying these criteria in concrete situations stems from differing standards and meanings people may have for such key terms as: distort, falsify, rational, reasonable, conceal, misrepresent, irrelevant, and deceive.

1. **Do not use false, fabricated, misrepresented, distorted, or irrelevant evidence to support arguments or claims.**
2. **Do not intentionally use specious, unsupported, or illogical reasoning.**
3. **Do not represent yourself as informed or as an "expert" on a subject when you are not.**
4. **Do not use irrelevant appeals to divert attention or scrutiny from the issue at hand. Among appeals that commonly serve such a purpose are: "smear" attacks on an opponent's character; appeals to hatred and bigotry; god and devil terms that cause intense but unreflective positive or negative reactions; innuendo.**
5. **Do not ask your audience to link your idea or proposal to emotion-laden values, motives, or goals to which it actually is not related.**
6. **Do not deceive your audience by concealing your real purpose, by concealing self-interest, by concealing the group you represent, or by concealing your position as an advocate of a viewpoint.**
7. **Do not distort, hide, or misrepresent the number, scope, intensity, or undesirable features of consequences or effects.**
8. **Do not use "emotional appeals" that lack a supporting basis of evidence and reasoning, or that would not be accepted if the audience had time and opportunity to examine the subject themselves.**
9. **Do not oversimplify complex, gradation-laden situations into simplistic two-valued, either-or, polar choices.**
10. **Do not pretend certainty where tentativeness and degrees of probability would be more accurate.**
11. **Do not advocate something in which you do not believe yourself.**

2. For example, see the following sources: E. Christian Buehler and Wil A. Linkugel, *Speech Communication for the Contemporary Student* (Harper and Row, 1975), pp. 30–36; Robert T. Oliver, *The Psychology of Persuasive Speech,* 2nd ed. (Longmans, Green, 1957), pp. 20–34; Wayne Minnick, *The Art of Persuasion,* 2nd ed. (Houghton Mifflin, 1968), pp. 278–287; Henry Ewbank and J. Jeffrey Auer, *Discussion and Debate,* 2nd ed. (Appleton-Century-Crofts, 1951), pp. 255–258; Wayne Thompson, *The Process of Persuasion* (Harper and Row, 1975), Ch. 12; Bert E. Bradley, *Fundamentals of Speech Communication,* 4th ed. (Wm. C. Brown Company Publishers, 1984), pp. 20–29.

To assess the degree of ethicality of specific *appeals to values,* consider the following questions that are rooted in standards central to ethical communication in our representative democracy: honesty, relevance, accuracy, fairness, and reasonableness. To what degree do the value appeals serve as relevant motivational reinforcement for a point or proposal that has an independent basis in reasonable evidence? To what degree do the value appeals serve a legitimate function of promoting social cohesion, of reinforcing audience commitment to ideas they already believe? With what degree of appropriateness are the consequences of commitment to the values clarified? To what degree do the value appeals serve as substitutes, as pseudoproof, for the factuality of an assertion? To what degree do the value appeals divert attention from more fundamental, pressing, or controversial matters? To what degree do the value appeals seem to promote, intentionally or not, unreflective stimulus-response reactions when the occasion demands reflective judgment?

What aspects of an *ideological "critique"* might aid in an ethical assessment of the speech? Such a critique questions the "taken for granted," unsettles the comfortable "naturalness" of things, illuminates the unnoticed, hidden or omitted, and questions assumptions about "just the way things are." A central goal of "critique" is to make us conscious of the functioning of power relationships as they operate to dominate or marginalize persons, such as women and ethnic minorities. Another goal is the empowerment of the voiceless or marginalized so that they can become meaningful participants in public discussion and debate on societal issues. Here are a few questions that might guide such an ideological critique. In what ways do the language, structure, evidence, argument, and value appeals in the speech attempt to alter or to reinforce existing power relationships? What spoken or unspoken assumptions about knowledge and power shape the communication norms governing who is entitled to speak, when, where, and on what topics? Can only "experts" or "authorities" speak on the topic? If so, should this be the case? Within the speech, what persons, groups, ideas, or organizations are given legitimacy, approval, rights, superiority, or status either overtly or because their position is unquestioned? What persons, etc., are directly or indirectly delegitimized, condemned, trivialized, or denied rights? What persons, etc., are ignored or dismissed as insignificant because they are not mentioned or taken into account but should have been?

We now turn to a list of some additional questions that we hope will stimulate your examination of various ethical issues as you assess a particular speech. To what degree should ethical standards for judging speeches be relative, flexible, and situation bound, or universal, inflexible, and absolute? Should there be different ethical standards for speechmaking in different fields such as politics, business, education, and religion? To what degree, if any, does the worthiness of the speaker's end justify the employment of communication techniques usually deemed ethically suspect? Does the sincerity of the speaker's intent release him or her from ethical responsibility for means and effects? Under what circumstances might intentional use of ambiguity be considered ethical? To what degree and for what reasons might we consider the use of "sexist" and "racist" language as unethical?

Conclusion

Sonja K. Foss reminds us in her *Rhetorical Criticism*: "We live our lives enveloped in symbols. How we perceive, what we know, what we experience, and how we act are the results of our symbol use and that of those around us. . . . One of the ways we can use to discover how symbols affect us is rhetorical criticism. We engage in the process of rhetorical criticism constantly and often unconsciously, but with some formal training we can become more adept and discriminating in its practice."

By focusing on contemporary American speeches, this book necessarily focuses on one particular kind of rhetorical practice. Speeches still form a significant portion of our communication environment, an environment constantly bombarding us with data, appeals, reasons, and judgments. Whether a speech seeks to create understanding, to advocate or reinforce values and value judgments, to resolve "factual" disputes, to generate concern for problems, or to secure acceptance of solutions—that speech seeks a specific response from a specific audience. Thus such speeches inherently involve some degree of "persuasive" intent, some degree of conscious concrete influence. As responsible citizens in a representative democracy, we are expected to develop skills in communicating our ideas and choices on matters of personal and public concern. Also we are expected to become discerning consumers of communication, to become perceptive evaluators of messages we receive.

FOR FURTHER READING

On the Art of Rhetoric

Brockriede, Wayne. "Dimensions of the Concept of Rhetoric." *Quarterly Journal of Speech,* February 1968, pp. 1–12.

Foss, Sonja K., and Griffin, Cindy L. "Beyond Persuasion: A Proposal for an Invitational Rhetoric." *Communication Monographs,* March 1995, pp. 2–18.

Foss, Sonja K., Foss, Karen A., and Trapp, Robert. *Contemporary Perspectives on Rhetoric.* 2nd ed. Waveland Press, 1991. A thorough exploration of the implications for rhetorical theory of the works of Kenneth Burke, I. A. Richards, Richard M. Weaver, Chaim Perelman, Stephen Toulmin, Ernesto Grassi, Jurgen Habermas, and Michel Foucault.

Foss, Sonja K., Foss, Karen A., and Griffin, Cindy L. *Feminist Rhetorical Theories.* Sage, 1999. A thorough exploration of the implications for rhetorical theory of the works of Cheris Kramarae, bell hooks, Gloria Anzaldua, Mary Daly, Starhawk, Paula Gunn Allen, Trinh T. Minh-ha, Sally Miller Gearhart, and Sonja Johnson.

Smith, Craig R. *Rhetoric and Human Consciousness: A History.* Waveland, 1998. Traces the historical development of theories of rhetoric by relating rhetoric to conceptions and issues of knowledge, power, politics, values, ethics, and human nature.

On the Ethics of Rhetoric

Jensen, J. Vernon. *Ethical Issues in the Human Communication Process.* Erlbaum, 1997. Examines ethical issues related to the communicator, message, medium, receivers, and situation.

Johannesen, Richard L. *Ethics in Human Communication.* 4th ed. Waveland Press, 1996. Explores varied perspectives, issues, and examples to foster skill in assessing degrees of ethicality.

Johannesen, Richard L. "Perspectives on Ethics in Persuasion." In Charles U. Larson, *Persuasion: Reception and Responsibility.* Wadsworth, 1998. Chapter 2.

On the Forms of Speeches

Cali, Dennis D. *Generic Criticism of American Public Address.* Kendall/Hunt, 1996. Discusses methods for analysis of various forms or genres of public speaking.

Campbell, Karlyn Kohrs, and Jamieson, Kathleen Hall. *Deeds Done in Words: Presidential Rhetoric and the Genres of Governance.* University of Chicago Press, 1990. Examines such forms of presidential discourse as inaugural addresses, state of the union messages, farewell addresses, and war rhetoric.

Walter, Otis M., and Scott, Robert L. *Thinking and Speaking.* 5th ed. Macmillan, 1984. Chapters 6–10 discuss speeches that deal with problems, causes, solutions, values, and definitions.

On the Critical Analysis of Speeches

Brock, Bernard L., Scott, Robert L., and Chesebro, James, eds. *Methods of Rhetorical Criticism: A Twentieth Century Perspective.* 3rd ed. Wayne State University Press, 1990. An anthology of essays illustrates varied approaches to the theory and practice of rhetorical criticism.

Cooper, Martha. *Analyzing Public Discourse.* Waveland Press, 1989. Of special interest are Chapters 7–9 on ethics, ideology/propaganda, and freedom of speech.

Foss, Sonja K. *Rhetorical Criticism: Explorations and Practice.* 2nd ed. Waveland Press, 1996. Presents critical methods that focus on context, message, or rhetor. Types of criticism illustrated are: neo-Aristotelian, generic, feminist, ideological, metaphoric, narrative, fantasy theme, pentadic, and cluster.

Hart, Roderick P. *Modern Rhetorical Criticism.* 2nd ed. Allyn and Bacon, 1997. Describes the rhetorical and critical perspectives; presents forms of criticism that analyze situations, ideas, argument, structure, and style; illustrates specialized forms of criticism (role, cultural, dramatistic, feminist, continental).

Johannesen, Richard L. "Attitude of Speaker Toward Audience: A Significant Concept for Contemporary Rhetorical Theory and Criticism," *Central States Speech Journal,* Summer 1974, 95–104.

Rybacki, Karyn, and Rybacki, Donald. *Communication Criticism: Approaches and Genres.* Wadsworth, 1991. Chapters 3–7 cover various methods and perspectives for criticism and Chapter 8 focuses on the rhetoric of public speaking.

Chapter Three

Speeches That Increase Understanding

The Nature and Importance of Speeches That Increase Understanding of Knowledge

As the rate of new knowledge continues to accelerate, and as local, national and world problems become increasingly complex, speeches that increase understanding of knowledge must continue to grow in number and significance. Speeches that serve this function are of different kinds: lectures, reports of research findings, treasurers' reports, the happy chef show, military and business briefings, and the evening TV weather report are all instances of this genre of rhetoric. Whenever speakers seek to create in the minds of their listeners an understanding of an event, concept, phenomenon, object, process, or relationship, they may be viewed as seeking to increase understanding of knowledge.

In certain instances, increasing understanding is a speaker's *primary* speech purpose. A professor of history, for example, may be totally content if his students understand the major forces that contributed to the beginning of the First World War. A computer systems engineer may be fully satisfied if installation procedures are understood by technical personnel. An accountant may be adequately rewarded if a company's executive officers understand the implications of a new federal tax regulation.

In other instances, increasing understanding is a speaker's *ancillary* purpose. For example, a sociologist may describe an event in order that he may urge social reform. A civil rights leader may narrate a story of social injustice in order to elicit a greater commitment to social tolerance. A senator may explain a piece of legislation as a prelude to urging adoption. A computer salesperson may give a thorough explanation of a new computer system before urging purchase.

From the perspective of the audience, it is often difficult to determine the extent to which a speech increases understanding rather than serving some other major purpose. Audience members listening to the same speech may come away feeling informed, persuaded to a new point of view, or even inspired to recommit their lives to cherished values. But a speaker who purports to increase understanding, whether as a primary or ancillary purpose, should be expected to meet several fundamental criteria.

Criteria for Evaluating Speeches That Increase Understanding

Four criteria are vital for evaluating speeches that seek to increase understanding. If a speaker fails to satisfy any of these four measures, the speaker's communication of information will be seriously impaired.

1. Is the information communicated accurately, completely and with unity?

Because genuine understanding by an audience is the informative speaker's goal, an *accurate, complete and unified* view of the subject must be presented. The speaker must select those items of information that an audience must have to gain understanding, and arrange them in a unified sequence and express them in an undistorted manner. Wilson, Arnold and Wertheimer have expressed this criterion in this way:

> The tests that listeners apply when talk seems intended to be predominantly informative are these: (1) Is the information *accurate?* Listeners want information that is true to fact in both detail and proportion. (2) Is the information sufficiently *complete?* Does the speaker cover the *whole* subject adequately? (3) Is the information *unified?* We want information that "hangs together" to form a whole of some sort. If we're to understand a wheel, we must understand not just that there are a hub, some spokes, and a rim, but we must understand also how their arrangement in relation to one another enables the wheel to *turn.* Speakers trying to inform need to pay special attention to how facets of the explained subject "fit together" to form or create the explained thing as a totality. If an explanation meets the three tests we have just given, listeners experience the satisfaction of "having been informed"[1]

2. Does the speaker make the information meaningful for the audience?

It is not enough that speakers know the essential components of a truth; they must transform their perceptions of facts and concepts into symbols that evoke understanding in those who listen. Even a highly motivated audience may lack the substantive, linguistic, and conceptual skills essential to understanding an idea presented in its pure form. Speakers must be faithful to both the integrity of the truth they seek to impart and to the demands of the particular audience they address.

These demands need not be incompatible, as an example will demonstrate. Let us assume that you wish to clarify the reasoning processes of induction and deduction to an audience of laborers who have come to your campus. You know that *induction* is a method of systematic investigation that seeks to discover, analyze, and explain specific instances or facts in order to determine the existence of a general law embracing them, whereas *deduction* is a process by which a particular conclusion about an instance is drawn from the application of a general law. In appraising your audience, you recognize that, although these terms are meaningful to you, they represent an unfamiliar level of conceptual abstraction to your audience. The rhetorical problem is clear; the solution is not.

As long ago as 1866, Thomas Henry Huxley faced exactly the same problem. The rhetorical choices that he made in explaining these processes to a group of English workingmen in his speech entitled "The Method of Scientific Investigation" are demonstrated in the following paragraphs.

---

1. John F. Wilson, Carroll, C. Arnold, and Molly Wertheimer, *Public Speaking as a Liberal Art,* 2nd ed. (Boston: Allyn and Bacon, 1990), pp. 190–191.

Suppose you go into a fruiterer's shop, wanting an apple—you take one up, and, on biting, you find it is sour; you look at it, and see that it is hard and green. You take another one and that too is hard, green, and sour. The shopman offers you a third; but, before biting it, you examine it, and find that it is hard and green, and you immediately say that you will not have it, as it must be sour, like those you have already tried.

Nothing can be more simple than that, you think; but if you will take the trouble to analyze and trace out into its logical elements what has been done by the mind, you will be greatly surprised. In the first place, you have performed the operation of induction. You found that, in two experiences, hardness and greenness in apples went together with sourness. It was so in the first case and it was confirmed by the second. True, it is a very small basis, but still it is enough to make an induction from; you generalize the facts, and you expect to find sourness in apples where you get hardness and greenness. You found upon that a general law, that all hard and green apples are sour; and that, so far as it goes, is a perfect induction. Well, having got your natural law in this way, when you are offered another apple which you find is hard and green, you say, "All hard and green apples are sour; this apple is hard and green, therefore this apple is sour." That train of reasoning is what logicians call a syllogism and has all its various parts and terms—its major premise, its minor premise, and its conclusion. And, by the help of further reasoning, which, if drawn out, would have to be exhibited in two or three other syllogisms, you arrive at your final determination. "I will not have that apple." So that, you see, you have, in the first place, established a law by induction, and reasoned out the special conclusion of the particular case.

In this instance, Huxley chose to impart only a very basic understanding of the processes of induction and deduction by showing them to be inherent in a commonplace happening familiar to the workers who comprised his audience. Although he simplified these processes, he did not misrepresent them. His illustration accurately portrays their essential nature. And it is complete in the sense of comprehensively demonstrating the specific purpose of the speech: to show that "there is not one here who has not in the course of the day had occasion to set in motion a complex train of reasoning of the very same kind, though differing of course in degree, as that which a scientific man goes through in tracing the causes of natural phenomena." Finally, his speech possesses unity in providing a systematic development through which the listener may gain a clear grasp of the total meaning.

In giving meaning to the knowledge that he wished to present, Huxley chose to move from a simple illustration to a complex generalization, to develop a common understanding of a process before attaching labels to it, and to use periodic summations of what had been discussed. Other speakers have used definition, restatement and repetition, clarity of organization, factual and hypothetical examples, synonyms and negation, comparison and contrast, analogies and statistics, description and narration, questions and answers. In addition to the foregoing linguistic techniques, they have used photographs and films, blackboards and diagrams, meaningful gestures and movement, and varied patterns of rate and pitch.

3.   Does the speaker create audience interest in the information being presented?

Because understanding is the goal of the speech designed to increase understanding, the speaker must create in the audience a reason for concentrating on the information that is being transmitted. Creating this interest is not always easy. Often the speaker must explain technical, detailed, and abstract concepts to an apathetic audience. In seeking to do so, the speaker can capitalize on the interest factors in content, language, and delivery. *Concrete* and specific terms and illustrations have more interest value for most listeners than vague generalities or abstract concepts. *Conflict* in the form of disagreements, threats, clashes, and antagonisms capture and hold an audience's attention. *Suspense* and *curiosity* in building to a climax, anticipating a conclusion, or asking intriguing questions can be used. Description or narration focusing on activity and movement capitalizes on *action*. The new, unusual, or unexpected reflect the *novelty* factor. On the other hand, listeners are also interested in things that are "close to home" and *familiar*. When carefully and appropriately used, *humor* may increase interest while explaining or highlighting a main point.

As a study of the choices that one speaker made, let us again return to Huxley's illustration. In appraising his audience, Huxley realized that, for average English workingmen of his time, the scientific method represented an esoteric construct of little interest or significance to all but the disciples of science. By making his individual audience member "you," the chief participant in his illustration, by choosing a familiar environment as the setting, and by selecting such suspense words as "suppose" and "you will be greatly surprised" as major transitional devices, he gave to his material a sense of vitality, realism, suspense, and urgency that it did not naturally possess. Huxley chose a hypothetical illustration for this purpose; others have selected metaphors, narratives, comparisons, contrasts, real and figurative analogies, and specific examples. Thus, a speaker who is inventive need not worry about losing the audience even when an unusual or difficult subject is involved.

4. Does the speaker show the audience that the information is important?

Beyond presenting information that is accurate, complete, unified, meaningful, and interesting, speakers must also get their audiences to feel that they should make such knowledge a permanent part of their storehouse of knowledge. In order to do so, speakers might clarify the relation of the information to the wants and goals of their audiences. They might point out ways in which the information can be used or applied, where this new knowledge fits within the context of information already considered worthwhile by the audience, and, if appropriate, where and how the audience can obtain additional information on the subject.

Given the vast array of information that may be communicated, the critic has a right to question the quality of the information that the speaker chooses to present. Student speakers often err by selecting speech topics that are trivial and lacking in real information value. Gruner, Logue, Freshley, and Huseman, in *Speech Communication in Society,* recall

> . . . a dreadful speech by a young man who spoke on and demonstrated how to use two simple types of can openers, one being the elementary "church key" type for opening beverage cans. Disappointed by his low grade he complained, "Well, the speech *did* contain information, didn't it?" The instructor replied: "Not for this audience; I'm sure they already know how to open cans." The instructor's reply could be paraphrased: "You instructed no one."[2]

An effective speech of this form presents information that is worth having to an audience that lacks such knowledge.

2. Charles R. Gruner, Cal M. Logue, Dwight L. Freshley, and Richard C. Huseman, *Speech Communication in Society* (Boston: Allyn and Bacon, Inc., 1972), p. 179.

Conclusion

Increasing understanding is one of the primary and ancillary functions that speeches serve. When speakers try to fulfill this purpose, they must be aware of the constraints that govern their speech behavior. They must choose information that is worth knowing. They must present the information with *accuracy, completeness,* and *unity.* They must be aware of the demands that varied audiences impose on the choices they make in giving *meaning, interest,* and *importance* to a body of knowledge. In other words, they must be faithful to the integrity of their perception of truth while adapting to the demands of their audiences.

FOR FURTHER READING

Lucas, Stephen. *The Art of Public Speaking.* 6th ed., McGraw-Hill, 1998. Chapter 14 presents guidelines for speaking to inform about objects, processes, events, and concepts.

Netter, Gwyn. *Explanations.* McGraw-Hill, 1970. Chapters 2–6 explore the main variations of explanation used in discourse: definitional, empathetic, scientific, and ideological.

Osborn, Michael, and Osborn, Suzanne. *Public Speaking.* 5th ed. Houghton Mifflin, 2000. Chapter 12 examines the functions, types, and structure of speeches to increase understanding.

Rowan, Katherine. "A New Pedagogy for Explanatory Public Speaking," *Communication Education,* 44 (July 1995): 236–250.

An American Prisoner of War in South Vietnam

◆ *James N. Rowe* ◆

For more than five years Major James N. Rowe was a prisoner of the Viet Cong. He was captured by the enemy when he was a Special Forces advisor in 1963 and was held prisoner in the Mekong region and the U Minh Forest. He devised a cover story about himself that kept the enemy from executing him, a fate which befell several others imprisoned with him. His cover story held up until 1968, when the enemy found out he had lied. Major Rowe felt that they received a biographical sketch with complete information about him and his family from the Peace and Justice Loving Friends of the National Liberation Front in America. This information put him on the list for execution. But on December 31, 1968, circumstances conspired that allowed Major Rowe to escape. A heavy American air strike shook up the guards. One of the Viet Cong groups panicked when United States gunships came into the area, and Major

---

◆ This speech is printed by permission of Major James N. Rowe.

Rowe took advantage of the confusion. He was picked up by an American helicopter pilot who almost mistook him for a member of the enemy because he was wearing the pajama-like garb of the Viet Cong. The beard that Major Rowe had grown during his imprisonment permitted the helicopter pilot to identify him as an American a second before pulling the trigger.

Major Rowe delivered his speech at the U.S. Army General Staff and Command College at Leavenworth, Kansas. The audience consisted primarily of students of the college—mostly majors and lieutenant colonels of the American Army, some Navy and Air Force personnel, and a significant number of Allied officers attending the college. [More information about Major Rowe's experiences can be found in his book, *Five Years to Freedom* (Boston: Little, Brown, 1971).]

This speech by Major Rowe is a personal narrative used to impart knowledge about Viet Cong prison camps and what an American prisoner of war lives through. In assessing the speech you will thus want to ask how well Major Rowe tells his story. Does he make effective use of suspense? Imagery? Action? Anecdotes? Is he able to organize his narrative effectively so it can easily be followed? How well does he draw increased understanding with general application from his story?

Major Rowe delivered this address extemporaneously and used no notes. The manuscript you are about to read is a transcript of an audio-tape recording. The extemporaneous style of Major Rowe is thus very apparent. What difficulties do you encounter in reading a speech with genuine oral style? You may want to discuss the statement "Good speeches don't read well."

On April 21, 1989, Col. "Nick" Rowe was assassinated by communist terrorists on the streets of Manila, the Philippines.

◆　◆　◆

1　The American prisoners of war are particularly close to those of us in the military, because the prisoners of war are members of the military. It could be any one of us, and I was one of those prisoners of war. I am Major Nick Rowe; I spent 62 months as a prisoner of the Viet Cong in South Vietnam. The issue of the prisoners of war has come to the forefront in our nation; and in bringing this issue to the forefront, we have found that it's not that American people don't remember, or that they don't care, it's that most of the people in our country don't know. And those of us who have come out feel that we have a particular duty, because we are speaking for 1,600 men who have no voices. So this afternoon I would like to bring you some insight into the prison camps and some insight into what an American prisoner of war lives through.

2　I was a Special Forces advisor in 1963 in Phuoc Hoa. I was in a camp approximately in this area and I was captured very near there in October of 1963. Shortly after capture, I was moved down in the Mekong region; I stayed in this region until January of 1965, when I was moved into the U Minh Forest. I stayed in the U Minh Forest from January 1965 through December of 1968, when I escaped. The camp I was held in was on canal 21 and canal 6. I was approximately fourteen kilometers from our old district capital. I was that close to Americans, and yet they couldn't get to me nor could I get to them. This is the most frustrating thing about being an American prisoner in South Vietnam.

3　The conditions that an American lives under are those that are structured by his captors, and there are several new aspects of captivity. It is not the Hogan's Heroes concept that many people have, because in South Vietnam and in North Vietnam, we found that an American prisoner of war is not a military prisoner, he is a political prisoner; and the Communists are dealing with American prisoners of war based on the Pavlovian theory—stimuli and response—the manipulation of human behavior. These are parameters that we have never dealt with before and are not prepared to deal with. The American prisoners find themselves being manipulated and being made more pliable by the Communists using principles that we have read about in Koestler's *Darkness at Noon,* perhaps in *1984;* these types of things that are never reality. But in prison camps in South Vietnam and in North Vietnam and in Laos, it is reality. An American prisoner of war has two main purposes for the Communists. First of all, propaganda; because in an age of ideological conflict, the most important thing is political opinion, and formation of political opinion, and this is done through propaganda. What more effective source do the Communists have for propaganda than an American prisoner of war? Through coercion, manipulation, or force, to cause that man to condemn our society, our government, our actions throughout the world; and then, as a representative of our system of government and our society, for him to confess to crimes against humanity. Think of the impact of this propaganda in either a Communist or nonCommunist country when contrasted with the same propaganda coming from a Communist source.

4   The second purpose of an American prisoner of war is that when the Communists finally do decide to negotiate, what better blue chip do they have to lay down on the table than an American prisoner of war, trading American lives for political gain—this is why they take an American prisoner of war. When I was captured, there were three of us, two of us Special Forces and one MAAG advisor, who were with a strike force company when we were overrun; all three of us were wounded and were taken prisoners. The other strike force wounded were shot by the VC. And yet an American was of value. In captivity we found, first of all, that we were political prisoners. We weren't military prisoners. This was typified during the initial interrogations. I was one of the first American officers captured in the Mekong Delta, and they really didn't know what to do with us. The first cadre who came in were hampered by the decided lack of ability to speak English, so they brought in a journalist-by-trade who spoke English, and used him as an interrogator. They had an S-2 who stayed across the canal from our camp in a cadre hut, and he was responsible for the interrogation. But since he couldn't speak English, he would write his questions down in Vietnamese, give them to this journalist, the interpreter, who would then translate them into English and come down to my cage. I was in the low-rent district right behind the camp, about thirty meters behind the camp, and he would come down and would sit down and ask me the questions. Anything I said he would write down verbatim. Then he would take the answers back and translate them from his Vietnamese-English dictionary back into Vietnamese to take to the S-2. Well, the first thing I discovered there was that he could deal with a large number of American prisoners, because the S-2 is in one place with the interpreter doing the legwork for him. And he got nothing for it.

5   About four to five weeks, six weeks, seven weeks, and the S-2 got upset, but he was apparently prevented from doing any more than threatening us. And when this little interpreter would come down and threaten, he would say, "I can kill you, I can torture you, I can do anything I want"; then he'd wince. So we knew he wasn't really serious; and I decided after a period of time, that since he had so much flexibility, it would be better to try and see if anything could be done to play with him, I had him come down one day, and I said, "Well, all right, Plato, I am ready to talk." We had nicknames for all of them, and he was very philosophical, so we nicknamed him Plato. I said, "All right, Plato, I am ready to talk." He beamed, pulled out extra paper and a new ballpoint pen, and sat down. I gave him four pages on the theory of laminar flow. This was to include calculus, integrated differential. I gave him pressure formulas—the weights, dams, storm gutters—the aerodynamic principles of air flow. I almost failed mechanical fluids at West Point, so it wasn't really that good anyway, but he copied it down verbatim. Everything I said he copied down, checking on spelling, and he took it back to his hut, and spent the next five days translating it from English into Vietnamese, coming down every day to check on the formulas and things like that; and I said, "Drive on, Plato, you are in good shape." Well, when he finished, he had a great volume, almost like *Khrushchev Remembers.* He took all of this great volume of paper over to the S-2. The enemy are very stoic individuals, and although I was thirty meters behind the camp, I soon heard screams from the S-2's hut. Not more than two minutes later, here came Plato scurrying down this little log walk with the S-2 right behind him. Obviously, the S-2 found out in a very short period of time what Plato had been doing, and it had erased his ability to deal with other American prisoners. Had the S-2 had the ability to deal with me as he wished, there wouldn't have been a tree high enough in the area for him to string me up to. But, I was a political prisoner, and the political cadre said no. Interrogation is secondary, indoctrination is primary. If they lose you through interrogation, they lose you for indoctrination; and so that was when we established what was of primary importance.

6   In dealing with an American prisoner of war their philosophy is that you can take any man and if you control the physical, you do not necessarily control that man; but if you can control and manipulate his mind, you will control the physical and the man. So this is what their target is, not necessarily physical torture, because they realize that indiscriminate physical torture can alienate a man, and once you have done that, he identifies you with the enemy, and you will never indoctrinate him. They will use physical torture, but they use it only to amplify the mental pressure. We found that a bruise will heal, a broken bone will heal, a wound will heal, but if they push you over the line mentally, or they break your spirit, then you are not coming back. That was the big battle. And that was what we had not been prepared for.

7   One of the first things that came up, and I will bring this up here because it is very important to members of the military, was the Code of Conduct. The Code of Conduct to me was a series of pictures in an orderly room. I had read them, I had gotten the T.I. and E. classes on Code of Conduct; it really wasn't that clear. I knew that I was supposed to give my name, my rank, my serial number, my date of birth, and then I thought I was supposed to shut up. This is the way it usually comes down to the troops. But this is a fallacy, because if you don't know the Code of Conduct when you're captured, the Communists will teach it to you. Because they teach our Code of Conduct to their cadre. And then they tell you while you're there, go ahead and follow it, but you will die if you do. They'll let you make your own decisions. What they are doing here is one of the first steps in breaking down a man's will to resist, because generally speaking, an individual feels if he goes beyond name, rank, serial number, and date of birth, he is a traitor. I know I felt it right at first. And this is the first question that comes up in a man's mind. What about the Big Four? How long do I last? Well, you hang onto the Big Four as long as you can, but the next line says, "I will evade answering further questions to the best of my ability." It does give you credit for having basic intelligence. And this is what a man does. Fortunately, I went to West Point, and they teach you ambiguity; this is one of the things that really comes in handy. When you get a B.S. degree from West Point, that is exactly what it is. I liked English up there, and that is where they teach you to say the same thing 25 different ways. So this is what the American is doing. He is hedging, working for a way to get around, or get under, or get through. But if an individual goes in thinking, if I break from name, rank, serial number, and date of birth, I am a traitor, the first thing they are going to do is instill a guilt complex into him that will beat him into the ground. I know, because we had an individual who felt, initially, that anything beyond name, rank, serial number, and date of birth, was a violation of a punitive article of the uniform code of military justice. Now, this is where a man feels, all right, I have broken; and then they say, "Well, you have broken once, you are going to be punished, you might as well go all the way." Once they've got their finger in that crack, you're in trouble. And they teach our Code of Conduct as a punitive article, if you don't know it before you go in, find out about it now and find out exactly what it is. Because they are going to tell you and they are going to try to convince you that it is a punitive article, once you violate anything, once you go beyond name, rank, serial number, and date of birth, you have violated the Code of Conduct and you are going to be punished. Then they have their foot in the door. And they say, "Drive on, because you are going to be punished anyway. Why not get out sooner and go home?" This is the thing that a person has to be aware of. Remember that the code says, "I will make no statements disloyal to my country, its allies, or detrimental to their cause." And that's the thing that you have to remember. But as far as name, rank, serial number, and date of birth, you hold it as long as you can, but they are going to move you off of it at one point or another. They have developed all types of evasive techniques. We are training our people now, finally, to include a calculated breakdown, where you plan ahead what you are going to say, and then you dole it out a little bit at a time over an extended period, buying time to escape.

8   The other thing I used is a cover story; and in this case, I realized I wasn't the bravest person, so I decided to devise something which would allow me to say, "I don't know," rather than "I can't tell you" or "I won't tell you." So, I employed first of all the old artillery kiss formula, keep it simple, stupid. Then I built a cover story that would allow me to say, "I don't know"; and in that cover story, I graduated from the United States Armed Forces Institute in Washington, D.C., as an engineer; I went there for four years, and gave them three years of service back. It was 1963 and I was ready to go be a civil engineer. Since I studied engineering, I was assigned to the Adjutant General. I went to Fort Belvoir afterward, and studied bridge building and house building and road building, and then I went to civilian seminars throughout the nation, again engineering subjects; finally I was assigned to a Special Forces attachment because of my outstanding capabilities as an engineer, and because they needed civil affairs project people. So this was my cover story which allowed me over the period of time to tell them, "I don't know," to a great volume of things, and to hide behind it.

9   So, what they are trying to do initially is find out who is this person that they have, what are his capabilities? And they come out with a very neat form, it is entitled, "Red Cross Index Data Card"; the first thing it says, military information: name, rank, serial number, and date of birth. And you think, great, that is what it is supposed to be. But they have a heavy dotted line; under it, it says, "Who did you train with in the United States, what was your unit in the United States, when did you come to Vietnam, who did you come with, how did you come, when did you land, where did you serve in Vietnam, what operations did you go on?" They want to know your educational background, your political background, your religious background; they want to know your mother, your father, your wife, your children; educational, religious, and political backgrounds for all of them; your hobbies and your sports. Then they give you four sheets of paper and they want a short biographical sketch. Now they are going to try and build a picture of this American. And they've taken American prisoners of war from Korea, from North Vietnam, and from South Vietnam. They try to fit these people into some sort of category, based on their background, the psychological category if you will, and this is column A. They've got different categories; column B is different environmental situations of the stimuli that have been applied to these different groups of Americans. In column 3 are the reactions they have gotten from them. So if they get a new man and they can categorize him, then they just look to column 3 to find out what they want him to do, and then they come back to column 2 to find out what they have to do to him to get him to do it. This again is stimuli and response.

10   Now, in the camp, the physical conditions in South Vietnam with the Viet Cong are primitive. I was in the U Minh Forest, the camps were temporary at best. You had two to three feet of standing water during the rainy season; in the dry season it sank out, and you were hunting for drinking water. We had two meals of rice a day, and generally we got salt and nuoc mam with them. We did get infrequent fish from the guards, but always the castoff that the guards didn't want. If we got greens, it was maybe one meal's worth every two or three months. Immediately vitamin deficiency and malnutrition were a problem. This is a thing you are going to fight the whole way through. And you are fighting on two sides. You are fighting a physical survival, and you are fighting for mental survival.

The physical survival is just staying alive. We found that we had to eat a quart pan of rice each meal, two meals a day, just to stay alive. We found that if we could put down everything we had, and I think the most difficult thing initially was the nuoc mam. It is high in protein value, but the VC don't have that much money to spend on nuoc mam. You don't get Saigon nuoc mam. Theirs is called ten-meter nuoc mam. You can smell it within ten meters, and it is either repulsive or inedible, depending on how long you have been there. But this was the type of thing you are eating for nutritional value, and not for taste. So you are fighting on that side.

11 Disease, this is always present. Dysentery, beri-beri, hepatitis, jaundice, lac—which is a fungus infection, I had all those while I was in. I had about 85 percent of my body covered with lac. And you find that depending on your political attitude, there is either very little medication or no medication.

12 This is another thing which was disturbing, as if your political attitude determines whether you will get medication and what your treatment will be. And you are either reactionary or progressive, or somewhere in between. You find that it is not a military type thing, it is purely political. And again, we are not prepared for this. The Geneva Convention, international law, the VC say, we don't recognize them. The only law you are subjected to is our law. And if you ever want to go home, you are going to have to be a good POW, and it is based upon your good attitude and behavior as prisoner and your repentance of your past misdeeds. That last one is a hooker, because that is a confession. So they set up perimeters, and they set up this dirty little world that they keep you in; then they throw the mental pressure on top of this.

13 Indoctrination, this is where they take an individual's beliefs, and his faiths, and his loyalties, and they challenge them, because they have to break all of these before they can influence him. This is where thought correction comes in, because thought correction is nothing more than creating confusion and doubt in a man's mind and filling the void that follows with answers to the questions that you have created for him. If you will take a man as an island, with little bridges running to the mainland, and his faiths, his beliefs, his loyalties, his ethics, his standards, are all these little bridges that link him to something, to his place in the universe. If they can cut these, then they are going to turn that man inside himself, and they are going to make him fight himself. And that's exactly what they want him to do. Because as soon as you compromise one of your beliefs, as soon as you compromise one of your loyalties, just to survive, then you are condemning yourself for it. That is exactly what they want. Because this is the pressure that doesn't stop. Physical torture, as soon as they stop it, you've got relief. But mental torture is something that will last 24 hours a day, and you do it to yourself.

14 One of the most vital things that came up was when men in the camp were asked, "Do you have a wife, do you have a family?" A couple of them answered, "Yes, we've got wives, we've got families." And the first thing that was asked was, "Do you think of your wife very often, do you think of your children, do you think of your family?" In an off-hand manner, we would respond, "Well, yah, we do, we are concerned, but we can't do anything about it." Then the guard would walk off. It didn't bother the individual for a couple of days, but pretty soon he started to think, and he began to wonder, "Is my wife all right, are my children all right, do they have enough money, are they sick, are they provided for?" and this was beginning to bother them, because they didn't know. Then the guard came down, and a little bit later, he would toss in another one; he would say, "How long does it take a woman in the United States to get a divorce after her husband is missing in action? Would your wife do this?" And of course, the immediate comment was, "No sweat. Not with my wife. She is going to hang in tight." Then he goes back to his cage at night, where he is by himself, and he lays there in that mosquito net, and he starts to think, and they give you plenty of time to think, and he begins to wonder, "Will she? What is it? What's the story? What's happening back there?" And he doesn't know. Next they go one step further, after he is going up the wall over these two questions, maybe a week later, he will come back, and he will say, "What is this we hear about immorality in your country? We read much about immorality. Do you know what your wife is doing?" And again, the first answer that comes out of the prisoner's mouth is what he believes, "My wife is straight, there's no problem." But then he goes back to his cage at night, and he begins to wonder: "I've been gone four years, I've been gone three years, what is happening back there?" You talk about frustration and anxiety, this is what does it to a man. This is a very subtle thumbscrew that they put on his mind, and then he tightens it down. And they don't even have to touch him. Because he doesn't know and he is in a prison camp. Now this works constantly. There is no getting away from these, and these are just everyday things.

15   Then you have the threats, and you find that anxiety comes in. When Plato said, "I can kill you, I can torture you, I can do anything I want," it really didn't mean anything. But in 1965, they moved us into the U Minh Forest and we met Mr. Hi. Mr. Hi was a political cadre, he was in charge of indoctrination, interrogation, and proselytizing of the enemy troops. He was a professor of English in Saigon before he joined the Revolution. We called him Mafia, and he fitted his name. Because when Mafia said I can kill you, I can torture you, I can do anything I want, he meant it. We met him in March 1965, Captain Humbert "Rock" Vercase and I both failed the initial interrogation indoctrination, we both went to punishment camps. I stayed in a starvation camp for six months, Rocky Vercase was executed in September of 1965. That was Mafia's lesson. When he said I can kill you, I can torture you, I can do anything I want, he meant it. And that was a lesson to all the American POW's. It was an entirely new ballgame. Here was a political cadre who was in charge of our lives; he could take us and he could do anything he wanted to with us. This is a hard lesson to learn. This was the new concept beginning in 1965, and this is what exists now.

16   The threat of violence, the anticipation of violence, the anxiety that goes with it, sometimes, in fact most of the time, is far more devastating than what follows. This is what they are doing. They'll take a man and they'll threaten and then they will watch him run himself up and down the ladder worrying about what is going to happen to him. This is the thing—when they get hold of your emotions, and they can run them up and down the scale like a yoyo; then they've got you ricocheting off the wall; and this is exactly what they want. Because now they've got you fighting on both fronts. They've got you fighting to stay physically alive, and they've got you fighting to maintain your sanity. At that point you're becoming pliable. Because they're dangling this carrot in front of you that says, "Comply, and go home." And they toss in a few extras. One of the cadre told me in 1968, "Merely because the war ends is no reason for you to go home. If your attitude is not correct, you may rest here after the war." And ties that in with something he said a few months before, "We are here to tell you the truth of the situation today, and if you do not believe us, we will tell you tomorrow. And if you do not believe us tomorrow, we will tell you the day after, and the day after, until one day, if you don't die first, you'll believe us, and then you can go home." And so you have that carrot dangling in front of you which is "Going Home," and that is something you really want to do, because the environment is so oppressive that you want to get out of it, and yet what he is telling you is that there is no way out except our way.

17   Well, there is a way, initially, and that's escape, but that's hard. I tried three times and failed, and a fourth time it took a B-52 strike, and Cobras and light observation helicopters to get me out, which is a rotten way to do it, but it worked. But this is the only other way an American has out at the immediate time. The people in the prison camps in North Vietnam are not so fortunate. Like Bob Frishman said one time, "You know, even if you do get out of the camp, where does a round-eye go in downtown Hanoi wearing striped pajamas?" So this is one thing that the prisoners in North Vietnam don't even have to hope for. The prisoners in South Vietnam have this to look forward to, if they are strong enough to do it. But generally speaking, you are kept so physically weak that you can't. Yet you keep trying. So you are closed in on from all sides, and they seem to give you the only way out. But to take their way means you are going to compromise everything you believe in.

18 Now there have been individuals who have done this without really believing it, just going along to get out. The cases are very few, and I think the Communists have found that the Americans are probably the most insincere group of people they have ever come in contact with. The only thing is when a man comes out, if this has actually happened, when he finds that freedom is something of a hollow thing, because he has given more to get that freedom than it was worth. He's got to live with himself the rest of his life. This is one thing people have to think about. I found, for myself, that under this pressure, you find that there is a tight, hard little core inside of everybody, and it is basically faith, a person with a faith in God. This is something they can't challenge, because they don't believe in God. You find that if you can attach your belief to something far above and beyond this dirty little world they've got you in, then you have an opportunity to remove yourself from it. Their understanding of faith or of God is purely ritual and dogma. They've studied our ritual. For instance, every Christmas, they'd come down, like Mafia would come down, and he gave me a candle. He said, "According to our policy, the Front respects the religious beliefs of the POW. Take this candle, go to your net, and burn it for Midnight Mass." And I said, "Look, Mafia, I'm a Protestant, I've already had my little service, and I really don't need a candle, I don't have Midnight Mass." He stuck the candle out and said, "Take it to your net and burn it, we respect your religious beliefs." So I took the candle, I went to my net, and I burned it, for a couple of minutes. This is what they understand about religion. But you find it's a very personal and a very simple communication between one man and his God. And that's all it requires. This is essential, because it removes you from this imprisonment. And you find, I think more importantly, that the Communists have stripped you of everything that identifies you. They strip you of your rank, your position, your money, of status, anything which allows you to identify yourself with material means, to identify yourself as a human being. They are trying to dehumanize you; you might as well be a handful of mud that they pick up off the ground. But faith in God is something that identifies you far more clearly than anything material that we have right now. Once you establish that, then you'll never lose your identity.

19 The second thing was faith in our country and faith in our government. And this they did attack very well. Initially, their Communist propaganda sources were not really effective because it was a Vietnamese writing for American consumption. When Radio Hanoi, the Radio Liberation, and all their bulletins and papers came across, they were using Webster's 1933. The words were either obsolete or obsolescent. I had to look some of them up when I got home to find out what they meant. What they are sending out is things that you will not accept because they are so far out. Like we lost 3,247 aircraft over North Vietnam, which includes five B-52's and three F-111A's. And they said one of the F-111A's was shot down by a girls' militia unit in Haiphong. So we read that and said, "Okay, fine, that's great." The next thing they came up with was that we lost more tanks and artillery than we actually had in Vietnam. Another one they came up with, two of the ones that I really liked, they said that the VC platoon in the Delta had defeated a South Korean company in hand-to-hand combat. I read through that and I sort of scratched my head on that one. The next thing they came up with was during the Tet offensive in 1968, a VC girls' militia squad in Hue, they were called the Twelve Daughters of the Perfume River, which flows through Hue, had defeated a Marine batallion. The first thing I asked the cadre was, "Well, was this hand-to-hand combat, too?" But you know, we read this, and it really didn't affect us.

20 But then, in 1966 and '67, they started dropping all their sources, and we started getting the Congressional Record, magazines, newspapers, articles from the United States. This is what really turned out to be the greatest morale-breaker in the camp. The fact that we were sitting here defending our country and our government and our system, not only against the Communist political cadre, but against individuals right within our own government. And it is difficult to defend yourself when somebody in your own government is calling you an aggressor. This was the greatest weapon that they had. I think this was the thing that was most devastating to my morale personally, because there was no way that I could contest it. This was coming from my country. How do you explain dissent to Communist cadre who have never had the right to dissent in their whole lives? It was something they couldn't understand. And yet even in this context one of the cadre said, "Very soon the people in your country will decide that your coming to Vietnam was a mistake. And at that time those of you who have died here will have died a useless death. And those who lead the Revolution in your country will be the heroes and the saviors. Why should you rot in a jungle prison camp when you can return to your home, join the Revolution, repent of your crimes, and live with your family?" And you sit there and you say, "Why?" And then you begin to evaluate; and I found that no matter how many negatives they came up with, on our side, we always had more positives than the system that they were advocating. And there was always a chance for change within our system, whereas in the system they offered there was no chance for change. We got everything about the demonstrations, the riots, and the anti-war movement. I looked at the groups, the photographs of the college students carrying VC flags, the American flags being desecrated, and the one thing I thought of was, well, what if these people did this in Czechoslovakia, or Hungary, or Communist China? And I thought, "Thank God they are in the United States and they've got the right to do it." But it was disturbing to me, because nobody wants to die for nothing.

21 The other thing that came up was a faith in the other American POWs. You find that these are the only friends you've got. The communist cadre are going to try to convince you that they are your friends, but you learn rapidly that all they are doing is exploiting you, they're using you as a tool. When you see an American prisoner giving up his meager ration of fish, just so another American who is sick can have a little bit more to eat, that is sacrifice. Because when you don't have anything and you give it up, or you have very little and you give it up, then you're hurting yourself, and that is true sacrifice. That's what I saw in the prison camp.

22 So those were the three things that I found were a sort of a basis for survival in this environment that's structured to break you down. The one thing they're finding out is that the American prisoners are first of all physically tougher than they ever expected. They read our society as materialistic, as being soft, as being apathetic, and yet they're finding that once they put these prisoners in this situation, and it's a battlefield just like any other, except it's more terrifying because you're fighting in the mind, they are finding that the American prisoners are hanging on. Everybody who has come out has said the same thing—there's three faiths, and these are the three things that stand strong. But the thing is, how long can these people hold up? In my camp, there were eight of us total over the five-year period. Contrary to the VC claims for humanitarian treatment, in my camp alone, out of eight of us, three died of starvation and disease, one was executed, three were released, one of whom was dying, and I escaped before I was executed. This is actuality. This is the fact contrasted with the promise.

23 Since my wife and I have been around the country, the one thing that civilians are asking is "Why doesn't the military do something for its own people? Why don't they do something to help those men?" We're starting. We just got a letter from Fort Knox the other day in Fort Campbell, and both of them are starting a Concern for POW drive; the whole posts are turning out. This is the type of thing that needs to be done, because it could be any one of us, and it could be any one of the military families of men on this post. I had one individual that told me on one occasion, "Why should we do it, when we've got too much other to do, the Red Cross, the Officers' Wives' Club, the various things that we have to do?" and the only thing I could think of was "Just pray to God that your husband doesn't get captured some day, and you have to ask somebody else for help." I think this is the saddest commentary, that the families and loved ones of these men have to go out and seek help, not only from the military community, but from the civilian community, for their husbands, and their fathers. This is to me something that needs to be changed, and it's not so much that the people don't care, it is just that most people don't know.

24 I'm thankful for the opportunity I had to come today, to perhaps enlighten you a little bit as to what does happen inside the camps. Thank you.

Inheriting the Earth:
Louis Farrakhan and the Nation of Islam

◆ *Ian M. Rolland* ◆

For many Americans, the essential elements of the Islamic faith remain a mystery. An even larger enigma, however, is understanding the key spokesman for the Nation of Islam, Louis Farrakhan. On February 3, 1995, Ian M. Rolland spoke to the Quest Club of Fort Wayne, Indiana with the general purpose of informing his audience about the Nation of Islam and Louis Farrakhan.

Ian Rolland is Chairman and CEO of the Lincoln National Insurance Corporation based in Fort Wayne. Educated at Depauw University and the University of Michigan, Rolland, a native of Fort Wayne, has been with Lincoln National since 1956. The Quest Club is an eighty-five year old luncheon organization that meets twice a month to hear presentation by members on historical, cultural, and political topics. Over one hundred of the leading civic and business leaders in Fort Wayne are members of the Quest Club.

Rolland begins his lengthy presentation with a clear "common ground" statement for his audience (1) that is reinforced with an engaging rhetorical question (2). While Rolland promises a focus on Farrakhan, his internal preview (3) suggests that listeners need to be first introduced to the larger "cast of characters" that created the Nation of Islam. Once established, does Rolland maintain this dramatic metaphor as a structural device throughout the presentation? How helpful are his internal summaries and transition devices (20, 28, 47, 61, 94) in this speech?

Following an historical summary of Islamic theology and its transition to America (4–14), Rolland provides biographical descriptions of W.D. Farad Muhammad, Elijah Muhammad, Malcolm X, and Warith Deen Mohammed (38–60). Rolland is careful at the beginning to compare and contrast how Elijah Muhammad's teachings differed from traditional "mainstream

◆ Ian M. Rolland, "Inheriting the Earth: Louis Farrakhan and the Nation of Islam," April 1, 1995, pp. 376–380. Reprinted with permission of *Vital Speeches of the Day* and the author.

Islam" (30–36). In addition, Rolland offers his audience colorful personal insights about each of these key individuals (44, 46, 58).

Karlyn Kohrs Campbell observes in the second edition of *The Rhetorical Act* (Belmont, California: Wadsworth, 1996) that "chronological organization argues that this topic . . . is best understood in terms of how it develops or unfolds through time, or that you cannot achieve a goal without following a certain sequence" (p. 249). Does Rolland achieve his goal with the historical narrative presented? Are all the historical details he includes interesting and meaningful?

Over half-way through the speech, Rolland finally begins his discussion of Louis Farrakhan (62–63). Following a biographical sketch of Farrakhan (68–73) Rolland confronts the more controversial aspects of the Nation of Islam leader. Are the statements made by Rolland "fair" regarding the claim that Farrakhan is a "racist or a 'hatemonger'" (33, 75–79)? How do you evaluate Rolland's brief use of irony (56)? Has Rolland, with his final references to a public opinion poll on Farrakhan's influence (96–98), been objective and "balanced" with his choice of information presented?

After reading Rolland's speech, were misconceptions that you had about the Nation of Islam or Louis Farrakhan clarified? What additional information could Rolland have presented that would have increased your understanding of this organization and its leaders?

1   After 200 years as a nation, America still fights an internal battle with racism, a widening gulf between the haves and have-nots, deterioration of the inner cities and the lives of those who live there.

2   The man you just saw—Louis Farrakhan—has an answer. It's an answer that has been repeated to thousands of black Americans since the early 1930s. And, while we might not always like what we hear, the real question is this: is his message worth listening to?

3   Today, you're going to hear about Louis Farrakhan. But you're also going to hear about a whole cast of characters preceding Farrakhan's rise as a leader of the Nation of Islam. They include:

- W. D. Farad Muhammad, a mysterious door-to-door silk peddler who founded the movement.
- Elijah Muhammad, who succeeded Farad as head of the group and over the next four decades built it into national power.
- Warith Deen Mohammed, Elijah's son, who was named to head the organization upon his father's death 20 years ago.
- And Malcolm X, perhaps the best known and most influential of all.

4   While different in many respects, each man had one goal in common: to recognize the anger and explain the disenfranchisement of black people—poor and middle class alike—while instilling group identity, self-respect and hope. The Nation of Islam addresses the issues of religion, racism, economic exclusion, drug abuse and destruction of the traditional family.

5   Both black people and white people should listen to what Farrakhan is saying. Blacks because he speaks to them—whites because he speaks AGAINST them—and both because his assessment of the world, whether right or wrong, can force us to more closely examine our own.

6   To understand the Nation of Islam, we first have to look at Islam itself.

7   Islam is the youngest of the three great monotheistic religions, but it has grown to 1.16 billion adherents worldwide—nearly a fourth of everyone alive today. The number of people who call themselves Muslims is second only to Christianity.

8   By definition, a Muslim is someone who has surrendered his or her whole being to God. Anyone can be accepted as a Muslim who professes that "there is no god but Allah, and Mohammed is his messenger."

9   Muslims are generally expected to adhere to the "Five Pillars" of the faith: Profession that there is no god but Allah, prayer five times a day, fasting during Ram-a-DON, almsgiving, and pilgrimage to Mecca, if the person is physically and financially able to make the trek.

10   Today, Islam is thought to be the fastest growing religion in the U.S., though it is difficult to find statistically valid numbers. Immigration and census figures from 1980—as well as estimates of the number of African-American Muslims in America—indicate that the number of Muslims living here was about 3.3 million at the time, or one and a half percent of the population. That would make Islam the third largest religion in the United States—after Judaism, with 3 percent of the population and Christianity, with 55 percent.

11   It's likely that this number rose to at least 4 million by 1986. If that rate holds steady, the number of Muslims in the United States in the next five years will have nearly doubled over the 1980 estimate, and could pass Judaism as the country's second largest faith.

12   Part of this growth can be attributed to the liberalization of immigration policies in the 1960s. But growth of Islam among indigenous African-Americans skyrocketed for another reason—Malcolm X. The Nation of Islam's spokesman during the 1950s and early 1960s, Malcolm X's eloquence and message of hope struck a chord with many black people who had grown impatient with the pace of civil rights.

13   Today, nearly one in three American Muslims are what were once generically referred to as "Black Muslims." And Malcolm X deserves much of the credit.

14   Still, Islam has a longer history in America than its recent growth might suggest. As many as one-fifth of the slaves brought to America were educated in some of the principles of Islam. And we know that slaves from West Africa and the Sudan practiced the religion secretly in both North and

South America during slavery. Louis Farrakhan, in promoting the need for black people to identify more closely with their origins, often uses this point to claim Islam is the natural religion of African-Americans.

15   In the black community, Islam has fulfilled a variety of needs. It spread as a religion, a vehicle of protest and as a means of self-identity. Conversion to Islam fit the separatist "nation-within-a-nation" school of thought that insisted blacks had a claim to America because it was built on the blood and labor of their ancestors.

16   As Islam spread in the black community, the non-orthodoxy of many Muslim groups became obvious, drawing criticism from more mainstream Muslims. The focus of these new groups was to give *poor* blacks especially—but also others—an identity apart from a system and society that was oppressive.

Ian M. Rolland

17   Islam gave many disenfranchised African-Americans a right that they felt Christianity did not give—the right to fight back against the oppressor. While the Koran forbids aggressive warfare, it allows Muslims to use force to rectify the injustices of others.

18   Islam also lent a structure to daily living and fostered development of communities based on collective needs, adherence to a strong moral code, respect for women and the family, authority for men and economic self-sufficiency.

19   Today, at least 17 distinct groups of African-American Muslims exist. Among those is Louis Farrakhan's Nation of Islam, with an estimated membership of anywhere from 20,000 to 100,000. The largest group, estimated at 1 million members, is led by Warith Deen Mohammed—son of Nation of Islam's former leader, Elijah Muhammad.

20   So where does the Nation of Islam fit within the context of Islam in general? Well, I think we have to start at the beginning. And in the beginning, was W.D. Farad Muhammad.

21   Farad founded the Nation of Islam in 1930. A silk peddler working the poor neighborhoods of Detroit, Farad gained converts during his door-to-door sales calls. He said he was an Arab born in Mecca, but his claim has never been substantiated. His origins—and his disappearance in 1934—remain clouded in mystery.

22   Farad built a following through stories of his homeland, which he said was also the original homeland of American black people. His ministry began with gentle cautions against eating certain foods and stories about how people in the homeland preserved their health. As people asked to hear more, he gradually introduced religious concepts and doctrine about the origin of black people in Asia and Africa. Eventually, his teachings became diatribes against Christianity and "blue-eyed devils."

23   When Farad vanished without a trace—apparently even the police were mystified—his teachings were advanced by his closest associate, Elijah Muhammad, who would rule the Nation of Islam for the next 41 years.

24   Elijah Muhammad was born in rural Georgia as Elijah Poole. His impression of race relations was formed early when, as a small boy walking through the woods, he stumbled upon the lynching of a black man by two whites. Elijah hid in the bushes as the man was beaten, then hanged from a nearby tree.

25   Maybe it was that image that helped him overcome a third-grade education, a hostile press, and an unsympathetic economic system. In any case, Elijah Muhammad built an admirable business operation and a significant religious movement that drew thousands of African-Americans between the 1950s and the 1970s.

26   Revered as god-like by some and a king by others, his teachings appealed to many blacks looking for meaning in their lives. The Nation of Islam's political and ideological appeal owed to its claims to Islam, black supremacy and the unity of black people against the white man.

27   Muhammad's Nation of Islam owed a debt to two movements of the early 1900s: The Moorish Science Temple established by Noble Drew Ali and the International Negro Improvement Movement of Marcus Garvey. But Elijah Muhammad's impact was more than the sum of those parts. He was the father of a social and political movement that to this day forces mainstream leaders to sit up and take notice.

28   In a minute, I'm going to discuss some of Elijah's religious teachings—some of them will sound quite strange. But before I do, it's important to note that his primary mission was not religious conversion. His main goal was to develop a group solidarity that could become strong enough to overcome oppression by whites.

29   To quote from one Muslim minister, the aim was to get "the white man's foot off my neck, his hand out of my pocket and his carcass off my back."

30 Consequently, Elijah Muhammad's teachings differed widely from mainstream Islam. In fact, many questioned whether it was Islam at all. Muhammad did not stress fulfillment of any of the five pillars, and his ministers relied more on the Bible than the Koran. While most Muslim organizations have been more or less egalitarian, the Nation of Islam was extremely hierarchal and its leadership centralized.

31 Muhammad taught that Farad, the Nation's founder, was God incarnate. He interpreted his OWN role as that of divine messenger, and espoused a doctrine both mythical and practical in his teachings:

32 According to Muhammad, blacks belong to the tribe of Shabazz, which came from space 66 trillion years ago. The white race was created 6,000 years ago by a black scientist named Yakub. Yakub, through genetic manipulation, created a number of races that were lighter, weaker and genetically inferior to the black man.

33 The lowest of this order is the Caucasian. The white man turned out to be a liar and a murderer—Elijah Muhammad called them white devils—but according to Elijah, Allah allowed the Caucasian to dominate the world as a test for the black race. This, by the way, is a theme that lived on in the sermons of Louis Farrakhan and which has contributed to his label as a racist.

34 Elijah Muhammad also taught that blacks are Allah's chosen people and will inherit the earth. White people—and Muhammad often specified Jews—are anxious to impede black people from achieving success. He believed the way out of repression wasn't integration, but self-sufficiency and separation.

35 Muhammad gave black people an identity apart from the existing "system." He reminded them that they were not Americans, but members of an "Asiatic nation from the tribe of Shabazz." New members were required to write a letter to him asking for permission to discard the "slave name" given to them by the white man by taking the last name "X."

36 Elijah Muhammad's success was built on his ability to instill pride of self and race, an emphasis on personal responsibility and morality, respect for the family, and abstinence from drugs, alcohol and pork.

37 These teachings drew substantial numbers of followers over the years, although it is difficult to pinpoint just how many. Elijah Muhammad once put the number at several hundred thousand, but his son, Warith, has said active membership never exceeded 10,000.

38 In building this movement, Elijah made use of a

- Strong charismatic and centralized leadership.
- He also designed a well organized militia, called the Fruit of Islam, which consisted of former servicemen. The Fruit of Islam was charged with the duty of protecting the community, the temples, and other institutions.

39 It was also accused of many misdeeds, including the assassination of Malcolm X. But in recent times there have been relatively few problems, despite the organization's continued high visibility.

40 Elijah Muhammad built a well-run, profitable business organization that comprised, among other things, a bank, a publishing facility, a fish import company, temples, apartment complexes and various small businesses. In all, the Nation's assets grew to an estimated $80 million to $100 million.

41 These businesses provided jobs for hundreds of people in the inner cities. Elijah Muhammad's former attorney estimates that the fish import business alone did $27 million to $30 million a year in trade and had cornered the distribution system at the time of Elijah's death in 1975.

42   In addition, Elijah established institutions originally called Universities of Islam, which continue to run a highly disciplined system of education. These schools are now called Sister Clara Muhammad schools after his wife.

43   And he established a national network of temples including some in the West Indies that continue to be very well organized under the direction of their ministers.

44   Stop for a minute and think about what Elijah Muhammad actually did. Over 41 years, a sharecropper's son with little education took a small, local, religious sect begun by a door-to-door salesman and transformed it into a nationwide, multi-million dollar organization that affected the lives of thousands of people.

45   Maybe it's not too surprising, then, that the mysticism that grew out of this movement during this time eventually attached to Elijah himself.

46   For example, many of his followers believe Elijah is still alive, and Louis Farrakhan has said that he did not physically die. Farrakhan tells of a vision in which he was beamed aboard a UFO. This craft docked in the Motherplane—a plane-like object a half-mile in diameter. And inside, Farrakhan heard Elijah speak, telling him that Ronald Reagan had met with the Joint Chiefs of Staff to plan a war against Libya. With that information, Farrakhan warned Libyan officials of an impending attack.

47   Elijah owed his success to his knowledge of the U.S. economic and political system, his business savvy, his charisma, and commitment to his cause. But he didn't build his organization all by himself, he had help. And his greatest help came from Malcolm X.

48   During the 1950s and early 1960s the Nation of Islam was, in the public mind, synonymous with the name Malcolm X. Until he left the organization, Malcolm X was its greatest success story, a former prison convict who became an internationally-known activist and political figure.

49   Elijah Muhammad's national spokesman until 1964, Malcolm X may be better known than any other member of the Nation of Islam. His detractors at the time criticized him for taking the spotlight from Elijah Muhammad, but he is credited for recruiting thousands of people into the organization.

50   His break with the Nation of Islam was precipitated by his move toward orthodox Islam and by his discovery that Elijah Muhammad had been involved in a number of extramarital affairs. He was assassinated in a Harlem dance hall in 1965 while speaking to followers, seven months after leaving the organization.

51   Some have blamed Malcolm X's assassination on the man who now leads the group—Louis Farrakhan. You probably read or heard about the arrest last month of one of Malcolm X's daughters, Qubilah Shabazz, on charges that she tried to hire someone to kill Farrakhan. She was four years old and in the room when her father was killed, and her mother—Betty Shabazz—has said publicly that she thinks Farrakhan had something to do with the assassination.

52   Farrakhan, in turn, has said that his public condemnation of Malcolm X probably contributed to the atmosphere that resulted in the assassination. However, he denies any direct role in the killing.

53   In the years after Malcolm X, Elijah Muhammad and the Nation of Islam took a quieter public posture.

54   Finally, in 1975—10 years after Malcolm X's assassination—Elijah Muhammad died. Shortly before his death, the ailing Muhammad named his successor—his son, Warith Deen Mohammed.

55   Ironically, Warith Deen had been expelled from the organization several times for speaking against his father's teachings. But Elijah gave his son one more chance, "rehabilitating" him on his deathbed, and naming him heir to the Nation.

56   If Elijah *is* still alive, you have to believe he regrets his decision.

57 Warith Deen's style contrasted sharply with that of his father. Like Malcolm X, Warith Deen was drawn to a more orthodox form of Islam, and he gradually decentralized the power structure his father had designed and gave less attention to the business side of the movement. Only a year after his father's death, Warith Deen declared that Elijah was not a prophet and consequently started to replace the theology of the Nation with orthodox Islam.

58 He also changed the spelling of his last name—instead of spelling it M-U-H-A-M-M-A-D, he changed it to M-O-H-A-M-M-E-D. In addition, he renamed his organization the World Community of Al-Islam in the West. Temples became mosques, ministers imams, and the islamic rituals began to be observed.

59 Leadership stopped preaching the race-tinged ideology that identified white people as devils, relaxed strict discipline and disbanded the Fruit of Islam militia. In 1980, the name changed finally from the World Community of Al-Islam to the American Muslim Mission.

60 Despite—or perhaps because of—his break with his father's teachings, Warith Deen's organization has grown to become the largest African American Muslim organization. While that in itself is a notable achievement, Warith Deen is notable for another reason. Without him, most of us probably would never have heard of Louis Farrakhan.

61 I want to take just a few seconds here to recap. There are so many people who are part of the story, that it's difficult to keep them straight. First there was Farad Muhammad, a door-to-door salesman who founded the organization. Elijah Muhammad took over when Farad disappeared in 1934, and Malcolm X was his national spokesman during the '50s and early '60s. Elijah's son, Warith Deen was placed at the top when Elijah died in 1975.

62 Now comes Farrakhan, who succeeded Malcolm as minister of the Nation's Harlem temple. When Warith Deen began to distance the group from his father's teachings, Farrakhan was horrified. He broke away, claiming for himself and other hard core followers of Elijah Muhammad the designation "Nation of Islam."

63 Farrakhan's group is just one of four now claiming to be the true Nation of Islam, but it is the largest and has the highest profile.

64 His numbers of followers is estimated at 20,000 on the low end to as many as 100,000—perhaps more than the Nation had at the time of Elijah Muhammad's death, but not nearly the estimated 1 million members of Warith's American Muslim Mission.

65 Oratorically gifted and passionate about his goals, Farrakhan is one of the most popular speakers on black college campuses today. He typically draws 15,000 to 20,000 people to his lectures, but attracted 60,000 to a speech he gave in Atlanta in 1992. In doing so, he outdrew the opening game of the World Series, taking place about a mile away.

66 Farrakhan can speak for two hours or more without the apparent use of notes, mesmerizing audiences with his alternate use of gravity and humor, compassion and anger, fact and hyperbole. He easily covers a huge range of subjects in his lectures.

67 The need for strong families, black economic empowerment, education, morality, the media, self-worth, and the white conspiracy against blacks are all common themes.

68 Farrakhan was born Louis Eugene Walcott in the Bronx in 1933. His mother was a West Indian domestic worker who raised him Episcopalian. His family moved to Boston, where he graduated from Latin High School with honors. He spent two years at college in North Carolina, where he also ran track.

69 But he loved music most of all. He became an accomplished violinist and, as a teenager, appeared on Ted Mack's Original Amateur Hour. In the 1950s he became a nightclub singer billed as "The Charmer," singing calypso songs and playing the violin.

70   He became aware of the Nation of Islam at a convention in Chicago. He later visited the Nation's temple in Harlem, where he heard Malcolm X speak. He decided to join and became Louis X.

71   Because Elijah Muhammad forbade members from being entertainers, Farrakhan abandoned his career. Some say he rejected a movie deal later signed by Harry Belafonte.

72   Farrakhan became Elijah Muhammad's minister of Temple 11 in Boston, while raising a family of nine children. He later went to New York, but was moved to Chicago by Warith Mohammed after his father's death.

73   Farrakhan has continued to run the Nation of Islam from Chicago. When Warith Muhammad's organization later filed bankruptcy, Farrakhan's organization bought Elijah's old flagship temple in Chicago and renamed it Mosque Maryam.

74   Outside his organization, Farrakhan is widely viewed as a racist, not only for some of his own public remarks but also for those made by his predecessors and contemporary aides. You may have heard about Khallid Abdul Muhammad, whom Farrakhan demoted last year after complaints about the reference to Jews as "bloodsuckers" and for insensitive comments about the Holocaust.

75   Farrakhan has denied that he is a racist or a "hate-monger," tagging Jews and other whites as hypocrites for criticizing *him* while they perpetuate racism against blacks.

76   In fairness to Farrakhan, a reading of his published speeches between 1984 and 1989 reveals much scapegoating, but little evidence of outright hate against anybody—nowhere does he advocate violence against any group. He often takes great pains to distinguish between hate of actions and hate of people, and in recent years has toned down what could be construed as racist language. Even some mainstream religious leaders say Farrakhan's remarks have been distorted by the media or taken out of context.

77   However, it is true that Farrakhan often blames Jews—sometimes without explaining his reasons—for many of the problems of African-Americans. His remarks can be inflammatory, such as calling Judaism "a gutter religion." And the Nation's natural affinity for Arab Muslims puts it at odds with Zionist causes, which many Jews interpret as anti-Semitic.

78   His disdain for homosexuals also remains clear. And in 1990 he accused whites of manufacturing AIDS and deliberately spreading it among blacks.

79   He doesn't allow white people to worship in his mosques, and he tolerates other members of the Nation who have little inhibition against expressing clearly racist beliefs. So, while Farrakhan may not be the seething hatemonger some would have the public believe, he hasn't done much to change his image as a bigot.

80   Despite all this, Farrakhan's harshest language—as well as his greatest encouragement—is reserved for his own audiences.

81   He tells his followers they feed white prejudice by allowing their communities to deteriorate—through teen pregnancies, drugs, violence, lack of respect for each other and lack of faith in God. He tells them they bear much of the blame for the way they are viewed and that they can't wait for the current system to bring them out of oppression—they must do it themselves.

82   His solution? A separate society based on Nation of Islam values and a black economic base in which African Americans become producers, not just consumers.

83   Farrakhan's lectures and sermons have strong religious components, and he uses the Bible and Koran almost equally in arguing his points. He's been known to preach Easter sermons on the need for renewal, and his home temple is Mosque Maryam—named for the mother of Jesus.

84   Taken by themselves, his pro-family, anti-drug arguments could come from any number of conservative religious figures or politicians. Unlike some of those conservative Christian leaders, however, Farrakhan actually appointed a woman as one of his ministers.

85   Farrakhan sounds quite mainstream at times, depending on the subject he is addressing.

86   Farrakhan says black people are God's chosen people, but that they have been "sleeping" while Allah allowed white people to dominate. He uses Biblical interpretation to prove this claim: The bondage of the Jews by the Egyptians, he says, is not historical fact but prophetic allegory—the Jews of the Bible weren't really the Jews of ancient times, but the blacks of today. Just as Moses was said to have led his people out of slavery, the time is at hand in which black people will be victorious over their white oppressors.

87   Farrakhan does not call himself a prophet—Mohammed of Arabia was, as Islam teaches, the last of the prophets—but he believes he is divinely chosen to bring his message to a black nation.

88   While Farrakhan has continued many of the traditional teachings of Elijah Muhammad, he has never shown the business acumen Elijah Muhammad demonstrated. It is not for lack of effort.

89   His regrouped Fruit of Islam militia is sometimes feared by outsiders, yet credited with cleaning up several inner city housing complexes that contracted with the group to eradicate drugs and violence. Despite some failures, in many cases these programs have made a significant impact in reducing drug trafficking and violence where they operate.

90   His success in other business areas has been limited. In 1985, he launched a new line of health and beauty-aid products made by POWER—People Organized and Working for Economic Rebirth.

91   While five black-owned companies had promised to make POWER products under the Clean 'N Fresh brand name, they later withdrew, reportedly for fear of alienating Jewish distributors.

92   Farrakhan persuaded Libyan leader Mo-Mar Khaddafi to lend POWER $5 million interest free. But distribution in high crime areas proved difficult because residents were reluctant to open their doors to solicitors and salespeople were afraid to go into those areas.

93   So the business side of Farrakhan's organization is struggling. While disappointed, Farrakhan has remained steadfast—never losing sight of his mission.

94   Farrakhan sees himself as Elijah Muhammad's heir: a messenger from God, sent to help African-American people take their rightful place as Allah's chosen people. His sentiments hit home with many in the black community in need of structure in their lives, unity with other blacks, inspiration for the future and who see no chance that the current power structure will ever meet their needs.

95   Farrakhan's biggest stumbling block to broader acceptance has been his refusal to compromise his beliefs, which many view as racist or unforgiving. His inability to shed this image has left him unable to bridge important gulfs between his organization and other black organizations who see his potential but shun the baggage that he brings.

96   While he is able to command large groups to hear his speeches, it is difficult to gauge how much influence he has in the general population. A *New York Times* poll last year showed that most blacks reject the notion that Farrakhan and the Nation of Islam represent their views, but they do share some of his racial beliefs. For example, only 15 percent said he and his organization represent the views of most blacks in America, but 40 percent said they agree that most Jews are against progress by blacks.

97   Sixty-six percent say most whites feel they are superior to blacks, and thirty-two percent said most whites want to keep blacks down.

98   Finally, twenty-three percent said they agree with Farrakhan that the government deliberately makes drugs easily available in poor black neighborhoods in order to harm black people.

99   From this standpoint, it appears he has the ears—and possibly the hearts—of many who cannot be formally counted as members of the Nation of Islam.

The Search for Common Ground in the Abortion Conflict: A Short Primer

◆ *Mary E. Jacksteit* ◆

Search for Common Ground (a non-profit, non-governmental organization) was founded in Washington, D.C. in 1982 and the European Center for Common Ground was founded in Brussels, Belgium in 1995. Both organizations operate programs that seek to transform how the world deals with conflict through moving away from adversarial approaches and toward cooperative solutions. In the international arena, Search for Common Ground has operated programs in Angola, Burundi, Iran, Macedonia, and the Ukraine. In the United States, it has operated programs on the subjects of race and of abortion.

At the time of this speech, Mary E. Jacksteit, who has degrees in political science, law, and conflict resolution, was the Project Director for the Search for Common Ground Network for Life and Choice. This project uses an approach of dialogue rather than debate in bringing together pro-life and pro-choice supporters and other concerned citizens. This approach aims at breaking down communication barriers and stereotypes, achieving understanding of opposing views, and "rehumanizing" (not dehumanizing) opponents. The approach also facilitates ways to explore shared concerns, such as teenage pregnancy or inadequate resources for women and children. Fundamental to the Common Ground approach on this topic is that no one ever is asked to change her or his belief about the core issue of abortion. At the end of 1999, the Network for Life and Choice project was

transferred from Search for Common Ground to the National Association for Community Mediation. You are urged to consider Jacksteit's speech in conjunction with the pro-choice speech by Faye Wattleton and the pro-life speech by Jerry Falwell, both in Chapter Seven.

On November 12, 1998 Mary E. Jacksteit delivered this speech at George Mason University in Fairfax, Virginia, to an undergraduate class in Conflict Resolution and Cross-Cultural Communication. Clearly her purpose is to increase the audience's level of understanding about what the Common Ground Network for Life and Choice is and does (3–4). At the outset, she clarifies the purposes of that program (2, 4–5).

Through varied methods she explains the key concept of "common ground" to make it more meaningful and understandable for the audience. She itemizes numerous brief examples (4). She presents simple diagrams (7, 9) that stress areas of overlap or points on a continuum rather than completely separate or polarized positions. And she defines by negation—by saying what "common ground" is not, namely, it is not a compromise (8).

Jacksteit also explains the basic processes that promote a search for common ground. Simple description of processes frequently is used (10, 11, 14–16). But a major method that Jacksteit employs to explain processes is the technique of comparison and contrast. She contrasts dialogue with mediation and with direct facilitation (1). Dialogue is contrasted with de-

◆ The text of this speech was provided by Mary E. Jacksteit and is printed with her permission.

bate twice (6, 10). And she contrasts ʻgenuine dialogueʻ with rhetorical questions and leading questions that only appear to promote interaction (12).

A crucial part of her speech is her description of how the program works in actuality. Partially she does this through brief examples (17–18). How are the language resources of alliteration and parallel structure used to strengthen her points? But Jacksteit also presents an extended illustration of how it works; she narrates a story (19–23). She emphasizes that this is not a unique or atypical example of success but is a representative example (24). What elements of the story particularly hold your attention? How would you evaluate the story in light of the discussion in Chapter Two (question 11) about narration as a noteworthy rhetorical strategy?

The speech could be analyzed by applying in some detail the criteria for evaluating speeches that increase understanding—criteria discussed earlier in the present chapter. (1) To what degree and in what ways is the information communicated accurately, completely, and with unity? (2) How does the speaker attempt to make the information meaningful for the audience? (3) How does the speaker create audience interest in the information being presented? (4) How does the speaker show the audience that the information is important? An excellent book that discusses communication approaches for bridging the gap between polarized moral viewpoints is W. Barnett Pearce and Stephen W. Littlejohn, *Moral Conflict: When Social Worlds Collide* (Sage, 1997).

◆ ◆ ◆

1   Somewhere beyond interest-based, negotiable issues are conflict areas that feature beliefs and values that are not subject to compromise. These "hot" values-based conflicts often result in exaggeration, mistrust, hyperbolic speech, and extreme stereotyping. Neither mediation that seeks movement towards a negotiated settlement nor highly directive facilitation aimed at collaborative problem-solving are usually effective in addressing the needs of these highly polarized parties.

2   By contrast, dialogue "puts a human face" on these conflicts. It alters the relationships between adversaries by changing their perceptions of one another and of the issues in conflict. Most critically, it narrows the perceived distance between the parties without threatening them with giving up their deepest held beliefs or losing their integrity. Dialogue seeks understanding, not agreement, and encourages discovery of areas of genuine overlap.

3   For nearly six years, Search for Common Ground has sponsored The Common Ground Network for Life and Choice (the Network) to promote dialogue between the two sides in the abortion debate. Much of this work has been at the community level where informal groups of pro-life (PL) and pro-choice (PC) people have come together. Sometimes this has been a reaction to intensified PC/PL conflict. In other instances local people have organized a dialogue effort out of a personal need for a different kind of conversation with their adversaries. Some of these groups have a relatively short life (six months to a year); others have gone on for years.

4   My purpose here is to explain what we mean by common ground and how we go about helping people discover it. **The goal** is to transform the *dynamics* of the abortion conflict, not settle or resolve the conflict. The idea is to reduce polarization and hostility and promote a level of trust between the adversaries so that they can—

- Gain a deeper understanding of the conflict over abortion and the motivations, interests and values reflected in people's positions;
- Coexist peacefully and with civility, with debate focused on the merits of their contrasting beliefs, not on stereotyped and dehumanized "enemies";

- Act together when it serves their mutual interests and the common good. This is the area we call the "common ground"—shared belief in the need for such things as:
  — preventing teen pregnancy;
  — providing practical assistance to people facing crisis/unwanted pregnancies;
  — renouncing violence against abortion providers;
  — building dialogue and conflict resolution skills in the larger community;
  — raising the level of knowledge and understanding about adoption;
  — reducing the conflict between family and work;
  — increasing male sexual responsibility.

5   Changing the relationships between the adversaries in this way contributes to a higher level of discourse on abortion and related issues, one that can reveal the elements of truth in each perspective (there are some) and the areas of overlapping values and interests where working together might make a difference. In turn this builds community, recognition of mutual interdependence and an understanding of how people with profound differences can live and work together to make a better world.

6   **What do we mean by a common ground approach?** *Dialogue* is at the heart of the common ground approach. Dialogue is different from debate. Debate is about persuading others that your views are "right" and that the views of others are "wrong." The goals of dialogue center around increasing understanding and being understood rather than persuading others and being "right." It is a process in which people are asked to respect and acknowledge the humanity of the people present regardless of their points of view. Dialogue in a sustained and polarized conflict is aimed at *changing the relationship* between people who see each other as demonized adversaries.

7   *The common ground approach is a search for what is genuinely shared.* We illustrate this by the image of two interlocking circles.

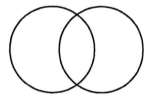

Each circle represents a point of view about abortion (one circle, pro-life, the other pro-choice). A common ground process recognizes the integrity of each circle as a complete set of concerns, beliefs and values around this issue. It focuses attention on and explores the *area of intersection or overlap.* This is where shared concerns, beliefs and values are located. The common ground "space" is also a perspective for examining differences where everyone works together to try to understand the conflict rather than facing off to argue. This tends to make the differences less threatening and more comprehensible. In our experience people always find the area of overlap larger than anticipated.

8   *Common ground is not compromise.* Searching for common ground is not about compromising to reach a middle position but about focusing on areas of *genuinely* shared values and concerns. People are not asked to change their views on abortion or pretend agreement where it does not exist.

9   A common ground approach encourages *looking beyond the labels and the stereotypes.* A common ground approach assumes that even in a polarized conflict, people's views fall on a continuum.

Pro-life _____|_____ Pro-choice

When people identify themselves as "pro-choice" or "pro-life," they are only placing themselves *somewhere* on the continuum other than the exact center. This idea of a continuum encourages awareness of how little we can assume about another person's set of beliefs if all we know about them is that they choose one label over the other. It allows recognition of the diversity on both sides and discovery that two given people with the same label may be as different by some other criteria as are two people with different labels because there are issues that cut across the pro-choice/pro-life divide. Capital punishment and welfare reform are examples. The continuum provides a way for people to nuance their own positions on abortion in ways that the labels do not. Encouraging people to think in terms of a continuum fosters curiosity, rather than assumptions, about what people believe.

10 A common ground approach *encourages connective thinking*. Debates tend to focus attention on the weaknesses of the speakers and to encourage a search for the flaws in what is said. In dialogue we ask people to engage in *connective thinking*—to focus attention on where they agree or resonate with the other's experience and/or beliefs, to listen for the pieces of truth in what is said. Where people place their focus really influences what they hear and remember.

11 Common ground dialogue *encourages the sharing of personal experience*. Personal experiences cannot be argued with like positions can be. Experiences are not agreed or disagreed with. They *are*. Hearing a person explain *how* they arrived at their pro-life or pro-choice positions invites understanding responses from those who hear them. They are a constructive place to begin.

12 Common ground dialogue *encourages genuine questions*. *Genuine questions* are questions asked in a spirit of real curiosity and a sincere interest in learning the answers. Rhetorical or leading questions are not genuine questions. They are questions where we already know the answers—we just want it said so we can make our rebuttal. They are statements disguised as questions that really cannot be answered. "Why don't pro-life people care about children after they are born?" "Why aren't pro-choice people concerned about women after they have the abortion?" These questions work as traps, not as openings to learning. A genuine question on the other hand invites an honest answer: "What do you pro-life activists do for the children who are born?" "Do you pro-choice activists concern yourselves with the longer-term impact abortion may have on a woman?"

13 Putting the common ground approach into practice. As you can imagine, people have great apprehension about involving themselves in a potentially ugly argument on abortion. They also often fear having their participation used against them (i.e., identified as weakness or concession), especially if they are full-time advocates. Common ground dialogue is designed to provide a safe space where productive conversations can take place. There are explicit ground rules that call for respectful speech and behavior, confidentiality, and an intention to seek understanding, not necessarily agreement. The common ground approach is described and explained to participants, just as I have done here. Other elements include having a balance of pro-choice and pro-life participants, active listening, speaking for oneself, personal storytelling, and dialogue structured by questions and assisted by a facilitator. Let me explain some of these elements.

Mary E. Jacksteit (Photo provided courtesy of Mary E. Jacksteit)

14 Creating a *PC-PL balance*. The need for balanced participation is critical, not only because both viewpoints need to be represented for a real dialogue to take place, but because meetings sponsored and designed by only one faction risk being perceived as stacked or as efforts to co-opt. The effort to get balanced participation becomes a common ground exercise in itself, pushing people to reach outside their comfort zone.

15 *Active listening*. This means the listener reflecting to the speaker what has been heard without comment, answer or interpretation. Two dynamics make active listening a key building block of the dialogue process. Often, people on both sides are so sure they know what each other is going to say that they either do not listen, or they listen with such a thick filter that only a portion of the message gets through. Secondly, due to the polarized nature of the abortion conflict, strong feelings are often very close to the surface. Even without "hot buttons" being pushed, certain kinds of statements can lead people to start talking "at" or "past" one another. Active listening is one effective way to address these situations, as it is powerful for a person on one side to have the experience of really being heard by someone on the other side.

16 The Role of *Facilitation*. A facilitator is there to make sure that participants have the conversation that they came to experience. Based on our experience and feedback from informal and formal evaluations, we know that facilitation is very important. The key is for the facilitator to be:

- Solely committed to the process, allowing the group to focus on the substantive conversation. This means staying out of the substantive dialogue and not injecting, however indirectly, the result that she/he thinks is desirable.
- Absolutely fair. To avoid a perception of bias, a facilitator has to play a neutral role. This means that ahead of time the person must honestly consider whether he/she can be even-handed and calm in a discussion relating to abortion and can use balanced language (*i.e.,* can avoid using the labels the sides use for their opponents, like anti-choice or pro-abortion).
- Compassionate and empathic. This puts participants at ease and models the attitude you hope to elicit from everyone.

Specific facilitator tasks are:

- Structuring and leading the dialogue process.
- Explaining, modeling, and coaching good communication skills.
- Enforcing ground rules.
- Suggesting and leading the group in other group processes as it moves to decision-making, or collaborative problem-solving and strategizing for an action project.

17 **What happens?** People opposed over abortion do find common ground. This is not because they are all "mushy middle" sorts of people. Common ground participants have included clinic directors, picketers, crisis pregnancy workers and lobbyists as well as social workers, nurses, ministers, stay-at-home moms and lawyers. They are full-time activists and they are people who relate to the abortion issue as a concern, not a vocation. The key is that they are open to try a new kind of conversation.

18 Through experience people develop the ability to talk respectfully and to support others in doing the same. They make friends with their "enemies" and develop respect for the seriousness and sincerity of viewpoints they do not share. They come to accept that a feminist can be pro-life and a religious person can be pro-choice. Out of these new understandings and relationships their idea of the possible changes. They do a range of things from dialogue, to education about common ground, to projects concerning adoption and teen pregnancy. They write articles and speak together when they have something to say that they believe will have greater impact coming from their joined voices. They are changed, and they become change agents.

19 I want to end by telling you about a real life common ground effort that will give all of these ideas some reality. The Quad Cities is a metropolitan area on the Iowa-Illinois border surrounding the cities of Davenport and Moline. Quad Cities Common Ground started when an *ad hoc* group of community activists came together in the spring of 1995 to confront the reality that two organizations had announced plans to open clinics to provide abortions—the first in many years in this metropolitan area. They found themselves on opposing sides, not just as bystanders but as people with high profiles in the local pro-choice and pro-life movements. They feared both the potential for violent confrontation and outside agitation, and destruction of the ties that had enabled them to join in addressing many social justice issues over the years.

20 After a series of meetings in which they openly talked about their differences and hopes and built trust among themselves, QCCG went public in an effort to have maximum impact. They held an all-day common ground dialogue for 50 people from different sectors of the community; they made a concerted outreach to the press and other media to explain the group's membership and goals, achieving TV, radio and print coverage; and they began to publicly model the civil and peaceful debate about the potential clinics that they hoped the community would embrace. A local community mediation center took on sponsorship of the group.

21 For close to four years QCCG has retained the active participation of such key activists as the social action director for the Catholic Diocese, and a clinic director. A broad spectrum of religious traditions and professional affiliations is represented. The group has weathered litigation, protests and counter-protests—activities in which many of them have participated in their advocate roles. Groundbreaking for the Planned Parenthood facility this past summer has kept the controversy in the forefront. Throughout this time they have regularly met for dialogue, and consistently injected their commitment to mutual respect and civility through their conduct on the sidewalk, at public hearings, during joint appearances on radio and TV, in local speaking engagements, and while taking part in frequent print media interviews.

22 QCCG also garnered significant national exposure. During the summer of 1997 Davenport Diocesan staff member, Dan Ebener invited clinic director Marilyn Cohen and another group member to join him in a presentation on common ground at a national Catholic pro-life directors' meeting in Texas in the summer of 1997. The *Wall Street Journal* and *Harper's* have both published articles about the group and QCCG was featured in a Peter Jennings' report on ABC World News Tonight. The group is active in national common ground efforts through the Network for Life and Choice. Through that vehicle, Marilyn Cohen co-authored a paper "Common Ground on Clinic Activism" with a pro-life activist from Buffalo, New York.

23 This year the group formed an Adoption Task Force that held a community dialogue to broaden understanding about adoption. Meetings over the period of a year have led to action plans focusing on education and information. Another QCCG initiative is a joint pro-life/pro-choice examination of the nature of the counseling given to women in clinics and in pro-life pregnancy support centers.

24 The vision, courage and boldness of these common ground activists in the Quad Cities are incredible, but not unique. They have colleagues around the country who are quietly bringing about change. We Americans have taken our pluralism for granted for too long. There is increasing anxiety about the ability of people with different norms, values and cultures to coexist in a positive and creative way that is not at the lowest common denominator but the highest. To support bridge-building and peace-making across these divides is a privilege. It is to participate in creating a hopeful future. I hope you will find opportunities to join in.

Chapter Four

Speeches That Affirm Propositions of Fact

The Nature and Importance of Speeches That Affirm Propositions of Fact

S peakers sometimes try to prove to the satisfaction of an audience that a proposition of fact is, in reality, true. While the preceding chapter was concerned with the art of interpreting established knowledge or original inquiry for the *enlightenment of an audience,* the present chapter is devoted to the principles involved in *establishing alleged truth in order to win agreement.* Earlier, the primary task for the speaker was to help an audience understand an event, process, concept, or inquiry; in this chapter, the speaker's efforts are directed toward seeking approval of the "facts" that are presented. In the previous speech form, the speaker might publicly analyze, "What is the present state of social security for the elderly?" In this chapter, the speaker seeks to gain acceptance of a conclusion: "The social security system as presently constituted will not survive the drain that will be placed on it by the baby-boomer generation."

The social environments that produce speeches affirming factual propositions are diverse. A district attorney may seek to establish the guilt of a labor leader charged with misuse of union funds. The president of a liberal arts college may try to convince the board of regents that faculty salaries are not equal to that of competing schools. A state legislator may attempt to prove to his or her constituency that the condition of state highways will deter expansion of the tourist industry. While in certain instances the affirmation of a proposition of fact is the sole purpose of a persuasive speech, at other times a speaker may affirm a fact as a means of affirming a value, creating concern for a problem, or gaining acceptance for a course of action. On the whole, matters of fact are more commonly argued in relation to one of those ends than they are as separate entities.

Matters of fact are not self-evident. In the common vernacular, the term *fact* connotes an incontrovertible truth. Thus the novitiate to the advocate's art seeks to stifle further argument by asserting, "It's a fact"—by which it is meant, "It is incontestable truth." But, "Matters of fact," Matthew Tyndal has observed, "are very stubborn things." Were all facts self-evident, there would be no such thing as a proposition of fact because the term *proposition* implies a statement about an unsettled or controversial state of affairs.

What, then, is a proposition of fact? A proposition of fact may be defined as a statement (a sentence with assertive content) that may be affirmed or denied through tests of *existence, occurrence,* or *causality.* The fact in question may concern an individual, an event, a process, a condition, a concept, or even a policy. Whatever the fact to be judged, however, the advocate is primarily interested in gaining listener acceptance that something was, is, or will be true. Consider these examples:

Proposition A: The Great Depression was caused by excessive speculation on the stock market.

Proposition B: The Japanese attack on Pearl Harbor was precipitated by United States failure to provide military safeguards.

Proposition C: Sightings of flying saucers are real events.

Proposition D: Marijuana smoking is physically harmless.

Proposition E: In the computer age, teacher-based classroom education will become obsolete.

Proposition F: Free agency will ultimately cause the demise of major league baseball.

Although these six propositions differ substantially in subject matter, they are all legitimate factual propositions. Propositions A and B concern matters of past causality. Propositions C and D concern matters of present existence and causality. Propositions E and F concern matters of future occurrence and future causality respectively.

Whatever the subject matter and tense of a factual proposition, its proposer is interested in gaining audience acceptance of an alleged truth. We do not argue about matters that are generally accepted to be true; for example, who today would argue "The world is a sphere"? None of us can touch it, see it, or feel it; we, nevertheless, accept its truthfulness. But we might argue about the proposition that "Global warming will be dangerous to human life in the next fifty years." The following section identifies the criteria that are especially relevant for evaluation speeches that affirm propositions of fact.

Criteria for Evaluating Speeches That Affirm Propositions of Fact

Because propositions of fact treat supposedly verifiable or predictable phenomena, the tests of speeches affirming such propositions are strongly concerned with the logical sufficiency of the affirmation.

1. Has the speaker adequately assessed the proof requirements of the factual proposition?

Implicit in a proposition of fact is the assumption that there are reasonable criteria with which to judge the truth of alleged events, states of being, causal relationships, and so on. Proof requirements are often field dependent; that is, they differ from one area of knowledge or profession to another. For example, the affirmation of a proposition of medical fact may require that standards on the observation and clinical diagnosis of patients be met. The affirmation of a proposition of historical fact, on the other hand, may require that standards relevant to sound historical research be met. Lawyers, behavioral scientists, chemists, mathematicians, and astronomers have all devised standards by which certain types of phenomena are to be judged. When talking to a specialized group about a specialized topic, the speaker can expect that the proposition will be judged by the special proof requirements established by that profession as a modus operandi.

In the world of ordinary discourse, the criteria by which propositions of fact are judged are less well defined. However, even the popular proposition of fact demands that the speaker employ responsible standards of assessment. If popular speakers fail to support their assertions or if they support them with emotional appeals and shallow truisms, they will be criticized for their faulty interpretation of the responsible proof requirements of their propositions. Enlightened lay critics do not excuse the maxims and pseudo-arguments of modern mass media advertisements even though they are aware of the logical permissiveness of the American consuming public.

2.   Has the speaker offered acceptable arguments in support of the proposition of fact?

Given that a speaker demonstrates awareness of the general proof requirements of a particular factual proposition, the next question to be raised is "Has the speaker offered relevant arguments— reasons for belief—in support of the proposition of fact?" Imagine, for example, that a district attorney seeks to affirm the proposition that "a labor leader is guilty of misusing union funds." Imagine, further, that our barrister has recognized that the particular proof demands that must be met are those of the bar rather than the public forum. We may then question whether the arguments that are selected support the conclusion that the labor leader is guilty of misusing union funds. We might expect, for example, that it would be argued that (1) the labor leader in question did spend union funds on nonunion activities, (2) legal precedence makes the misuse of union funds a criminal offense, and (3) the expenditure of the funds in question is classifiable as a misuse in light of legal precedence. Should our lawyer fail to offer any of these arguments or should irrelevant nonlegal arguments be offered in their place, we may deny that a convincing case in support of the proposition has been made.

In the world of everyday discourse, the specific argument or arguments necessary for the establishment of a factual proposition are largely dependent on the criteria of sufficiency employed by the listener/critic receiving the argument. As an enlightened critic, the listener should consider the possible reasons that make the argument advanced questionable. Assume, for instance, the following argument:

Proposition (claim):   Capital punishment is not an effective deterrent to crime.

Reason (justification):   The states that have capital punishment have more serious crimes per capita than the states that do not have capital punishment.

Will you accept this argument? What possible exceptions or reservations to this argument might you legitimately raise? Should you note that there are serious differences between the states that have capital punishment and those that do not, you are well on your way to discrediting the argument. Should you know that the capital-punishment states are highly populated urban areas, while the noncapital-punishment states are essentially rural and less populous, you may raise one important reservation to the argument. Should you know that the states with capital punishment have a higher incidence of poverty, unemployment, and racial antagonism, you may raise another serious reservation.

Thus, in evaluating an argument, the critic must ask whether there is cause to question the sufficiency of it. If there are reasonable reservations and if the speaker has failed to refute them, the argument may be denied.

3. Has the speaker provided adequate evidence in support of arguments?

In some fields of argument, the nature of adequate evidence is carefully specified. For example, the rules of evidence of the American bar are rather carefully specified. In the courtroom, there are rules governing the admissibility and inadmissibility of evidence. Historians, scientists, and behavioral scientists also have some clear notion of what constitutes sound evidence and what does not.

However, in the world of ordinary discourse, evidential requirements are less well known and less well defined. Perhaps the most distinctive characteristic of ordinary arguments on propositions of fact is the reliance of the speaker upon secondary information and uncontrolled, unsystematic observation. Thus, the popular speaker often bases arguments on the *testimony* of others, well-known or verifiable *specific instances,* and *statistical data.* Sometimes speakers use a *literal analogy* or describe a *cause-effect relationship.*

In using *testimony,* the speaker draws evidence from the statements of others. One interesting example of testimonial evidence occurred in the championship debate at the National College Debate Tournament at West Point in 1960. John Raser of San Diego State College sought to prove that "Eventually the public and the nation always get their way in national policy." Having stated what he hoped to prove Mr. Raser went on to say:

> Now that sounds like a strong statement, but I've got more than a few people who tell me it's true. . . . I'd first like to turn to Robert H. Jackson, the former Supreme Court Justice, who should know if anyone does. He said, in *Vital Speeches* in October 1953, that "The practical play of the forces of politics is such that judicial power has often delayed but never permanently delayed the persistent will of substantial majorities." In other words, the majority always gets its way. Let's turn to some more support. Professor Jack W. Peltason, University of Illinois . . . [in] his book *The Federal Courts and the Political Processes,* states, "In almost every decision in which the judges have imposed a check on Congress in the name of the Constitution, in one way or another Congress eventually has done what the judges told them they could not do and should not do." . . . Let's turn to further support of this idea that judges can't really thwart national policy. James MacGregor Burns, and the same man, Jack Walter Peltason, told us that, in their joint effort, *Government by the People,* published in 1954, "Judges have no armies or police to execute their laws; they have no authority to levy taxes to support their activities. In the long run they must adapt themselves to the nature and demands of government by the people." Now what do we draw from this? Simply that the Supreme Court does not thwart national policy because always eventually the policies which the people apparently want and always the policies which Congress endorses eventually are put into effect.

In this example, a college debater uses three pieces of testimony to support his point. In evaluating a speaker's use of testimony, the critical listener should employ some of the popular tests of testimonial evidence: (1) Was the source of the testimony in a position to observe? (2) Was the source of the testimony competent to observe? (3) Was the source of the testimony biased? (4) Was the source of the testimony qualified? (5) Was the source of the testimony consistent with other sources and with himself or herself on previous occasions? and (6) Is the testimony sufficiently recent?

In using *specific instances* as evidence, the speaker provides well-known or verifiable examples that demonstrate the truth of the proposition or of a claim leading to the proposition. An excellent example of the use of specific instances can be found in a speech delivered by Richard Nixon well before his catastrophic involvement in the Watergate affair. As vice president under Dwight Eisenhower, Nixon visited Russia, and during his stay there delivered an important "Address to the Russian People."

In an effort to prove that United States efforts to assure peace had been thwarted by the Soviet government, Nixon effectively drew upon a series of specific instances.

> . . . It is possible that many of you listening to me are not aware of the positive programs the United States has proposed which were designed to contribute to peace. Let me tell you about just a few of them and what happened to them:
>
> We had a monopoly on the atomic bomb when on June 14, 1946, we submitted the Baruch plan for international control of atomic energy. What happened? It was rejected by the USSR.
>
> At the Summit Conference in Geneva on July 21, 1955, President Eisenhower made his offer of open skies aerial inspection. What happened? It was rejected by the USSR.
>
> On May 1, 1958, the United States offered an Arctic aerial inspection plan to protect both nations from surprise attack. What happened? It was rejected by the USSR. I realize that your government has indicated reasons for its rejection of each of these proposals. I do not list these proposals for the purpose of warming over past history but simply to demonstrate the initiative our government has taken to reduce tensions and to find peaceful solutions for differences between us.

An equally good example of the use of specific instances occurs in a speech by Phyllis Jones Springen on "The Dimensions of the Oppression of Women."

> An infuriating example of unequal pay for equal work concerned a New Jersey manufacturer. Their chief financial officer was a woman paid $9,000 a year. When she left, they had to pay a man $20,000 a year to do her job. When he left they hired another woman at $9,000. When she left, they hired a man at $18,000. According to the recruiter, they were all good at the job.

In evaluating specific instances used as evidence in support of factual propositions, the critic should raise such questions as these: (1) Was a sufficient number of instances presented? (2) Were the instances presented typical instances? and (3) Are there any negative instances that should be accounted for?

In using *statistical data,* the speaker draws evidence from studies that have surveyed large numbers of cases and reported data numerically. Charles Schalliol has sought to demonstrate that "The increasing size of our metropolitan areas is compounding our air pollution problem" by citing relevant statistics.

> Since 1940, our population has grown by 50,000,000, the use of energy had quadrupled, disposable income has increased 60%—yet—our air supply remains the same. In such a setting air pollution is a murderer. According to Edward Parkhurst, a noted health authority, death rates are "consistently higher in the central cities of 50,000 and over than in places under 10,000 and in rural areas in nonmetropolitan districts." The Census Bureau further establishes that life expectancy is three years greater in the rural states than in the urban states.

In evaluating a speaker's use of statistics, the enlightened critic asks: (1) Do these statistics come from a reliable source? (2) Are these statistics based on a reliable sample? (3) Were these statistics accurately and completely reported? and (4) Are they presented in a meaningful form?

In demonstrating a *literal analogy,* the speaker typically compares two things or instances that belong to the same category or classification (two nations, people, corporations, etc.) to show that because the two actually are similar in several major relevant elements, something known to exist in the first instance probably exists (or will exist) in the second. You might contend, for example, that because England and the United States are similar in language, general economic system, and general political system, and because so-called "socialized medicine" is working in Great Britain, it probably would work in the United States. In evaluating the soundness of a speaker's literal analogy, the critic could ask some of the standard questions: (1) Are the known elements of both similar enough? (2) Are the known similarities relevant to the issue-at-hand? (3) Are significant relevant differences ignored? (4) Does the element assumed to exist in the first instance but unknown in the second actually exist in the first? (5) Do essential points of similarity outweigh essential points of difference?

In asserting a *cause-effect relationship,* the speaker contends that one factor (or set of factors) directly contributes to the occurrence of another factor (or set of factors); in some sense the first causes (or will cause) the second. As a variation, a given effect or circumstance is described as the result of a certain cause. Sometimes use of words such as "because," "due to," or "if . . . then" can alert us to possible cause-effect arguments. Jenkin Lloyd Jones, in a speech titled "Let's Bring Back Dad: A Solid Value System," suggested a number of cause-effect relationships, including the following. At one point he described "neo-Socialist" university professors who are "hostile" to the free enterprise business system "because they have never had any experience with it." At another point he asked concerning some Black families, "Why are our ghetto societies in such chaos? Because the man walks off when it gets tough." Jones concluded the speech by predicting a cause-effect relationship:

> . . . If enough American dads were to resolve to become partisan dads, unashamed to hold moral standards, willing to take the time to communicate values, then the chances of raising a new generation that would live in the agony of social chaos, or worse yet, lose their liberties for generations yet to come, will be substantially diminished.

To assess the soundness of any asserted cause-effect relationship, the critic could inquire: (1) Might there be multiple causes, several significant contributing and interrelated influences, rather than just the one asserted? (2) Might there be a chain or sequence of causal factors to consider, not just the asserted one as the immediate cause? (3) Is the speaker confusing a causal connection either with *chronology* (one thing simply happened after another) or with *correlation* (two things vary together in predictable ways, but *both* may be the effects of some unknown cause)? (4) Might there be additional positive or negative effects to consider other than the single effect identified? (5) Can the asserted cause-effect relationship be supported by evidence such as scientific studies, expert testimony, or other factual examples of the relationship?

Conclusion

In certain instances of persuasive discourse, speakers seek to prove to the satisfaction of their audiences that particular propositions of fact are really true. When evaluating such speeches, the critic should consider *whether the speaker has adequately assessed the proof requirements of the factual proposition, whether acceptable arguments in support of the proposition of fact have been offered, and whether adequate evidence in support of the argument has been provided.*

FOR FURTHER READING

Campbell, Karlyn Kohrs. *The Rhetorical Act.* 2nd ed. Wadsworth, 1996. Chapters 7 and 8 discuss the resources of evidence and argument that a public speaker might use.

Cooper, Martha. *Analyzing Public Discourse.* Waveland Press, 1989. Chapter 3 examines issues of fact, value, and policy and Chapter 6 discusses standards for sound evidence and reasoning.

Herrick, James A. *Argumentation: Understanding and Shaping Arguments.* Gorsuch Scarisbrick, 1995. Chapter 10 discusses reasoning about causes of events and problems.

Inch, Edward S., and Warnick, Barbara. *Critical Thinking and Communication: The Use of Reason in Argument.* 3rd ed. Macmillan, 1998. Chapters 7–11 discuss claims of fact, value, and policy and types of evidence and reasoning.

Lucas, Stephen E. *The Art of Public Speaking.* 6th ed. McGraw-Hill, 1998. Chapter 7 discusses supporting ideas with examples, statistics, and testimony. Chapter 15 examines questions of fact, value, and policy in persuasion.

Osborn, Michael, and Osborn, Suzanne. *Public Speaking.* 5th ed. Houghton Mifflin, 2000. Chapter 6 explains the use of supporting materials such as facts, testimony, examples, and narrative. Chapter 14 discusses evidence, proof, and sound argument.

Rieke, Richard D., and Sillars, Malcolm O. *Argumentation and Critical Decision Making.* 4th ed. Addison Wesley, 1997. Chapter 7 examines the use of factual instances, statistics, and expert testimony and notes the field-dependent nature of some standards for sound argument.

A Black President: When?

◆ Carl B. Stokes ◆

In 1967 Democrat Carl B. Stokes was elected to a two year term as mayor of Cleveland, Ohio. Thus he became the first African-American elected mayor of a major U.S. city. After a second term, he did not seek re-election. In the 1970s he worked as a TV anchor in New York City. You may find his autobiography, *Promises of Power* (1973), of interest. When he died, April 4, 1996 of throat cancer at age 68, he was serving as U.S. ambassador to the Seychelles Islands which are a British possession northeast of Madagascar in the Indian Ocean.

On February 19, 1993, while serving as a judge of the Cleveland Municipal Court, Carl Stokes presented this speech at a luncheon forum of the Columbus, Ohio, Metropolitan Club. This organization promotes free speech and fair debate by sponsoring weekly forums on a broad range of current political, cultural, civic, and international issues. Spirited question-and-answer

◆ Carl B. Stokes, "Racial Equality and Appreciation of Diversity in Our Urban Communities: How Far Have We Come? A Black President: When?" April 1, 1993, pp. 357–361. Reprinted with permission of *Vital Speeches of the Day.*

periods typically follow a speaker's presentation. Columbus Metropolitan Club members represent such fields as government, law, finance, health care, real estate, marketing, and public relations, but the weekly forums also are open to the general public.

Carl Stokes clearly is arguing a proposition of future fact–of future occurrence: An African-American will be elected President of the United States "in the near future," perhaps "within the next 20 years" (3, 45, 55). At the beginning of the speech, he forecasts the theme he will develop at length through factual examples and specific instances (4–5).

Over half of the speech (largely the first half) is Stokes' personal narrative of his first-hand experience with significant events (7–36). The narrative embodies extensive use of specific instances for factual support. This narrative captures and sustains audience attention. We all like to hear captivating stories, especially when they reflect personal emotions (23), depict the overcoming of obstacles (14–15, 17–18, 29, 32), and reflect elements of tension, opposition, and tragedy (20, 24–31). Stokes also narrates the story of Cleveland and his experiences as mayor as a "microcosm" of broader national issues, problems, and progress (6, 39). His story is to be taken as illustrative of and evidence for his larger points.

In the last third of the speech, Stokes employs a roughly chronological history of examples of African-American political progress to demonstrate a factual trend that supports his prediction (45). Some of the examples are more fully developed as a sort of landmark event (40–42, 44, 47–49). How adequately does Stokes demonstrate the significance of these landmark events? Some specific instances are used to prove that racism in America is practiced inconsistently (50–53, 56). At various points in the speech, Stokes uses a quick, tight-knit, cumulative listing of examples to strengthen an argument (33, 35, 38, 39) or to summarize previous instances (54).

It is clear, then, that throughout the speech Stokes employs examples and instances as his major type of evidence. How might you apply the test questions for reasonable use of specific instances to Stokes' usage? (1) Was a sufficient number of instances presented? (2) Were the instances presented typical instances? (3) Are there any negative (contradictory, inconsistent) instances that should have been mentioned or accounted for?

As might be expected, Stokes also employs a cause-effect argument implied in such words as "compounded" and "making" (33) and employs statistical data (17, 18, 43). Where appropriate apply the tests for soundness of cause-effect argument and for statistical evidence. Note, too, how Stokes uses parallel phrasing ("It means that . . .") to sharpen his conclusion (56).

One final question remains. Based on Carl Stokes' arguments and evidence, do you believe that an African-American will be elected President in the near future of approximately twenty years? Why?

◆ ◆ ◆

1   Twenty-five years ago, people told me that a black man could not be elected mayor of a major American city—particularly if the population of that city was majority white. I asked them "why not." They told me "because its never been done." I did it.

2   Today, the question tantalizing our nation, is when, if ever, the United States will elect an African American as its President. It seems to me that the discussion of the election of a black president is not "if" or "when," but "who." "When" is necessarily subordinate to and conditioned upon the unique persona of "who" will be that maker of history.

3   But there is no question in my mind that there will be an African American elected President of the United States. And it could easily occur within the next twenty years.

4   One hundred thirty years ago, the ratification of the Thirteenth Amendment began a remarkable political odyssey for the black people of this country. From an enslaved people, they have become

an integral component in the election of Governors, Senators, and Presidents—as President Clinton and former President John F. Kennedy would attest.

5   And with the passage of the 1965 Voters Rights Act, they have projected themselves into every elective and appointed office in the land—with the only exception being that of the presidency and vice-presidency of the nation.

6   Cleveland, Ohio, which I was once honored to serve as its mayor, is a microcosm of that latter development.

7   Many years ago, 26 to be exact, there was international media and public reaction to my being elected as Mayor of Cleveland. I was delighted, happy, and gratified.

8   But seemingly ignored by everyone was that the year I was elected, 1967, Edward Brooke had been serving as a member of the U.S. Senate for almost five years—the first black to be elected to that body in this century.

9   And Brooke's election to the U.S. Senate followed his state-wide election as Attorney General of the Commonwealth of Massachusetts. That despite there being only a 3 percent black population in Massachusetts; that Brooke was a Republican in a largely Democrat-leaning state; and that he was in an interracial marriage in a heavily Catholic, European-Ethnic state. Lots of traditional reasons there that he not be elected. But he was.

10   Brooke's election as a state official and then to the Senate was not lost on me as I was planning my own race for the mayoralty of my city—63 percent white, almost all of them conservative Eastern European ethnics. In fact, his experiences helped convince me that I could win, although there were some major differences in that Brooke's candidacy for the U.S. Senate did not excite the same fears from a white constituency that mine did for mayor.

11   A U.S. Senator, though powerful, exercises no direct control over his constituency. He is physically removed in Washington, his vote one of many. But the mayor lives "down the street," he has authority over the police (white), he spends the city tax dollar, and he decides when and where the snow is going to be plowed or not plowed. Those fears had to be frontally faced by me and allayed in the campaign. And they were.

12   I had long studied the ethnic political history of Massachusetts, Connecticut and New York. I understood that the visible color difference added a problem that the immigrant groups didn't have. But the ever-increasing numbers of black people in my and other central cities, coupled with the "white-flight," was creating the same demographic opportunities for a black person to seize City Hall, as had occurred for an Italian, LaGuardia, an Irishman, Hague, and the Polish mayor, Cermak in their era.

13   The task was to maximize my black vote, get as many white votes as I could, and to minimize white-fear reactions that would cause a majority voter turn-out for my white opponent. It would have been easier had my opponent been less accomplished.

14   Seth Taft, my Republican opponent, was the grandson of President and former U.S. Chief Justice William Howard Taft. My grandfather was born into slavery in 1859 in the state of Georgia. Taft had been educated at private Ivy League schools, graduated from Yale Law School, and was a partner in the eighth largest law firm in the U.S.

15   I attended public schools, spent a year at all-black West Virginia State College, earned my law degree from Cleveland Marshall Law School, and was a single-practitioner with my brother.

16   We had a hard-fought but clean campaign. Taft knew that he was going to benefit from much of the white vote solely because he was white—or that I was black. But not once did he make that appeal. Correspondingly, I made no appeal to the black voter on the basis of race—obviously, I knew that the black people also were not blind. So, to the extent such things are possible, Taft and I had a clean campaign—certainly one that was free of any overt racial appeal. He and I were friends before

that campaign, during the campaign, and remain friends to this day. The problem after winning the election was: how to govern.

17   It was not easy. Cleveland had been identified in national surveys as second only to Chicago in racial segregation. The population of 800,000 was balkanized into 33 wards—23 white and 10 black. The mayoralty term of two years was legislated insecurity. The federal government had cut off urban renewal funds due to shortcomings by the prior administration. There was no political organization in the city: the two daily newspapers had been credited over the previous 40 years with having elected mayors. Neither paper had a black person serving in an editorial or policy-making position. There were no black anchor people on the three local television stations and no black political reporters.

18   I was a black man elected to run a majority-white city with a national reputation for racism; with white people in control of the city council, the various media, and all of the business, financial, and commercial institutions. And with a 93 percent white police force. The odds of success were dramatically short from the outset.

19   But had it not been for one fatal mishap, Cleveland would have been a national role model for cities, and a microcosmic view of a black presidency.

20   The middle 1960s was a time of great national turmoil. Students throughout the nation were taking over university facilities and violently protesting the Viet Nam War. Dr. King and his followers were under attack in Illinois and Tennessee as they made their shift from civil rights to fighting racism in the labor unions, in residential housing, and other areas of economic concern. Rioting and looting had become commonplace in all the major cities. The mainly white police forces were at swords-point with the black communities. The Kerner Commission came out with its finding that America was fast becoming two societies: One white and one black, separate and unequal. Unemployment and inflation were on the increase and the resultant economic insecurity was causing short tempers nationally.

21   Then, as though all of these national tensions had come to one focus in Cleveland's neighborhood of Glenville, white police and a group of young black nationalists, both sides armed with rifles, shot it out. Three policemen were killed and nine suffered permanently disabling wounds. Seven of the young black men were killed. The worst nightmare of any mayor, had actually happened only ten months into my first term.

22   The news came to me over a police radio in my car, just as we were pulling away from my home to go to the Glenville area where we'd learned shortly before that there was a potential of trouble. "One policeman is down and still being hit by rifle fire . . ." the dispatcher's voice said. Seconds later he added that one civilian "was down" from police fire after fleeing from the house from which the nationalists were firing. The "Glenville Shoot-out" was underway.

23   I sat unmoving in the back seat of my car listening to the broadcast. There was no need now for me to go to the area. The war that both groups had wanted, was on. Tears of frustration and helplessness rolled down my cheeks as I sat there, miles away from the scene, powerless to stop those damn fools whose mutual hatreds were killing each other—and the hopes of a city. I then became angry, and cursed out loud, because I knew that this armed conflict would shut down all our delicately-crafted plans for integrated housing, affirmative action in jobs, and cooperation from a majority-white city council.

24   No one had to tell me, at that instant, that all of the worst fears of the white people had actually happened: their white police were under attack from black men. I also knew that, as the black mayor, I would be personally blamed for the tragedy. I understood that the police were viewed by many of my white constituents as their "line of defense" against "them," the black people. And now—without regard as to how the battle began, or who shot first, the white perception would be that it would never have happened if a black man had not been mayor.

25   And that is what happened. The radio talk shows were jammed with hate calls, now that it was "acceptable" for the white bigots to surface and to attack and blame the black mayor. Vitriolic letters to the editor from white readers and op-ed criticisms followed in all the local papers. Every taxi driver had his or her own personal insight as to how and what happened.

26   And the rumors escalated to the certainty that I had personally armed the militants and dispatched them to their war with the police.

27   But Glenville wasn't over the next morning. We still had to bury the dead and visit the wounded. Store windows had to be boarded up and fires extinguished from the local reaction to the small war. And a decision had to be made as to how to avoid a repeat of the previous night's violence. There was anger in the streets among other young black nationalists about their colleagues who had been killed the night before. And the white policemen were distraught with anger over the officers who had fallen. Both sides were vowing revenge.

28   I made the decision that the best way to avoid the almost certain armed conflict, and loss of lives, was to withdraw all white police officers from the Glenville area. I had arrived at that conclusion after a day-long consultation with dozens of black community leaders. To keep the peace that night, I assigned all of our black city police officers to the area accompanied by black deputy sheriffs, and supplemented them with a corp of 500 black community leaders—ministers, athletes, gang leaders, school teachers, Boy Scout leaders, and other activists.

29   It worked. No shots were fired that night. No lives were lost. The following night, and thereafter, the regularly assigned white police officers were returned to the area, together with members of the national guard, and, with tempers having cooled, there were no more covert incidents. The bloodshed had ended.

30   But the political damage was deep and proved to not be reversible. A major, innovative public-private sector program that depended upon and had been receiving funding from the business community, dried up. The racial lines in the city council hardened, and the passage of any legislation of significance became the occasion for confrontation and obstruction that had no relation to the subject of the bill.

31   Any hope of softening the long-established racial divisions in the city was over. The bright promise of the partnership of a young, black mayor and a majority white city population, being able to fashion new ways of racial cooperation, was not to be.

32   Nonetheless, I was reelected in 1969, by a wider margin and with more white votes than in my first election.

33   However, the local problems I have described were being sorely compounded by our national problems. In 1967 it had seemed that the cities could be turned around. But by 1970, in the early months of my second term, the national economy had worsened, and we were headed for even more problems than before. Local governments' lack of resources, the revolt against taxes, the high crime rate, the seemingly inexorable slide of housing, bridges and highways into decay and deterioration, the continued flight from the cities by even the marginally affluent, the increasing unemployment and labor problems—all these things were making cities virtually unmanageable.

34   It became clear to me and other big-city mayors who had been the cutting-edge in battling the urban crisis, that the nation no longer had the will to commit the resources and priorities that the problems of major central cities demanded.

35   The time for activist mayors committed to achieving change and reform had passed. Most of us were unwilling to be overseers whose function would be to preside over the absolute demise of neighborhoods; increased social and physical sicknesses from drugs; new and old diseases and little or no health care; a renewal of rioting in the streets; soaring crime rates; the rise of an underclass highlighted by generational welfare; dysfunctional public school systems; the flow of jobs to the suburbs; increased infant mortality; the city infrastructure falling apart; the middle-class gone; and the poor battling the poor for anything left in deserted downtowns, vacant office buildings, and vandalized and empty former factories.

36 Over half of the mayors elected between 1960 and 1970, did not run for reelection. New York City's activist mayor, John Lindsay, announced his retirement. Boston's mayor, Kevin White, Mayor Tommy Delasandro of Baltimore, and I met and decided that we would make a "statement" by the three of us jointly announcing that we would not stand for reelection. A few days later, White recanted, saying that he "could not imagine life not being mayor." Delesandro and I were left to go it alone. On April 16, 1971, I announced that I would not run again for mayor and my retirement from politics.

37 During my years at city hall, the local and national black political scene changed dramatically. Following my tenure, the acknowledged, most powerful politician in Cleveland during fifteen years in which the city had three white mayors, was a black man, George Forbes, the President of City Council.

38 The current mayor, Michael White, is black. And so is the elected county prosecutor, the president and superintendent of the public school system, and a member of Congress, Louis Stokes, my older brother. Other black men and women head the metropolitan housing authority, the community college, the state's lottery commission, and one of America's oldest and most prestigious philanthropic organizations, the Cleveland foundation.

39 Without many Americans being overly conscious of it, that pattern of black political participation is being replicated nationwide. California's Speaker of the House of Representatives, Willie Brown, has dictated and/or manipulated that state's policies for over a decade. Other black men have led their legislatures in New Jersey and Pennsylvania. California and Colorado have elected black Lieutenant Governors. The southern states of Mississippi, Georgia, and Alabama have elected black men and women to offices ranging from mayor, congressperson, and county commissioners, to that old citadel of power in southern communities: The Sheriff.

40 The centerpiece of this non-violent, political revolution is, of course, Douglas Wilder, the elected Governor of the Commonwealth of Virginia. A black man.

41 In 1661, while still a colony, Virginia was the first to pass statutory recognition of slavery. And its unremitting struggle against the Union as the oldest of the Confederate states is a matter of history. Yet, in 1986, Doug Wilder was elected its Lieutenant Governor, and in 1990, the over 85 percent white population of Virginia elected Wilder their Governor over his white opponent, the elected Attorney General.

42 What a feat. This country had quietly gone from slavery in 1865, to the election of a black man in 1990 to the chief executive officer of one of its fifty states.

43 In the interim, over 300 black men and women have been elected mayor of their cities—indeed, the six largest cities in our nation have been led by African American mayors; the number of black congresspersons has ballooned from none in 1990, to 40 today, many of them chairs of major committees; most state legislatures have black members occupying varying degrees of power; the school boards and city councils in every large city are led or dominated by their black elected members; several states have black officials elected state-wide; the police chiefs of most of the largest industrial cities are black; black judges, elected and appointed, are serving from the municipal level to the highest state courts, and in the Federal district and appellate courts, and the U.S. Supreme Court; and the current Chairman of the Joint Chiefs of Staff of the U.S. military forces is a black man, General Colin Powell.

44 General Powell's current position as head of the military is of great significance to one of my generation. When I was in the U.S. Army from 1945 to 1947, there were only a few black lieutenants, almost no captains, black majors or colonels, and with the exception of Benjamin O. Davis, Sr., generals were not to be thought of. We were totally segregated in our living quarters and training facilities. We were generally denied the opportunity to serve in combat, and relegated to driving trucks. Today, 45 years later, the boss of all the armed services, an African American, General Colin Powell.

45   It is the totality of these events in American history that support the thesis of an African American President in the near future.

46   In the preliminaries to last year's presidential election, there was serious talk among Republicans about replacing Vice-President Quayle with General Powell. There was even talk among Democrats of drafting Powell. It wasn't done, by either party. But not because it was considered any longer to be unthinkable. Several of the recognized, political-savvy news columnists and commentators speculated on the positives Powell could bring to the vice-presidential slot—especially after Operation Desert Storm. In politics, once that an idea becomes realistic and pragmatic, its just a question of time before one or the other political party uses it.

47   In 1967, the conventional political wisdom was that I could not be elected mayor. The black and white voters of Cleveland proved them wrong. In the 1988 Democratic primaries, over a six months period, the white and black voters in states from Maine to Colorado, chose Jesse Jackson over four of his five white opponents. In a campaign that began with derision from many national columnists and commentators, Jackson was the surviving candidate against the ultimate nominee, Michael Dukakis, and garnered over 6 million votes.

48   As you read the results in the various state primary votes, Jackson won some primaries, and consistently ran second and third in others. The significance, of course, is that everyone in America—those who voted for him, and those who didn't—knew that he was a black man. In those primary elections, white voters had a choice of five other seasoned, capable, and responsible candidates—all white. But a consistent, sizable number of white voters from states throughout the union, knowingly cast their ballot for the black man over most of his counterparts. Their votes stamped him, indelibly, as being the best-qualified—regardless of his being black!

49   An equally telling realization late in the 1988 primaries that Jackson had become a serious, potential winner of the Democratic nomination, was the public conversion of Sam Donaldson and his fellow television political reporters, from derision and scorn, early on, to subsequent heated discussions of whether Jackson or Dukakis would get the necessary electoral votes to win the Democratic nomination.

50   Racial bias, prejudice and discrimination are institutionalized in our nation. But a consistent feature of racism is its inconsistency.

51   There is no other way to explain Massachusetts electing a black Republican to be its state law enforcement official, and then being elected as its United States Senator, while black candidates in Boston were being rejected out-of-hand by white voters in their campaigns for city council.

52   Again it is the inconsistency of racism that helps explain last year's election of Illinois', and America's, first African American woman to the United States Senate.

53   Carol Mosley-Braun, a resident of Chicago, the most segregated city in the nation, defeated a white, well-financed Republican, in a two-person race, white against black, in a state renowned for its down-state conservatism, and some Ku Klux Klan activity. Nonetheless, white Illinoisans voted for Braun over a perfectly acceptable and qualified white male.

54   This black woman has now been elected to the second-highest office in our land. Wilder presides over one of our fifty states. Willie Brown still heads the legislative body of our most populous and diverse state. And Colin Powell is directing the U.S. armed forces in the United Nations' historically unprecedented humanitarian excursion in Somalia.

55 It therefore takes no leap of faith, nor convoluted reasoning, to project that an African American can and will be elected President of the United States in the near future. African Americans already have been accorded electoral approval at all but the highest level in our country.

56 This does not mean that racial bias and prejudice is not existent in the political market place. It means that racial animosities are not uniform and not universally employed. It means that more often than noticed, America's acknowledged racism, is well off-set by a fundamental decency in a nation still molding the kind of democracy it wants to be. It means that there is a framework in this country within which the individual can cause the system to respond to his or her appeal to the best that is in us. It means that the opportunity to rise to one's level is a fact; that the precept that "all men are created equal" had credence when viewed from the realities of those who have succeeded; and that the democratic principles on which this nation was formed, continue to evolve and expand and to fulfill the promise of a Democracy that has yet to reach full bloom.

Human Resource Management Issues in the '90s

◆ *Christine D. Keen* ◆

One of the most frequently heard terms in American business in the past decade has been human resource management, for many think that proper management of human resources is the key to an effective business enterprise. It is thus that the Society for Human Resource Management, consisting of human resource, personnel, and industrial relations executives, attempts to promote the advancement of human resource management. In this vein, Christine D. Keen, Issues Manager for the Society for Human Resource Management, delivered the following address to its National Conference at Atlanta, Georgia, June 25, 1990.

This tightly organized, factual prediction speech, which begins with a quotation from Yogi Berra and ends with one from Shoshana Zuboff, consists of two sections, the first being devoted to three predictions about today's Baby Boomers

(1–24) and the second consisting of four scenarios for the changing times (25–33). A speaker wishing to predict must make the predictions seem both plausible and probable. To do this the speaker must look to present trends that seem to be deviating from the past and discern those trends that are the most likely to develop. Examine how Keen uses data from the present to support her predictions. Are all her predictions sufficiently developed to be both plausible and probable? Can you offer different predictions and different scenarios? Of what use are such attempts at predictions?

Finally, at the dawn of a new decade, you are urged to look backward to judge how accurate her predictions for the 1990s proved to be in actuality. For each prediction, was she largely on-target, slightly off-target, or significantly wrong? If a prediction proved clearly off-target

◆ This speech is reprinted by permission from *Vital Speeches of the Day,* October 1, 1990, pp. 752–754.

or wrong, what factors might account for that? The speaker's use of faulty evidence, incomplete evidence, or illogical reasoning? Intervening events or circumstances that could not reasonably have been foreseen by the speaker?

1   When asked about an upcoming series, Yogi Berra supposedly once said, "I try never to make predictions, especially about the future." But I've never been very good about following commonly accepted wisdom, so that's exactly what I'm going to do. I'm going to chance some predictions about how the workplace may change over the next 10 or 15 years.

2   Let me start by asking you a question: how many of you were born sometime between 1946 and 1964? You're the Baby Boom generation, and during the '90s the work force and the workplace will come to be dominated by the Baby Boomers—demographically, hierarchically, and psychologically. The Boomers already make up 55 percent of the work force, but during the '90s they will be moving into senior management. They will be policy-setters, and their attitudes and philosophies will govern the workplace.

3   I think we could see three broad trends developing over the next ten years which have, at their root, the differences between the Baby Boomers and the generation which preceded them.

4   First, we are seeing a shift toward putting more importance on family relationships and less on work. During the '70s and '80s the Boomers deferred marriage and children in order to develop their careers. They were ambitious and worked long and hard. But the restructurings of the last several years have taught them an important lesson: you cannot rely on your job as your source of self-validation. If all you've got is your career, when you lose your job, you lose your sense of self.

5   Consequently, the Boomers are now shifting from "In Search of Excellence" to "in search of meaning." They are seeking non-career avenues of self fulfillment, including family relationships, volunteer work and the personal growth movement. Not too surprisingly, the birth rate is rising again: last year there were more babies born in the U.S. than in any year for the past 25. The fertility rate went up 2 percent, which means, in layman's terms, women are having more children.

6   And perhaps even more revealing, we are starting to hear more comments—from men and women—like "unless I'm inventing a cure for AIDS or something, my work is not worth missing my kids grow up." Or "I married you for you, not for your paycheck." Don't get caught in the trap of thinking this is just a "women's thing." Men may not articulate it, but a recent study of employees at Fortune 500 companies showed men were three times as likely to cite children as a reason for leaving a position as women were.

7   During the '90s we may see parents—male and female—scaling back their devotion to their jobs or dropping out of the traditional 9 to 5 work force entirely.

8   Where are they going to go? This brings me to my second broad trend: the emergence of the independent work force.

9   We are moving toward a point when we may have individual contracts with each of our employees. Employees may, in fact, become more akin to independent contractors, negotiating schedules, responsibilities, and rates of pay. We are already seeing a trickle-down effect, for example, from the severance contracts we gave senior executives in the '80s—more middle managers are now insisting on similar written guarantees.

10   Likewise, many companies are broadening their experiments with flextime. A hospital in Dallas, for example, is using a "work three, get one free" approach to recruiting nurses. The nurses work nine months a year, get to choose any three months they would like off, and have benefits for a full year. (This approach has, by the way, increased employment inquiries by 100 percent.)

11 Meanwhile, some European companies are taking the flextime approach to its logical conclusion. Whereas flextime generally lets you choose which 8 hours a day you want to work, and the compressed work week lets you choose which 40 hours a week you want to work (say, four 10 hour days), European companies are pioneering the flexyear: an employee chooses which 2000 or so hours he or she wants to work during the year.

12 The computer, the modem and the fax machine are allowing employees to choose not just when but where they work.

13 Further, the independent employee wants to determine his or her compensation package—not just the money, but the benefits. Flexible or cafeteria benefit plans have, in part, appealed to this desire. The '90s, though, could go in one of two opposite directions: a smorgasbord of mandated and optional benefits or no benefits at all.

14 Congress is actively interested in the possibility of taxing the value of employee benefits as income. Already, tuition assistance benefits are taxed in many cases, and the new child care bill awaiting President Bush's signature contains a provision taxing the value of employer-provided child care benefits for couples with a household income of $70,000 or more. Are benefits going to be an effective recruiting tool if their value is taxed. Perhaps companies would be wiser to get rid of their benefits entirely and compensate employees with more cash—after all, that's more the way we compensate consultants and independent contractors in the first place.

15 Further, the movement toward an independent work force may be accelerated by the Boomers' emphasis on independence and self-reliance. More outplaced middle managers are choosing to chuck corporate life entirely and go into business for themselves than ever before. Half of a recent graduating class of MBAs said they expect to work for themselves one day. Moonlighting is at its highest level in 30 years. Two factors will be feeding the entrepreneurial urge of the independent employee during the '90s; career plateaus and inheritance.

16 The Boomers are plateauing earlier than the previous generation. This is true for a couple of reasons: (1) there are more Boomers and fewer middle management positions for them to aspire to, and (2) much of the job growth over the last 15 years has been in small firms which often do not have the well-developed corporate ladder larger firms might. Second, in another 10 years the Boomers are expected to have more of the necessary capital to invest in their own businesses—not because of any saving they did, but because they will have inherited their parents' considerable assets.

17 How are you going to respond to the challenges and opportunities posed by the independent work force?

18 My third broad trend for the '90s and beyond is a complete redefinition of employment rights and responsibilities.

19 The Boomers do not share their parents attitudes about the role of business in society. "Big business" still carries a negative connotation. This generation doesn't think twice about targeting the deep pockets of business if they think they've been wronged. And they think they've been wronged a lot.

20 The Boomers tend to believe they should not have to waive their Constitutional rights in order to make a living. They believe in rights to privacy, due process, and freedom of speech in the workplace. They believe employees should not be fired without a good reason. They believe in meritocracy—the best should be rewarded without regard for age, gender, race, position, or seniority.

21 The ramifications of these attitudes will reverberate throughout the workplace. We can reasonably expect more concern about testing, for example. Polygraphs are all but gone, and there is movement afoot to ban psychological testing as well. Drug testing is still a thorny subject, and genetic testing could be a powder keg in the '90s.

22   We can also expect more erosion of employment-at-will doctrine. We may see more whistleblowing and more challenges to separation agreement waivers.

23   We will definitely see a call for a more equitable sharing of the benefits and burdens of the company's success and failure. That means linking pay more clearly with individual performance. It may mean generous severance compensation if the termination is not related to performance. It could even mean demands for reform of exorbitant CEO pay packages.

24   These three trends—the renewed emphasis on family, the independent work force and the redefinition of rights and responsibilities—may apply to some but certainly not all of your work force during the '90s. I'd like to sketch very quickly for you four other scenarios to watch for during the '90s.

25   First, the official bilingual or multilingual workplace. Immigration levels are at their highest levels this century, and for most of these immigrants, English is a second language—if they know it at all. We may see the development of a bilingual or multilingual workplace out of necessity or out of government intervention.

26   At Digital Equipment Corp.'s Boston plant, for example, 350 employees speak 19 different languages. Company announcements are printed in English, Chinese, French, Spanish, Portuguese, Vietnamese and Haitian Creole. Other companies are finding they need to teach employees English or teach managers Spanish.

27   Some people apparently feel employers are not reacting to this problem quickly enough on their own. A new law in Iowa requires all business to hire interpreters if 10 percent or more of their workplace speaks no English. This is the first law I am aware of which requires accommodation of a language handicap.

28   In the second scenario, tuition assistance for dependents becomes to the late '90s what child care was to the mid '80s. Tuition has been outpacing inflation for the last 10 years, and federal support for financial aid has halved since 1980. The leading edge of the baby boomlet—the children of the Baby Boomers—will be 13 this year. It was the birth of these same children which turned child care into a political issue and ushered in employer-provided child care benefits.

29   The Boomers have high expectations of their kids. Eighty-six percent expect their kids to go to college. Yet only 54 percent are saving for it. As was the case with child care, employers could be asked to come up with the rest.

30   In the third scenario, employers may step up dramatically their importation of skilled workers because the domestic work force cannot meet the demands for quantity or quality. Canada, for example, which currently has a higher national unemployment rate than the U.S., could be one pool to tap in the '90s (Canadians tend to be well educated, speak English, and free movement of labor may be encouraged by the U.S.-Canada free trade agreement.)

31   Finally, we may see a resurgence of unions during the '90s. Organized labor has spent much of the last decade reinventing itself to appeal to a changing work force. They have been successful in capitalizing on mainstream family issues such as health care, child care, parental leave and housing affordability. Unions have a rising approval rating among the general public, particularly among younger people, and have a rising rate of victory in union elections.

32   Women, minorities, immigrants, service sector workers and even white collar workers are being targeted by organized labor in an attempt to reach out to pockets of the work force which do not typically join unions. Employers should not be too sure that their work force is immune to the charms of a repositioned labor movement, particularly if workers feel their interests are at odds with management's—and evidence is that feeling is growing.

33 Issues for the '90s—the good, the bad and the ugly. How things develop over the next 10 years depends in large part on how we respond today. I read a quote from Shoshana Zuboff, a Harvard business school professor, a few months ago: "The future creeps in on small feet." Here at SHRM we are trying to not only track the footprints; we're trying to help you head them off.

The President Did Not Obstruct Justice

◆ *Cheryl Mills* ◆

Making what the *Washington Post* termed her "public debut" in front of the nation and 100 United States Senators, little-known White House attorney Cheryl Mills delivered a spirited defense of President Bill Clinton in the Senate chamber on January 20, 1999. Mills was the second of Clinton's attorneys who spoke on that day to defend the President against Articles of Impeachment presented by managers from the House of Representatives. These historic proceedings marked only the second time an American President had to face the members of the Senate sitting as a court of impeachment.

The dramatic presence of Mills, a 33-year-old African-American woman, stood in stark contrast to the 13 middle-aged white male managers from the House who had previously argued for impeaching the president. After her presentation, however, the *Chicago Tribune* noted that Mills "stood out for her oratory" and that "some senators had tears in their eyes." (*The Chicago Tribune*, January 21, 1999, section 1, p. 14).

The daughter of a career Army officer, Mills grew up on various military bases around the world. She earned her undergraduate degree from the University of Virginia and later graduated from Stanford University Law School. Mills joined the Clinton pre-election presidential transition team in 1992. After Clinton's victory, she rose quickly through the ranks to become a senior member of the Office of White House Counsel.

As in any legal proceeding, the charges presented in the impeachment trial against Bill Clinton revolved around the interpretation of facts. Specifically, Mills' lengthy presentation was structured as a formal rebuttal to the second article of impeachment in which the House mangers charged the President with obstruction of justice in an effort to conceal his illicit sexual relationship with Monica Lewinsky. (See *The New York Times*, January 21, 1999, pps. A1 & A15.)

Mills begins her defense of Clinton by expressing her pride in having worked six years for the White House (1–2). Her introduction further makes significant use of enactment (3, 5) where she presents herself as "proof that the American dream still lives." You may wish to compare Mills' use of enactment with that of

◆ The text of this speech is reprinted from the *Congressional Record*, Vol. 145, #9 (January 20, 1999), pp. S824–S830.

Barbara Jordan's "Democratic Convention Keynote Address" in Chapter Eight.

After praising and elaborating on the "the rule of law," (6–10) Mills previews her "walk through the facts" (11, 12). How effectively does Mills' lengthy introduction prepare her audience "called to judge the facts?" Does Mills enhance her credibility as an advocate by using enactment? The first set of facts confronted by Mills concerns the gifts allegedly given by Clinton to Lewinsky (14–20). How well does she refute and establish her own version of the facts about these gifts to the president (22–49)? Do you find Mills' recounting of the evidence, mainly personal testimony, in defense of the president compelling (42–48)? How credible are *her* interpretations of the facts about Clinton actions? Has Mills presented a fair version of the "stubborn facts" (50–52) in defense of the president? Does Mills adequately demonstrate why the president's actions are not illegal as provided in the specific instances cited in Federal law (54–56)?

Many speeches that affirm propositions of fact include reasonable criteria for the definition of key terms essential to the argument being presented. Does Mills present a reasonable explanation of the phrase "corruptly persuade" (57)? Does Mills present adequate proof that Clinton did not commit witness tampering (58–61)? How compelling are Mills' arguments that the House managers may have "overreached" with their claims about Ms. Currie's testimony (63–76)?

Mills concluded her presentation by addressing the claim that by not removing the President from office, the national commitment to civil rights and sexual harassment legislation would be questioned (77–78). Does the narrative about Clinton's grandfather (80–81) adequately support Mills' claim about Clinton's commitment to civil rights? How appropriate are the analogies (84) Mills uses to put Clinton's lack of "perfection" into perspective? Does Mills effectively summarize her argument in the closing paragraphs (85–89)?

On August 8, 1999, Cheryl Mills was offered the opportunity to become Chief White House Counsel. According to the *Chicago Tribune*, Mills declined the offer in order to return to private practice. (See the *Chicago Tribune*, August 9, 1999, Section 1, p. 6.)

◆ ◆ ◆

1   Mr. Chief Justice, managers from the House of Representatives. Members of the Senate, good afternoon. My name is Cheryl Mills, and I am deputy counsel to the President. I am honored to be here today on behalf of the President to address you.

2   Today, incidentally, marks my 6-year anniversary in the White House. I am very proud to have had the opportunity to serve our country and this President.

3   It is a particular honor for me to stand on the Senate floor today. I am an Army brat. My father served in the Army for 27 years. I grew up in the military world, where opportunity was a reality and not just a slogan. The very fact that the daughter of an Army officer from Richmond. VA, the very fact that I can represent the President of the United States on the floor of the Senate of the United States, is powerful proof that the American dream lives.

4   I am going to take some time to address two of the allegations of obstruction of justice against President Clinton in article II: First, the allegation related to the box of gifts that Ms. Lewinsky asked Ms. Currie to hold for her; second, the allegation related to the President's conversation with Ms. Currie after his deposition in the Jones case. Tomorrow my colleague, Mr. Kendall, will address the remaining allegations of obstruction of justice.

5   Over the course of the House managers' presentation last week, I confess I was struck by how often they referred to the significance of the rule of law. House Manager Sensenbrenner, for example, quoted President Theodore Roosevelt stating. "No man is above the law and no man is below it. . . ." As a lawyer, as an American, and as an African American, it is a principle in which I believe to the very

core of my being. It is what many have struggled and died for, the right to be equal before the law without regard to race or gender or ethnicity, disability, privilege, or station in life. The rule of law applies to the weak and the strong, the rich and the poor, the powerful and the powerless.

6 If you love the rule of law, you must love it in all of its applications. You cannot only love it when it provides the verdict you seek. You must love it when the verdict goes against you as well. We cannot uphold the rule of law only when it is consistent with our beliefs. We must uphold it even when it protects behavior that we don't like or is unattractive or is not admirable or that might even be hurtful. And we cannot say we love the rule of law but dismiss arguments that appeal to the rule of law as legalisms or legal hair-splitting.

7 I say all of this because not only the facts but the law of obstruction of justice protects the President. It does not condemn him. And the managers cannot deny the President the protection that is provided by the law and still insist that they are acting to uphold the law. His conduct, while clearly not attractive, or admirable, is not criminal. That is the rule of law in this case.

8 So as my colleagues and I discuss obstruction of justice against the President, we ask only that the rule of law be applied equally, neutrally, fairly, not emotionally or personally or politically. If it is applied equally, the rule of law exonerates Bill Clinton.

9 That said, I want to begin where Manager HUTCHINSON left off this weekend during a television program. The evidence does not support conviction of the President on any of the allegations of obstruction of justice. On the record now before the Senate, and that which was before the House, Manager HUTCHINSON said, "I don't think you could obtain a conviction or that I could fairly ask for a conviction." We agree. We agree. There are good reasons for Manager HUTCHINSON's judgment. And the most important, the evidence in the record and the law on the books, does not support the conclusion that the President obstructed justice.

10 Now, I know that Manager McCOLLUM begged you in his presentation to not pay attention to details when the President's case was put forward. He went so far as to implore you not to get hung up on some of the details when the President and his attorneys try to explain this stuff—"The big picture is what you need to keep in mind, not the compartmentalization." Manager McCOLLUM was telling you, in effect, not to pay attention to the evidence that exonerates the President—"Don't pay attention to the details that take this case out of the realm of activities that are prohibited by the law."

11 But the rule of law depends upon the details because it depends upon the facts and it depends upon the fairness of the persons called to judge the facts. I want to walk through the big picture and I want to walk through the facts.

12 I first want to discuss the real story, and then I want to focus on all those inconvenient details, or what Manager BUYER called those stubborn facts that didn't fit the big picture that the House managers want you to see.

13 Manager BARR suggested the fit between the facts and the law against the President in this case is as precise as the finely tuned mechanism of a Swiss watch. But when you put the facts together, they don't quite make out a Swiss watch; in fact, they might not even make good sausage.

14 So what is the big picture? The big picture is this: The President had a relationship with a young woman. His conduct was inappropriate. But it was not obstruction of justice. During the course of their relationship, the President and the young woman pledged not to talk about it with others. That is not obstruction of justice. The President ended their relationship before anyone knew about it. He ended it not because he thought it would place him in legal jeopardy: he ended it because he knew it was wrong. That is not obstruction of justice.

15 The President hoped that no one would find out about his indiscretion, about his lapse in judgment. That is not obstruction of justice, either. One day, however, long after he had ended the relationship, he was asked about it in an unrelated lawsuit, a lawsuit whose intent, at least as proclaimed by those who were pursuing it, was to politically damage him. That was their publicly announced goal. So he knew, the President knew that his secret would soon be exposed. And he was right.

16 It was revealed for public consumption, written large all over the world against his best efforts to have ended the relationship and to have put right what he had done wrong. That is the real big picture. That is the truth. And that is not obstruction of justice.

17 So let's talk about the allegation of obstruction of justice, about the box of gifts that Ms. Currie received from Ms. Lewinsky. I want to begin by telling you another true story, the real story of the now famous gifts.

18 It takes place on December 28, 1997. On that day the President gave Ms. Lewinsky holiday gifts. During her visit with the President, Ms. Lewinsky has said that she raised the subpoena that she had received from the Jones lawyers on the 19th and asked him, what should she do about the gifts. The President has said he told her, whenever it was that they discussed it, that she would have to give over whatever she had. He was not concerned about the gifts because he gives so many gifts to so many people. Unbeknownst to the President, however, Ms. Lewinsky had been worrying about what to do with the gifts ever since she got the subpoena. She was concerned that the Jones lawyers might even search her apartment so she wanted to get the gifts out of her home.

19 After Ms. Lewinsky's visit with the President, Ms. Currie walked her from the building. Then or later, either in person or on the phone. Ms. Lewinsky told Ms. Currie that she had a box of gifts that the President had given her that she wanted Ms. Currie to hold because people were asking questions. In the course of that conversation, they discussed other things as well. Ms. Currie agreed to hold the box of gifts. After their discussion, Ms. Lewinsky packed up some but not all of the gifts that the President had given her over time. She kept out presents of particular sentimental value as well as virtually all of the gifts he had given her that very day on the 28th.

20 Ms. Currie went by Ms. Lewinsky's home after leaving work, picked up the box that had a note on it that said, "Do not throw away," and she took it home. Ms. Currie did not raise Ms. Lewinsky's request with the President because she saw herself as doing a favor for a friend. Ms. Currie had no idea the gifts were under subpoena.

21 So Ms. Lewinsky's request hardly struck her as criminal.

22 This story that I just told you is obviously very different from the story presented by the House managers. How can I tell such a story that is so at odds with that which has been presented by the House managers? The answer lies in the selective reading of the record by the House managers. But theirs is not the only version of the facts that needs to be told. So what details did they downplay or discard or disregard in their presentation to create allegations of obstruction of justice?

23 To be fair, the House managers acknowledged up front that their case is largely circumstantial. They are right. Let's walk through the House managers' presentation of the key events which they gave to you last week. Let's look at exhibit 1 which is in the packet that has been handed out to you.

24 First key fact: On December 19, Monica Lewinsky was served with a subpoena in the Paula Jones case. The subpoena required that she testify at that deposition in January 1998 and also to produce each and every gift given to her by President Clinton.

25 Second event: On December 28, Ms. Lewinsky and the President met in the Oval Office to exchange Christmas gifts, at which time they discussed the fact that the lawyers in the Jones case had subpoenaed all of the President's gifts.

26 Third key fact: During the conversation on the 28th, Ms. Lewinsky asked the question whether she should put away outside her home or give to someone—maybe Betty—the gifts. At that time, according to Ms. Lewinsky, the President responded, "Let me think about it."

27 Fourth fact they presented to you. That answer led to action. Later that day, Ms. Lewinsky got a call at 3:32 p.m. from Ms. Currie who said, "I understand you have something to give me or that the President has said you have something for me." It was the President who initiated the retrieval of the gifts and the concealment of the evidence.

28 Fifth event they presented: Without asking any questions, Ms. Currie picked up the box of gifts from Ms. Lewinsky, drove to her home, and placed the box under her bed.

29 That is what the House managers told you last week. Now, let's go through their story piece by piece. On December 19, Monica Lewinsky was served with a subpoena in the Jones case. The subpoena required her to testify at a deposition in January 1998, and also to produce each and every gift given to her by the President. This statement is factually accurate. It does not, however, convey the entire state of affairs. Ms. Lewinsky told the FBI that when she got the subpoena she wanted the gifts out of her apartment. Why? Because she suspected that lawyers for Jones would break into her apartment looking for gifts. She was also concerned that the Jones people might tap her phone. Therefore, she wanted to put the gifts out of reach of the Jones lawyers, out of harms way. The managers entirely disregarded Ms. Lewinsky's own independent motivations for wanting to move the gifts.

30 Let's continue. On December 28, 1997, Ms. Lewinsky and the President met in the Oval Office to exchange Christmas gifts, at which time they discussed the fact that the lawyers in the Jones case had subpoenaed all of the gifts from the President to Ms. Lewinsky. During conversation on December 28, Ms. Lewinsky asked the President whether she should put away the gifts out of her house some place, or give them to someone, maybe Betty. At that time, according to Ms. Lewinsky, the President said, "Let me think about it."

31 The House managers have consistently described the December 28 meeting exactly this way, as did the majority counsel for the House Judiciary, as did the Office of Independent Counsel. It has been said so often that it has become conventional wisdom. But it is not the whole truth. It is not the full record. Ms. Lewinsky actually gave 10 renditions of her conversation with the President. All of them have been outlined in our chart. Invariably, the one most cited is the one least favorable to the President. But even in that version, the one that is least favorable to the President, no one claims he ordered, suggested, or even hinted that anyone obstruct justice. At most, the President says, "Let me think about it." That is not obstruction of justice.

32 But what about the nine other versions? Some of the other versions which I have never heard offered by the House managers, versions that maybe you, too, have never heard, are the ones that put the lie to the obstruction of justice elevation.

33 Let's look at exhibit 2 which is in your material. You may have never heard, for example, this version of their conversation. This is Ms. Lewinsky speaking.

It was December 28th and I was there to get my Christmas gifts from him . . . and we spent maybe about 5 minutes or so, not very long, talking about the case. And I said to him, "Well, do you think" . . . and I don't think I said get rid of, but I said, "Do you think I should put away or maybe give to Betty or give someone the gifts?" And he—I don't remember his response. It was something like, "I don't know," or "hmm" or there was really no response.

34 You also may not have heard this version. This is a juror speaking, a grand juror speaking to Ms. Lewinsky.

The Juror: Now, did you bring up Betty's name or did the President bring up Betty's name?

35 And this is at the meeting on the 28th.

Ms. LEWINSKY: I think I brought it up. The President wouldn't have brought up Betty's name because he really didn't—he really didn't discuss it. . . .

36 And you probably have not heard this version.

Lewinsky advised that Clinton was sitting in a rocking chair in the study. Lewinsky asked Clinton what she should do with the gifts Clinton had given her and he either did not respond or responded "I don't know." Lewinsky is not sure exactly what was said, but she is certain that whatever Clinton said, she had no clear image in her mind of what to do next.

37 Why haven't we heard these versions? Because they weaken an already fragile circumstantial case. If Ms. Lewinsky says that the President doesn't respond at all, then there is absolutely no evidence for the House managers' obstruction of justice theory, even under their version of events. So these versions get disregarded to ensure that the House managers' big picture doesn't get cluttered by all those details. It is those facts, those stubborn facts, that just don't fit.

38 But the most significant detail the managers disregard because it doesn't fit is the President's testimony. The President testified that he told Ms. Lewinsky that she had to give the Jones lawyers whatever gifts she had. Why? As the House managers predicted we would ask, because it is a question that begs to be asked, why would the President give Ms. Lewinsky gifts if he wanted her to give them right back? The only real explanation is he truly was, as he testified, unconcerned about the gifts. The House managers want you to believe that this gift giving was a show of confidence; that he knew Ms. Lewinsky would conceal them. But then why, under their theory, ask Ms. Currie to go pick them up? Why not know that Ms. Lewinsky is just going to conceal them? Better still, why not just show her the gifts and tell her to come by after the subpoena date has passed?

39 It simply doesn't make sense. The President's actions entirely undermine the House managers' theory of obstruction of justice.

40 But let's continue with their version of events. That answer, the "Let-me-think-about-it" answer, that answer led to action. Later that day, Ms. Lewinsky got a call at 3:32 p.m. from Ms. Currie who said, "I understand you have something to give me or the President said you have something to give me." It was the President who initiated the retrieval of the gifts and the concealment of the evidence.

41 Here is where the House managers have dramatically shortchanged the truth because the whole truth demands that Ms. Currie's testimony be presented fairly.

42 In telling their story, the managers do concede that there is a conflict in the testimony between Ms. Lewinsky and Ms. Currie, but they strive mightily to get you to disregard Ms. Currie's testimony by telling you that her memory on the issue of how she came to pick up the gifts was "fuzzy"—fuzzy. In particular, Manager HUTCHINSON told you:

I will concede there is a conflict in the testimony on this point with Ms. Currie. Ms. Currie, in her grand jury testimony, had a fuzzy memory, a little different recollection. She testified that, the best she can remember, Ms. Lewinsky called her, but when she was asked further, she said that maybe Ms. Lewinsky's memory is better than hers on that issue.

That is what the House managers want you to believe about Ms. Currie. That is not playing fair by Ms. Currie. It is not playing fair by the facts. Why? Because Ms. Currie was asked about who initiated the gift pick-up five times. Her answer each time was unequivocal—5 times. From the first FBI interview just days after the story broke in the media, to her last grand jury appearance, Ms. Currie repeatedly and unwaveringly testified that it was Ms. Lewinsky who contacted her about the gifts.

43 Her memory on this issue is clear. What does she say? Let's look at exhibit 3, the first time she is asked:

> Lewinsky called Currie and advised she had returned all gifts Clinton had given to Lewinsky, as there was talk going around about the gifts.

44 The second time:

> Monica said she was getting concerned and she wanted to give me the stuff the President had given her, or give me a box of stuff. It was a box stuff.

45 Third time, and this was a prosecutor asking Ms. Currie the question:

> Just tell us for a moment how this issue first arose, and what you did about it, and what Ms. Lewinsky told you.

> Ms. CURRIE: The best I remember, it first arose with conversation. I don't know if it was over the phone or in person; I don't know. She asked me if I would pick up a box. She said Isikoff had been inquiring about the gifts.

46 The fourth time:

> The best I remember, she said she wanted me to hold these gifts—hold this—I'm sure she said gifts, a box of gifts—I don't remember—because people were asking questions, and I said fine.

47 The fifth time:

> The best I remember is, Monica called me and asked me if she can give me some gifts, if I would pick up some gifts for her.

48 The last time, the fifth time, when a grand juror completely misstated Ms. Currie's testimony regarding how the gift exchange was initiated by suggesting that the President had directed her to pick up the gifts. Ms. Currie was quick to correct the juror:

> Question: Ms. Currie, I want to come back for a second to the box of gifts and how they came to be in your possession. As I recall your earlier testimony the other day, you testified that the President asked you to telephone Ms. Lewinsky. Is that correct?

> Answer: Pardon? The President asked me to telephone Ms. Lewinsky?

> JUROR: Is that correct?

Ms. CURRIE: About?

JUROR: About the box of gifts. I am trying to recall and understand exactly how the box of gifts came to be in your possession.

Ms. CURRIE: I don't recall the President asking me to call about a box of gifts.

JUROR: How did you come to be in possession of the box of gifts?

Ms. CURRIE: The best I remember. Ms. Lewinsky called me and asked me if she can give me the gifts— if I would pick up some gifts for her.

49 The record reflects that Ms. Currie's testimony on this issue was clear—five times—every time she was asked.

[*Editor's Note:* At this point Mills moves into an extended discussion of the alleged gifts. Mills asks her audience to compare the details of Ms. Currie's account versus that of Ms. Lewinsky. Mills concludes that both versions are substantially the same.]

50 I believe I can best sum up by using the words of Manager BUYER who quoted President John Adams. "Facts are stubborn things. Whatever may be our issues, or inclinations, or the dictates of our passions, they cannot alter the state of the facts and the evidence."

51 Those stubborn facts. Manager BUYER went on to say, "I believe John Adams was right." Facts and evidence. Facts are stubborn things. You can color the facts, like calling Ms. Currie's memory fuzzy. You can shade the facts by not telling you the length of that supposed corroborating phone call. You can misrepresent the facts by giving only 1 of 10 versions of Ms. Lewinsky's testimony about the President's response to her question about the gifts. You can hide the facts, like not telling you of Ms. Lewinsky's personal motivation for wanting the gifts. But the truthful facts are stubborn: they won't go away. Like the telltale heart, they keep pounding. And they keep coming. They won't go away. Those stubborn, stubborn facts. They show that this was not obstruction of justice.

52 I now will talk about the President's conversation with Ms. Currie on January 18. It is not difficult to understand these events if you have lived a life in which you are the subject of extraordinary media attention and extraordinary media scrutiny. Most American lives are not like that. Our jobs and our personal lives are not usually the subject for daily media consumption. As Senators, you obviously know well what that life is like.

53 On January 18, the President talked to Ms. Currie about the Jones deposition and in particular about his surprise at some of the questions the Jones lawyers had asked about Ms. Lewinsky. In the course of their conversation, the President asked Ms. Currie a series of questions and made some statements about his relationship with Ms. Lewinsky, all of which seemed to seek her concurrence, or reaction, or her input.

54 The managers' theory is that the President, by his comments, corruptly tried to influence Ms. Currie's potential testimony in the Jones case in violation of the obstruction of justice law. They acknowledge that the President knew nothing about the independent counsel's investigation. So they have focused on the Jones case as the place to lodge their obstruction of justice allegation. Ms. Currie was not scheduled to be a witness in that case. And, as you will see, the President had other things on his mind.

55 Before I go into the facts surrounding these conversations, I want to first focus briefly on the law, as the managers did in their presentation. There are two relevant obstruction of justice statutes: 18 U.S.C. 1503, which is the general obstruction of justice statute; and 18 U.S.C. 1512, the more specific statute which prohibits witness tampering.

56 There are differences between these two statutes, but for our purpose their essential elements are similar. Both require the Government to prove that the person being accused, one, acted knowingly; two, with specific intent; three, to corruptly affect and influence. In 1503, and corruptly persuade, in 1512, either the due administration of justice, under 1503, or the testimony of a person in an official proceeding, under 1512, to try to persuade the testimony of a person in an official proceeding. For conviction, each and every element must be proven beyond a reasonable doubt. If the prosecution fails to prove even one element, the jury is obliged to acquit. In this case, none of the elements is present.

[*Editor's Note:* For the next several paragraphs, Mills provides a detailed review and extensive quotation from case law and the U.S. Federal Code.]

57 So I want to begin by focusing on the "corruptly persuade" elements of witness tampering. What does it mean to corruptly persuade? The term is vague, and the legislative history on the specific point is not very clear. We do know it means more than harassing, which is described as badgering or pestering conduct, since 1512 makes intentional harassment a misdemeanor, a lesser offense than "corruptly persuade," which is a felony. The U.S. Attorneys' Manual gives some guidance. A prosecution under 1512 would require the Government to prove beyond a reasonable doubt, one, an effort to threaten, force or intimidate another person and; two, an intent to influence the person's testimony. Thus, "corruptly persuade" for career prosecutors requires some element of threat or intimidation or pressure.

58 Keeping that overview in mind, let's look at the facts. On January 17, 1998, the President called Ms. Currie after his deposition and asked her to meet with him the following day. On January 18, the President and Ms. Currie met, and the President told her about some of those surprising questions he had been asked in his deposition about Ms. Lewinsky. In the course of their conversation, according to Ms. Currie, the President posed a series of questions and made statements including: You were always there when she was there, right? We were never really alone. You could see and hear everything. Monica came on to me, and I never touched her, right? And she wanted to have sex with me, and I can't do that.

59 Our analysis of this issue could stop here. There is no case for obstruction of justice. Why? There is no evidence whatsoever of any kind of threat or intimidation. And as we discussed, the U.S. Attorney's Manual indicates that without a threat or intimidation, there is no corrupt influence. Without corrupt influence, there is no obstruction of justice. But the evidence reveals much more. Not only does the record lack any evidence of threat or intimidation, the record specifically contains Ms. Currie's undisputed testimony which exonerates the President of this charge. This is Ms. Currie's testimony and is the fourth exhibit in the materials.

60 Question to Ms. Currie:

Now, back again to the four statements that you testified the President made to you that were presented as statements, did you feel you were pressured when he told you those statements?

None whatsoever.

Question: What did you think, or what was going through your mind about what he was doing?

Ms. Currie:

At the time I felt that he was—I want to use the word shocked or surprised that this was an issue, and he was just talking.

Question: That was your impression, that he wanted you to say—because he would end each of the statements with "Right?," with a question.

Ms. Currie:

I do not remember that he wanted me to say "Right." He would say, "Right?" and I could have said. "Wrong."

Question: But he would end each of these questions with a "Right?" and you could either say whether it was true or not true.

Correct.

Did you feel any pressure to agree with your boss?

None.

61 The evidence on this issue is clear. There was no effort to intimidate or pressure Ms. Currie, and she testified that she did not feel pressured. Betty Currie's testimony unequivocally establishes that the managers' case lacks any element of threat or intimidation. There is no evidence, direct or circumstantial, that refutes this testimony. This is not obstruction of justice.

62 But let's not stop there. Let's look at the intent element of the obstruction of justice laws—in other words, whether the President had the intent to influence Ms. Currie's supposed testimony, or potential testimony.

63 In an attempt to satisfy this element of the law, the managers overreached in their presentation to create the appearance that the President had the necessary specific intent. They argue that, based upon the way he answered the questions in the Jones deposition, he purposely referred to Ms. Currie in the hopes that the Jones lawyers would call her as a corroborating witness. Therefore, according to their theory, he had the specific intent.

64 The facts belie their overreaching. The House managers suggested to you that the President increased the likelihood that Ms. Currie would be called as a witness by challenging the plaintiff's attorney to question Ms. Currie. A review of the transcript, however, shows that the President's few references to Ms. Currie were neither forced nor needlessly interposed. They were natural, appropriate; they were responsive. Indeed, the only occasion when he suggested the Jones lawyers speak to Ms. Currie is when they asked if it was typical for Ms. Currie to be in the White House after midnight. He understandably said, "You have to ask her." Hardly a challenge. It is a reasonable response to an inquiry about someone else's activities.

65 The managers' conjecture about the President's state of mind, however, falls on an even more basic level. If you believe the managers' theory, if you believe that the President went to great lengths to hide his relationship with Ms. Lewinsky, then why on Earth would he want Ms. Currie to be a witness in the Jones case? If there was one person who knew the extent of his contact with Ms. Lewinsky, it was Ms. Currie. While she did not know the nature of his relationship with Ms. Lewinsky, Ms. Currie did know and would have testified to Ms. Lewinsky's visits in 1997, the notes and messages that Ms. Lewinsky sent the President, the gifts that Ms. Lewinsky sent the President, and the President's support of the efforts to get Ms. Lewinsky a job. With just that information, it would have only been a matter of time before the Jones lawyers discovered the relationship—not that they needed Ms. Currie's testimony; they didn't need it for any of this. Ms. Tripp was already on the December 5, 1997, witness list, and she was already scheduled for a deposition.

66 So why would the President want her to testify? The answer is simple. He didn't. The President was not thinking about Ms. Currie becoming a witness in the Jones case. Indeed, she is the last person the President would have wanted the Jones lawyers to question. And even if the Jones lawyers had wanted to question Ms. Currie, it is highly unlikely they would have been allowed to do so, given the posture of the case at that time.

67 Judge Wright ordered the parties in August of 1997 to exchange names and addresses of all witnesses no later than December 5, 1997. Ms. Currie was not on their final witness list. Moreover, the cutoff date for all discovery was January 30. By the time the President's deposition was over, it was really too late to call Ms. Currie as a witness.

68 Finally, you need to remember that in the context of the Jones case Ms. Currie was, at best, a peripheral witness on a collateral matter that the court ultimately determined was not essential to the core issues in the case. She had only knowledge of a small aspect of a much larger case—all the more reason not to view her as a potential witness.

69 The President was not thinking about Ms. Currie becoming a witness in the Jones case. So what was the President thinking? The President explained to the grand jury why he spoke to Ms. Currie after the deposition. It had nothing to do with Ms. Currie being a potential witness. That was not his concern. The President was concerned that his secret was going to be exposed and the media would relentlessly inquire until the entire story and every shameful detail was public. The President's concern was heightened by an Internet report that morning that he spoke to Betty which alluded to Ms. Lewinsky and to Ms. Currie and to issues that the Jones lawyers had raised. The President was understandably concerned about media inquiries, a concern everyone who lives and serves in the public eye likely can understand.

70 In trying to prepare for what he saw as the inevitable media attention, he talked to Ms. Currie to see what her perceptions were and what she recalled. He talked to her to see what she knew.

71 Remember, some of the questions that the Jones lawyer asked the President were so off base. For example, they asked him about visits from Ms. Lewinsky between midnight and 6 a.m. where Ms. Currie supposedly cleared her in. The President wanted to know whether or not Ms. Currie agreed with this perception or whether she had a different view, whether she agreed that Ms. Lewinsky was cleared in when he was present or had there been other occasions that he didn't know about. He also wanted to assess Ms. Currie's perception of the relationship. He knew the first person who would be questioned about media accounts, particularly given that she was in the Internet report, was going to be Ms. Currie.

72 The House managers did the President a disservice in suggesting in the end that his five pages of testimony about why he spoke to Ms. Currie ultimately amounts to a four-word sound bite to refresh his recollection. He obviously said a lot more.

73 Why did they say that? Because they needed to establish intent, and the testimony and the facts do not show intent. That is the truth. That is all of the facts.

74   The President's intent was never to obstruct justice in the Jones case. It was to manage a looming media firestorm, which he correctly foresaw. As the President told the grand jury, "I was trying to get the facts and trying to think of the best defense we could construct in the face of what I thought was going to be a media onslaught."

75   He was thinking about the media. That is the big picture. That is not obstruction of justice.

76   In the end, of course, you must make your own judgments about whether the managers have made a case for convicting the President of obstructing justice on either of these allegations. We believe they have not, because the facts, those stubborn facts, don't support the allegations. Neither does the rule of law. We are not alone in that conclusion.

[*Editor's Note:* Mills next refers to the text of videotape testimony presented by a bipartisan panel of prosecuters to the House Judiciary panel. The testimony reviewed the accounts of Ms. Currie and Ms. Lewinsky over the alleged gifts.]

77   Before I close, I do want to take a moment to address a theme that the House managers sounded throughout their presentation last week—civil rights. They suggested that by not removing the President from office, the entire house of civil rights might well fall. While acknowledging that the President is a good advocate for civil rights, they suggested that they had grave concerns because of the President's conduct in the Paula Jones case.

78   Some managers suggested that we all should be concerned should the Senate fail to convict the President, because it would send a message that our civil rights laws and our sexual harassment laws are unimportant.

79   I can't let their comments go unchallenged. I speak as but one woman, but I know I speak for others as well. I know I speak for the President.

80   Bill Clinton's grandfather owned a store. His store catered primarily to African Americans. Apparently, his grandfather was one of only four white people in town who would do business with African Americans. He taught his grandson that the African Americans who came into his store were good people and they worked hard and they deserved a better deal in life.

81   The President has taken his grandfather's teachings to heart, and he has worked every day to give all of us a better deal, an equal deal.

82   I am not worried about the future of civil rights. I am not worried because Ms. Jones had her day in court and Judge Wright determined that all of the matters we are discussing here today were not material to her case and ultimately decided that Ms. Jones, based on the facts and the law in that case, did not have a case against the President.

83   I am not worried, because we have had imperfect leaders in the past and will have imperfect leaders in the future, but their imperfections did not roll back, nor did they stop, the march for civil rights and equal opportunity for all of our citizens.

84   Thomas Jefferson, Frederick Douglass, Abraham Lincoln, John F. Kennedy, Martin Luther King, Jr.—we revere these men. We should. But they were not perfect men. They made human errors, but they struggled to do humanity good. I am not worried about civil rights because this President's record on civil rights, on women's rights, on all of our rights is unimpeachable.

85   Ladies and gentlemen of the Senate, you have an enormous decision to make. And in truth, there is little more I can do to lighten that burden. But I can do this: I can assure you that your decision to follow the facts and the law and the Constitution and acquit this President will not shake the foundation of the house of civil rights. The house of civil rights is strong because its foundation is strong.

86   And with all due respect, the foundation of the house of civil rights was never at the core of the Jones case. It was never at the heart of the Jones case. The foundation of the house of civil rights is in the voices of all the great civil rights leaders and the soul of every person who heard them. It is in the hands of every person who folded a leaflet for change. And it is in the courage of every person who changed. It is here in the Senate where men and women of courage and conviction stood for progress, where Senators—some of them still in this chamber: some of them who lost their careers—looked to the Constitution, listened to their conscience, and then did the right thing.

87   The foundation of the house of civil rights is in all of us who gathered up our will to raise it up and keep on building. I stand here before you today because others before me decided to take a stand, or as one of my law professors so eloquently says, "because someone claimed my opportunities for me, by fighting for my right to have the education I have, by fighting for my right to seek the employment I choose, by fighting for my right to be a lawyer," by sitting in and carrying signs and walking on long marches, riding freedom rides and putting their bodies on the line for civil rights.

88   I stand here before you today because America decided that the way things were was not how they were going to be. We, the people, decided that we all deserved a better deal. I stand here before you today because President Bill Clinton believed I could stand here for him.

89   Your decision whether to remove President Clinton from office, based on the articles of impeachment, I know, will be based on the law and the facts and the Constitution. It would be wrong to convict him on this record. You should acquit him on this record. And you must not let imagined harms to the house of civil rights persuade you otherwise. The President did not obstruct justice. The President did not commit perjury. The President must not be removed from office.

Chapter Five

Speeches That Affirm Propositions of Value

The Nature and Importance of Speeches That Affirm Propositions of Value

The centrality of values to human existence and to the communication process is acknowledged by Richard M. Weaver, a rhetorical theorist and critic, and by Kenneth Boulding, social critic and economist. In his *The Ethics of Rhetoric,* Weaver contends, "It is the nature of the conscious life of man to revolve around some concept of value. So true is this that when the concept is withdrawn, or when it is forced into conflict with another concept, the human being suffers an almost intolerable sense of being lost." Boulding, in *The Image,* argues:

> . . . The value scales of any individual or organization are perhaps the most important single element determining the effect of the messages it receives on its image of the world. If a message is perceived that is neither good nor bad it may have little or no effect on the image. If it is perceived as bad or hostile to the image which is held, there will be resistance to accepting it.

On the other hand, when a message reinforces a value that is cherished, auditors are likely to be receptive to the position being advanced.

During the past four decades, values have been very much in conflict in American society. Activists have questioned war as a legitimate method of resolving international disputes, poverty as a necessary consequence of a complex economic order, and civil obedience as an unquestioned obligation of responsible citizenship. Americans of all ages have become more compellingly aware of their own values. Some have sought to translate new values into working political and economic practices. Others, threatened by the aggressiveness of reformers, have reasserted their own traditional values as the appropriate way for civilized community life. Hopefully this continuing dialogue about values will meet Richard Weaver's test of public discourse in its finer moments: " . . . Rhetoric at its truest seeks to perfect men by showing them better versions of themselves, links in that chain extending up toward the ideal. . . ."

Not all propositions of value, however, concern the crucial issues of modern social existence. While some speakers affirm propositions related to war or peace, prosperity or poverty, and human love or bigotry, others affirm propositions of value related to artistic excellence, academic achievement, or even, via the mass media, the taste of colas and toothpastes. Propositions of value pervade all facets of human life.

Recall that in Chapter 2 a value was defined as a conception of "The Good" or "The Desirable" which functions sometimes as a goal motivating our behavior and sometimes as a standard for evaluating means to achieve ends. You may wish to reread the comments in that chapter explaining the line of critical analysis that asked: "To what degree do the speaker's ideas harmonize with the audience's relevant values?"

Sometimes speakers urge adoption of a new value, or adoption of a new perspective through redefining an old value. Some speakers aim to reinforce and reenergize audience commitment to values already held. Often speakers offer their value judgment of something (such as a book, film, play, or speech) as valid for audience belief. On occasion a speaker must defend his or her character and reputation against criticism. Such a speech of personal defense aims at refuting negative value judgments concerning the speaker's honesty, integrity, ethics, morals, and public responsibility.

Speakers also affirm values in speeches not primarily devoted to values. A speaker presenting information to enhance audience understanding will show that the information is valuable because it is relevant and useful. To generate listener concern about a problem, a speaker must show that the situation threatens or violates basic relevant audience values. To secure audience acceptance of a policy as a solution to a problem, a speaker must show that the policy is consistent with or enhances central audience values. And, contrary to the popular notion, "facts" do not "speak for themselves." *Humans* present and interpret matters agreed upon as factual in light of their own related values.

Whatever the particular proposition of value, the advocate seeks listener agreement that something meets or does not meet a specific value standard. Unlike the proposition of fact, which is affirmed or denied through tests of existence, occurrence, or causality, the proposition of value is affirmed through tests of *goodness* or *quality*. A value standard may be applied to an individual, an event, an object, a way of life, a process, a condition, or even to another value. Consider the following examples:

Proposition A: All popular music is trash.

Proposition B: Prohibition against same sex unions is an outmoded value.

Proposition C: Richard Nixon was a great man.

Proposition D: War is immoral.

Proposition E: A speaker who uses primarily emotional appeals is unethical.

Proposition F: Civil disobedience is always bad.

Proposition G: President Clinton was irresponsible in his handling of the Monica Lewinsky affair.

These propositions of value differ in subject matter being valued or devalued. However, each affirms or denies something measured against standards rooted in listener values. Like all propositions of value, those noted above include a word or words that imply a value dimension—"is trash," "is an outmoded value" "was a great man," "is immoral," "is unethical," "is bad," "was irresponsible." Because the meanings associated with such evaluative terms are deeply rooted, saturated with emotion, and wrapped in tradition, the task of the advocate seeking to affirm a proposition of value frequently is an incredibly difficult one. And equally difficult is the task of judging such speeches.

Criteria for Evaluating Speeches That Affirm Propositions of Value

1. Has the speaker demonstrated or is it assumed by the audience that he or she is a person of high credibility with respect to the proposition being advocated?

When the speaker leaves the realm of empirically verifiable fact and enters the realm of culturally-based and often abstractly-defined values, the assessment by listeners becomes increasingly dependent on their perceptions of the speaker's expertness and trustworthiness. In stressing the potency of speaker ethos, Aristotle wrote: "As a rule we trust men of probity more and more quickly about things in general, while on points outside the realm of exact knowledge, where opinion is divided, we trust them absolutely."

Listeners tend to believe statements about values and value judgments made by speakers they admire and respect. But different audiences and cultures value different qualities in speakers. A college professor of economics arguing that American advertising is unethical may be considered an expert by an audience of high school sophomores, a starry-eyed idealist by an audience of business people, and an extreme liberal by an audience of college Young Republicans.

Although most communication scholars agree that the speaker who is considered by an audience as highly credible has an advantage over the speaker whose ethos is low, they do not always agree on the exact factors determining speaker prestige. In *Principles of Speaking,* for example, Hance, Ralph, and Wiksell list *competence,* which "grows out of a combination of mental ability, know-how, intelligence, understanding, experience with the subject, and knowledge"; *good character,* which is "made up of honesty, integrity, sincerity, fairness, and similar qualities that meet the standards of listeners"; and *good will,* which "consists of friendliness, likeableness, rapport, warmth, and being 'in' with the audience." In *The Art of Persuasion,* Minnick includes confidence and poise, physical energy, sincerity and conviction, mental alertness, intelligence and knowledge, fairness and justice, self-discipline, even temper and restraint, sympathy and understanding, decisiveness, dynamism, and similarity to audience values and beliefs. For further discussion of the importance of source credibility, you may want to read again in chapter 2 the line of critical inquiry which asked: "To what degree is the speaker perceived as a highly credible source on the subject?"

Among the questions you may wish to ask about the advocate of a proposition of value are these: Is the speaker a person who embodies the qualities of character, intelligence, and experience most admired by the audience? Does the speaker's life demonstrate commitment to the value she or he advocates or applies? Does the speaker have the training and experience to qualify for making the value judgment expressed?

2. Has the speaker advanced acceptable criteria for the assessment of the proposition of value?

The criteria for assessing a proposition of value differ from those for assessing a proposition of fact. The criteria for the latter are essentially empirical or quasi-empirical, whereas those for the former are steeped in feelings and related values. For example, consider the following proposition:

Proposition of fact: Capital punishment is not an effective deterrent to crime.

Proposition of value: Capital punishment is morally bad.

In the first case, widely accepted criteria for judgment involve tests of empirical reality. Has capital punishment led to a reduction in serious crimes in states where it has been tried? Do states with capital punishment have lower rates of serious crimes than equivalent states that do not have capital punishment? Have carefully controlled, systematic studies demonstrated that potential criminals consider the consequences of their crimes before committing them? In the second instance, the criteria for judgment are rooted in earlier value commitments. Is the taking of human life, for whatever cause, contrary to values fundamental to the Judeo-Christian ethic, to human decency, or to communal life?

In attempting to gain acceptance of a proposition of value, a speaker has a number of rhetorical options available for stressing the appropriateness of his or her value criteria. The speaker can show that the value standards used or values advocated are consistent with other values already held by the audience. The speaker might show that the value advocated has produced desirable consequences in the past when adhered to; this involves using *another* value standard to demonstrate "desirability." Sometimes speakers use examples and testimony to show that "good" persons generally have accepted the advocated value and "bad" or less desirable persons have rejected it. Or the value being advocated may be *contrasted* with its undesirable opposite (disvalue) or with a less desirable value. And some speakers offer to an audience a *hierarchy* of values by verbally indicating that the value advocated or defended is *better than* other specific values. Finally, a speaker might argue that socially undesirable consequences will result from continued adherence to old, outmoded values.

Speakers need not fail when their value judgments run counter to the values of the audience. When in 1932 Franklin D. Roosevelt spoke to San Francisco's Commonwealth Club, a group of businessmen with conservative economic values, he began with a careful historical review of the values that had produced industrial America. Then he pointed out that these values had served the nation well but were no longer consistent with our best national interest. In 1886, Southerner Henry W. Grady, in an address to members of the New England Society, sought to erase their long-standing hostility toward the South by praising the spirit of Lincoln and by urging commitment to national values rather than to regional loyalties. Admittedly persuading about values is a complex task, but it is one that a perceptive and sensitive speaker can accomplish to some degree.

In evaluating a speech affirming a proposition of value, the enlightened listener must carefully consider the criteria for judgment that he or she is being asked to accept. Is the value advocated for acceptance or application clearly and exactly specified? Does the speaker demonstrate that the value is reasonable and relevant for the subject at hand? Is the value or value judgment only asserted or implied without clear and reasonable support or demonstration? To what degree do the value appeals serve a legitimate function of promoting social cohesion, of reinforcing audience commitment to ideas they already believe? With what degree of appropriateness are the consequences of commitment to the values clarified? To what degree do the value appeals serve as substitutes, as pseudoproof, for the factuality of an assertion? To what degree do the value appeals divert attention from more fundamental, pressing, or controversial matters? To what degree do the value appeals seem to promote, intentionally or not, unreflective stimulus-response reactions when the occasion demands reflective judgment?

3. Has the speaker presented a fair view of what is being evaluated?

It should be apparent that a speaker may be eminently qualified to judge and may have acceptable criteria of judgment in mind and yet may have a distorted view of what is being judged. Propositions of value usually are emotion-laden and a speaker's bias may impair her or his ability to depict fairly the object being judged.

Propositions of value often depend on the previous acceptance or establishment of a proposition of fact. Thus the critic must consider whether the advocate has met adequate criteria for the assessment of fact that portrays what the advocate is judging. Should the speaker be interested in evaluating an event, we first must be assured that the event has been portrayed accurately. Similarly, should the speaker wish to assign a value to a work of art, a belief, an individual, an institution, an action, or another value, we should inquire about the accuracy with which the object being judged is described. Faced with an object described in two-valued, either-or, no-middle-ground terms, the critical listener must consider whether such a description is accurate and adequate for the situation.

Conclusion

The climate of public debate in America during the late 20th Century reflects "an unwillingness, if not a psychological inability, to make and defend judgments of better and worse." Emmanuel Mesthene, a professor of philosophy, elaborates on his view by condemning the widespread hesitancy to "argue a position or justify an action on the basis of judgments of relative worth, whether of morality, of art, of individuals, or of institutions." To what extent do you agree with his contentions? Are value judgments or advocacy of values far too rare in contemporary public discourse?

No matter how frequently we are exposed to value-oriented messages, and because values play such an important role in decisions related to individual and social well-being, the enlightened listener/critic must consider carefully the evaluative messages received each day. In assessing speeches that affirm propositions of value, the critic should consider (1) *whether the speaker is a person of high credibility with respect to the proposition being advocated,* (2) *whether the speaker has advanced acceptable criteria for the assessment of the proposition, and* (3) *whether the speaker has presented a fair view of what is being evaluated.*

FOR FURTHER READING

Chen, Guo-Ming, and Starosta, William J. *Foundations of Intercultural Communication.* Allyn and Bacon, 1998. Chapter 3 explores the role of values in intercultural and multicultural communication.

Ehninger, Douglas, and Hauser, Gerard. "Communication of Values." In Carroll Arnold and John Bowers, eds. *Handbook of Rhetorical and Communication Theory.* Allyn and Bacon, 1984, Chapter 4.

Fisher, Walter R. "Toward a Logic of Good Reasons." *Quarterly Journal of Speech,* December 1978, 376–384.

Harrell, Jackson; Ware, B. L.; and Linkugel, Wil A. "Failure of Apology in American Politics: Nixon on Watergate." *Speech Monographs,* November 1975, 245–61. Analyzes Nixon's first two Watergate speeches from the perspective of the bases of political authority and the theory of apology.

Inch, Edward S., and Warnick, Barbara. *Critical Thinking and Communication: The Use of Reason in Argument.* 3rd ed. Allyn and Bacon, 1998. Chapter 10 discusses advocating and opposing value propositions.

McCroskey, James C. *An Introduction to Rhetorical Communication.* 7th ed. Allyn and Bacon, 1997. Chapter 5 examines theory and research on the speaker's ethos or credibility.

McEdwards, Mary G. "American Values: Circa 1920–1970." *Quarterly Journal of Speech,* April 1971, pp. 173–80. Illustrates how basic American values have remained relatively constant.

Mesthene, Emmanuel G. "On the Importance of Judging Between Better or Worse." *National Forum,* LXIX (Summer 1979): 4–8.

Rieke, Richard D., and Sillars, Malcolm O. *Argumentation and Critical Decision Making.* 4th ed. Addison Wesley, 1997, Chapter 8. After explaining the nature of values, the authors describe in detail six traditional and nontraditional American value systems.

Rokeach, Milton. *The Nature of Human Values.* Macmillan, 1970. A theoretical discussion of what values are and an empirical description of major contemporary American value commitments.

Sillars, Malcolm O. *Messages, Meanings, and Culture: Approaches to Communication Criticism.* Harper/Collins, 1991. Chapter 7 considers criticism of values in discourse.

Walter, Otis M., and Scott, Robert L. *Thinking and Speaking.* 5th ed. Macmillan, 1984. Pages 95–97 survey some contemporary American values and Chapter 10 discusses persuading about values.

Ware, B. L., and Linkugel, Wil A. "They Spoke in Defense of Themselves: On the Generic Criticism of Apologia." *Quarterly Journal of Speech.* October 1973, 273–83. Examines the rhetorical strategies and tactics available to speakers in defending their personal character against negative value judgments.

Weaver, Richard M. *The Ethics of Rhetoric.* Regnery, 1953, Chapter 9. Weaver's discussion of "ultimate terms" in the rhetoric of the era illuminates the persuasive potency of values and disvalues as they appear in the form of societal "god terms" and "devil terms."

For the World to Live, "Europe" Must Die

◆ *Russell Means* ◆

In the Summer of 1980, Russell Means, a member of the Ogala Lakota tribe, of the Sioux nation, addressed several thousand people during the Black Hills International Survival Gathering held on the Pine Ridge Reservation in South Dakota. This meeting was held to protest the pollution and exploitation of American Indian lands throughout the West. For most of those in his audience, Means' ethos, his level of source credibility, would be extremely high. Their perceptions of his personal qualities, such as expertness and trustworthiness, would be very positive. He co-founded the activist American Indian Movement (AIM). He organized activist groups in cities and on reservations. He played a major role in the protest occupation of Wounded Knee, South Dakota, in the Spring of 1973. In the course of his various activities, he has been injured, shot, and jailed. Although now he downplays his leadership role (46), his audience would listen carefully to his advice because of their high esteem for him as a leader.

The central issue, according to Means, is the clash between two antagonistic value systems, between two opposite world views—the European and the traditional American Indian tribal. A revolution in value commitments is needed, and he offers a persuasive definition of what we should mean by the label "revolution" (21, 23, 33–34).

◆ Reprinted with permission from *Mother Jones* magazine, December, 1980, pp. 24–38.

An attack on the European-American value system comprises the bulk of Means' address. He pinpoints some of the values he feels are central to the European mind-set: step-by-step logical thinking (7); mechanical image of nature and humans (8); material gain (10); scientific despiritualization of nature and humans (11); and arrogant elevation of humans above other animate and inanimate things (29–30). The values of progress, development, victory, and freedom, all highly prized in the European cultural view, Means depicts as actually undesirable, as disvalues (12).

One major strategy used by Means to undermine European values is to describe the dangerous consequences of following such values (11–12, 18–19, 24, 25–26). Assess the soundness of the cause-effect reasoning he uses to make such arguments. Means contends very specifically that Marxism is only a different version of the European cultural tradition and, as such, is just as flawed as capitalism or Christianity (21–23, 27). As another rhetorical strategy he itemizes objectionable groups and individuals who embody the undesirable European values (38).

To a lesser extent, Means discusses a few of the specific values central to the traditional American Indian world view: the universe as complex and spiritual (7); "being" a good person (10); and the interrelation of all humans and facets of nature (29–31, 40). To what degree would the speech have been strengthened by a more complete discussion of the values central to the Indian world view? Might Means' audience already have understood and assumed the validity of some key values not discussed? Means mentions a few groups that seem to embody the praiseworthy tribal value system (39). The labels Means chooses heightens the stark contrast between the antagonistic value stances: "death culture" (41) versus "correct peoples" (32). Means' fundamental belief is that the strength to resist and overturn Europeanization flows from commitment to traditional American Indian tribal values (5, 34).

In December 1985, along with other members of the New American Indian Movement, Means went to Nicaragua to join Indians native to Nicaragua in fighting that country's Marxist Sandinista government (*Chicago Tribune*, December 28, 1985, Sec. 1, p. 3). Means argued that the Marxist government could not deal fairly with Nicaraguan Indians because "Marxists are racists."

For an analysis of the broad historical and cultural context within which Means advocates Native American values, see Richard Morris and Philip Wander, "Native American Rhetoric: Dancing in the Shadows of the Ghost Dance," *Quarterly Journal of Speech,* 76 (May 1990): 164–191. The clash of the Lakota and European cultures and value systems in the late 1800s in the American West is depicted vividly in the 1990 academy award film, "Dances With Wolves," produced by, directed by, and starring Kevin Costner.

◆ ◆ ◆

1 The only possible opening for a statement of this kind is that I detest writing. The process itself epitomizes the European concept of "legitimate" thinking; what is written has an importance that is denied the spoken. My culture, the Lakota culture, has an oral tradition, so I ordinarily reject writing. It is one of the white world's ways of destroying the cultures of non-European peoples, the imposing of an abstraction over the spoken relationship of a people.

2 So what you read here is not what I've written. It's what I've said and someone else has written down. I will allow this because it seems that the only way to communicate with the white world is through the dead dry leaves of a book. I don't really care whether my words reach whites or not. They have already demonstrated through their history that they cannot hear, cannot see; they can only read (of course, there are exceptions, but the exceptions only prove the rule). I'm more concerned with American Indian people, students and others, who have begun to be absorbed into the white world through universities and other institutions. But even then it's a marginal sort of concern. It's very possible to grow into a red face with a white mind; and if that's a person's individual choice, so be it, but I have no use for them. This is part of the process of cultural genocide being waged by Europeans against American Indian peoples today. My concern is with those American Indians who choose to resist this genocide, but who may be confused as to how to proceed.

3   (You notice I use the term *American Indian* rather than *Native American* or *Native indigenous people* or *Amerindian* when referring to my people. There has been some controversy about such terms, and frankly, at this point, I find it absurd. Primarily it seems that *American Indian* is being rejected as European in origin—which is true. But *all* of the above terms are European in origin; the only non-European way is to speak of Lakota—or, more precisely, of Oglala, Brulé, etc.—and of the Diné, the Miccosukee and all the rest of the several hundred correct tribal names.)

4   (There is also some confusion about the word *Indian,* a mistaken belief that it refers somehow to the country, India. When Columbus washed up on the beach in the Caribbean, he was not looking for a country called India. Europeans were calling that country Hindustan in 1492. Look it up on the old maps. Columbus called the tribal people he met "Indio," from the Italian *in dio,* meaning "in God.")

5   It takes a strong effort on the part of each American Indian *not* to become Europeanized. The strength for this effort can only come from the traditional ways, the traditional values that our elders retain. It must come from the hoop, the four directions, the relations; it cannot come from the pages of a book or a thousand books. No European can ever teach a Lakota to be Lakota, a Hopi to be Hopi. A master's degree in "Indian Studies" or in "education" or in anything else cannot make a person into a human being or provide knowledge into the traditional ways. It can only make you into a mental European, an outsider.

6   I should be clear about something here, because there seems to be some confusion about it. When I speak of Europeans or mental Europeans, I'm not allowing for false distinctions. I'm not saying that on the one hand there are the by-products of a few thousand years of genocidal, reactionary, European intellectual development which is bad; and on the other hand there is some new revolutionary intellectual development which is good. I'm referring here to the so-called theories of Marxism and anarchism and "leftism" in general. I don't believe these theories can be separated from the rest of the European intellectual tradition. It's really just the same old song.

7   The process began much earlier. Newton, for example, "revolutionized" physics and the so-called natural sciences by reducing the physical universe to a linear mathematical equation. Descartes did the same thing with culture. John Locke did it with politics, and Adam Smith did it with economics. Each one of these "thinkers" took a piece of the spirituality of human existence and converted it into a code, an abstraction. They picked up where Christianity ended; they "secularized" Christian religion, as the "scholars" like to say—and in doing so they made Europe more able and ready to act as an expansionist culture. Each of these intellectual revolutions served to abstract the European mentality even further, to remove the wonderful complexity and spirituality from the universe and replace it with a logical sequence: one, two, three, Answer!

8   This is what has come to be termed "efficiency" in the European mind. Whatever is mechanical is perfect; whatever seems to work at the moment—that is, proves the mechanical model to be the right one—is considered correct, even when it is clearly untrue. This is why "truth" changes so fast in the European mind; the answers which result from such a process are only stop-gaps, only temporary, and must be continuously discarded in favor of new stop-gaps which support the mechanical models and keep them (the models) alive.

9   Hegel and Marx were heirs to the thinking of Newton, Descartes, Locke, and Smith. Hegel finished the process of secularizing theology—and that is put in his own terms—he secularized the

religious thinking through which Europe understood the universe. Then Marx put Hegel's philosophy in terms of "materialism," which is to say that Marx despiritualized Hegel's work altogether. Again, this is in Marx' own terms. And this is now seen as the future revolutionary potential of Europe. Europeans may see this as revolutionary, but American Indians see it simply as still more of that same old European conflict between *being* and *gaining*. The intellectual roots of a new Marxist form of European imperialism lie in Marx'—and his followers'—links to the tradition of Newton, Hegel, and the others.

   10 *Being* is a spiritual proposition. *Gaining* is a material act. Traditionally, American Indians have always attempted to *be* the best people they could. Part of that spiritual process was and is to give away wealth, to discard wealth in order *not* to gain. Material gain is an indicator of false status among traditional people, while it is "proof that the system works" to Europeans. Clearly, there are two completely opposing views at issue here, and Marxism is very far over to the other side from the American Indian view. But let's look at a major implication of this; it is not merely an intellectual debate.

   11 The European materialist tradition of despiritualizing the universe is very similar to the mental process which goes into dehumanizing another person. And who seems more expert at dehumanizing other people? And why? Soldiers who have seen a lot of combat learn to do this to the enemy before going back into combat. Murderers do it before going out to commit murder. Nazi SS guards did it to concentration camp inmates. Cops do it. Corporation leaders do it to the workers they send into uranium mines and steel mills. Politicians do it to everyone in sight. And what the process has in common for each group doing the dehumanizing is that it makes it all right to kill and otherwise destroy other people. One of the Christian commandments says, "Thou shalt not kill," at least not humans so the trick is to mentally convert the victims into nonhumans. Then you can proclaim violation of your own commandment as a virtue.

   12 In terms of the despiritualization of the universe, the mental process works so that it becomes virtuous to destroy the planet. Terms like *progress* and *development* are used as cover words here, the way *victory* and *freedom* are used to justify butchery in the dehumanization process. For example, a real-estate speculator may refer to "developing" a parcel of ground by opening a gravel quarry; *development* here means total, permanent destruction, with the earth itself removed. But European logic has *gained* a few tons of gravel with which more land can be "developed" through the construction of road beds. Ultimately, the whole universe is open—in the European view—to this sort of insanity.

   13 Most important here, perhaps, is the fact that Europeans feel no sense of loss in all this. After all, their philosophers have despiritualized reality, so there is no satisfaction (for them) to be gained in simply observing the wonder of a mountain or a lake or a people *in being*. No, satisfaction is measured in terms of gaining material. So the mountain becomes gravel, and the lake becomes coolant for a factory, and the people are rounded up for processing through the indoctrination mills Europeans like to call schools.

   14 But each new piece of that "progress" ups the ante out in the real world. Take fuel for the industrial machine as an example. Little more than two centuries ago, nearly everyone used wood—a replenishable, natural item—as fuel for the very human needs of cooking and staying warm. Along came the Industrial Revolution and coal became the dominant fuel, as production became the social imperative for Europe. Pollution began to become a problem in the cities, and the earth was ripped open to provide coal whereas wood had always simply been gathered or harvested at no great expense to the environment. Later, oil became the major fuel, as the technology of production was perfected through a series of scientific "revolutions." Pollution increased dramatically, and nobody yet knows what the environmental costs of pumping all that oil out of the ground will really be in the long run. Now there's an "energy crisis," and uranium is becoming the dominant fuel.

15 Capitalists, at least, can be relied upon to develop uranium as fuel only at the rate at which they can show a good profit. That's their ethic, and maybe that will buy some time. Marxists, on the other hand, can be relied upon to develop uranium fuel as rapidly as possible simply because it's the most "efficient" production fuel available. That's *their* ethics, and I fail to see where it's preferable. Like I said, Marxism is right smack in the middle of the European tradition. It's the same old song.

16 There's a rule of thumb which can be applied here. You cannot judge the real nature of a European revolutionary doctrine on the basis of the changes it proposes to make within the European power structure and society. You can only judge it by the effects it will have on non-European peoples. This is because every revolution in European history has served to reinforce Europe's tendencies and abilities to export destruction to other peoples, other cultures, and the environment itself. I defy anyone to point out an example where this is not true.

17 So now we, as American Indian people, are asked to believe that "new" European revolutionary doctrine such as Marxism will reverse the negative effects of European history on us. European power relations are to be adjusted once again, and that's supposed to make things better for all of us. But what does this really mean?

18 Right now, today, we who live on the Pine Ridge Reservation are living in what white society has designated a "National Sacrifice Area." What this means is that we have a lot of uranium deposits here, and white culture (not us) needs this uranium as energy production material. The cheapest, most efficient way for industry to extract and deal with the processing of this uranium is to dump the waste by-products right here at the digging sites. Right here where we live. This waste is radioactive and will make the entire region uninhabitable forever. This is considered by industry, and by the white society that created this industry, to be an "acceptable" price to pay for energy resource development. Along the way they also plan to drain the water table under this part of South Dakota as part of the industrial process, so the region becomes doubly uninhabitable. The same sort of thing is happening down in the land of the Navajo and Hopi, up in the land of the Northern Cheyenne and Crow, and elsewhere. Thirty percent of the coal in the West and half of the uranium deposits in the U.S. have been found to lie under reservation land, so there is no way this can be called a minor issue.

19 We are resisting being turned into a National Sacrifice Area. We are resisting being turned into a national sacrifice people. The costs of this industrial process are not acceptable to us. It is genocide to dig uranium here and drain the water table—no more, no less.

20 Now let's suppose that in our resistance to extermination we begin to seek allies (we have). Let's suppose further that we were to take revolutionary Marxism at its word: that it intends nothing less than the complete overthrow of the European capitalist order which has presented this threat to our very existence. This would seem to be a natural alliance for American Indian people to enter into. After all, as the Marxists say, it is the capitalists who set us up to be a national sacrifice. This is true as far as it goes.

21 But, as I've tried to point out, this "truth" is very deceptive. Revolutionary Marxism is committed to even further perpetuation and perfection of the very industrial process which is destroying us all. It offers only to "redistribute" the results—the money, maybe—of this industrialization to a wider section of the population. It offers to take wealth from the capitalists and pass it around; but in order to do so, Marxism must maintain the industrial system. Once again the power relations within European society will have to be altered, but once again the effects upon American Indian peoples here and non-Europeans elsewhere will remain the same. This is much the same as when power was redistributed from the church to private business during the so-called bourgeois revolution. European society changed a bit, at least superficially, but its conduct toward non-Europeans continued as before. You can see what the American Revolution of 1776 did for American Indians. It's the same old song.

22   Revolutionary Marxism, like industrial society in other forms, seeks to "rationalize" all people in relation to industry—maximum industry, maximum production. It is a materialist doctrine that despises the American Indian spiritual tradition, our cultures, our lifeways. Marx himself called us "precapitalists" and "primitive." *Precapitalist* simply means that, in his view, we would eventually discover capitalism and become capitalists; we have always been economically retarded in Marxist terms. The only manner in which American Indian people could participate in a Marxist revolution would be to join the industrial system, to become factory workers, or "proletarians" as Marx called them. The man was very clear about the fact that his revolution could occur only through the struggle of the proletariat, that the existence of a massive industrial system is a precondition of a successful Marxist society.

23   I think there's a problem with language here. Christians, capitalists, Marxists. All of them have been revolutionary in their own minds, but none of them really mean revolution. What they really mean is a continuation. They do what they do in order that European culture can continue to exist and develop according to its needs.

24   So, in order for us to *really* join forces with Marxism, we American Indians would have to accept the national sacrifice of our homeland; we would have to commit cultural suicide and become industrialized and Europeanized.

25   At this point, I've got to stop and ask myself whether I'm being too harsh. Marxism has something of a history. Does this history bear out my observations? I look to the process of industrialization in the Soviet Union since 1920 and I see that these Marxists have done what it took the English Industrial Revolution 300 years to do; and the Marxists did it in 60 years. I see that the territory of the USSR used to contain a number of tribal peoples and that they have been crushed to make way for the factories. The Soviets refer to this as "The National Question," the question of whether the tribal peoples had the right to exist as peoples; and they decided the tribal peoples were an acceptable sacrifice to industrial needs. I look to China and I see the same thing. I look to Vietnam and I see Marxists imposing an industrial order and rooting out the indigenous tribal mountain people.

26   I hear a leading Soviet scientist saying that when uranium is exhausted, *then* alternatives will be found. I see the Vietnamese taking over a nuclear power plant abandoned by the U.S. military. Have they dismantled and destroyed it? No, they are using it. I see China exploding nuclear bombs, developing uranium reactors and preparing a space program in order to colonize and exploit the planets the same as the Europeans colonized and exploited this hemisphere. It's the same old song, but maybe with a faster tempo this time.

27   The statement of the Soviet scientist is very interesting. Does he know what this alternative energy source will be? No, he simply has faith. Science will find a way. I hear revolutionary Marxists saying that the destruction of the environment, pollution, and radiation will all be controlled. And I see them act upon their words. Do they know *how* these things will be controlled? No, they simply have faith. Science will find a way. Industrialization is fine and necessary. How do they know this? Faith. Science will find a way. Faith of this sort has always been known in Europe as religion. Science has become the new European religion for both capitalists and Marxists; they are truly inseparable, they are part and parcel of the same culture. So, in both theory and practice, Marxism demands that non-European peoples give up their values, their traditions, their cultural existence altogether. We will all be industrialized science addicts in a Marxist society.

28   I do not believe that capitalism itself is really responsible for the situation in which American Indians have been declared a national sacrifice. No, it is the European tradition; European culture itself is responsible. Marxism is just the latest continuation of this tradition, not a solution to it. To ally with Marxism is to ally with the very same forces that declare us an acceptable cost.

29 There is another way. There is the traditional Lakota way and the ways of the other American Indian peoples. It is the way that knows that humans do not have the right to degrade Mother Earth, that there are forces beyond anything the European mind has conceived, that humans must be in harmony with *all* relations or the relations will eventually eliminate the disharmony. A lopsided emphasis on humans by humans—the Europeans' arrogance of acting as though they were beyond the nature of all related things—can only result in a total disharmony and a readjustment which cuts arrogant humans down to size, gives them a taste of that reality beyond their grasp or control and restores the harmony. There is no need for a revolutionary theory to bring this about; it's beyond human control. The nature peoples of this planet know this and so they do not theorize about it. Theory is an abstract; our knowledge is real.

30 Distilled to its basic terms, European faith—including the new faith in science—equals a belief that man is God. Europe has always sought a Messiah, whether that be the man Jesus Christ or the man Karl Marx or the man Albert Einstein. American Indians know this to be totally absurd. Humans are the weakest of all creatures, so weak that other creatures are willing to give up their flesh that we may live. Humans are able to survive only through the exercise of rationality since they lack the abilities of other creatures to gain food through the use of fang and claw.

31 But rationality is a curse since it can cause humans to forget the natural order of things in ways other creatures do not. A wolf never forgets his or her place in the natural order. American Indians can. Europeans almost always do. We pray our thanks to the deer, our relations, for allowing us their flesh to eat; Europeans simply take the flesh for granted and consider the deer inferior. After all, Europeans consider themselves godlike in their rationalism and science. God is the Supreme Being; all else *must* be inferior.

32 All European tradition, Marxism included, has conspired to defy the natural order of things. Mother Earth has been abused, the powers have been abused, and this cannot go on forever. No theory can alter that simple fact. Mother Earth will retaliate, the whole environment will retaliate, and the abusers will be eliminated. Things come full circle, back to where they started. *That's* revolution. And that's a prophecy of my people, of the Hopi people, and of other correct peoples.

33 American Indians have been trying to explain this to Europeans for centuries. But, as I said earlier, Europeans have proven themselves unable to hear. The natural order will win out, and the offenders will die out, the way deer die when they offend the harmony by overpopulating a given region. It's only a matter of time until what Europeans call "a major catastrophe of global proportions" will occur. It is the role of American Indian peoples, the role of all natural beings, to survive. A part of our survival is to resist. We resist not to overthrow a government or to take political power but because it is natural to resist extermination, to survive. We don't want power over white institutions; we want white institutions to disappear. *That's* revolution.

34 American Indians are still in touch with these realities—the prophecies, the traditions of our ancestors. We learn from the elders, from nature, from the powers. And when the catastrophe is over, we American Indian peoples will still be here to inhabit the hemisphere. I don't care if it's only a handful living high in the Andes. American Indian people will survive; harmony will be reestablished. *That's* revolution.

35 At this point, perhaps I should be very clear about another matter, one which should already be clear as a result of what I've said. But confusion breeds easily these days, so I want to hammer home this point. When I use the term *European,* I'm not referring to a skin color or a particular genetic structure. What I'm referring to is a mind-set, a world view that is a product of the development of European culture. People are not genetically encoded to hold this outlook; they are *acculturated* to hold it. The same is true for American Indians or for the members of any other culture.

36 It is possible for an American Indian to share European values, a European world view. We have a term for these people; we call them "apples"—red on the outside (genetics) and white on the inside (their values). Other groups have similar terms: Blacks have their "oreos"; Hispanos have "coconuts" and so on. And, as I said before, there *are* exceptions to the white norm: people who are white on the outside, but not white inside. I'm not sure what term should be applied to them other than "human beings."

37 What I'm putting out here is not a racial proposition but a cultural proposition. Those who ultimately advocate and defend the realities of European culture and its industrialism are my enemies. Those who resist it, who struggle against it, are my allies, the allies of American Indian people. And I don't give a damn what their skin color happens to be. *Caucasian* is the white term for the white race; *European* is an outlook I oppose.

38 The Vietnamese Communists are not exactly what you might consider genetic Caucasians, but they are now functioning as mental Europeans. The same holds true for Chinese Communists, for Japanese capitalists or Bantu Catholics or Peter "MacDollar" down at the Navajo Reservation or Dickie Wilson up here at Pine Ridge. There is no racism involved in this, just an acknowledgment of the mind and spirit that make up culture.

39 In Marxist terms I suppose I'm a "cultural nationalist." I work first with my people, the traditional Lakota people, because we hold a common world view and share an immediate struggle. Beyond this, I work with other traditional American Indian peoples, again because of a certain commonality in world view and form of struggle. Beyond that, I work with anyone who has experienced the colonial oppression of Europe and who resists its cultural and industrial totality. Obviously, this includes genetic Caucasians who struggle to resist the dominant norms of European culture. The Irish and the Basques come immediately to mind, but there are many others.

40 I work primarily with my own people, with my own community. Other people who hold non-European perspectives should do the same. I believe in the slogan, "Trust your brother's vision," although I'd like to add sisters into the bargain. I trust the community and the culturally based vision of all the races that naturally resist industrialization and human extinction. Clearly, individual whites can share in this, given only that they have reached the awareness that continuation of the industrial imperatives of Europe is not a vision, but species suicide. White is one of the sacred colors of the Lakota people—red, yellow, white and black. The four directions. The four seasons. The four periods of life and aging. The four races of humanity. Mix red, yellow, white, and black together and you get brown, the color of the fifth race. This is a natural ordering of things. It therefore seems natural to me to work with all races, each with its own special meaning, identity, and message.

41 But there is a peculiar behavior among most Caucasians. As soon as I become critical of Europe and its impact on other cultures, they become defensive. They begin to defend themselves. But I'm not attacking them personally; I'm attacking Europe. In personalizing my observations on Europe they are personalizing European culture, identifying themselves with it. By defending themselves in *this* context, they are ultimately defending the death culture. This is a confusion which must be overcome, and it must be overcome in a hurry. None of us have energy to waste in such false struggles.

42 Caucasians have a more positive vision to offer humanity than European culture. I believe this. But in order to attain this vision it is necessary for Caucasians to step outside European culture—alongside the rest of humanity—to see Europe for what it is and what it does.

43 To cling to capitalism and Marxism and all the other "isms" is simply to remain within European culture. There is no avoiding this basic fact. As a fact, this constitutes a choice. Understand that the choice is based on culture, not race. Understand that to choose European culture and industrialism is to choose to be my enemy. And understand that the choice is yours, not mine.

44 This leads me back to address those American Indians who are drifting through the universities, the city slums, and other European institutions. If you are there to learn to resist the oppressor in accordance with your traditional ways, so be it. I don't know how you manage to combine the two, but perhaps you will succeed. But retain your sense of reality. Beware of coming to believe the white world now offers solutions to the problems it confronts us with. Beware, too, of allowing the words of native people to be twisted to the advantage of our enemies. Europe invented the practice of turning words around on themselves. You need only look to the treaties between American Indian peoples and various European governments to know that this is true. Draw your strength from who you are.

45 A culture which regularly confuses revolution with continuation, which confuses science and religion, which confuses revolt with resistance, has nothing helpful to teach you and nothing to offer you as a way of life. Europeans have long since lost all touch with reality, if ever they were in touch with it. Feel sorry for them if you need to, but be comfortable with who you are as American Indians.

46 So, I suppose to conclude this, I should state clearly that leading anyone toward Marxism is the last thing on my mind. Marxism is as alien to my culture as capitalism and Christianity are. In fact, I can say I don't think I'm trying to lead anyone toward anything. To some extent I tried to be a "leader," in the sense that the white media like to use that term, when the American Indian Movement was a young organization. This was a result of a confusion I no longer have. You cannot be everything to everyone. I do not propose to be used in such a fashion by my enemies; I am not a leader. I *am* an Oglala Lakota patriot. That is all I want and all I need to be. And I am very comfortable with who I am.

A Just War

◆ *George Bush* ◆

Prior to the start of the war with Iraq on January 16, 1991, many "advocates and opponents of war resorted—at least implicitly—to the distinctions and categories of just-war thinking" (*Newsweek,* February 11, 1991, p. 47). On January 28, 1991, in an address to over 1000 delegates at the conservative National Religious Broadcasters annual conference in Washington, D.C., President George Bush explicitly and at length employed the "just war" doctrine to defend American and coalition military action. He advocates the value judgment that the war with Iraq "is a just war" (8, 22) and he applies the traditional value criteria for such a war.

President Bush is speaking to a friendly audience (2, 4) and he reinforces values (3) and policy positions that he and the audience share (5–6). As he begins his argument, he employs antithetical phrasing to underscore the moral conflict involved and he describes the roots of the just war doctrine in Greco-Roman philosophy and Christian theology (8). A morally just

◆ The text of this speech is reprinted from *Weekly Compilation of Presidential Documents,* 27 (February 4, 1991): 87–89.

war, the doctrine holds, should be waged only: (1) for a morally just cause; (2) when approved by a legitimate authority; (3) as a last resort when all peaceful alternatives have been exhausted; (4) when the good achieved outweighs the bad side-effects; (5) when the war is waged with just means; and (6) when there is a reasonable chance for success.

To develop his contention that the war with Iraq is a noble and just cause, Bush discusses the purposes and motivations of American military action (9–10, 13). Toward the end of the speech, he uses a quotation from Abraham Lincoln to stress again the morality of the cause (24). The President then cites twelve United Nations resolutions and the united agreement of twenty-eight nations from six continents to show that the war is approved by legitimate authority (11–12).

Bush employs a compact summary of statistics and examples to demonstrate that peaceful diplomatic efforts have been exhausted (14–15). In contrast, in his speech to the nation on January 16 announcing the start of the war, the thrust of his argument focuses not only on exhausted diplomatic efforts but also on the failure of economic and political sanctions against Iraq. In fact the tone of that speech is very pragmatic and his rationale is not at all placed in the context of a morally just war. Bush's speech on January 16 stresses pragmatic necessity—circumstances now dictate that we have no choice but to go to war with Iraq. Why might the President have used a primarily pragmatic justification in announcing the war and a full-blown moral argument here?

That the greater good of thwarting the threat posed by Saddam Hussein can be achieved through just means with minimal bad side-effects is a contention developed through Bush's pledge to minimize casualties, act humanely, and "avoid hurting the innocent" (16–17). Finally, Bush argues that there is a reasonable chance of success—that victory can be achieved—by pledging that it will be a relatively short and decisive war (not another Vietnam) and by reminding the audience of the high quality of America's military forces (18–19).

In what ways and to what extent do you agree or disagree that Bush proved his value judgment that the war with Iraq was a morally just war? Also consider the role in war rhetoric throughout American history of what critic Robert Ivie terms "images of savagery"—images of "cunning but otherwise irrational enemies who are driven to circumvent all the restraints of international law and of human principles in order to impose their will on others." (See Robert L. Ivie, "Images of Savagery in American Justifications for War," *Communication Monographs,* 47 (November 1980): 279–294; also see Ivie, "Presidential Motives for War," *Quarterly Journal of Speech,* 60 (October 1974): 337–345.) What rhetorical functions in this speech might be served by such images as "naked aggression"; "the rape, the pillage, the plunder"; "wanton, barbaric bombing of civilian areas"; and "indiscriminate use" (9, 13–14, 17)? Also see David E. Decosse, *But Was It Just? Reflections on the Morality of the Persian Gulf War* (New York: Doubleday, 1992); Kathleen M. German, "Invoking the Glorious War: Framing the Persian Gulf Conflict Through Directive Language," *Southern Communication Journal,* 60 (Summer 1995): 292–302.

This speech by President Bush to the National Religious Broadcasters was given on the morning of January 28 and was covered live only by the CNN television network. On the evening of the next day, January 29, 1991, via major network television and radio coverage, President Bush presented the annual State of the Union message to the nation. In his lengthy State of the Union speech on both domestic and international topics, Bush does indirectly and implicitly touch on some of the standards for a just war but does not explicitly and clearly apply the just war criteria. In place of the tone of morality pervading the January 28 speech, there remains in the State of the Union address a simple summary alluding to the more complex argument of the previous day: "Our cause is just. Our cause is moral. Our cause is right." The morning hour and the coverage only on CNN severely limited the exposure of the general citizenry to the explicit just war argument of Bush's January 28 speech. Why might the President have decided not to use the same explicit and overtly developed just war argument in his State of the Union address to the nation the next night?

◆ ◆ ◆

1   Thank you, President Rose, thank you, sir, and Executive Director Gustavson—all. First, let me salute your leadership of the NRB: Billy Graham and Jerry Falwell, Pat Robertson, James Dobson, Chuck Colson; and FCC Commissioners: Sikes and Duggan and James Quello.

2   This marks the fifth time that I've addressed the annual convention of the National Religious Broadcasters. And once again, let me say it is, for both Barbara and me, an honor to be back here.

3   Let me begin by congratulating you on your theme of declaring His glory to all nations. It's a theme eclipsing denominations and which reflects many of the eternal teachings in the Scripture. I speak, of course, of the teachings which uphold moral values like tolerance, compassion, faith, and courage. They remind us that while God can live without man, man cannot live without God. His love and His justice inspire in us a yearning for faith and a compassion for the weak and oppressed, as well as the courage and conviction to oppose tyranny and injustice.

4   And I'm very grateful for that resolution that has just been read prior to my speaking here.

5   Matthew also reminds us in these times that the meek shall inherit the Earth. At home, these values imbue the policies which you and I support. Like me, you endorse adoption, not abortion. And last year you helped ensure that the options of religious-based child care will not be restricted or eliminated by the Federal Government.

6   And I commend your concern, your heartfelt concern, on behalf of Americans with disabilities, and your belief that students who go to school to nourish their minds should also be allowed to nourish their souls. And I have not lessened my commitment to restoring voluntary prayer in our schools.

7   These actions can make America a kinder and gentler place because they reaffirm the values that I spoke of earlier, values that must be central to the lives of every individual and the life of every nation. The clergyman Richard Cecil once said, "There are two classes of the wise: the men who serve God because they have found Him, and the men who seek Him because they have not found Him yet." Abroad, as in America, our task is to serve and seek wisely through the policies we pursue.

8   Nowhere is this more true than in the Persian Gulf where—despite protestations of Saddam Hussein—it is not Iraq against the United States, it's the regime of Saddam Hussein against the rest of the world. Saddam tried to cast this conflict as a religious war, but it has nothing to do with religion per se. It has, on the other hand, everything to do with what religion embodies: good versus evil, right versus wrong, human dignity and freedom versus tyranny and oppression. The war in the Gulf is not a Christian war, a Jewish war, or a Moslem war; it is a just war. And it is a war with which good will prevail. We're told that the principles of a just war originated with classical Greek and Roman philosophers like Plato and Cicero. And later they were expounded by such Christian theologians as Ambrose, Augustine, Thomas Aquinas.

9   The first principle of a just war is that it support a just cause. Our cause could not be more noble. We seek Iraq's withdrawal from Kuwait—completely, immediately, and without condition; the restoration of Kuwait's legitimate government; and the security and stability of the Gulf. We will see that Kuwait once again is free, that the nightmare of Iraq's occupation has ended, and that naked aggression will not be rewarded.

10   We seek nothing for ourselves. As I have said, U.S. forces will leave as soon as their mission is over, as soon as they are no longer needed or desired. And let me add, we do not seek the destruction of Iraq. We have respect for the people of Iraq, for the importance of Iraq in the region. We do not want a country so destabilized that Iraq itself could be a target for aggression.

11   But a just war must also be declared by legitimate authority. Operation Desert Storm is supported by unprecedented United Nations solidarity, the principle of collective self-defense, 12 Security Council resolutions, and in the Gulf, 28 nations from 6 continents united, resolute that we will not waver and that Saddam's aggression will not stand.

12   I salute the aid—economic and military—from countries who have joined in this unprecedented effort, whose courage and sacrifice have inspired the world. We're not going it alone, but believe me, we are going to see it through.

13   Every war—every war—is fought for a reason. But a just war is fought for the right reasons, for moral, not selfish reasons. Let me take a moment to tell you a story, a tragic story, about a family whose two sons, 18 and 19, reportedly refused to lower the Kuwaiti flag in front of their home. For this crime, they were executed by the Iraqis. Then, unbelievably, their parents were asked to pay the price of the bullets used to kill them.

14   Some ask whether it's moral to use force to stop the rape, the pillage, the plunder of Kuwait. And my answer: Extraordinary diplomatic efforts having been exhausted to resolve the matter peacefully, then the use of force is moral.

15   A just war must be a last resort. As I have often said, we did not want war. But you all know the verse from Ecclesiastes—there is "a time for peace, a time for war." From August 2, 1990—last summer, August 2d—to January 15, 1991—166 days—we tried to resolve this conflict. Secretary of State Jim Baker made an extraordinary effort to achieve peace: more than 200 meetings with foreign dignitaries; 10 diplomatic missions; 6 congressional appearances; over 103,000 miles traveled to talk with, among others, members of the United Nations, the Arab League, and the European Community. And sadly, Saddam Hussein rejected out of hand every overture made by the United States and by other countries as well. He made this just war an inevitable war.

16   We all know that war never comes easy or cheap. War is never without the loss of innocent life. And that is war's greatest tragedy. But when a war must be fought for the greater good, it is our gravest obligation to conduct a war in proportion to the threat. And that is why we must act reasonably, humanely, and make every effort possible to keep casualties to a minimum. And we've done so. I'm very proud of our military in achieving this end.

17   From the very first day of the war, the allies have waged war against Saddam's military. We are doing everything possible, believe me, to avoid hurting the innocent. Saddam's response: wanton, barbaric bombing of civilian areas. America and her allies value life. We pray that Saddam Hussein will see reason. To date, his indiscriminate use of those Scud missiles—nothing more than weapons of terror, they can offer no military advantage—weapons of terror—it outraged the world what he has done.

18   The price of war is always high. And so, it must never, ever, be undertaken without total commitment to a successful outcome. It is only justified when victory can be achieved. I have pledged that this will not be another Vietnam. And let me reassure you here today, it won't be another Vietnam.

19   We are fortunate, we are very fortunate, to have in this crisis the finest armed forces ever assembled, an all-volunteer force, joined by courageous allies. And we will prevail because we have the finest soldiers, sailors, airmen, marines, and coastguardsmen that any nation has ever had.

20   But above all, we will prevail because of the support of the American people, armed with a trust in God and in the principles that make men free—people like each of you in this room. I salute Voice of Hope's live radio programming for U.S. and allied troops in the Gulf, and your Operation Desert Prayer, and worship services for our troops held by among others, the man who over a week ago led a wonderful prayer service at Fort Myer over here across the river in Virginia, the Reverend Billy Graham.

21 America has always been a religious nation, perhaps never more than now. Just look at the last several weeks—churches, synagogues, mosques reporting record attendance at services; chapels packed during working hours as Americans stop in for a moment or two. Why? To pray for peace. And I know—of course, I know—that some disagree with the course that I've taken, and I have no bitterness in my heart about that at all, no anger. I am convinced that we are doing the right thing. And tolerance is a virtue, not a vice.

22 But with the support and prayers of so many, there can be no question in the minds of our soldiers or in the minds of our enemy about what Americans think. We know that this is a just war. And we know that, God willing, this is a war we will win. But most of all, we know that ours would not be the land of the free if it were not also the home of the brave. No one wanted war less than I did. No one is more determined to seize from battle the real peace that can offer hope, that can create a new world order.

23 When this war is over, the United States, its credibility and its reliability restored, will have a key leadership role in helping to bring peace to the rest of the Middle East. And I have been honored to serve as President of this great nation for 2 years now and believe more than ever that one cannot be America's President without trust in God. I cannot imagine a world, a life, without the presence of the One through whom all things are possible.

24 During the darkest days of the Civil War, a man we revere not merely for what he did but what he was, was asked whether he thought the Lord was on his side. And said Abraham Lincoln: "My concern is not whether God is on our side, but whether we are on God's side." My fellow Americans, I firmly believe in my heart of hearts that times will soon be on the side of peace because the world is overwhelmingly on the side of God.

25 Thank you for this occasion. And may God bless our great country. And please remember all of our coalition's armed forces in your prayers. Thank you, and God bless you.

Caring for Creation:
Religion and Ecology

◆ *Russell E. Train* ◆

As Chairman of the World Wildlife Fund and Conservation Foundation, Russell Train represents an organization with over 300,000 members—an organization that seeks to protect the biological resources on which human well-being depends. On May 18, 1990 Train presented this address at the closing session of the North American Conference on Religion and Ecology

◆ This speech is reprinted with permission from *Vital Speeches of the Day,* August 15, 1990, pp. 664–666.

held in Washington, D.C. As is true of other speeches in this anthology, this speech legitimately could be evaluated from several critical viewpoints. It could, as discussed in Chapter 6, be analyzed primarily as attempting to create concern for environmental problems (12–14).

In our view, however, this speech primarily advocates propositions of value—it offers value judgments and advocates adoption of certain desirable values in contrast to less desirable values. After stressing that organized religion generally has been oblivious to and silent on environmental issues (3–4) and illustrating possible cooperative efforts (6), Train argues both early and late in the speech that organized religion should be the primary vehicle for instilling environmental values in people (4, 19, 22). He criticizes the value priorities imbedded in the Roman Catholic Church's birth control policies for contributing to ecological problems (11–12). Note his use of alliteration—the repetition of the same initial sound, usually a consonant, in a series of words in proximity. Often used to make an idea more memorable or to associate several positive or negative ideas, here alliteration stimulates negative associations (degrade, deface, desecrate, destroy). Train urges organized religion to readjust its value priorities to show equal concern for human and ecological issues (16). Very overtly he advocates specific values to be taught by organized religion (19) and he encourages adoption of them by describing the positive consequences of holding those values (20).

A key strategy in advocating his values and value judgments is the emphasis through diverse techniques in the interrelation and interdependence of human welfare and environmental welfare (15, 16). He develops the "web of life" metaphor (7) and presents creative twists on two common phrases: "facts of life" (9) and "right to life" (15). Train overtly employs representative examples (9–"their number could be almost infinite") and he accumulates a lengthy list of examples to underscore the massiveness of the threats to the environment (10).

Finally, consider the role of speaker credibility in this address. In what ways might some of his statements (2, 7) strengthen or weaken his credibility with his audience?

◆ ◆ ◆

1   It is a privilege to address this closing event of the Conference on Caring for Creation on the subject of "Religion and the Environment." Following so many splendid speakers, it is highly doubtful that I will offer you anything very original. Anyway, someone has said that "the only secret of being original is not to reveal your sources."

2   I am neither a theologian nor a philosopher. For a good many years of my life, I was a relatively active layman in the Episcopal Church here in Washington, although something of a "backslider" in more recent years. It may have some significance that my absence from regular attendance at Sunday services dates back almost exactly to the time my wife and I purchased a farm on the Eastern Shore of Maryland. Suddenly, my weekends no longer included formal religious observance in church but instead were filled with the enjoyment of fields and woods and water, the presence of wildlife, the rhythm of the seasons. And for the past 30 years I have been part of the environmental movement, both in government and in the private sector.

3   During much of this time, I have been puzzled—to say the least—by what has seemed to me the almost total obliviousness of organized religion toward the environment. It has been nothing less than extraordinary. Here we have had one of the most fundamental concerns to agitate human society within living memory—certainly in North America and Europe and increasingly around the globe. Here we have issues that go to the heart of the human condition, to the quality of human life, even to humanity's ultimate survival. Here we have problems that can be said to threaten the very integrity of Creation. And yet the churches and other institutions of organized religion have largely ignored the whole subject.

4   Of course, a number of thoughtful persons have over the past twenty years or so explored the interrelationship of religion and the environment, of human spirituality and nature. However, until recently, organized religion has remained largely silent and on the sidelines. Yet our churches, synagogues, temples, and mosques should be a principal vehicle for instilling environmental values in our planet's people. And, believe me, it is very much a matter of values.

5   To be fair, I must point out that the organized environmental movement has on its side largely ignored the potentially central role that religion can have in bringing about a new harmony between man and nature. Hopefully, an active partnership is now arising between the environmental and religious communities. This conference will help build that partnership.

6   It was in 1986 that the World Wide Fund for Nature (formerly called the World Wildlife Fund and still so called in the United States and Canada) brought together at Assisi representatives of the five major religions of the world—Christian, Jewish, Moslem, Hindu and Buddhist—to explore the development of a single, unified statement of religious responsibility toward nature. As you know, while a single statement did not prove practical at that time, each religion did its own statement consonant with its own beliefs and traditions, and these have been published in the *Assisi Declarations.* The Assisi experience was an exciting one, and it has been highly influential in bringing different religious groups to address their responsibility toward nature. In 1988, Pope John Paul II and the Dalai Lama met in Rome to discuss issues of "world peace, spiritual values, and protection of the earth's natural environment." A number of other initiatives have and are occurring, and I will not try to enumerate them here. At long last, religion seems to be awakening to the environment. I am delighted on this occasion to acknowledge that our honored guest, H.R.H. The Duke of Edinburgh, was the principal moving force in bringing about Assisi and its continued follow-up.

7   I said earlier that I am neither a theologian nor a philosopher. Nor am I a scientist. Yet I know that our human life, its quality and its very existence, are totally dependent upon the natural systems of the Earth—the air, the water, the soils, the extraordinary diversity of plant and animal life—systems all driven by the energy of the sun. We could not exist without the support of these natural systems. Nor could any of the other forms of life with which we share the Earth. These are facts over which it seems to me there can be no argument. We are all part of a living community that is mutually dependent. All life exists in an infinitely complex set of interrelationships—truly a "web of life"—that we disturb at our peril.

8   We depend upon the air to supply us with oxygen we must breathe—oxygen that in turn is produced by the microorganisms in the surface of the ocean and by the vegetative cover of the land, particularly its tropical forests, often referred to as the "lungs of the planet." We depend for our sustenance on the productivity of the soil, whose fertility is in turn sustained by the nitrogen-fixing ability of soil bacteria. The humus essential to productive soils is of course the product of the work of other bacteria, beetles, worms, and such. (Size is clearly no measure of the importance of one's role in the planetary scheme. In fact, it is truly the little things that run the world!) Our grains and other crops, our orchards, and much of the world's forests depend for pollination and, thus, their continued existence upon insects, birds, and bats among other mammals—often highly specialized to serve the needs of a particular species of plant. The most valuable fruit crop of southeast Asia is *durian,* a $100 million-a-year crop, and it is pollinated entirely by bats. Birds and bats are responsible for eliminatng a high proportion of the world's destructive insects and weed seeds—far more than all the insecticides and herbicides we apply. Only last week, I read a news report that in Pakistan a species of owl, considered there a bird of ill omen, is responsible for controlling the rats and mice that would otherwise destroy a large part of the grain crop. A majority of our North American bird species, which provide us with such valuable (and free) services, migrate to Mexico and farther south in the winter. A number of these species are in substantial decline because of the destruction of the tropical forests on which they depend for winter habitat. And, of course, it is on the tropical forests that the entire planet depends for much of the production of oxygen and much of the sequestration of carbon which together in turn help maintain the life-sustaining quality of the global atmosphere.

9   These are a few examples—and their number could be almost infinite—to illustrate the dependence of human and other life on the natural systems of the Earth as well as the intricate interdependence of the living community as a whole. I feel it is important to be explicit about such examples because our increasingly urban population tends to take human self-sufficiency for granted and lives in almost total ignorance of the true "facts of life."

10   Given the historic tendency of the human race to put its own self-interest ahead of everything else and usually to measure that self-interest in the near term rather than the long term, it is probably not surprising that the natural systems of the Earth are under such dire threat today. You are no doubt familiar with the litany of environmental threats. A partial one would include the destruction of tropical forests, the loss of productive soils, the spread of deserts, declining supplies of fresh water, the depletion of ocean fisheries, the pervasive pollution of air, land and water, the accelerating extinction of species, the likelihood of global warming, and the depletion of the life-protecting stratospheric ozone layer. It should be pointed out that, in the case of stratospheric ozone depletion, which could have a catastrophic impact on life on Earth, the cause is purely and simply human technology—our refrigerants, air conditioners, fire extinguishers, spray propellants, etc. Finally, overarching all the other environmental threats, of course, is the burgeoning human population. And here again we clearly have no one to blame but ourselves, and here it is not so much our technology as the lack of its use.

11   As critical and seemingly intractable as environmental problems are today with 5.3 billion people on the face of the Earth, these problems will be compounded exponentially as we move inevitably to 11.3 billion and very likely to 14 billion by the end of the next century. And yet, Pope John Paul is reported to have declared last week in Mexico:

> If the possibility of conceiving a child is artificially eliminated in the conjugal act, couples shut themselves off from God and oppose His will.

12   Personally, I find it difficult to accept that it is the will of God that humanity should degrade, deface, desecrate, and ultimately, perhaps, destroy His Creation on Earth. Yet that is the course on which we are embarked. Almost every significant threat to the environment is contributed to and compounded by human numbers. Moreover, whatever other adverse impacts on the natural environment may result from the growth in sheer human numbers, such growth is necessarily accompanied by a reduction in space for other species, in the opportunity for other forms of life. Natural ecosystems do not have the capacity to absorb infinite numbers of species.

13   To me, the most grievous assault on the Earth's environment is the destruction of species—both plant and animal. It is the destruction of life itself, life which has evolved over hundreds of millions of years into a diversity of forms that stagger the imagination, life of a beauty and complexity that fill one with awe and wonder, life in which the Creation is surely manifest.

14   Some scientists today estimate that there are up to 30 million species of life on the Earth. Twenty to 30 percent of these are projected to vanish forever over the next very few years due in large part to human action and especially to the destruction of tropical forests. The eminent biologist, E. O. Wilson, has said: "The sin our descendants are least likely to forgive us is the loss of biological diversity."

15 We hear much today about the "right to life" and the phrase as normally employed seems to extend only to human life, as if the rest of life is somehow irrelevant. I have tried to develop the point that human life cannot exist in isolation from other forms of life, that our existence is, in fact, dependent upon those other forms of life. We are, indeed, part of a community of life and our apparent dominance as a species should not be permitted to obscure that fact. Putting it bluntly, anthropocentrism is simply irrational. And yet that is the thrust of much of our traditional religious thought and teaching, particularly in the West.

16 I do not suggest that the Christian church abandon its concern for humanity but that it give at least equal time to the rest of God's Creation and do so not as a concern that is separate and apart, but as one that recognizes that the welfare of any part, including the human part, is inseparable from the welfare of the whole; that it is the community as a whole for which we must necessarily care. We really have no other option in this regard. If we truly care for the human condition, then we must necessarily care for the rest of Creation on which humanity's well-being and even existence so clearly depend.

17 It is not enough in my mind to say that we should act as good stewards of the Earth. Stewardship suggests that we have a management responsibility and that smacks too much to me of the same anthropocentrism that has gotten us into trouble in the first place. After all, the planet got along very well indeed for a very long time without our managerial assistance. Indeed, you might say that the Earth has been a far better steward of the human race than vice versa. If the living community of the Earth operated on a democratic basis, I have no doubt the other members would quickly vote us out.

18 There is no doubt that humanity is now the dominant species on the Earth although there is no assurance that this is a permanent status. After all, *homo sapiens* has only been here about 250,000 years, a blink of the eye in evolutionary terms. Humanity today holds the fate of most other life in its hands, a reality that is awesome and should be humbling. Unfortunately, we are more apt to feel such power a mark of our success. I am afraid we have our values pretty much backwards in this regard.

19 And here it is, it seems to me, that the church should define its special role in environmental matters. In my own experience, family, school, and church were the principal transmitters of values in my early life. The church will seldom have the expertise and, thus, the credibility to involve itself in the increasingly technical and complex debates over environmental issues, whether involving clean air, toxic wastes, tropical forests, etc., but it does have the credibility and the historic mission of articulating and teaching values to society. The church should assume a major responsibility for teaching that we humans, individually and collectively, are part of the living community of the Earth that nurtures and sustains us; that humanity as well as all life depends for its very being upon the healthy functioning of the natural systems of the Earth; that all living things, including humans, are interdependent; that we have the duty, collectively and individually, to care for God's Creation and that in it lie all the creative possibilities for life now and in the future. These are precepts that could provide the substance for an Eleventh Commandment: Thou shalt cherish and care for the Earth and all within it.

20 Of course, adoption of such a set of values would require a fundamental change in the way we look at the world around us and at our relationship with it. Such values would be decidedly human values, not self-centered but providing positive guidelines for creative human outreach to the world and all within it. Such values would provide a logical framework within which human society can address the entire range of environmental problems facing the planet. And these values would provide the essential spiritual energy for effective action to address these problems.

21 And so it seems to me that the major challenge to religion as it addresses the environment is to give leadership to human understanding and acceptance of these essentially ecological values. It should do so in the curriculum of its seminaries, in the liturgy of its services, in its preaching from the pulpit, and in its teaching of the young. I suspect that a contributing factor in the failure of religion up to now to address these matters is that the clergy has not felt at home with them. Basic courses in ecology should be required in the seminaries and, as a matter of fact, throughout our education system. After all, ecology is nothing more than Creation at work.

22   Over the past twenty years, we have seen concern for environmental values institutionalized throughout much of our society—in government at all levels, in business, in the professions, in international agencies, in citizen environmental action, among other areas. It is now high time for the oldest human institutions of all, our religions, to make concern for nature—Caring for Creation—a central part of their doctrine and practice. I firmly believe that doing so could help revitalize society's commitment to religion, particularly among the young, and would help establish these fundamental values on which the future of the Earth and of ourselves so clearly depends.

The Environmental Movement: A Skeptical View

◆ *Virginia I. Postrel* ◆

"To a large degree, however, green ideology is not about facts. It is about values, and the environmental movement is about enforcing those values through political action." This argument highlights the central theme developed by Virginia I. Postrel in her speech to the City Club of Cleveland on June 19, 1990. As editor of *Reason Magazine,* she addressed an audience of men and women in leadership roles in the businesses and industries of Cleveland. *Reason Magazine* is published by the Reason Foundation which has as its goal the promotion of individualist philosophy and free market economic principles.

In taking a "skeptical view," Postrel identifies and attacks the central value underlying the "green" ideology of most environmental activists (7, 14–15, 29). Stasis or sustainability is the core value in a static view of "an ecosystem that has reached an unchanging climax stage." The

values that a speaker advocates or condemns should be presented accurately and fairly. To what degree do you believe Postrel does so? Note that she is sensitive to the complexity of ideologies (11–12) and wants to demystify the green ideology (9–10).

Postrel's major strategy in attacking the core value of the green ideology is presentation of multiple undesirable consequences of adhering to that value (17). Green values, she contends, typically are enforced through government policies—often a single prescribed solution (18, 29). Green ideology overemphasizes both a crisis mentality (26–28) and feelings of guilt/sin (31–32). In the name of simplicity, green ideology promotes regression rather than progress (35–37). And most undesirable of all, green ideology leads to extreme and radical programs for remaking human nature (41–43, 47–48, 51–52). Note how effectively she uses alliteration to as-

◆ This speech is reprinted with permission from *Vital Speeches of the Day,* September 15, 1990, pp. 729–732.

sociate the environmental movement with a negative concept: "environmentalists tolerate totalitarians in their midst."

Postrel's extensive use of quotations invites evaluation by a rhetorical critic. What type of person does she typically quote? What persuasive functions do such quotations seem to serve? Evidence to prove a point? Illustration to clarify a point? Would you question her use of any of the quotations? If so, on what grounds?

Often through contrast and antithesis, Postrel advocates a desirable value system to guide concern for the environment (19–20, 49). Her ideology embodies individual choice in pollution control, a dynamic and growth-oriented view, governmental encouragement of innovation, and the "common" or "ordinary" desire for a cleaner world through "tradeoffs," but not at all costs (7, 50).

Compare Virginia Postrel's speech with the previous one by Russell Train. Explore the ways in which the value systems advocated by them may be similar or clearly in conflict. Would Postrel probably condemn the values advocated by Train (19)? Why? Would she probably categorize the World Wildlife Fund as representative of the green movement? Note her statement: "Grassroots activists criticize the 'Gang of 10,' the large, well-funded environmental groups."

◆ ◆ ◆

1   On Earth Day, Henry Allen of the *Washington Post* published a pointed and amusing article. In it, he suggested that we've created a new image of Mother Nature:

> A sort of combination of Joan Crawford in *Mildred Pierce* and Mrs. Portnoy in *Portnoy's Complaint,* a disappointed, long-suffering martyr who makes us wish, at least for her sake, that we'd never been born.

> She weeps. She threatens, She nags. . . .

> She's a kvetch who makes us feel guilty for eating Big Macs, dumping paint thinner down the cellar sink, driving to work instead of riding the bus, and riding the bus instead of riding a bicycle. Then she makes us feel even guiltier for not feeling guilty enough.

> *Go ahead, use that deodorant, don't even think about me, God knows I'll be gone soon enough, I won't be here to see you get skin cancer when the ozone hole lets in the ultraviolet rays . . .*

2   I think all of us can see that Allen is on to something. There's a lot of truth in his picture of the new Mother Nature.

3   The question is, Where did this New Mother Nature come from? And how does this picture of nature affect—even warp—the way we deal with environmental issues?

4   Americans have historically been a can-do people, proud of our Yankee ingenuity. We believe in solving problems. Based on our history, you'd expect to see us tackling environmental problems the way John Todd took on sewage sludge.

5   Todd is an environmental biologist who became concerned about the toxic sludge that comes out of sewage plants. Based on his biological research, he realized that the sludge could be cleaned up by mixing it with certain microbes. The microbes would metabolize it and produce clean water. Todd now has a pilot plant in Providence, Rhode Island, and he estimates that such a system could handle all of that city's sludge with 120 acres of reaction tanks—a modest number.

6   Now, if you're like me, you think this is great. Here is a bona fide environmental problem. An ingenious man with an environmental conscience has come along, put his ingenuity and training to work, and *solved the problem.* But rather than applauding Todd's solution, many of his friends in the environmental movement have stopped speaking to him. "By discovering a solution to a man-made offense," writes Gregg Easterbrook in *The New Republic,* "he takes away an argument against growth."

7   Todd's practical environmentalism has run up against what I refer to as "green" ideology. This ideology is distinct from the common desire for a cleaner world—that's why it can lead people to condemn solutions like Todd's. It is also different from the traditional doctrines of either the left or the right: It combines elements from each with a values system of its own.

8   This green ideology underlies many of the environmentalist critiques and policy recommendations that we see today. Now, I'm not suggesting that environmentalists are engaged in some sort of grand conspiracy or are governed by some lockstep system of thought. What I *am* suggesting is that if you want to understand a political movement, it's a good idea to read its theorists and find out who its intellectual heroes are.

9   Green ideology is not mysterious. Anybody can go to the library and read the books that define it.

10   Green ideology is not some fringe theory cooked up in California. Like many important ideas in American history, it is largely imported from Britain and Germany. It is, increasingly, one of the most powerful forces in our culture. We may even adopt parts of it without realizing their origins. To be informed citizens, we ought to know something about it.

11   First of all, a caveat. Ideologies are messy. They tend to associate disparate ideas in unexpected ways. What's more, people who share the same general ideological viewpoint rarely agree on everything. No two conservatives or liberals or libertarians or even Marxists believe exactly the same thing. And political movements are almost always riven by internal conflict (you should read some of the things the abolitionists said about each other).

12   The environmental movement is no different. Purist greens who distrust political compromise berate Washington-based groups that lobby for legislation. The Green-Greens, who aren't leftist, attack the Red-Greens, who are. Grassroots activists criticize the "Gang of 10," the large, well-funded environmental groups.

13   And perhaps the biggest *philosophical* split is between "deep ecology" and other forms of environmentalism. Deep ecologists advocate a mystical view of the natural world as an end in itself, not made for human beings. They criticize traditional conservationism, as well as leftist "social ecology," for emphasizing the environment's value to people.

14   Most environmental activists—the rank and file—combine some of each outlook to create a personal viewpoint. They can do this because, deep down, the greens aren't as divided as they sometimes like to think.

15   Every ideology has a primary value or set of values at its core—liberty, equality, order, virtue, salvation. For greens, the core value is stasis, "sustainability" as they put it. The ideal is of an earth that doesn't change, that shows little or no effects of human activity. Greens take as their model of the ideal society the notion of an ecosystem that has reached an unchanging climax stage. "Limits to growth" is as much a description of how things *should* be as it is of how they are.

16   That is why there is no room in the green world for John Todd and his sewage-cleaning microbes. Todd hasn't sought to stop growth. He has found a way to live with it.

17   The static view has two effects on the general environmental movement: First, it leads environmentalists to advocate policies that will make growth hard on people, as a way of discouraging further development. Cutting off new supplies of water, outlawing new technologies, and banning new construction to increase the cost of housing are common policies. And, second, the static view leads environmentalists to misunderstand how real environmental problems can be solved.

18 Consider how we regulate air pollution. Since the 1977 Clean Air Act, Americans spend some $30 billion a year just to comply with the 1977 Clean Air Act—with very little to show for it. Current policy dictates *specific technologies*—for example, smokestack scrubbers for coal-burning power plants. The plants can't just use cleaner coal. And cars have to have catalytic converters. If someone comes up with a cheaper or more efficient way to get the same result, the government says, Sorry. We've picked our one true technology. You can't sell yours.

19 Now, for decades economists have suggested that we take a different approach to regulating pollution. Set an overall allowable level, they say, then let companies decide how to achieve it. Let them buy and sell permits that regulate the amount of pollution they can emit: If you wanted to build a new plant, you'd have to buy some permits from somebody else who was closing their plant or reducing their pollution. The economy could grow without increasing the total amount of pollution. Companies would have to pay a price for the pollution they put out. And plant managers would have an economic incentive to adopt—or even develop from scratch—pollution-saving technologies.

20 Most environmentalists, however, hate, loath, and despise this whole idea. They call it a "license to pollute." Emissions trading treats pollution as a cost, a side effect to be controlled, rather than an outright evil, a sin. It allows growth. And it lets individual choice, not politics, determine exactly which technologies will be adopted to control pollution. It takes a *dynamic* view, rather than a static one. Over time, it assumes, people will come up with better and better ways to deal with pollution. And, it assumes, we ought to *encourage* those innovations.

21 People rarely adopt a new technology because it makes life worse. But nowadays we tend to pay more attention to the dangers or pollution from new technologies. We take the old technologies' disadvantages for granted. So, for example, we forget that the automobile actually made city life cleaner.

22 By creating a market for petroleum-derived gasoline, the car also encouraged the production of heating oil and natural gas—much cleaner fuels than the coal people used to use to heat homes and businesses. And, thanks to the automobile, cities no longer have to dispose of tons of horse manure every day.

23 Extrapolating from his own time, a British writer in 1885 described the future of London:

> It is a vast stagnant swamp, which no man dare enter, since death would be his inevitable fate. There exhales from this oozy mass so fatal a vapour that no animal can endure it. The black water bears a greenish-brown scum, which forever bubbles up from the putrid mud of the bottom.

24 Clearly, modern environmentalists have no monopoly on dire predictions of disaster. From this particular fate we were saved by the automobile.

25 A dynamic view sees the pluses of change as well as the minuses. And it appreciates how new, unforeseen technologies or social changes can allay current problems.

26 By contrast, the environmental movement has been built on crisis. Around the turn of the century, Americans were terrified of the growing lumber shortage. A 1908 New York *Times* headline read: "Hickory Disappearing, Supply of Wood Nears End—Much Wasted and There's No Substitute." Actually, as prices rose, the railroad—the major consumers of wood—did find substitutes. And more efficient ways of using wood.

27 Meanwhile, however, Gifford Pinchot used the specter of a "timber shortage" to get the U.S. Forest Service started. There was, of course, no such shortage, unless you take the static view. And a growing number of both economists and environmental activists now see Pinchot's legacy of central planning and federally managed forest lands as an economic and enviromental disaster.

28 Contrary to the doomsayers, both past and present, people have a knack for innovating their way out of "crises"—if they have both the permission and the incentive to do so. So we find that people developed petroleum as whale oil became scarce, that farmers turn to drip irrigation as water prices rise, and that drivers bought fuel-efficient cars when gas prices went up.

29 To a large degree, however, green ideology is not about facts. It is about *values,* and the environmental movement is about enforcing those values through political action. Green politics, write British greens Jonathon Porritt and David Winner, "demands a wholly new ethic in which violent, plundering humankind abandons its destructive ways, recognizes its dependence on Planet Earth, and starts living on a more equal footing with the rest of nature. The danger lies not only in the odd maverick polluting factory, industry, or technology, but in the fundamental nature of our economic systems. It is industrialism itself—a 'super-ideology' embraced by socialist countries as well as by the capitalist West—which threatens us."

30 If we look around, we can see the effort to remake "violent, plundering humankind" in a number of current initiatives. Take recycling. On one level, it seems like common sense. Why waste resources? That's certainly true with aluminum, which takes huge amounts of electricity to make in the first place and very little energy to recycle. But then there's glass. Both making glass in the first place and melting it down for recycling take about the same amount of energy. The only other thing new glass takes is sand—and we have plenty of that. Unless you're worried about an imminent sand crisis, there's little reason to recycle glass. It doesn't even take up much room in landfills.

31 But, of course, glass—like other forms of packaging—is convenient. Getting people to recycle it is a way of reminding them of the evils of materialism and the folly of convenience. As Jeremy Rifkin's little booklet *The Greenhouse Crisis: 101 Ways to Save the Earth* advises shoppers: "Remember, if it's disposable and convenient, it probably contributes to the greenhouse effect." On a scientific level, this is ridiculous. But as a value statement it conveys a great deal. Convenient disposable products are the creations of an affluent, innovative, industrial society that responds to consumer demands. In a static, green world, we would forego incandescent lighting for fluorescent bulbs and clothes dryers for clothes lines. We would give up out-of-season fruits and vegetables, disposable diapers (of course), free-flowing shower heads, and other self-indulgent pleasures.

32 If green ideology is guilt transformed into politics, we might wonder why people adopt it. Partly, I think green ideology appeals to many people's sense of frustration with modern life. Technology is too complicated, work too demanding, communication too instantaneous, information too abundant, the pace of life too fast. Stasis looks attractive, not only for nature but also for human beings.

33 E. F. Schumacher put it this way in *Small Is Beautiful,* a central work of green theory. "The pressure and strain of living," he wrote, "is very much less in, say, Burma than it is in the United States, in spite of the fact that the amount of labour-saving machinery used in the former country is only a minute fraction of the amount used in the latter."

34 Jeremy Rifkin describes the green coalition as "time rebels," who "argue that the pace of production and consumption should not exceed nature's ability to recycle wastes and renew basic resources. They argue that the tempo of social and economic life should be compatible with nature's time frame." Rifkin, therefore, can't stand computers. They go too fast.

35 To slow economy and society to the approved *adagio,* the greens have some fairly straightforward prescriptions: Restrict trade to the local area. Eliminate markets where possible. End specialization. Anchor individuals in their "bioregions," local areas defined by their environmental characteristics. Shrink the population. Make life simple again, small, self-contained.

36 It is a vision that can be made remarkably appealing, for it plays on our desire for self-sufficiency, our longing for community, and our nostalgia for the agrarian past. We will go back to the land, back to the rhythms of seedtime and harvest, back to making our own clothes, our own furniture, our own tools. Back to barnraisings and quilting bees. Back to a life we can understand without a string of Ph.D.s.

37 "In living in the world by his own will and skill, the stupidest peasant or tribesman is more competent than the most intelligent workers or technicians or intellectuals in a society of specialists," writes Wendell Berry, an agrarian admired by both greens and cultural conservatives. Berry is a fine writer; he chooses words carefully; he means what he says. We will go back to being peasants.

38 These are, of course, harsh words. And we aren't likely to wake up as subsistence farmers tomorrow. But an economy, like an ecology, is made up of intricate connections. Constantly tinkering with it—cutting off this new technology here, banning that product there—will have unintended consequences. And sometimes, one suspects, the consequences aren't all that unintended.

39 Take electricity. Environmentalists, of course, rule out nuclear power, regardless of the evidence of its safety. But then they say coal-powered plants can cause acid rain and pollution, so they're out, too. Oil-fired plants release greenhouse gases (and cost a bundle, too). Hydroelectric plants are no good because they disrupt the flow of rivers.

40 Solar photovoltaic cells have always been the great hope of the future. But making them requires lots of nasty chemicals, so we can expect solar cells to be banned around the time they become profitable. Pretty soon, you've eliminated every conceivable source of electricity. Then your only option is to dismantle your industry and live with less: the environmentalist warning of impending shortages becomes a self-fulfilling prophecy.

41 And, make no mistake about it, many environmentalists have a truly radical agenda. "It is a spiritual act to try to shut down DuPont," says Randall Hayes, director of the Rainforest Action Network. From the appealing ads his group runs to solicit donations to save the rainforests, you'd never guess he had that goal in mind.

42 And consider the remarkably frank book, *Whatever Happened to Ecology?*, by longtime environmental activist Stephanie Mills, recently published by Sierra Club Books. Mills garnered national attention in 1969, when she delivered a college commencement address entitled "The Future Is a Cruel Hoax" and declared she'd never have children. The book traces the evolution of the environmental movement and of her ideas since then. Today, she and her husband live on a farm in northern Michigan, where they pursue their bioregionalist ideal of "reinhabiting" the land by restoring some of its wildness and blocking future development. A journalist, not a theorist, Mills speaks not only for herself but for the intellectual movement of which she is a part. Her words are chilling:

> We young moderns resort to elaborate means of getting physical experience. Yogic practice, fanatical running, bicycling, competitive sports, bodybuilding. All of these recreations are voluntary and may not cultivate the endurance necessary for the kind of labor required to dismantle industrial society and restore the Earth's productivity.

Are voluntary . . . the endurance necessary . . . the labor required . . . dismantle industrial society. The prose is pleasant, the notions it contains disturbing. She continues:

> One summer afternoon a few days after a freak windstorm, I made a foray out to buy some toilet paper. (Every time I have to replenish the supply of this presumed necessity, I wonder what we're going to substitute for it when the trucks stop running.)

43   *When the trucks stop running.* There is a history of the future buried in those words, fodder for several science-fiction novels—but no explanation of when and why the trucks will stop. Or who will stop them.

44   People don't want to be peasants: The cities of the Third World teem with the evidence. And certainly, the typical subscriber to the *Utne Reader* (a sort of green *Reader's Digest* with a circulation of 200,000 after only six years of publication) doesn't envision a future of subsistence farming—much less the hunter-gatherer existence preferred by deep ecologists. More to the reader's taste is, no doubt, the cheery vision offered by Executive Editor Jay Walljasper.

> It's 2009. Nuclear weapons have been dismantled. Green publications have huge circulations. Minneapolis has 11 newspapers and its own currency ("redeemable in trout, walleye, or wild rice"). Sidewalk cafés sell croissants and yogurt. A local ordinance decrees a 24-hour workweek. Cars are nearly nonexistent (a delegation from the "People's Independent Republic of Estonia" is in town to help design better ski trails for commuters). Citizens vote electronically. The shopping mall has become a nature preserve.

45   Walljasper is clearly having fun—after all, he puts Aretha Franklin's face on the $10 bill—and he doesn't consider any of the tough questions. Like how all those magazines and newspapers exist without printing plants or paper mills. How the Estonians got to town without airplanes or the fuel to run them (Jeremy Rifkin specifically names the Boeing 747 as the kind of product that can't be produced in the small-is-beautiful factories of the coming "entropic age.") How the chips to run the electronic voting got etched without chemicals. Where the chips were made. How a 24-hour workweek produced the sustained concentration needed to write software or the level of affluence that allows for restaurant croissants.

46   And, above all, Walljasper doesn't explain why after millennia of behaving otherwise, humans simply gave up wanting *stuff.* If the Walljasper of 2009 still overloads on reading material, why should we assume that people whose fancy runs toward fast food and polyester (or fast cars and silk) would be struck with a sudden attack of bioregionally approved tastes? How *exactly* did that shopping mall disappear?

47   "The root of the solution has to be so radical that it can scarcely be spoken of," says movie director and British green John Borrman. "We all have to be prepared to change the way we live and function and relate to the planet. In short, we need a transformation of the human spirit. If the human heart can be changed, then everything can be changed."

48   We have heard this somewhere before—in, for example, the promise of a "New Soviet Man." People are forever seeking to change the human heart, often with tragic results.

49   The greens want people to give up the idea that life can be better. They say "better" need not refer to material abundance, that we should just be content with less. Stasis, they say, can satisfy our "vital needs." They may indeed convince some people to pursue a life of voluntary simplicity, and that is fine and good and just the thing a free society ought to allow. Stephanie Mills is welcome to her organic farm.

50   But most of us do not want to give up 747s, or cars, or eyeglasses, or private washing machines, or tailored clothing, or even disposable diapers. The "debased human protoplasm" that Stephanie Mills holds in contempt for their delight in "clothes, food, sporting goods, electronics, building supplies, pets, baked goods, deli food, toys, tools, hardware, geegaws, jim-jams, and knick-knacks" will not happily relinquish the benefits of modern civilization. Many ordinary human beings would like a cleaner world. They are prepared to make sacrifices—*tradeoffs* is a better word—to get one. But ordinary human beings will not adopt the Buddha's life without desire, much as E. F. Schumacher might have ordained it.

51 At its extreme, green ideology expresses itself in utter contempt for humanity. Reviewing Bill McKibben's *The End of Nature* in the *Los Angeles Times,* National Park Service research biologist David M. Graber concluded with this stunning passage:

> Human happiness, and certainly human fecundity, are not as important as a wild and healthy planet. I know social scientists who remind me that people are part of nature, but it isn't true. Somewhere along the line—at about a billion years ago, maybe half that—we quit the contract and became a cancer. We have become a plague upon ourselves and upon the Earth. It is cosmically unlikely that the developed world will choose to end its orgy of fossil-energy consumption, and the Third World its suicidal consumption of landscape. Until such time as Homo sapiens should decide to rejoin nature, some of us can only hope for the right virus to come along.

52 It is hard to take such notions seriously without sounding like a bit of a kook yourself. But there they are—calmly expressed in the pages of a major, mainstream, Establishment newspaper by an employee of the federal government. When it is acceptable to say such things in polite intellectual company, when feel-good environmentalists tolerate the totalitarians in their midst, when sophisticates greet the likes of Graber with indulgent nods and smiles rather than arguments and outrage, we are one step farther down another bloody road to someone's imagined Eden.

53 Thank you.

The Ethics of Protest: Is It Right to Do Wrong?

◆ *Lee W. Baker* ◆

Lee W. Baker has had extensive public relations experience first in corporate managerial positions with Allis-Chalmers Co. and then as president of his own public relations firm in Milwaukee and later in Denver. He has maintained continued interest in ethical issues related to public relations specifically and to public discourse generally. He has served as an editorial board member for the *Journal of Mass Media Ethics.* You may want to read his book, *The Credibility Factor: Putting Ethics to Work in Public Relations* (1993).

On November 1, 1995 Lee Baker, then retired, addressed the monthly Business Ethics Forum at Trinity United Methodist Church in Denver, Colorado. The audience numbered 60–70 persons and his speech was followed by a lively question-and-answer period.

◆ Lee W. Baker, "The Ethics of Protest: Is it Right to Do Wrong?" February 1, 1996, pp. 252–255. Reprinted by permission from *Vital Speeches of the Day* and the author.

In his introduction, Baker establishes a positive relationship with his audience by citing instances familiar to most of them (1–2). Later he encourages this relationship by overtly inviting the audience to judge whether they agree with him (4, 18). Clearly Baker primarily focuses on propositions of value in the speech. He offers ethical judgments of various types of social protest tactics. He advocates a set of ethical standards to guide evaluation of protest tactics. At the outset, he makes careful distinctions before proceeding to his major arguments (3–4).

In the first half of the speech, Baker uses an extended illustration of the social protest tactics of animal rights activist groups such as PETA and ALF (4–10). This lengthy illustration allows him to reveal personal motivations (4), to dramatize the extremism of the tactics, to make vivid the range of tactics he condemns, and to criticize hypocrisy (4, 10). As a type of evidence, consider his example in paragraph 7: "A Michigan state police officer also has talked about what he called a 'real problem,' a string of hunter deaths in Michigan-Ohio-Indiana areas." Is Baker arguing by implication that these deaths were caused by animal rights protestors? If so, how reasonable is the evidence he offers?

In a major segment of the speech (11–17), Baker categorizes unethical protest tactics and presents them in an implied rank order from most unethical to least unethical. He highlights the categories by using verbal signposts to mark them (12, 13, 15, 16, 17). In this major segment, Baker continues to rely extensively on examples and specific instances both for proof and for clarification. To Baker's massive use of examples throughout the speech, apply the standard tests for reasonableness of specific instances: (1) Was a sufficient number of instances presented? (2) Were the instances presented representative of the type of instances being discussed? (3) Were there any negative or counter-instances omitted that need to be discussed?

Near the end of the speech, Baker advocates adoption of a specific set of values to guide our evaluations of the ethics of protest tactics. He outlines the standards (18–21) and then summarizes them (21). How do the numerous examples he presents earlier in the speech measure up to these ethical standards? Would his argument have been clearer if he had presented his ethical standards first and then applied them to his categories of unethical protest tactics? Baker's premise is that the ethical standards to be met by protestors "are the same accepted ethical standards—no higher or lower—as acknowledged by the other segments of society" (18). One scholar of social protest who disagrees with this premise is Steven Goldzwig in his article, "A Social Movement Perspective of Demagoguery: Achieving Symbolic Realignment," *Communication Studies*, 40 (Fall 1989): 202–228. Baker also contends that protestors must exhaust all available peaceful means before turning to illegal or extreme tactics. Do you agree? Why?

You may want to compare Baker's speech with one made on the same topic of social protest ethics in 1968 by Franklyn S. Haiman, "The Rhetoric of 1968: A Farewell to Rational Discourse," and reprinted in two sources: Wil A. Linkugel, R. R. Allen, and Richard L. Johannesen, *Contemporary American Speeches*, 4th ed. (Dubuque, IA: Kendall/Hunt, 1978), pp. 156–169; Richard L. Johannesen, *Ethics in Human Communication*, 2nd ed. (Prospect Heights, IL: Waveland Press, 1983), pp. 177–190. At what points would Baker and Haiman agree and at what points would they disagree? Whose analysis do you find most reasonable and why? On the ethics of social protest, also see Richard L. Johannesen, *Ethics in Human Communication*, 4th ed. (Waveland, 1996), pp. 90–96.

◆ ◆ ◆

1   You've probably all watched or participated in protest actions. Their numbers surely reached a peak during the Vietnam War, when college campuses were alive with students challenging U.S. government leaders. In the Denver area, Rocky Flats has been the locale for many protesters; the

Statehouse steps are a frequently-used stage; when President Clinton was here recently protesters marched outside the downtown hotel where a fundraising dinner was underway.

2   What do protesters want to paraphrase Dr. Freud's question? Well, they want you on their side, they want your support. To win you over, they use every form of communication and a variety of methods. You're familiar with many of the causes. Protesters may work through the democratic process, such as petitions to public officials and the ballot box, or take their causes to the public through picketing, parades, rallies, signs, handbills and paid ads; or directly to target representatives through angry confrontations. Sometimes, but not always, the protest group is a David challenging a Goliath, the little guy against the Establishment, which may be big business or big government, or established educational or religious institutions. In the West, such issues as cattle grazing and other uses of public lands, or those related to saving of endangered species and wetlands, or conservation of forests, fuel the causes. At times, protesters seem full of a holier-than-thou attitude, create the impression that everyone is out of step except them, that only their beliefs or credos are the right ones. They not only oppose beliefs counter to theirs, they make little room for the people who have them. Also, at times, it seems protesters are acting to satisfy desires for personal notoriety and attention as much or more than to spread the word about their issues.

3   Let me add that there are many good things about protests and their leaders. Many achieve their goals to bring about changes that benefit society and human lives. I hope I come across as selective as I focus on what to me are unethical protests. I'm not tarring all protests with an unethical brush or label.

4   My subject, "The Ethics of Protest," grew from early reactions to what I read and heard about the organization called People for the Ethical Treatment of Animals. I first became aware of PETA, to use the acronym, five or six years ago. I found that it then and since engaged in rather shocking protest activities for an organization that used the word "Ethical" in its title. You might presume from such usage that it shared a generally accepted view of ethical conduct and had an ethics record others would acclaim. Well, I found differently. See if you agree. After taking a look at People for the Ethical Treatment of Animals, I'll move on to an ethical examination of some other kinds of individual and group protests. As I do this, let me add, I'm commenting about the tactics of these individuals and organizations and not their issues. A discussion of issues, some highly explosive, might require several more of these meetings. Fair enough?

5   PETA is a nonprofit charity organization founded in 1980 to plead the cause of animal rights before policy-makers and the public. It particularly targets what it calls factory farm raising and slaughtering of animals for human consumption, and the use of animals in experimentation.

6   Here are a few protest activities conducted in the name of animal rights. A few months ago PETA's vegetarian campaign coordinator from the Washington headquarters was in Denver attempting to unload a truck full of manure in front of the Colorado Convention Center. She was protesting against the World Meat Congress that was meeting there. Signage on the side of the truck said, "Meat Stinks." Police arrested her before she completed the job. At a dog show, PETA protesters opened the cages of several of the show dogs and turned them loose; they also put anti-freeze in the water bowls of some cages. One of the protesters said, "A dead dog is better than a caged dog." Add to this such incidents as PETA protesters throwing paint or blood onto fur coats worn by women walking down the street. Or, consider this: A protester against the use of fashion furs appearing on David Letterman's show wearing leather shoes. This protester the day before had been arrested with others from PETA for vandalizing the offices of fashion designer Karl Lagerfeld, who uses fur. As part of its program, PETA makes claims found to be without substance. For instance, it says minks have their testicles electrocuted. The industry standard—said to be rigidly adhered to—is to euthanize the creatures by either carbon mon-

oxide or lethal injection. That's the procedure used in animal shelters. Medical authorities deny PETA claims of unnecessarily harsh treatment for animals in research. And they vouch for the need for animal experimentation to reveal valuable data in the development of medicines and health procedures. PETA terms guide dogs for the blind "akin to slavery."

7   There's another animal rights group, the Animal Liberation Front, that has been blamed for the firebombing of an animal-research lab at Michigan State University. Police reported an estimate of $200,000 in damages and the destroying of 30 years' worth of primary research data. A similar incident occurred at Washington State University a year earlier. There were grand jury indictments in Michigan against alleged perpetrators, whom I believe, are still at large. PETA issued a news release, said to have been provided by the ALF, on the disaster. A Michigan state police officer also has talked about what he called a "real problem," a string of hunter deaths in Michigan-Ohio-Indiana areas. Last year, the Animal Liberation Front planted incendiary devices in four downtown Chicago department stores.

8   A British journalist reports animal rightists placed incendiary bombs under cars of those whose work involves the use of animals, also 42 letter-bombs and 61 mousetraps, devices sent in parcels designed to slice off the fingers of whomever opens them. Another dimension in the fight for animal rights was provided by vegetarians who broke into the shop of a German butcher. They smashed equipment worth $21,000 and painted the message, "Meat is murder, animal killer," on the shop windows.

9   Subsequently, they slashed the butcher's tires and left a phone message, "Yesterday your store, tomorrow you."

10   These activities of animal rights proponents may have met their goal of grabbing the public's attention. But at what costs? In the flouting of high moral and ethical conduct they trampled on others' rights and inflicted harm.

11   The pattern of thinking that led me to have questions about PETA prompted me to look at the ethical aspects in protest actions of other groups that sought public understanding and even endorsement for their concerns and programs. I found numerous instances in which they too brought harm to citizens and portions of society. Here are a few of the ways. I've sorted them into several categories, but as I go through them you'll recognize that the instances often fit into more than one.

12   Number one. I reserve the top place on the chart of the most damaging kinds of protest for actions that endanger the lives of others. We're all familiar with the acts of zealous protesters that brought injuries to staff employees and the loss of lives at abortion clinics. Since 1993, at least five who work in abortion clinics—two doctors and three clinic staff members—have been killed. Save-the-forest protesters have driven spikes deep into trees in the northwest, endangering the lives of lumbermen. New Orleans police had a two-day sickout to protest unresolved issues in contract negotiations with the city. (The right to collectively bargain was one of the issues.) A police department spokesman put the absences at more than 50 percent. On one shift 70 percent of the assigned officers stayed home. While there are no figures available on the negative effects to citizens' lives, can't we assume there were some? In 1970, during the height of the student protest against the Vietnam war, the Army Math Research Center at the University of Wisconsin in Madison was bombed. One student working there was killed, four others injured. Most of the contents, including a $1.5 million computer, were destroyed. Math research that was conducted there had nothing to do with military projects. We can include in this category the perpetrators of the Oklahoma City and World Trade Center bombings, and the Unabomber.

13   Second, as a category, are the protests that damage property and cut off income for individuals and employers. In a tiny town in Alabama last year, a fire believed to have been arson burned down a high school whose principal's stand against mixed-race dating had casued racial turmoil. The principal had threatened to cancel the school prom if interracial couples attended. The 25-year-old son of a

protest leader, arrested for setting the fire, was acquitted just last week. While the identity of the protester who set the fire may never be known, the community suffered a real loss. In another kind of protest, there were the economic pressures applied by farm workers in California in the 1980s. They called on the public to boycott lettuce and grapes in the hope that reduced sales would help them gain concessions from the owners. Then there was the famous Alar case, in which a meticulously-conceived protest plan by the Natural Resources Defense Council swept apples from the bins of super markets and frightened families and school officials. Entertainment personalities led the chorus: Apples sprayed with Alar could cause cancer; children were most at risk. Mothers poured apple juice down sink drains. Apples were removed from school lunchrooms. Normalcy began to return when a joint announcement from the USDA, EPA and FDA declared apples safe. Meanwhile, apple growers lost $100 million and dozens of family-owned orchards went bankrupt.

14   Here's an unusual case from Germany. The Benetton Group, an Italian clothing manufacturer, ran ads with themes of human tragedy and suffering. Among photographs in its ads were a man's arm tattooed with the words "HIV positive," a dying AIDS patient, a war cemetery, an oil soaked seabird, children toiling in a South American sweat shop and the bloody uniform of a Croatian soldier. Benetton said the ads were designed to raise awareness about social issues. Licensees of many of its stores in Europe disagreed—as did customers. They found them offensive, tasteless and insensitive, as did 84 percent of those responding to a German magazine poll. Customers at the four stores of one dealer joined the protest. They applied blood-red tape over his store windows to block out the Benetton name. At the center of the Xs formed by the tape was this message: "No more Benetton, because we condemn the scandalous advertising using misery, war, sickness and death." And they boycotted the stores. The merchant said the boycott cost him some $600,000 in lost sales. So he refused to pay Benetton that amount. However, a judge ordered him to pay the full bill plus interest.

15   I give third place for harm to the intimidation, coercion and harassment that stem from the fervor of protesters. Former Defense Secretary Robert McNamara said in his book published earlier this year that his vacation home near Snowmass, Colo., was a target for anti-war protesters who twice tried to burn it down in 1967. The FBI believed there were several attempts at arson at the house in later years. Blueprints of his home were found in a Berkeley, Calif., garage of the Symbionese Liberation Army after heiress-turned-revolutionary Patty Hearst was arrested for her work with the SLA. We know that physicians in Colorado and around the country who perform abortions have received death threats. Many have been stalked. Some doctors wear bullet-proof vests and helmets and have 24 hour security. A recent anti-abortion, pro-life strategy is the filing of malpractice suits against doctors, which harass them and intimidate their patients. In Denver, no clashes or damage to life or property occurred in the protests that led to the demise of the Columbus Day parade in 1992. But coercive pressures and threats by leaders of the American Indian Movement resulted in its cancellation by the Italian-American organizations. The decision was made in the interest of safety after a face-off between marchers and protesters shortly before the parade hour. The press reported a death threat against the man who would have been dressed as Columbus.

16   Next, protesters deprive others of their citizen rights. As Patrick Buchanan announced his candidacy for the Republican presidential nomination earlier this year in New Hampshire, four protesters leaped on the stage. They halted his speech with shouts and accused him of being a racist. Buchanan tusselled with one at the podium before they were hustled away by his supporters. Newt Gingrich had a similar experience in Chicago, where demonstrators protesting proposed Republican cuts in social programs forced him to stop speaking several times. In Georgia, Gingrich was met with such ardent protesters that the event he was attending had to be canceled. Speakers such as Buchanan and Gingrich have a First Amendment right to be heard. There have been instances in which protesters were so vociferous that police were called and, concerned about the safety of the speakers, said it would be best if they left. These instances illustrate what's called "the heckler's veto." If someone's right to assemble and speak becomes shattered by hecklers, the First Amendment has been violated. It's the responsibility of the police to remove the protesting hecklers rather than urge the speakers to disperse under fire.

17 As a fifth category are protesters who cause inconvenience, disruption and unwanted bother in the lives of consumers and businesses. The effects are often hard to evaluate without more information about the circumstances. A couple of examples: Striking employees of Air France disrupted the schedules of international travelers by closing down the largest airport in Paris and partially shuttering another. Who knows if a passenger failed to arrive in time at the bedside of a dying family member? Or if the tardiness of a business representative forced a potential agreement to vanish? Lives of crew members and ground forces surely were unnecessarily upset. And what was the loss to Air France? In Mexico City, dozens of masked men protested California's Proposition 187 that curbs benefits to illegal aliens by invading a McDonald's restaurant. They threw cash registers to the floor, smashed windows, overturned tables and spray-painted anti-American slogans. Fortunately, no customers were injured, though there may have been a case or two of indigestion caused by the excitement. At Rutgers University last February, 400 student protesters seeking the dismissal of the school's president descended on the gymnasium floor during half-time of a basketball game with the University of Massachusetts. They refused to budge and officials called off the remainder of the game—to the disappointment and frustration of the players and fans. Object of the protesters' wrath was a comment of the president they found to be a racial slur, made at a faculty meeting the previous November. Incidentally, the board of directors meeting three days later in a special session, open to the news media and broadcast live by CNN, voted to keep the president.

18 Each of these examples illustrates the lack of ethics in protest movements. What are the ethical standards that protesters should meet? They are the same accepted ethical standards—no higher or lower—as acknowledged by other segments of society. I know, someone out there may be asking, accepted by whom? Well, accepted by me for one, by you, I hope, by all who prize conduct based on high moral values. Here are components of those standards. First, fairness. Fairness is a key quality in ethical social behavior—fairness expressed as a matter of reciprocity. In order to receive fair treatment one should give fair treatment. Confucius, the Chinese philosopher and teacher, expressed it this way: "Do not do to others what you would not want others to do to you." The Golden Rule calls for a more positive stance, "Do unto others as you would have others do to you." Admittedly, the state of being fair can be subject to different meanings and definitions. But I think those precepts form the basis for an objective definition. Do you agree with me that in the examples I've mentioned, there often was failure to observe fairness?

19 Observing respect is another basic ingredient in ethical conduct. Respect for the basic rights of others. Refusal to act in a manner that reduces or tramples on the rights of others. Respect for the law is also a basic. I cited numerous occasions in which protesters committed illegal acts. Some of you may say, sometimes protesters do need to take drastic action to get attention—and that this may mean breaking the law. But this reaction is most likely a cop out. Don't protesters sometimes travel the illegal route without exhausting all available peaceful means to get the attention and results they seek? Keep in mind that perhaps the largest protest in our country's history—until a few weeks ago—was the peaceful "I Have A Dream" march and rally of Martin Luther King, Jr., in Washington in 1963. That generated a tremendous wallop. Then, in October, we witnessed the even larger—and also peaceful—million man march.

20 Further, ethical individuals or organizations engaged in protests should be honest, should avoid misrepresentation of facts, lying, deceit and subterfuge, or manipulation. In a couple of earlier instances, we found protesters who made truth a victim. Another kind of case: A small group of protesters gather at their appointed spot, their placards at the ready. All is quiet until the television crews arrive and turn on their lights. Then the signs go up, the chanting starts, the leader shakes a fist at a distant target and tape depicting this spirited protest is ready for the evening news. As the lights go off, the protesters resume their relaxed mode.

21 And there's no place in protests for the activists to gloss over faulty conduct by saying, "The ends justify the means." Situational ethics and relativism have become too much accepted today as the platform for excusing questionable ethics. You may have trouble abiding by Immanuel Kant's moral imperative: What is right is right. All deception is morally wrong. He may seem too inflexible. Yet following as closely as possible his strict rules of moral conduct is preferable to reaching for the lowest possible level of ethics. Advancing the ethical standards of society requires that all must strive for what's right and what's fair, for mutal respect of rights, for honesty.

22 Protesters have no right to advance their cause with unethical methods and tactics. Though spurred by excess exuberance and fierce dedication, they shouldn't be so deluded that they believe they're entitled to unethical shortcuts. Those who disagree with or are neutral about the goals of a protest group have the right to their beliefs without being subject to pressure—economic, emotional or physical—from members of the movement. They should not feel impelled to restrict their movements or actions, including speech, because of fear churned by protesters.

23 Let's keep before us the outline of what's morally acceptable, the manner in which people of conscience and moral responsibility act, instead of looking for excuses to do wrong in the name of accomplishing what we believe is right.

The New World of Medical Ethics: Our Duty Lies Both to the Individual and the Population

◆ *Richard D. Lamm* ◆

"Governor Gloom" was the nickname earned by Richard D. Lamm during his terms as governor of Colorado (1974–1986). According to James S. Kunen (*People*, January 20, 1986, 46–50), Lamm's "typically apocalyptic speeches" won him a reputation as a doomsayer. Lamm sees himself in the role of an Old Testament prophet who warned of disaster unless people reformed their ways. Thus Lamm's speechmaking might be analyzed as illustrating the tradition of the American contemporary secular "jeremiad" (after the Old Testament prophet Jere-

◆ Richard D. Lamm, "New World of Medical Ethics: Our Duty Lies Both to the Individual and the Population," July 1, 1993, pp. 549–553. Reprinted by permission from *Vital Speeches of the Day* and the author.

miah) as a form or genre of public discourse. See, for example, Richard L. Johannesen, "The Jeremiad and Jenkin Lloyd Jones," *Communication Monographs,* 52 (June 1985): 156–171.

On March 27, 1984 Lamm captured national media attention when he made the following comment concerning the ethical and economic implications of high technology medicine that often permits costly and painful prolongation of our lives: "We've got a duty to die and get out of the way with all our machines and artificial hearts and everything else like that and let the other society, our kids, build a reasonable life." An excellent analysis of inaccurate news media coverage of his comment is Sue O'Brien, "The 'Duty to Die' Controversy: Taking Care with Health Care Reporting," in Philip Patterson and Lee Wilkins, eds., *Media Ethics: Issues and Cases,* 2nd ed. (Dubuque, IA: Brown & Benchmark, 1994), pp. 31–33.

Author or co-author of three books, Lamm also is a lawyer and accountant. Since leaving the office of governor, Lamm has been Director of the Center for Public Policy and Contemporary Issues at the University of Denver. He presented the following speech on April 17, 1993 in San Francisco at the International Bioethics Institute during the Third Annual Congress of Healthcare Ethics and Ethics Committees.

This speech clearly argues a proposition of value. Lamm advocates adoption of a new set of values to guide medical ethics (3). And he itemizes for clarity the six new value orientations that he advocates (11, 18, 24, 30, 36, 46).

Lamm uses a variety of lines of argument to develop his central theme of necessary shift from individual-centered values to community-centered values (57–58). The old individual-oriented values, by themselves, are outmoded as norms for medical ethics (4–6). The new community-oriented values are contrasted with the old (27–28). He contends that there should be a balanced duty both to the individual and the community (32, 64). But also note that in other places he implies that the community values should be given some degree of priority in the hierarchy of values related to medical care (28, 54, 55). A

book that explores the on-going tensions in American culture between individualism and community is Robert N. Bellah, et al., *Habits of the Heart: Individualism and Commitment in American Life* (1985).

A secondary theme is that economic resources available for medical care in this country are not unlimited (7, 28, 50–52). Lamm argues not only that maximum citizen access to medical care is vital but also that there must be rationing or prioritizing of economic resources for what is covered. Two analyses of the rationing of medical care are Daniel Callahan, *Setting Limits* (1987) and Robert Blank, *Rationing Medicine* (1988).

At strategic points Lamm employs statistics to support his analysis (6, 40, 43–44). But his most extensive use of evidence involves expert testimony (14, 16, 20–23, 34–35, 49–51). Considering the nature of his audience, how adequate are the statistics and testimony when judged by the tests of clarity, accuracy, relevance, recency, representativeness, and documentation of sources? For example, how well does he identify and present the qualifications and competency of the experts he quotes?

Lamm uses a variety of language resources to clarify and dramatize his points. He opens and concludes with parables—stories from ordinary life from which a moral message is extracted (1–2, 59). Although used few times, his literal analogies sharpen his points (19, 42). How well do his numerous uses of vivid metaphors function to clarify, reinforce, make memorable, or otherwise strengthen his statements (5, 9, 17, 32, 47–48, 57, 60–61)? Notable also is Lamm's use of antithesis—the phrasing of two opposing or competing items into sharp, terse contrast with one item of the pair given clear preference over the other (6, 7, 28, 39). In the conclusion of the speech, he employs one lengthy series of antitheses to summarize the necessary shifts in values and policy (62) and another lengthy series to underscore the need for early access and prevention more than later, more expensive, treatment and maintenance (63).

◆ ◆ ◆

1   I should start with a parable. In the Christian tradition, there is the story about Saint Martin of Tours who in the Medieval Ages was riding his horse, alone and cold, through the deepening night toward the walled city which was his destination. Right outside the gate to the city, Saint Martin of Tours met a cold and starving beggar. In an act of charity that lives in Christian tradition, Saint Martin of Tours divided his cloak in half and gave that with half of his dinner to the cold and starving beggar. It was clearly the ethical and moral course to take. It has served as an example of Christian charity for centuries.

2   Yet Brecht, in his play "Mother Courage," raises the issue of what if, instead of one cold and starving beggar, there were 40. Or, if you like, 100. What then is the duty of an ethical and moral person? It obviously does not make any sense to divide one's cloak into 40 or 100 painfully inadequate pieces. There is no reason to choose one among the many cold and starving beggars, and it is hard to solve this dilemma other than perhaps saying a prayer for them all as you ride past them into the city.

3   It is my passionate belief that this parable applies to the dilemma we are faced with in health care. There is a new set of realities with which we are confronted; and we must develop a new set of values and a new way of looking at health care if we are to resolve the implications of this brave new world of health care.

4   A whole new world has formed while we were busy inventing, developing, discovering, and innovating. A new world where our current and past values so agonizingly developed are no longer sustainable.

5   Ultimately, our health care ethics are tethered to the economic life support system of our economy. We cannot deliver medically what we do not earn economically. The arm bone of health care is connected to the backbone of the economy.

6   The medical values developed by the world's largest creditor nation with an economy that doubled every 30 years, with 9 percent of its citizens over 65, and modest biotechnology cannot now be sustained by the world's largest debtor nation that has already borrowed $4.3 trillion from its children and grandchildren, whose average worker has had no real growth in wages in 20 years; who has 12 percent of its population over the age of 65, and has incredibly expensive biotechnology.

7   No nation can long import more than it exports, borrow more than it earns, and spend medically what it does not produce economically.

8   Proust once observed that the real voyage of discovery lay not in discovering new worlds, but in seeing with new eyes.

9   I see a health care world where nothing we have done for the past 40 years has even dented the volcanic upward thrust of health care costs—a world of medical innovation that has become a fiscal black hole that threatens to bankrupt our children—a world where our medical miracles are fiscal failures.

10   Medical technology does *not* save us money, as a genre. "Cured" is a marvelous word, but it also means "alive to die later of something else." We have reduced mortality, but dramatically increased morbidity. Where we used to die inexpensively of the first or second disease, we now die expensively of the fifth or sixth disease having consumed far more resources. A new world has formed.

11   *Value Change No. 1:* Stop the egoism about the U.S. having "the finest health care system in the world."

12   It is often said, almost as a mantra, that the United States has the best health care system in the world. Whenever I hear this I am reminded of the historian who said that the 14th Century was a wonderful century, except for the Hundred Year War.

13 America has much to be proud of in its health care system; but like the rooster that knew the sun came up just to hear him crow, it overstates its case. Clearly, the United States has the most sophisticated and the best medical technology. I believe we have the best doctors. Yet, other industrialized countries have healthier people and lower health care costs. These countries deliver more health care services to more people more often, with less administrative hassle for substantially less money. Their doctors have more clinical freedom, and polls show both doctors and citizens in those countries are more satisfied.

14 As one of the most respected health care experts has found:

> In comparison with other major industrial countries, health care in the United States costs more per person and per unit of service, is less accessible to a large portion of its citizens, is provided at a more intensive level, and offers comparatively poor gross outcomes.

15 The test of a system is not the quality of its individual parts, but the effectiveness and efficiency of the total system. Like the man who knew seven languages, but had nothing to say in any of them—technical proficiency is not enough. You cannot have a good health care system without dedicated and brilliant doctors. Yet, dedicated and brilliant doctors are not enough to make a good health care system. A system can be flawed even if it is made up of individually spectacular parts. Clearly, the United States has a system which contains many spectacular parts. Yet, as society has come to recognize, the system contains two major flaws: 1. It leaves 35–37 million Americans uninsured, and an equal number underinsured; and 2. Cost.

16 The lack of access in America is well-known, but still worth repeating. We should take care we do not become hardened to these numbers. George Bernard Shaw once said, "The mark of a truly educated man (person) is to be moved deeply by statistics." In 1992, Louis Harris and Associates conducted a survey and found:

- Approximately 23 million Americans needed medical care but did not get it in the last 12 months. Approximately 18 million could not get medical care for financial reasons.
- Last year, 54 million people postponed care they thought they needed for financial reasons.
- About 7 million Americans were denied health insurance because of a prior medical condition.
- Nearly 22 million Americans said they themselves, or someone else in their family, or both, had been refused health care during the last year because they didn't have insurance or couldn't pay.

17 These figures are a national disgrace. They show that for all our technical proficiency, our system contains major flaws. The largest flaw is lack of access, and the access problem is the ugly stepchild of the problems with out-of-control costs. We must start to understand that these two flaws are not blemishes of an otherwise ethical delivery system—but fatal flaws that go to the heart of the system.

18 *Value Change No. 2:* Health care must be seen as a social good.

19 The first value issue involving access is to ascertain whether health care is a social good or a private commodity. It is important to first decide the context in which other decisions are made. Is health care a private commodity like a car or clothing? Or, is it a social good like education or a police department? I believe this is actually a question of community values.

20 I believe the hipbone of access is attached to the backbone of the values of our society. However imperfect, we have a democracy which eventually responds to public will. The problem is that we are schizophrenic about health care—we want everybody to have everything, but we do not want any more taxes and no more shifted costs. It we are to solve this problem of access, we shall have to form a new public consensus confirming that access is important. As Lawrence J. O'Connell, President & CEO of an ethics think tank, said:

> All the talk from the campaign trail and the Oval Office is superficial. That is because it sidesteps the fact that before health care reform can succeed, we need to reexamine the fundamental societal values that gave birth to the health care system we have today.

21 Our values must recognize that today uninsured Americans clearly have access to poorer medicine and poorer health. Blendon finds:

> Despite considerable amounts of uncompensated care provided by hospitals and physicians, Americans without health insurance face major barriers to the receipt of needed health services. Although they suffer from higher rates of ill health than the insured population, the uninsured report fewer hospitalizations and fewer visits to a physician, shorter hospital stays, and fewer discretionary in-patient hospital treatments and tests, at higher costs. The uninsured also experience higher mortality rates when hospitalized than persons with health insurance coverage who have similar diagnoses.

22 The human toll was—and is—incredible though often unobserved. As John Kitzhaber has said:

> Legislatures never had to confront the victims of silent rationing or be accountable for the very human consequences. It was like high level bombing where the crew never sees the faces of the people they are killing.

23 In light of the foregoing, modern health reforms state that health care is not a private good, but is a social good—and should be available to all. As Charles Dougherty has argued for universal access:

> The argument is simple but powerful. Respect for the incalculably great value of each person creates a duty not only to refrain from destroying health . . . but also a duty to take reasonable steps to preserve and restore health by ensuring access to basic health care. Failing to act on this duty, by allowing lives to be shortened or diminished in quality because of lack of access to basic health care, expresses callow disregard for the dignity of human life.

24 *Value Change No. 3:* Access must go from a secondary value to a primary value.
25 Reinhard Priester, in a very thoughtful article, has stated:

> Since WWII, U.S. health policy has consistently subordinated access to other values, most notably to professional autonomy, patient autonomy, and consumer sovereignty.

26 This is consistent, says Priester, with other American values, for in our past and present, "individualism and personal autonomy have superseded community values in American society."

27 At least six values, focused on the individual, have had a major role in shaping our current health care system. These values have guided decisions of both individuals and policy makers in structuring our health care system. These values are:

1. **Professional Independence: The importance of health professionals, especially physicians, to regulate their own work and to determine what is medically appropriate.**
2. **Consumer Freedom: The importance of individuals to be able to choose their own insurance company, health organizations, and physicians.**
3. **Patient Autonomy: The importance of individuals to be informed about their medical and surgical options and to accept or refuse the advice given.**
4. **Patient Advocacy: The importance of health professionals to act in the best interest of their patients, not the hospital's, the insurance company's, or the community's.**
5. **High Quality: The service of health professionals is expected to meet the highest standards of competence and compassion.**
6. **Availability: The importance of having access to all (including the latest) that medicine and surgical technology has to offer.**

28 Priester suggests, given the new world of limited resources and unlimted demands, that we have to add four new values which put a priority on community good:

7. **Resource Scarcity: There is a limit that can be spent on health and medical care if we wish not to undermine other important social needs.**
8. **Universal Access: Society has a responsibility to provide access to all citizens regardless of income, job status, state of illness, and so forth.**
9. **Personal Responsibility: Individual citizens have a responsibility to the community for staying well and keeping cost down.**
10. **Efficiency: The money spent on health care should help people stay well or get well. It should not be spent on needless administration or treatments that are not effective.**

29 Reforming the health care system will require that we consider these and other values which have given birth to the American health care system.

30 *Value Change No. 4:* We must start to value not only the individual, but also the whole society.

31 The bottom line of modern health care is that there is no bottom line. Modern men and women of medicine now have the capability to spend unlimited resources in heroic, and sometime vain attempts to extend life. Theoretically, one could now spend all of his or her available time and money in the pursuit of health.

32 Since health care is a public policy bottomless pit, we cannot build the new system looking only at the needs of the individual. We must never forget or abandon the individual, but we must look also at the needs of the entire population. There is an evolving new equation in this shift and it will come only after considerable ethical debate.

33 Using resources for one patient necessarily means that fewer resources will be available to treat others.

34 But it is coming. The Section on Health Care Systems of the American Hospital Association issued a report that found:

Health care in the U.S. should be redesigned around the needs of the population, not the needs of providers. "Population" is a broader term than patient, which has been our concern. We should all commit to a health population as one fundamental objective, then organize ourselves to support that objective. The measure of our success should be health status, not full hospitals; manageable cost per capita, not profitability for thousands of separate provider units; value, not just cost control.

35 As Victor Fuchs has said: "The difference between what is beneficial for the indivdual and what is beneficial to the society as a whole is the key element in the current health care debate."

36 *Value Change No. 5:* In the new world of health care, reform for community hospitals will owe a duty to the community.

37 The same analysis applies to hospitals. In the United States, hospitals focus almost entirely on the patients *within* the hospital. There seems to be little awareness of—let alone, a sense of responsibility for—the community. A community should have geographical accountability. And, it would be considered unethical and wrong for community hospitals to make large profits, while other people in the community are going without needed medical services.

38 Related to the sin of gluttony is the sin of excess. What if Saint Martin of Tours had come by in a camper stuffed with donated food and found six starving beggars and did nothing. Just passed on by.

39 America has a new sin—the sin of excess in the face of need.

40 Half empty hospitals hire marketing people and run expensive advertising campaigns—to win market share from a neighboring half empty hospital who has hired a public relations firm and does expensive promotional spots on television—blocks away from women without prenatal care and children without vaccines. Half of the hospitals in Colorado are empty, filled with marketing people and advertising geniuses who are desperately trying to beat neighboring half empty hospitals.

41 In the new world of health care, spending money to advertise your hospital would be like taking your neighborhood crime protection money away to advertise your police department.

42 A hospital is a community asset—like a fire department. If there are too many, they should be closed; not advertised.

43 I am not here to criticize California. Colorado has 2.8 hospital beds per 1,000 people—53 percent are empty. We have 21 hospitals that do open heart surgery; many of them doing less than 50 a year (one a week), when 250 is the minimum number Medicare says is needed for proficiency.

44 California also has 2.8 hospital beds per 1,000 people. Southern California and Colorado have 2.8 hospital beds per 1,000 people. HMOs operate at 1.5 hospital beds per 1,000 enrollees. California has 118 open heart units and 400 MRI machines.

45 The most health producing ethical decision many Colorado hospitals could make is to close their doors or merge.

46 *Value Change No. 6:* You cannot say "yes" to new needs to health care, unless you also say "no."

47 There is a yin and yang to the issue of access: The issue is part expansion (people into the system) and part contraction (what is covered). We must expand the who and limit the what; we must give with one hand and take away with the other.

48 Access to health care could be a fiscal black hole into which we could pour unlimited societal resources. If we are going to grant universal access, we must put limits on what is covered. Health care is infinitely expandable.

49 It is estimated that in any given month:

Approximately three-fourths of the population have an acute or chronic illness that leads to some action such as the restriction of activity or the taking of medication. Of these persons who report an illness during the month, approximately one-third seek medical consultation. Although, in general, illnesses that occur more dramatically or that cause greater discomfort or restriction of activity are more likely to lead to medical care, there is substantial overlap between the illnesses of treated and untreated persons.

50   While all politicians and many health care experts avoid the subject, increasingly society is recognizing a new world of limts:

Plainly, a positive right of access must be a limited right. Society is obliged only to provide basic care, not everything that medicine can offer. Defining basic care sets the moral limits of what government must provide or subsidize.

51   David Hadorn observes:

As costs continue to escalate out of control, nothing is more certain than that an increasing number of patients will be forced to go without potentially life-extending or quality of life-enhancing treatments.

Preister further adds:

While everyone ought to have access to health care this does not require univeral access to all potentially beneficial care. No society can afford to provide every service of potential benefit to everyone in need.

52   Thus, the easy part of the access question is arranging access. The hard part is defining "access to what" and figuring out how to pay for the new access.
53   A world of universal access is a world of choices and trade offs.

Using resources for one patient necessarily means that fewer resources will be available to treat others.

54   We are thus left, in this new and strange world, with the task of deciding not what is "beneficial" to a patient (which is a medical decision), but what is "appropriate" or "cost effective" (which is partly a social economic and a fairness decision). We shall have to balance quality of life with quantity of life, costs and benefits; preventive medicine versus curative medicine. We are, unfortunately but realistically, into prioritizing medicine. Medicine will never be the same.
55   Once we admit that we cannot pay for everything, we must ask ourselves not only what does a patient need, but how do we spend our resources to buy the maximum health for the largest number of citizens? This will inevitably impinge on a physician's judgement on what is the best medical treatment for an individual patient; when and where to admit patients to hospitals and when to discharge; under what conditions and symptoms are certain diagnostic or therapeutic procedures appropriate; and what prescriptions are appropriate under certain circumstances. It is the world of DRG writ large.
56   If the key to expansion of coverage is a matter of values so also the key to defining "appropriate" or "basic" healthcare is larely a matter of values. The access question shifts the question from *who* is covered to *what* is covered.
57   This is an ethical earthquake to existing medical values. Providers in America have been trained to monomaniacally focus only on the patient. In the new world of access:

Providers should not do everything that may benefit an individual patient, since doing so may interfere with the ability of other patients to obtain basic services; rather, providers should treat each patient with a full range of resources as is compatible with treating patients yet to come.

58 The illusion of unlimited resources has been very counter productive for America. Once we admit that resources are limited, a whole new dialogue emerges. When we recognize that we cannot do everything we start to ask: What do we do to maximize the health of the community? Both individuals and the community are important, but the emphasis shifts from individual centered to community centered.

59 I end with another parable, but it is also a true story. Harvey Cushing, the famous surgeon and after whom the Cushing Lectures are named, made an international reputation in his allegiance to quality. He badgered his profession to a higher standard of self-effacement, railed against the debasement of clinical skills and overemphasis on research and pursuit of personal gain. We honor him to this day because those were, and remain, important points. Yet, Harvey Cushing served as a surgeon during World War I and at Ypres. Although the Allied mortality was as much as 50,000 soldiers a day, not counting the wounded, Cushing refused to operate on any more than two patients a day, arguing that to do so would have lowered his standard of care for his patients—a standard which made sense in one time became strikingly insensitive, and I suggest even unethical, in another when confronted with a different reality. The ethical claims for professional autonomy based on such standards of professional ethics have had the effect of supporting widespread distribution inequities. These inequities are clearly a form of rationing that have been condoned implicitly by the professional ethics in the name of professional autonomy.

60 Many of the condemnations we hear today of perspective payment systems and how they will "ration" medicine contain a similar sense of unreality. The high standards are laudatory, but they should not be used as an excuse to not meet other pressing needs. High standards should never be used to make a problem worse. At some point, every ethical doctor has to lift their eyes from the patient in front of them and survey the needs of the whole battlefield.

61 America is right now at the beginning of a debate about the entire battlefield. Our system needs challenging. We have built up a health care system that better serves the needs of the providers than the public. We must substantially revamp our values and goals in health care.

62 We must move part of our existing emphasis:

Individual patient to population as a whole.

Acute care to chronic care.

Specialized care to primary care.

Institution based to ambulatory based.

Technology oriented to humanistically oriented.

Individual provider to team provider.

Cost unaware to cost aware.

Governed professionally to governed managerially.

63 We are spending millions of dollars on esoteric improvements at the margin in American medicine while spending pennies on the access problem where we could buy far more health. We give some people too much health care and others too little. We have money for Ecmo machines, but not prenatal care. We spend incredible amounts of money on kidney dialysis, but practically nothing on educating people to stop smoking and abusing alcohol. We have far too many MRI machines, but 30 percent of the women in America give birth without adequate prenatal care in their first trimester.

64   Our duty lies both to the individual and population; to the patient and to all citizens. In a world of unconstrained demands and limited resources, we must adapt ourselves to the new world of medical ethics.

Three Speeches of Apology

◆ *Bill Clinton* ◆

A speech of apology (an *apologia*) is a speech of personal defense of character. The questioning or criticism of a person's motives, ethics of behavior, or reputation is qualitatively different than the challenging of an individual's policies or ideas. An attack on a person's character, on his or her values as a human being, seems to demand a direct response that seeks to purify the speaker's personal image.

According to B. L. Ware and Wil Linkugel (*Quarterly Journal of Speech*, October 1973, pp. 273–283), apologetic discourse commonly involves one or more of four main strategies: denial, bolstering, differentiation, and transcendence. *Denial* involves explicit denial of an alleged negative action or relationship and may also involve denial of conscious intent. In *bolstering* the speaker uses reinforcement of or identification with a value, action, or viewpoint that the audience views positively in order to counterbalance the alleged negative behavior. In *differentiation* the speaker uses separation or differentiation of the alleged negative behavior from some broader context to show that the behavior was not typical or normal and thus should

be viewed less negatively. In *transcendence* the speaker moves the audience's focus away from the specific alleged negative behavior toward some larger, more abstract, more important, more positively valued need or issue that demands immediate attention.

In his book, *Accounts, Excuses, and Apologies* (State University of New York Press, 1995), William Benoit discusses numerous additional strategies including attacking the accuser, corrective action, and mortification. The speaker *attacks the accuser* by claiming negative behavior on the part of the accuser; the accuser is just as bad, if not worse, than the accused. The strategy of *corrective action* involves the speaker promising to mend his or her ways and make changes so that the alleged behavior will not happen again. In *mortification* the speaker admits personal responsibility or blame and asks forgiveness. The speaker may express regret, say he or she is sorry, or apologize to those harmed.

The general issue of Bill Clinton's ethical and moral character was made a central focus of the national news media throughout his campaigns and two terms as President. One major

◆ The texts of these speeches were obtained from President Clinton's White House web page.

component of that issue was the so-called Monica Lewinsky Affair. Three times in January 1998 President Clinton claimed he had not had sexual relations, a sexual relationship, or any improper relationship with Monica Lewinsky, a White House intern. But seven months later, in a nationally televised address from the White House on August 17, Clinton admitted he had engaged in an "inappropriate relationship." As you read this first apologetic speech, note the strategies he employs to defend his character and image. He employs mortification or self-blame in paragraphs 3 and 5 by admitting a relationship and having misled people. How does he characterize or label his actions, his responsibility, and his regret? Also in paragraph 5 he uses bolstering by identifying with motivations that he hopes many citizens would empathize with and understand as typically human. In paragraph 4 he uses denial to block accusations of encouraging perjury or obstruction of justice. Clinton attacks the accuser in paragraphs 6 and 7 by condemning the wide-ranging investigations of independent counsel Kenneth Starr. How reasonable are the grounds upon which he condemns Starr's investigations? Clinton makes a major appeal in paragraph 8 that the matter now solely is a private matter. To what degree would you agree? How, also in paragraph 8, does he make minimal use of the corrective action strategy? Finally, in paragraphs 9 and 10, he employs transcendence. How does he attempt to shift audience focus away from his specific behavior toward larger and more important issues?

Commentators and editorialists in the news media faulted Clinton's August 17 speech on several grounds. Some said he spent too much time on vindictive attacks on Kenneth Starr and devoted not enough time and detail to admitting blame and expressing remorse. Others emphasized that he never did say he was "sorry" and he did not specifically apologize to others he misled such as Congress, his staff and advisors, political supporters, and the American public. Democratic U.S. Senators, such as Joe Lieberman, Daniel Patrick Moynihan, and Bob Kerrey, publicly criticized Clinton's behavior, his insufficient expression of sorrow, and his lack of recogni-

tion of his influence as a role model for American youth. However, a series of public opinion polls taken shortly following the speech indicated that a majority of those surveyed believed he had done enough to explain his relationship with Lewinsky and believed that it was a private matter (*Washington Post National Weekly Edition,* August 24, 1998, pp. 4, 8–12).

After the August 17 speech, a political science professor at Rutgers University, Ross Baker, noted that a single speech rarely pulls a politician out of a crisis. Rather, said Baker, Clinton needed to follow "the repentance-sinner stage" over a period of time to recover the trust of citizens (*Washington Post National Weekly Edition,* August 24, 1998, p. 8). Indeed Clinton gradually seemed to recognize that a series of messages of contrition and redemption were needed. At a September 2 news conference in Moscow, Russia, he expressed his "profound regret to all who were hurt and all who were involved." At a September 4 news conference in Dublin, Ireland, he said he was "sorry" about his "bad mistake." On September 9 he told a Florida audience that he had let them, his family, and his country down but was "trying to make it right." Most of the day on September 10 Clinton used to apologize to his Cabinet members and his staff.

On the morning of September 11, 1998, at a routinely scheduled White House breakfast for religious leaders televised on CNN, Clinton presented a second, more extensive, speech of apology. His use of mortification is spread throughout the speech (3, 4, 6, 11). How does he describe his sense of blame and thus attempt to redeem his character? Note that the word "sorry" is not Clinton's directly but part of a quotation he uses. Similarly, the strategy of corrective action occurs throughout the speech (5, 6, 11, 12). What corrective actions does he specify and how adequate would you judge them to be? In the middle of the speech (7), how does he use transcendence as a strategy? How does he employ bolstering (9, 13–14) to identify with actions and ideas positively valued by the audience? Where does he make only a brief and indirect attack on his accuser, Kenneth Starr? In what way might his mention that he did not use speechwriters in preparation (2) work to increase his ethos or credibility? Finally, how appropriately and adequately does he recognize his role-model function (10)?

On December 11, 1998, a short time before members of the House Judiciary Committee started voting that day on possible articles of impeachment, Bill Clinton gave his third speech of apology, a brief statement presented in the White House Rose Garden. Although short, it again included extensive and direct expressions of sorrow, shame, and remorse. This use of mortification occurs throughout the speech (1, 2, 4, 6). What choices of language does he employ to underscore the intensity of his self-blame? In the conclusion, he employs transcendence to shift audience focus away from his specific actions toward larger and more important matters (8). What words does he choose to stress this point? This speech also is an appeal for the House, and perhaps later the Senate, to defeat impeachment attempts and to consider a formal but less harsh censure of him (5, 7). What word choices and comparison does he use to strengthen this appeal?

◆ ◆ ◆

Statement by the President. August 17, 1998

1 THE PRESIDENT: Good evening. This afternoon in this room, from this chair, I testified before the Office of Independent Counsel and the grand jury. I answered their questions truthfully, including questions about my private life—questions no American citizen would ever want to answer.

2 Still I must take complete responsibility for all my actions, both public and private. And that is why I am speaking to you tonight.

3 As you know, in a deposition in January I was asked questions about my relationship with Monica Lewinsky. While my answers were legally accurate, I did not volunteer information. Indeed, I did have a relationship with Ms. Lewinsky that was not appropriate. In fact, it was wrong. It constituted a critical lapse in judgment and a personal failure on my part for which I am solely and completely responsible.

4 But I told the grand jury today, and I say to you now, that at no time did I ask anyone to lie, to hide or destroy evidence, or to take any other unlawful action.

5 I know that my public comments and my silence about this matter gave a false impression. I misled people, including even my wife. I deeply regret that. I can only tell you I was motivated by many factors: first, by a desire to protect myself from the embarrassment of my own conduct. I was also very concerned about protecting my family. The fact that these questions were being asked in a politically inspired lawsuit which has since been dismissed was a consideration, too.

6 In addition, I had real and serious concerns about an independent counsel investigation that began with private business dealings 20 years ago—dealings, I might add, about which an independent federal agency found no evidence of any wrongdoing by me or my wife over two years ago.

7 The independent counsel investigation moved on to my staff and friends, then into my private life, and now the investigation itself is under investigation. This has gone on too long, cost too much, and hurt too many innocent people.

8 Now this matter is between me, the two people I love most—my wife and our daughter—and our God. I must put it right, and I am prepared to do whatever it takes to do so. Nothing is more important to me personally. But it is private. And I intend to reclaim my family life for my family. It's nobody's business but ours. Even Presidents have private lives.

9 It is time to stop the pursuit of personal destruction and the prying into private lives, and get on with our national life. Our country has been distracted by this matter for too long. And I take my responsibility for my part in all of this; that is all I can do. Now it is time—in fact, it is past time—to move on. We have important work to do—real opportunities to seize, real problems to solve, real security matters to face.

10   And so, tonight, I ask you to turn away from the spectacle of the past seven months, to repair the fabric of our national discourse and to return our attention to all the challenges and all the promise of the next American century.

11   Thank you for watching, and good night.

Remarks by the President at Religious Leaders Breakfast. September 11, 1998

1   THE PRESIDENT: Thank you very much, ladies and gentlemen. Welcome to the White House and to this day to which Hillary and the Vice President and I look forward so much every year.

2   This is always an important day for our country, for the reasons that the Vice President said. It is an unusual and, I think, unusually important day today. I may not be quite as easy with my words today as I have been in years past, and I was up rather late last night thinking about and praying about what I ought to say today. And rather unusual for me, I actually tried to write it down. So if you will forgive me, I will do my best to say what it is I want to say to you—and I may have to take my glasses out to read my own writing.

3   First, I want to say to all of you that, as you might imagine, I have been on quite a journey these last few weeks to get to the end of this, to the rock bottom truth of where I am and where we all are. I agree with those who have said that in my first statement after I testified I was not contrite enough. I don't think there is a fancy way to say that I have sinned.

4   It is important to me that everybody who has been hurt know that the sorrow I feel is genuine: first and most important, my family; also my friends, my staff, my Cabinet, Monica Lewinsky and her family, and the American people. I have asked all for their forgiveness.

5   But I believe that to be forgiven, more than sorrow is required—at least two more things. First, genuine repentance—a determination to change and to repair breaches of my own making. I have repented. Second, what my bible calls a "broken spirit"; an understanding that I must have God's help to be the person that I want to be; a willingness to give the very forgiveness I seek; a renunciation of the pride and the anger which cloud judgment, lead people to excuse and compare and to blame and complain.

6   Now, what does all this mean for me and for us? First, I will instruct my lawyers to mount a vigorous defense, using all available appropriate arguments. But legal language must not obscure the fact that I have done wrong. Second, I will continue on the path of repentance, seeking pastoral support and that of other caring people so that they can hold me accountable for my own commitment.

7   Third, I will intensify my efforts to lead our country and the world toward peace and freedom, prosperity and harmony, in the hope that with a broken spirit and a still strong heart I can be used for greater good, for we have many blessings and many challenges and so much work to do.

8   In this, I ask for your prayers and for your help in healing our nation. And though I cannot move beyond or forget this—indeed, I must always keep it as a caution light in my life—it is very important that our nation move forward.

9   I am very grateful for the many, many people—clergy and ordinary citizens alike—who have written me with wise counsel. I am profoundly grateful for the support of so many Americans who somehow through it all seem to still know that I care about them a great deal, that I care about their problems and their dreams. I am grateful for those who have stood by me and who say that in this case and many others, the bounds of presidency have been excessively and unwisely invaded. That may be. Nevertheless, in this case, it may be a blessing, because I still sinned. And if my repentance is genuine and sustained, and if I can maintain both a broken spirit and a strong heart, then good can come of this for our country as well as for me and my family. (Applause.)

10   The children of this country can learn in a profound way that integrity is important and self-ishness is wrong, but God can change us and make us strong at the broken places. I want to embody those lessons for the children of this country—for that little boy in Florida who came up to me and said that he wanted to grow up and be President and to be just like me. I want the parents of all the children in America to be able to say that to their children.

11   A couple of days ago when I was in Florida a Jewish friend of mine gave me this liturgy book called, "Gates of Repentance." And there was this incredible passage from the Yom Kippur liturgy. I would like to read it to you: "Now is the time for turning. The leaves are beginning to turn from green to red to orange. The birds are beginning to turn and are heading once more toward the south. The animals are beginning to turn to storing their food for the winter. For leaves, birds and animals, turning comes instinctively. But for us, turning does not come so easily. It takes an act of will for us to make a turn. It means breaking old habits. It means admitting that we have been wrong, and this is never easy. It means losing face. It means starting all over again. And this is always painful. It means saying I am sorry. It means recognizing that we have the ability to change. These things are terribly hard to do.

12   But unless we turn, we will be trapped forever in yesterday's ways. Lord help us to turn, from callousness to sensitivity, from hostility to love, from pettiness to purpose, from envy to contentment, from carelessness to discipline, from fear to faith. Turn us around, O Lord, and bring us back toward you. Revive our lives as at the beginning, and turn us toward each other, Lord, for in isolation there is no life."

13   I thank my friend for that. I thank you for being here. I ask you to share my prayer that God will search me and know my heart, try me and know my anxious thoughts, see if there is any hurtful-ness in me, and lead me toward the life everlasting. I ask that God give me a clean heart, let me walk by faith and not sight.

14   I ask once again to be able to love my neighbor—all my neighbors—as my self, to be an instrument of God's peace; to let the words of my mouth and the meditations of my heart and, in the end, the work of my hands, be pleasing. This is what I wanted to say to you today.

15   Thank you. God bless you. (Applause.)

Statement by the President. December 11, 1998

1   THE PRESIDENT: As anyone close to me knows, for months I have been grappling with how best to reconcile myself to the American people, to acknowledge my own wrongdoing and still to maintain my focus on the work of the presidency.

2   Others are presenting my defense on the facts, the law, and the Constitution. Nothing I can say now can add to that. What I want the American people to know, what I want the Congress to know is that I am profoundly sorry for all I have done wrong in words and deeds. I never should have misled the country, the Congress, my friends or my family. Quite simply, I gave into my shame.

3   I have been condemned by my accusers with harsh words. And while it's hard to hear yourself called deceitful and manipulative, I remember Ben Franklin's admonition that our critics are our friends, for they do show us our faults.

4   Mere words cannot fully express the profound remorse I feel for what our country is going through, and for what members of both parties in Congress are now forced to deal with.

5   These past months have been a tortuous process of coming to terms with what I did. I under-stand that accountability demands consequences, and I'm prepared to accept them. Painful though the condemnation of the Congress would be, it would pale in comparison to the consequences of the pain I have caused my family. There is no greater agony.

6 Like anyone who honestly faces the shame of wrongful conduct, I would give anything to go back and undo what I did. But one of the painful truths I have to live with is the reality that that is simply not possible. An old and dear friend of mine recently sent me the wisdom of a poet, who wrote, "The moving finger writes, and having writ moves on. Nor all your piety, nor wit shall lure it back to cancel half a line. Nor all your tears wash out a word of it."

7 So nothing—not piety, nor tears, nor wit, nor torment—can alter what I have done. I must make my peace with that. I must also be at peace with the fact that the public consequences of my actions are in the hands of the American people and their representatives in the Congress. Should they determine that my errors of word and deed require their rebuke and censure, I am ready to accept that.

8 Meanwhile, I will continue to do all I can to reclaim the trust of the American people and to serve them well. We must all return to the work, the vital work, of strengthening our nation for the new century. Our country has wonderful opportunities and daunting challenges ahead. I intend to seize those opportunities and meet those challenges with all the energy and ability, and strength God has given me.

9 That is simply all I can do—the work of the American people.

10 Thank you very much.

President Clinton and the Independent Counsel's Investigation

◆ Joe Lieberman ◆

After President Clinton's August 17, 1998 first speech of apology, dissatisfaction with the inadequacy of tone and remorse in that speech steadily grew among Democrats. Finally, on September 3, 1998, Joe Lieberman, the second-term Senator from Connecticut, and a man widely respected by both political parties for his integrity, reasonableness, and candor, delivered on the floor of the Senate what *Newsweek* (September 14, 1998, p. 28) termed "a blistering 24 minute sermon" that "excoriated the president over the Lewinsky matter." Political columnist Charles Kruthammer judged it "the only full-scale serious speech on this issue yet offered in either house of Congress" (*Chicago Tribune*, November 30, 1998, Sec. 1, p. 17). A *Chicago Tribune* editorial (September 5, 1998, Sec. 1, p. 22) noted that "eloquence—rhetoric infused with wisdom, compassion, and conviction" was rare in the Senate. But the editorial argued that Lieberman "delivered one of the most eloquent—and courageous—speeches the Senate has heard in many years, and one the country desperately needed to hear." Because Lieberman spoke not about

◆ The text of this speech was taken from the U.S. Senate Internet web site of Senator Lieberman.

legality but about "duty, honor, and morality," the speech was a denunciation of Clinton "more powerful than any legal indictment ever could be."

At the outset (1) and in several other places (4, 20), Lieberman makes clear his personal perspective. He offers a reluctant and difficult judgment as a friend and supporter of Bill Clinton and recognizes that no person, himself included, is perfect. Nevertheless, the speech clearly focuses on value judgments, not legal judgments, of Clinton's behavior (6, 7). Indeed Lieberman declares that Clinton's personal affair and his lies were immoral, harmful, and wrong (11, 24). He condemns the hypocrisy of Clinton's actions (15) and rejects Clinton's attempt to use the excuse of typically human motivations to lessen the blame for his deceptions (16).

Lieberman declares that his speech is motivated by responsibility to his constituents and to his conscience (6) and note how he employs the stylistic resource of alliteration to underscore his point. Also he is motivated by deep disappointment and anger at being personally betrayed (3) and because of more general damage to the country (4).

At length Lieberman argues that the President must be held accountable to higher values and ethics than other citizens (21). As supporting arguments leading to this conclusion, first he contends that any President's private life is a proper matter of public concern (8–10). Second, he argues that the President may provide a unique role-model for American youth, a point Clinton agreed with in his second speech of apology. To what extent, and why, do you agree with Lieberman that a President should be held to higher standards, that the President's private life is a public matter, and that the President serves a significant role-model function?

Lieberman proves amazingly accurate (18, 26) in his warning that Clinton's deceptions perhaps had fatally destroyed his credibility and trust on policy issues. Cynics argued that after the first (August 17) and third (December 11) speeches of apology, Clinton had ordered air attacks on international terrorist bases (August 20) and on Iraq (December 16) as tactics to divert public attention from his personal failings.

Lieberman employs parallel structure (22) to highlight three reasons why Clinton's August 17 speech was a failure. He concludes that Clinton's admission of responsibility in that speech simply was inadequate (23). At the time of Lieberman's speech, does he favor rebuke/censure or impeachment/resignation for Clinton (24–26)?

In order to prove or to clarify various points, Lieberman relies heavily on the use of expert testimony from three political science scholars of the presidency and two revered past presidents (9, 18, 21, 28). How well does his usage meet the standard tests for reasonableness of expert testimony? Analyze, also, the degree of effectiveness Lieberman demonstrates in strengthening his concluding appeal through the stylistic resources of alliteration and antithesis (29).

In the Senate, immediately following Lieberman's speech, Senators Daniel Patrick Moynihan and Bob Kerrey spoke to echo most of Lieberman's condemnations. On September 4, the day after Lieberman's speech, at a news conference in Dublin, Ireland, President Clinton said he was "sorry" about his "bad mistake." And at a number of places in his second speech of apology on September 11, Clinton seemed to be responding to some of the criticisms initiated by Lieberman.

◆   ◆   ◆

1   Mr. President, I rise today to make a most difficult and distasteful statement, for me probably the most difficult statement I have made on this floor in my ten years in the Senate.

2   On August 17th, President Clinton testified before a grand jury convened by the Independent Counsel and then talked to the American people about his relationship with Monica Lewinsky, a former White House intern. He told us that the relationship was "not appropriate," that it was "wrong," and

that it was "a critical lapse of judgment and a personal failure" on his part. In addition, after seven months of denying that he had engaged in a sexual relationship with Ms. Lewinsky, the President admitted that his "public comments . . . about this matter gave a false impression." He said, "I misled people."

3   My immediate reaction to this statement was deep disappointment and personal anger. I was disappointed because the President of the United States had just confessed to engaging in an extramarital affair with a young woman in his employ and to willfully deceiving the nation about his conduct. I was personally angry because President Clinton had by his disgraceful behavior jeopardized his Administration's historic record of accomplishment, much of which grew out of the principles and programs that he and I and many others had worked on together in the New Democratic movement. I was also angry because I was one of the many people who had said over the preceding seven months that if the President clearly and explicitly denies the allegations against him, then, of course, I believe him.

4   Since that Monday night, I have not commented on this matter publicly. I thought I had an obligation to consider the President's admissions more objectively, less personally, and to try to put them in a clearer perspective. And I felt I owed that much to President Clinton, for whom I have great affection and admiration, and who I truly believe has worked tirelessly to make life tangibly better in so many ways for so many Americans.

5   But the truth is, after much reflection, my feelings of disappointment and anger have not dissipated. Except now these feelings have gone beyond my personal dismay to a larger, graver sense of loss for our country, a reckoning of the damage that the President's conduct has done to the proud legacy of his presidency, and ultimately an accounting of the impact of his actions on our democracy and its moral foundations.

6   The implications for our country are so serious that I feel a responsibility to my constituents in Connecticut, as well as to my conscience, to voice my concerns forthrightly and publicly, and I can think of no more appropriate place to do so than the floor of this great body. I have chosen to speak particularly at this time, before the Independent Counsel files his report, because while we do not know enough to answer the question of whether there are legal consequences from the President's conduct, we do know enough to answer a separate and distinct set of questions about the moral consequences for our country.

7   I have come to this floor many times in the past to speak with my colleagues about my concerns, which are widely-held in this chamber and throughout the nation, that our society's standards are sinking, that our common moral code is deteriorating, and that our public life is coarsening. In doing so, I have specifically criticized leaders of the entertainment industry for the way they have used the enormous influence they wield to weaken our common values. And now because the President commands at least as much attention and exerts at least as much influence on our collective consciousness as any Hollywood celebrity or television show, it is hard to ignore the impact of the misconduct the President has admitted to on our children, our culture and our national character.

8   To begin with, I must respectfully disagree with the President's contention that his relationship with Monica Lewinsky and the way in which he misled us about it is "nobody's business but" his family's and that "even presidents have private lives," as he said. Whether he or we as a people think it fair or not, the reality in 1998 is that a president's private life is public. Contemporary news media standards will have it no other way. Surely this President was given fair warning of that by the amount of time the news media has dedicated to investigating his personal life during the 1992 campaign and in the years since.

9   But there is more to this than modern media intrusiveness. The President is not just the elected leader of our country, he is, as presidential scholar Clinton Rossiter observed, "the one-man distillation of the American people," and "the personal embodiment and representative of their dignity and majesty," as President Taft once said. So when his personal conduct is embarrassing, it is so not just for him and his family. It is embarrassing for us all as Americans.

10   The President is also a role model, who, because of his prominence and the moral authority that emanates from his office, sets standards of behavior for the people he serves. His duty, as the Rev. Nathan Baxter of the National Cathedral here in Washington said in a recent sermon, is nothing less than the stewardship of our values. So no matter how much the President or others may wish to "compartmentalize" the different spheres of his life, the inescapable truth is that the President's private conduct can and often does have profound public consequences.

11   In this case, the President apparently had extramarital relations with an employee half his age, and did so in the workplace, in vicinity of the Oval Office. Such behavior is not just inappropriate. It is immoral. And it is harmful, for it sends a message of what is acceptable behavior to the larger American family, particularly to our children, which is as influential as the negative messages communicated by the entertainment culture. If you doubt that, just ask America's parents about the intimate and often unseemly sexual questions their young children have been asking and discussing since the President's relationship with Ms. Lewinsky became public seven months ago.

12   I have had many of those conversations in recent days, and from that I can conclude that many parents feel much as I do, that something very sad and sordid has happened in American life when I cannot watch the news on television with my ten-year-old daughter any more.

13   This is unfortunately familiar territory for America's families in today's anything-goes culture, where sexual promiscuity is too often treated as just another lifestyle choice with little risk of adverse consequences. It is this mindset that has helped to threaten the stability and integrity of the family, which continues to be the most important unit of civilized society, the place where we raise our children and teach them to be responsible citizens, to develop and nurture their personal and moral faculties.

14   President Clinton is well aware of this threat and the broad public concern about it. He has used the bully pulpit over the course of his presidency to eloquently and effectively call for the renewal of our common values, particularly the principle of personal responsibility, and our common commitment to family. And he has spoken out admirably against sexual promiscuity among teenagers in clear terms of right and wrong, emphasizing the consequences involved.

15   All of which makes the President's misconduct so confusing and so damaging. The President's relationship with Ms. Lewinsky not only contradicted the values he has publicly embraced over the past six years. It has compromised his moral authority at a time when Americans of every political persuasion agree that the decline of the family is one of the most pressing problems we as a nation are facing.

16   Nevertheless, I believe the President could have lessened the harm his relationship with Ms. Lewinsky has caused if he had acknowledged his mistake and spoken with candor about it to the American people shortly after it became public in January. But as we now know, he chose not to do this. His deception is particularly troubling because it was not just a reflexive and understandably human act of concealment to protect himself and his family from the "embarrassment of his own conduct," as he put it, when he was confronted with it in his deposition in the Paula Jones case, but rather the intentional and premeditated decision to do so.

17   In choosing this path, I fear that the President has undercut the efforts of millions of American parents who are naturally trying to instill in our children the value of honesty. As most any mother or father knows, kids have a singular ability to detect double standards. So we can safely assume that it will be that much more difficult to convince our sons and daughters of the importance of telling the truth when the most powerful man in the nation evades it. Many parents I have spoken with in Connecticut confirm this unfortunate consequence.

18   The President's intentional and consistent misstatements may also undercut the trust that the American people have in his word, which would have substantial ramifications for his presidency. Under the Constitution, as presidential scholar Richard Neustadt has noted, the President's ultimate source of authority, particularly his moral authority, is the power to persuade, to mobilize public opinion and build consensus behind a common agenda, and at this the President has been extraordinarily effective. But that power hinges on the President's support among the American people and their faith and confidence in his motivations, his agenda, and ultimately his personal integrity. As Teddy Roosevelt once explained, "My power vanishes into thin air the instant that my fellow citizens who are straight and honest cease to believe that I represent them and fight for what is straight and honest; that is all the strength I have."

19   Sadly, with his deception, President Clinton may have weakened the great power and strength of which President Roosevelt spoke. I know this is a concern that many of my colleagues share, that the President has hurt his credibility and therefore, perhaps, his chances of moving his agenda forward. But I believe that the harm the President's actions have caused extend beyond the political arena. I am afraid that the misconduct the President has admitted may be reinforcing one of the most destructive messages being delivered by our popular culture—namely that values are essentially fungible. And I am afraid that his misconduct may help to blur some of the most important bright lines of right and wrong left in our society.

20   I do not raise these concerns as self-righteous criticism. I know that the President is far from alone in the wrongdoing he has admitted. We as humans are all imperfect. We are all sinners. Many have betrayed a loved one, and most of us have told lies. Members of Congress have certainly been guilty of such behavior, as have some previous Presidents. We try to understand the profound complexity and difficulty of personal relationships, which gives us pause before passing judgement on them. We all fall short of the standards our best values set for us. Certainly I do.

21   But the President, by virtue of the office he sought and was elected to, has traditionally been held to a higher standard. This is as it should be, because the American president is not, as I quoted earlier, just the one-man distillation of the American people but the most powerful person in the world, and as such the consequences of misbehavior by a President, even private misbehavior, are much greater than that of an average citizen, a CEO, or even a Senator. That is what I believe presidential scholar James Barber, in his book, *The Presidential Character,* was getting at when he wrote that the public demands "a sense of legitimacy from, and in, the Presidency. . . . There is more to this than dignity, more than propriety. The President is expected to personify our betterness in an inspiring way, to express in what he does and is (not just what he says) a moral idealism which, in much of the public mind, is the very opposite of politics."

22   Just as the American people are demanding of their leaders, though, they are also fundamentally fair and forgiving, which is why I was so hopeful the President could begin to repair the damage done with his address to the nation on the 17th. But like so many others, I came away feeling that he for reasons that are thoroughly human had squandered a great opportunity that night. He failed to clearly articulate to the American people that he recognized how significant and consequential his wrongdoing was and how badly he felt about it. He also failed to show that he understood his behavior has diminished the office he holds and the country he serves, and that it is inconsistent with the mainstream

American values that he has advanced as President. And he failed to acknowledge that while Mr. Starr, Ms. Lewinsky, Mrs. Tripp, and the news media have all contributed to the crisis we now face, his presidency would not be in peril if it had not been for the behavior he himself described as "wrong" and "inappropriate."

23   Because the conduct the President has admitted to was so serious and his assumption of responsibility on August 17th so inadequate, the last three weeks have been dominated by a cacophony of media and political voices calling for impeachment, or resignation, or censure, while a lesser chorus implores us to "move on" and get this matter behind us.

24   Appealing as the latter option may be to many people who are understandably weary of this crisis, the transgressions the President has admitted to are too consequential for us to walk away and leave the impression for our children and for our posterity that what President Clinton acknowledges he did within the White House is acceptable behavior for our nation's leader. On the contrary, as I have said at length today, it is wrong and unacceptable and should be followed by some measure of public rebuke and accountability. We in Congress—elected representatives of all the American people—are surely capable institutionally of expressing such disapproval through a resolution of reprimand or censure of the President for his misconduct, but it is premature to do so, as my colleagues of both parties seem to agree, until we have received the report of the Independent Counsel and the White House's response to it.

25   In the same way, it seems to me, talk of impeachment and resignation at this time is unjust and unwise. It is unjust because we do not know enough in fact and will not until the Independent Counsel reports and the White House responds to conclude whether we have crossed the high threshold our Constitution rightly sets for overturning the results of a popular election in our democracy and bringing on the national trauma of removing an incumbent President from office. For now, in fact, all we know for certain is what the President acknowledged on August 17th. The rest is rumor, speculation, or hearsay—much less than is required by Members of the House and Senate in the dispatch of the solemn responsibilities that the Constitution gives us in such circumstances.

26   I believe that talk of impeachment and resignation now is unwise because it ignores the reality that while the Independent Counsel proceeds with his investigation, the President is still our nation's leader, our Commander-in-Chief. Economic uncertainty and other problems here at home, as well as the fiscal and political crises in Russia and Asia and the growing threats posed by Iraq, North Korea, and worldwide terrorism, all demand the President's focused leadership. For that reason, while the legal process moves forward, I believe it is important that we provide the President with the time and space and support he needs to carry out his most important duties and protect our national interest and security.

27   That time and space may also give the President additional opportunities to accept personal responsibility for his behavior, to rebuild public trust in his leadership, to recommit himself to the values of opportunity, responsibility and community that brought him to office, and to act to heal the wounds to our national character.

28   In the meantime, as the debate on this matter proceeds, and as the investigation continues, we would all be advised to heed the wisdom of Abraham Lincoln's second annual address to Congress in 1862. With the nation at war with itself, Lincoln warned, "If there ever could be a proper time for mere catch arguments, that time is surely not now. In times like the present, men should utter nothing for which they would not willingly be responsible through time and eternity."

29   I believe we are at such a time again today. With so much at stake, we too must resist the impulse toward "catch arguments" and reflex reactions. Let us proceed in accordance with our nation's traditional moral compass, yes, but in a manner that is fair and at a pace that is deliberate and responsible. Let us as a nation honestly confront the damage that the President's actions over the last seven months have caused, but not to the exclusion of the good that his leadership has done over the past six years nor at the expense of our common interests as Americans. And let us be guided by the conscience of the Constitution, which calls on us to place the common good above any partisan or personal interest, as we now work together to resolve this serious challenge to our democracy. Thank you.

Chapter Six

Speeches That Create Concern for Problems

The Nature and Importance of Speeches That Create Concern for Problems

Social existence gives rise to problems that threaten the perpetuation of the group and the welfare of its members. A problem might be described as a defect, difficulty, barrier, need, threat, state of dissatisfaction, or undesirable situation that people perceive as requiring removal, adaptation, or solution. The ability of groups and individuals to perceive and understand the nature and importance of the problems they face is one measure of a society's maturity and strength. If a society is unable to comprehend the significance of its problems, it has little chance of solving them.

Speakers often address audiences for the primary purpose of creating concern for problems. Whereas speeches advocating values are designed to develop value standards and value judgments in the minds of listeners, speeches trying to create concern for problems focus on specific social situations calling for remedial action. The mayor of a large city, for example, may seek to arouse public concern about gang violence. A sociologist may attempt to create concern for teen pregnancies. A politician may try to arouse sympathy for the plight of the "working poor."

Sometimes a speaker focuses on a problem merely to generate audience concern. Other times, speakers identify problems as a prelude to advocating specific policies or solutions. In any case, we face potential personal and public problems at virtually every turn: alcoholism, drug abuse, racial conflict, unemployment, suicide, pollution, discrimination against minorities, political deception, deceptive advertising, automobile accidents, and rising crime rates.

While the proposition of fact asserts that something is true or false and the proposition of value asserts that something has or lacks merit, the speech attempting to create concern for a problem asserts that specific social conditions should be perceived or defined as problems. Consider the following examples:

Proposition A: Medicare fraud is a serious problem nationwide.

Proposition B: The national debt is America's most pressing social problem.

Proposition C: All parents should be concerned by the increased availability of hardcore pornography.

Proposition D: Student alcohol abuse is a serious campus problem.

Proposition E: The depiction of violence on television programs oriented toward children merits public concern.

Proposition F: The increasing rate of traffic fatalities on Highway 12 warrants action by the state legislature.

Although the speech that creates concern for a problem usually depends on the affirmation of subsidiary propositions of fact and value, the basic purpose of such a speech is to invite attention to a problem needing solution.

Criteria for Evaluating Speeches That Create Concern for Problems

1. Has the speaker presented a compelling view of the nature of the problem?

The philosopher John Dewey emphasized the importance of this criterion when he wrote: "The essence of critical thinking is suspended judgement; and the essence of this suspense is inquiry to determine the nature of the problem before proceeding to attempts at its solution." To depict compellingly the nature of a problem, a speaker must prove that a certain state of affairs actually does exist. The nature is explained by focusing on the major elements of the problem and on its symptoms or outward manifestations.

Naturally a complete view of a problem includes a thorough exploration of the causes (the contributing influences) which combine to produce the state of affairs. Some problems are rooted in defective structures, personnel, or policies; other problems stem from inadequate goals, standards, and principles; still others derive from "outside" threats, opponents, or enemies. Remember, also, that social problems seldom are the result of a single cause. Rather, although one contributing factor may be described as the primary or the immediate cause, several contributing factors usually combine in primary-secondary and immediate-remote relationships. Finally, a compelling view often stems from describing the intensity and/or the widespread scope of the problem.

In exploring the nature of a problem, speakers may assume the role of social informant. When they do, the success of their speeches is governed, in part, by the same constraints imposed on speakers seeking to increase understanding. They must choose those supporting materials that best demonstrate the nature of the problem: analogy and illustration, expert testimony and factual example, description, definition, and narration. Their messages are subject to the same criteria suggested in Chapter 3: Is the information communicated accurately, completely, and with unity? Does the speaker make the information meaningful for the audience? Does the speaker create audience interest in the information presented? Has the speaker shown the audience that the information is important?

In a speech called "Mingled Blood," Ralph Zimmerman, a college student and a hemophiliac, chose to use definition and description to illuminate the nature of hemophilia:

What is this thing called hemophilia? Webster defines it as "a tendency, usually hereditary, to profuse bleeding even from slight wounds." Dr. Armand J. Quick, Professor of Biochemistry at Marquette

University and a recognized world authority on this topic, defines it as "a prothrombin consumption time of 8 to 13 seconds." Normal time is 15 seconds. Now do you know what hemophilia is? . . .

What does it really mean to be a hemophiliac? The first indication comes in early childhood when a small scratch may bleed for hours. By the time the hemophiliac reaches school age, he begins to suffer from internal bleeding into muscles, joints, the stomach, the kidneys. This latter type is far more serious, for external wounds can usually be stopped in minutes with topical thromboplastin or a pressure bandage. But internal bleeding can be checked only by changes in the blood by means of transfusion or plasma injections. If internal bleeding into a muscle or joint goes unchecked repeatedly, muscle contraction and bone deformity inevitably result.

Along with increasing understanding about a problem, speakers also may affirm propositions of fact related to the problem. When speakers seek to prove propositions of fact in developing a compelling view of the problem, their efforts are subject to the same criteria suggested in Chapter 4: Has the speaker adequately assessed the proof requirements of the factual proposition? Has the speaker offered acceptable arguments in support of the proposition of fact? Has the speaker provided adequate evidence in support of the arguments?

2. Has the speaker shown the significance of the problem for the specific audience?

In addition to gaining an understanding of the nature of the problem, an audience must also be convinced that the problem has significance for them individually or collectively. Thus, value judgments must augment factual demonstrations. To demonstrate that Medicare fraud is extensive, a factual state of affairs must be established. To demonstrate that Medicare fraud poses a threat or is an undesirable situation, a judgment must be made in light of societal value standards. When a speaker affirms a proposition of value in showing the significance of a problem, the criteria suggested in Chapter 5 usually are relevant: Has the speaker demonstrated, or is it assumed by the audience, that he or she is a person of high credibility with respect to the proposition? Has the speaker advanced acceptable criteria for the assessment of the proposition? Has the speaker presented a fair view of what is being evaluated?

A problem is not really a problem to an audience until they perceive it as such. A situation may exist, and the audience may even know that it does, but in their eyes it remains nothing more than a lifeless fact until they view it as something that threatens or violates their interests and values. The members of an audience who have just been informed that many Native Americans endure substandard economic, educational, and health conditions may greet this knowledge with indifference. Although they may accept the situation as actual, they have not perceived it as a problem for themselves, either as individuals or as members of society.

In the background of public debate on societal issues are values which, according to Robert B. Reich, in his book, *Tales of a New America* (Times Books, 1987, p. 6), often are unstated, disguised, or taken for granted. These values, typically embodied in narrative "morality tales," influence when we "declare a fact to be a problem, how policy choices are characterized, how the debate is framed." Reich emphasizes: "Public problems don't exist 'out there.' They are not discrete facts or pieces of data awaiting discovery. They are the consequences of our shared values. Without a set of common moral assumptions we would have no way of identifying or categorizing problems and their possible solutions." Clearly a problem is "created" for an audience through their own perceptual processes. An audience labels something as a problem only when they perceive a strong link between a situation (real or imagined) and their relevant basic values which they see as undermined or threatened by that situation. Speakers and listeners employ values as standards to "define" something as a problem.

What approaches could a speaker use to show the significance of a problem? Ralph Zimmerman concluded that for many listeners it is sufficient to show that the problem brings danger, degradation, or suffering to those who directly experience it. Thus he depicted hemophilia as a source of suffering for those afflicted by it:

> I remember the three long years when I couldn't even walk because repeated hemorrhages had twisted my ankles and knees to pretzel-like forms. I remember being pulled to school in a wagon while other boys rode their bikes, and being pushed to my table. I remember sitting in the dark empty classroom by myself during recess while the others went out in the sun to run and play. And I remember the first terrible day at the big high school when I came on crutches and built-up shoes carrying my books in a sack around my neck. . . . And how well I remember the endless pounding, squeezing pain. When you seemingly drown in your own perspiration, when your teeth ache and bombs explode back of your eyeballs; when darkness and light fuse into one hue of gray; when day becomes night and night becomes day—time stands still—and all that matters is that ugly pain.

Although the most hardened pragmatist might state that the problem is of little social importance because when Zimmerman spoke in 1955 there were only 20,000 to 40,000 hemophiliacs in the United States, most Americans, committed to the worth of the individual human, would agree with Zimmerman that "if society can keep a hemophiliac alive until after adolescence, society has saved a member."

Guided by the actual nature of the problem and by relevant standards of ethics, a speaker may choose from a variety of potential strategies to create audience concern. Here we present a few such strategies, some adapted from the writings of Otis M. Walter. To show that the problem directly or indirectly harms the audience addressed (economically, socially, morally, physically) is an approach often used. Sometimes the problem is described as a unique, immediate, and pressing one demanding speedy recognition, diagnosis, and treatment; or it is described as an important contemporary manifestation of a timeless, continuing, larger problem always faced by humanity. Awareness of the problem may be emerging only gradually in the public consciousness and an audience might be urged to be in the vanguard of citizens concerned about it. On the other hand, the audience might be asked to join large numbers of fellow citizens who already recognize the problem.

Through use of historical examples, a speaker could argue that the failure of past societies to recognize the same or a similar problem caused them harm. Often this argument is embodied in an analogy to the decline and fall of the Roman Empire. The ways in which the problem contributes to or interacts with other societal problems could be demonstrated. If the problem is now in the embryonic stage, audiences could be warned that if it is not treated it will steadily worsen and perhaps become unsolvable. On occasion, a problem of concern for those affected takes on added significance when shown also to be working for the political or psychological advantage of our opponents or enemies. If the audience and the people harmed by the problem both have similar goals, values, needs, and fears, the audience could be made to feel that they might just as easily have experienced the problem themselves ("There but for the grace of God go I"). A speaker could show that the problem is acknowledged as vital by those whom the audience regards highly, such as public officials, statesmen, religious leaders, or experts on the subject.

The harmful economic, political, social, religious, or moral consequences of leaving the problem unsolved could be stressed. The problem could be shown as one of physical survival or security; or it could be shown as a problem threatening the enhancement or growth of the human spirit. A problem becomes of concern when it causes our society and its institutions to function at less than normal expected effectiveness. Sometimes the problem legitimately is described as stemming from conflict between an accepted but outmoded belief or value and existing circumstances. Finally, speakers often depict the problem as a high priority one—more crucial than most other problems faced by them or society.

Conclusion

In *Constructing the Political Spectacle,* Murray Edelman, a political scientist, reminds us: "Problems come into discourse and therefore into existence as reinforcements of ideologies, not simply because they are there or because they are important for well-being. They signify who are virtuous and useful and who are dangerous or inadequate, which actions will be rewarded and penalized." Problems, continues Edelman, "constitute people as subjects with particular kinds of aspirations, self-concepts, and fears, and they create beliefs about the relative importance of events and objects." Edelman concludes that problems "are critical in determining who exercise authority and who accept it. They construct areas of immunity from concern because those areas are not seen as a problem."

In our society people often seek to generate concern about problems, both great and small. At certain times the speaker's sole purpose is to set the stage for private thought or public discussion. At other times the speaker seeks to arouse interest in a problem to prepare the audience for accepting a specific solution. In either case, the speaker must present *a compelling view of the nature of the problem* and *the reasons that it is significant for the particular audience.*

FOR FURTHER READING

Dewey, John. *How We Think.* D. C. Heath, 1910, pp. 72–74. Concisely explains the importance of understanding the nature of problems.

Edelman, Murray. *Constructing the Political Spectacle.* University of Chicago Press, 1988. Chapter 2 probes the symbolic construction and ideological bases of social problems.

Herrick, James A. *Argumentation: Understanding and Shaping Arguments.* Gorsuch Scarisbrick, 1995. Chapter 10 discusses evaluating reasoning about causes of events and problems.

Jensen, J. Vernon. *Argumentation: Reasoning in Communication.* Van Nostrand, 1981. Chapter 4 suggests potential lines of argument basic to presenting the nature of a problem.

Walter, Otis M., and Scott, Robert L. *Thinking and Speaking.* 5th ed. Macmillan, 1984. Chapters 6 and 7 focus on suggestions for persuading about problems and causes.

Walter, Otis M. *Speaking Intelligently.* Macmillan, 1976, Chapters 2, 3, 4, and pp. 216–21. An exploration of the nature of societal problems and causes of such problems, along with suggested strategies for persuading about problems and causes.

Pesticides Speech

◆ *César Chávez* ◆

Noted speakers—whether they are presidents of large corporations, heads of public service organizations, major government officials, or leaders of social movements—frequently are called upon to speak on the same general topic to numerous but varied audiences. Politicians during major campaigns often face the same demand. One approach such speakers sometimes take is to present a "generic" speech—a speech containing the same general information and arguments regardless of audience but with opportunities in the speech for a modest amount of concrete adaptation to each specific audience. For one discussion of such generic or "stock" political campaign speeches, see Judith S. Trent and Robert V. Friedenberg, *Political Campaign Communication* 3rd ed. (Prager, 1995), pp. 156–160.

This speech by César Chávez is a generic speech. It contains standard or basic arguments on the topic suitable for diverse audiences and occasions with two places noted for specific audience adaptation: "insert names" (1) and "insert additional pitches" (18). There are no mentions in the text of the speech of a specific audience or occasion. The text simply is dated 1-9-90 and labeled as "Pesticides Speech for César Chávez." Other texts of speeches presented by Chávez provided by his office indicate specific audiences and occasions and some of the speeches make numerous adaptations to the audiences.

César Chávez was born in 1927 in Arizona and in 1962 in California founded the National Farm Workers Association (later called United Farm Workers of America). This was a labor union noted for its aggressive but nonviolent advocacy of the rights and safety of migrant farm workers. In numerous social protest efforts spanning four decades, Chávez often has utilized the pressure tactic of consumer boycott of the purchase of farm produce such as lettuce or grapes. Although in this speech he does urge adoption of a policy—the boycott of table grapes—and he does indicate its potential effectiveness (15–18), the bulk of the speech primarily aims at creating concern for a problem rather than describing in detail a program of action. César Chávez died on April 23, 1993.

In presenting a compelling view of the problem, Chávez answers the question—Why grapes?—by demonstrating the scope of the problem. He employs statistics to show how widespread the problem is (4, 10) and argues that the problem threatens farm workers, their children, and consumers (5–6, 10). Statistics such as 800 percent and 1200 percent above normal index the intensity of the problem (8–9). Expert testimony is used in several places, including use of so-called "reluctant" testimony from grower and government sources (2, 6, 14). What are the causes of the problem? Chávez clearly identifies two: grape grower greed (2–3, 12, 18) and inaction and misaction by state and federal gov-

---

◆ The text of this speech was provided by President César Chávez's office at the national headquarters of the United Farm Workers of America.

ernments (12–14). For Chávez, government "is part of the problem."

Chávez attempts to generate audience concern for the problem by vividly depicting the danger, degradation, and suffering of people who directly experience the problem. First, he lists the general physical harms: "cancer, DNA mutations, and horrible birth defects" (6). Second, and at length, he "humanizes" the "technical" problem of pesticides with examples of real people and groups (7–11). Note his skillful use of alliteration to make his argument memorable: "*children* are dying . . . *slow, painful, cruel* deaths in towns called *cancer clusters*" (8). And note his use of parallel phrasing to summarize his point (11).

Of special interest to the rhetorical critic is Chávez's strategy of associating the pesticides and policies he condemns with so-called "devil terms" that carry intense negative force because they represent violations of fundamental human values. He establishes associations with nerve gas (6-World War I German use and use by Saddam Hussein against Kurds in Iraq in 1988); with agent orange (6-a chemical with harmful physical side-effects used to strip leaves from trees during the Vietnam War); with killing fields (10-allusion to the 1984 film of the same name that depicted mass slaughter of Cambodian civilians by Communist terrorists); and, sarcastically, with Idi Amin (Uganda's bloody dictator) and Adolf Hitler (13). How adequately and legitimately do you believe that he establishes these associations?

In what ways and to what degree might the lack in a generic speech of arguments and appeals specifically intended for a specific audience lessen Chávez's, or any speaker's, ability to create concern for the problem she or he describes? Here recall the discussion of the second suggested criterion for evaluating speeches that create concern for problems: Has the speaker shown the significance of the problem for the specific audience? In addition, are there any ethical issues involved in the use of generic speeches? If so, what might they be and on what grounds? For an analysis of Chávez's rhetoric, see John C. Hammerback and Richard J. Jensen, *The Rhetorical Career of César Chávez* (Texas A & M University Press, 1998).

◆ ◆ ◆

1   Thank you very much, I am truly honored to be able to speak with you. I would like to thank the many people who made this possible for their kindness and their hospitality. (insert names)

2   Decades ago, the chemical industry promised the growers that pesticides would create vast new wealth and bountiful harvests. Just recently, the experts learned what farm workers, and the truly organic farmers have known for years. The prestigious National Academy of Sciences recently concluded an exhaustive five-year study which showed that by using simple, effective organic farming techniques, *instead of pesticides,* the growers could make *more money,* produce *more crops,* and *protect the environment*!

3   Unfortunately, the growers are not listening. They continue to spray and inject hundreds of millions of pounds of herbicides, fungicides, and insecticides onto our foods.

4   Most of you know that the United Farm Workers have focussed our struggle against pesticides on table grapes. Many people ask me "Why grapes?" The World Resources Institute reported that over three hundred thousand farm workers are poisoned every year by pesticides. Over half of all reported pesticide-related illnesses involve the cultivation or harvesting of table grapes. They receive *more* restricted-use application permits, which allow growers to spray pesticides known to threaten humans, than *any* other fresh food crop. The General Accounting Office, which does research for the U.S. Congress, determined that *34* of the *76* types of pesticides used *legally* on grapes pose potential human health hazards and could *not be detected* by current multi-residue methods.

5   My friends, grapes are the most dangerous fruit in America. The pesticides sprayed on table grapes *are killing America's children.* These pesticides *soak* the fields, *drift* with the wind, *pollute* the water, and are *eaten* by unwitting consumers. These poisons are designed to kill life, and pose a very real threat to consumers and farm workers alike.

6   The fields are sprayed with pesticides like captan, a fungicide believed to cause cancer, DNA mutation, and horrible birth defects. Other poisons take a similar toll. Parathion and phosdrin are *"nerve gas"* types of insecticides, which are believed to be responsible for the majority of farm worker poisonings in California. The growers spray sulphites, which can trigger asthmatic attacks, on the grapes. And even the growers own magazine, *The California Farmer,* admitted that growers were *illegally* using a very dangerous growth stimulator, called *Fix,* which is quite similar to *Agent Orange,* on the grapes.

7   This is a very technical problem, with very *human* victims. One young boy, Felipe Franco, was born without arms or legs in the agricultural town of McFarland. His mother worked for the first three months of her pregnancy picking grapes in fields that were sprayed repeatedly with pesticides believed to cause birth defects.

8   My friends, the central valley of California is one of the wealthiest agricultural regions in the world. In its midst are clusters of children dying from cancer. The children who live in towns like McFarland are surrounded by the grape fields that employ their parents. The children contact the poisons when they play outside, when they drink the water, and when they hug their parents returning from the fields. *And the children are dying.* They are dying *slow, painful, cruel* deaths in towns called *cancer clusters.* In cancer clusters like McFarland, where the childhood cancer rate is *800 percent* above normal.

9   A few months ago, the parents of a brave little girl in the agricultural community of Earlimart came to the United Farm Workers to ask for our help. Their four-year-old daughter, Natalie Ramirez, has lost one kidney to cancer and is threatened with the loss of another. The Ramirez family knew about our protests in nearby McFarland and thought there might be a similar problem in their home town. Our union members went door to door in Earlimart and found that the Ramirez family's worst fears were true. There are at least *four* other children suffering from cancer and similar diseases which the experts believe were caused by pesticides in the little town of Earlimart, a rate *1200 percent* above normal. In Earlimart, little Jimmy Caudillo died recently from leukemia at the age of three.

10   The grape vineyards of California have become America's Killing Fields. These *same* pesticides can be found on the grapes you buy in the store. Study after study, by the California Department of Food and Agriculture, by the Food and Drug Administration, and by objective newspapers, concluded that up to *54 percent* of the sampled grapes contained pesticide residues. Which pesticide did they find the most? *Captan,* the same carcinogenic fungicide that causes birth defects.

11   My friends, *the suffering must end.* So *many* children are dying, *so many* babies are born without limbs and vital organs, *so many* workers are dying in the fields.

12   The growers, and the supermarket owners, say that the government can *handle* the problem, can *protect* the workers, can *save* the children. It *should,* but it *won't.* You see, agribusiness is *big business.* It is a *sixteen billion* dollar industry in California alone. Agribusiness contributed very heavily to the successful campaign of Republican Governor George Deukmajian. He has rewarded the growers by turning the Agricultural Labor Relations Board into a tool for the growers, run by the growers. The Governor even vetoed a bill that would have required growers to warn workers that they were entering recently sprayed fields! And only *one percent* of those growers who *are caught* violating pesticide laws were even fined in California.

13   President Bush is a long-time friend of agribusiness. During the last presidential campaign, George Bush ate grapes in a field just *75 miles* from the cemetery where little Jimmy Caudillo and other pesticide victims are buried, in order to show his support for the table grape industry. He recently gave a speech to the Farm Bureau, saying that it was up to the *growers* to restrain the use of dangerous pesticides.

That's like putting *Idi Amin,* or *Adolf Hitler,* in charge of promoting *peace* and *human rights.*

14   To show you what happens to pesticides supposedly under government control, I'd like to tell you more about captan. Testing to determine the acceptable tolerance levels of captan was done by Bio-Tech Laboratories, later found *guilty* of falsifying the data to the E.P.A. The tolerance level set was *ten times* the amount allowed in Canada. Later, government agencies tried to ban captan, but were mysteriously stopped several times. Finally, the government banned captan on 42 crops, but *not on grapes.* Even the General Accounting Office found that the government's pesticide testing is wholly inadequate. The government is *not* the answer, it is part of the problem.

15   If we are to protect farm workers, their children, and consumers, we must use *people power.* I have seen many boycotts succeed. The Reverend Martin Luther King, Jr., who so generously supported our first fast, led the way with the bus boycott. And with *our* first boycott, we were able to get DDT, Aldrin, and Dieldrin banned, in our first contracts with grape growers. Now, even more urgently, we are trying to get deadly pesticides banned.

16   The growers and their allies have tried to stop us with *lies,* with *police,* with *intimidation,* with *public relations agencies,* and with *violence.* But *we cannot be stopped.* In our *life and death struggle* for justice, we have turned to the court of last resort: the American people.

17   At last we are winning. Many supermarket chains have stopped selling or advertising grapes. Millions of consumers are refusing to buy America's most dangerous fruit. Many courageous people have volunteered to help our cause or joined human chains of people who fast, who go without food for days, to support our struggle. As a result, *grape sales keep falling.* We have witnessed truckloads of grapes being dumped because no one would stoop low enough to buy them. As demand drops, so do prices and profits. This sort of economic pressure is the only language the growers understand.

18   We are winning, but there is still much work to be done. If we are going to beat the greed and power of the growers, we must work *together. Together,* we can end the suffering. *Together,* we can save the children. *Together,* we can bring justice to the killing fields. I hope that you will join our struggle, for it is *your* struggle too. The simple act of boycotting table grapes laced with pesticides is a powerful statement the growers understand. *Please, boycott table grapes.* For your safety, for the workers, *we must act,* and *act together.* (insert additional pitches)

19   Good night, and God bless you.

Men and Women Getting Along:
These Are Times That Try Men's Souls

◆ *Bernice R. Sandler* ◆

On March 26, 1991 Bernice Sandler spoke to several hundred students and faculty at Illinois State University in Normal, Illinois, at a meeting sponsored by the university's Women's Studies Program. Since 1971 Bernice Sandler has been Director of the Project on Status and Education of Women of the Association of American Colleges. Among the many awards received by Sandler are the Women Educators award for activism and the Anna Roe award from Harvard University. The Association of American Colleges promotes "humane and liberating learning," improves public understanding of the value of a liberal education, and explores issues affecting women in higher education.

In a style that relies on informal and colloquial language, Bernice Sandler creates audience concern for the problem of peer harassment on campuses of women by men, especially sexual harassment (6). Even before she identifies her specific topic, she alerts the audience to the difficulty of discussing such a sensitive topic (2–4). She employs a broad range of rhetorical resources to stimulate audience concern. Occasionally she places the problem in the broader context of peer harassment of ethnic groups and of gays and lesbians (5–6, 35). She defines the problem by discussing the range of its manifestations (7), by straightforward explanation (16), and by stressing the role of language choice in our definitions (40). In addition to respect, humaneness, and equality, what other values does she depict as being threatened or violated?

To illustrate the nature and scope of the problem, Sandler profusely employs examples (8–10, 17–18, 21–22, 25–28). Sometimes these examples stem from her personal experience (31–33, 39). In evaluating her use of examples, consider whether a sufficient number of examples was presented, whether the examples were typical instances, and whether there are counter-examples that should be taken into account. At one point she contends that "when things have a name, you know that they are not unusual occurrences, but that they happen often, in many places at many times" (9). To what extent do you accept this argument as an index of the typicality or representativeness of examples?

In order to elaborate one important dimension of the problem, she often illustrates the differing perceptions of the same behavior held by women and men (11, 15, 18, 23–24, 35, 42). How effective would this approach probably be? Why? Another rhetorical resource used to support her analysis is statistics (13–14, 21, 24, 40). How adequately does she substantiate the source and credentials of the research "studies" she draws upon? Or does she seem to assume that the audience simply will rely on her own credibility and honesty? Sandler attempts to avoid over-generalizations (11–12) and to draw careful distinctions (16). How adequately do you believe she does so?

As means of connecting the problem to the experience of her audience, she uses statistics

---

◆ The text of this speech was provided by Bernice Sandler.

(40), a hypothetical example (41), and a lengthy series of final questions that skillfully underscore the value choices facing the students, especially the men (46). Note particularly her adept use of "role reversal" examples to encourage men to empathize with the problem from the perspective of women (17, 19). A rhetorical critic immediately should note as important her extensive use throughout the speech of questions to provoke thought, as transitions or forecasts, or to underscore conclusions. How well do you believe she employs questions to serve these or other functions?

At length Bernice Sandler analyzes the major causes or "reasons" for the problem (36–42). And at various points she discusses the effects of the problem (12, 39, 43–45)—effects which in one way or another reflect devaluation or debasement of women. Consider how adequately she recognizes multiple and interrelated contributing causes, avoids confusing a causal connection with either chronology or correlation, recognizes both immediate causes and a chain or sequence of causes, explores major relevant effects, and employs sound evidence to support her arguments on causes and effects.

Finally, examine her strategy of dispelling sexual "myths" that unfortunately too often are used to justify sexual harassment (20, 21, 29–30). In what ways is this also an exploration of causes that contribute to the problem? And note that Sandler condemns the "it's just in fun" rationalization used as an excuse.

1   As everyone knows, the word "men" applies to women as well, and surely these are times that try women's souls as well. Since the days of Adam and Eve, men and women have had trouble getting along. Scholars—psychologists, sociologists, philosophers—indeed almost everyone has some opinion as to what the problems are. So when I venture into this territory, it is with some trepidation because everyone has opinions about what the problems are and what needs to be done, if anything.

2   I want to start off with a question. Do you remember when it was okay for the boys to tease the girls? People laughed—at least the boys laughed. The girls may have been uncomfortable, but nobody took this kind of teasing too seriously. In fact many people thought of it—some still do—as cute, as "boys will be boys," and as natural, normal, behavior.

3   Well, it is not okay anymore. And when big boys do it—men—in this institution or in the workplace, it may well be illegal in many instances. And so tonight, I'm going to talk about some of the negative aspects of men and women getting along. It is not an easy subject to talk about, and many of you may not like or agree with what you hear.

4   It's a subject that is hard for me to talk about, because most of the time I like to joke around, and it's hard for me to joke about this subject. But I hope you will listen and give some thought to this not only because it is important but also because it ultimately relates to what you want to get out of your college experience, and how you will relate to people who are not like you.

5   Ideally the college experience as a whole should help students not only acquire knowledge but also build skills and confidence, learn how to make good choices in life, and particularly how to handle differences, including those of race, class, gender and sexual orientation. All too often, colleges and universities fail in helping men and women meet the challenge of learning to get along. College is a lot more than just going to classes. The social learning that happens outside of the classroom is just as important as what happens inside. The wide range of experiences you have with friends and acquaintances is not only complementary but critical to what you will be learning in the next few years.

6   There is a darker side to campus life, often unnoticed, or if it is acknowledged, it is ignored or brushed off as "normal behavior." That darker side is peer harassment, whether it is men harassing women, men and women harassing gay and lesbian students, women harassing men, but particularly

the harassment of women by men students, and that is what I'm going to be talking about tonight. That's the darker side of campus life: peer harassment. For too many students the relationships between men and women are not always positive. Too many women experience hostility, anger, and sometimes even violence from male students.

7   Peer harassment covers a wide range of behaviors. At one end of the scale, peer harassment consists of so-called teasing, sexual innuendos, even obscenities—a sort of sexual bullying, both physical and verbal, often made in the guise of humor. At the other end, is explicit sexual harassment, up to and including sexual aggression, with rape as the most extreme form of peer harassment. Let me give you some examples, both serious and mild, of what I mean, although even mild ones can seriously affect a woman.

8   A woman raises something about women's issues in a class. The men in the class hiss and laugh at her. She is effectively silenced, even though theoretically in a classroom students are supposed to feel free to bring up any issues.

9   Here is another example. A lot of things happen in cafeterias. A group of men regularly sit at a table facing the cafeteria line. As the women go through the line the men loudly discuss the women's sexual attributes—size of breast and how she would act during intercourse—and then they hold up cards, rating each woman from 1 to 10. It's called "scoping," and when things have a name, you know that they are not unusual occurrences, but that they happen often, in many places at many times. Some women do not come to the cafeteria unless they can find a friend and pretend that they don't hear the men; other women skip meals altogether if the men are there.

10   Here is another example. A fraternity pledge approaches a woman student he has never seen before, and bites her on the breast, a practice called "sharking." And another. A group of men simultaneously expose themselves, or in another variation they simply surround a woman, demand that she bare her breasts, and do not allow her to leave the circle until she has done so.

11   I want to be sure that you all understand that not all men harass women students. And certainly not all women students experience this behavior. But just as certainly, on every campus, there are too many men treating women in ways that are disrespectful. That is an old-fashioned word, but I don't know what else to call this behavior, behavior that is invasive and can only be described as emotional and psychological harassment. Often however, the men do not describe their behavior this way. They are just having a good time. If a woman doesn't like it and she takes offense, the men probably say, "She just doesn't have a sense of humor." Yet to the woman, such behaviors can poison her college experience.

12   These behaviors are not universal; they don't occur all the time. And while men can also be harassed by women—that's the subject of another talk—not tonight—women are the majority of the peer harassment victims. What is interesting is that even though the women are harassed by men because they *are women,* not all women recognize these behaviors as harassment. Nevertheless, when these experiences occur again and again, and when they are either unnoticed, ignored by faculty and administrators, or even condoned by other students and some college officials, men and women alike receive the message that women are not to be treated with respect—that women can be treated with disdain and it does not matter to anyone.

13   How much of a problem are we talking about? Well, there have been a few studies—not many—but from the best information we have, somewhere between 70–90 percent of women students have experienced some behavior from male students to which they reacted negatively. 70–90 percent! In contrast, sexual harassment of women students by faculty and staff has a far lower incidence. 20–30 percent of women undergraduates report some form of sexual harassment from someone in authority, with only two percent reporting actual threats or bribes for unwanted sexual activity.

14 Additionally, widespread harassment of women by fraternities has been documented on virtually every campus that has examined fraternity life in the last five years. There is also another group of men that are likely to harass women. Anyone want to guess? Yes. Athletes—and not the swimming team, not the golf team, but the football and basketball teams, occasionally rugby, wrestling, or lacrosse.

15 Much of peer harassment is sexual harassment. In general, sexual harassment involves unwanted sexual attention, and there are a lot of men who think that all women want this and are flattered by any kind of sexual attention, especially if a woman does not indicate any displeasure about the behavior. You see this at construction sites, where, when a woman walks by, the men show their "manliness" by hooting and hollering at her, but this happens elsewhere as well. Now why doesn't the woman indicate any displeasure? Why doesn't she just say "Hey guys, knock it off. I don't like this." Sometimes she thinks if she says anything like that the behavior will get worse. Her strategy is to ignore it because she really wants the behavior to stop; in contrast, his perception is that she must really like it because she didn't say anything.

16 All sexual attention is not sexual harassment. Certainly when men and women are together, sexual attraction is possible, and people will express that attraction. Sexual attention becomes harassment when it is persistent or unwanted or personal boundaries are crossed. What may be appropriate in a continuing relationship is inappropriate coming from a stranger or new acquaintance as in the following examples:

17 Inappropriate personal remarks such as comments about a woman, her body, or sexual activities. Comments such as "You've got great breasts" from a stranger are not perceived as compliments because they depersonalize women—they reduce women to being *only* a sexual object. Her breasts become the most important part of her and it ignores her individuality or humanity. If you are a male person, try to think how you might feel if the first thing someone said to you after being introduced— say, you're a swimming star at a swimming meet, and the first thing someone said when they met you was "You've got a great penis."

18 Unwanted touching or kissing. Women have had their breasts grabbed or have been hugged and kissed by people they did not know well, especially at parties. Sometimes people say that women "ask" for this behavior. "Look at the clothes she wore." This is a good example of how men's clothing and women's clothing are seen very differently. Now women wear clothing to be in style and for their self-esteem, but men, when they see women's clothing, often assume that she is looking for sex. She could be wearing tight pants or loose pants, lowcut clothes or a high neck, ruffles, short skirts, long skirts, short sleeves, long sleeves—indeed whatever a woman wears may be viewed by some men as a sexual invitation. A woman could be wearing an old burlap potato sack and there will be some guy who'll look at her and say, "Wow—this is the sexiest potato sack I've ever seen and she obviously wants to have sex, and she obviously wants to have sex with me."

19 Interestingly, men's clothing does not communicate that at all. You're on a campus, and I'm sure you all have seen guys wearing jeans that are so tight that you can surely see the size and shape of the sexual apparatus. But a guy would be shocked if some woman—or man—came up to him and— grabbed—his penis, and when he said, "Hey what's going on here?" the person responded, "Well, look at the way you're dressed. You're asking for it."

20 Women's clothing does not communicate a sexual invitation. It does communicate "I am a woman" but it doesn't give anyone else permission to grab or touch. It doesn't signal what a woman wants or what she will do. This is what I call the clothing myth and it essentially views sexual harassment, and to some extent rape, as an extension of biological drives. "She was so beautiful, I just couldn't help myself." It ignores the issue of power which I'll talk about later, but it also shifts the responsibility for the harassment or the rape to the victim. *She* is the one that is causing the men to harass her. It's her fault, not his. The women are causing the men to harass them.

21   Another example is persistent sexual attention. Asking a woman for a date or sex repeatedly, even if the woman has said "no." Here we see the operation of another myth, that a woman says "no" when she really means "yes." So there is no way a woman can say "no," and many men feel it incumbent upon themselves to turn that "no" into a "yes." Someone did research on this and it turns out that most women have never said "no" when they meant "yes," and of the 15 or 20 percent that had said "no" when they meant "yes," almost all of these had said "no" when they meant "yes" only one time. So it is a relatively rare phenomenon for women to say "no" when they really mean "yes."

22   Another thing that happens are requests for sexual activity, such as men shouting obscene sexual invitations through an open dormitory window. This, like other forms of harassment, tells a woman that her individuality doesn't matter. She is being viewed only in terms of her sexuality.

23   Now, sometimes when sexual harassment or rape occurs, the man involved says, "Well, she asked for it." And when you ask questions about this, he usually refers to her clothing or her behavior. A woman smiled; he views it as a sexual invitation. A woman talked to him; and he views it as a sexual invitation. Indeed men often mistake a woman's friendliness as a sexual invitation.

24   Someone did a study on this. They taped several conversations of men and women talking to each other, and then showed the segments to a group of men and women and asked them to decide for each segment whether the woman was being friendly or was "coming on" to the guy. The women who view the video say for each segment, "She's being friendly, she's being friendly, she's being friendly." The men, in contrast, say "She's coming on to the guy, she wants to have sex with him, she's coming on strong." So we have a misperception here. Women are more likely to see friendliness and men are more likely to see sexual invitations. Think of how this affects the relationships between men and women.

25   Another example is a sexually demeaning climate, such as leaving pornographic materials in a woman's mailbox or in front of her dormitory door. Sometimes there are sexist posters or pictures or bumper stickers. At one fraternity party there was a poster on the door which said "No fat chicks allowed." Since 75 percent of young women believe that they are overweight, at least 75 percent of the women were offended.

26   Sexist graffiti can be on desks and walls, in library carrels or on cafeteria tables. Often the graffiti may also be racist or anti-semitic, or offensive to gays and lesbians. The graffiti can stay for years, often offending generations of students because most institutions ignore it. Syracuse University has one of the few programs to periodically examine the campus for graffiti and remove it. The only other example I know of graffiti being removed occurred at Brown University, where on the wall of the women's restrooms, women have begun to write the names of male students who have raped women students. These names are removed each day.

27   Let me give you an example of offensive graffiti. One university has a "free expression tunnel" which connects both sides of the campus which is divided by a railroad track. There is a painting of a Raggedy Ann doll, mutilated and bruised, with blood streaming between the doll's legs, and the statement, "I raped Raggedy Ann." What do women feel when they walk by this several times daily? And what do men feel as they see it? And is this the kind of free expression we should be encouraging?

28   Other examples of the chilly climate for women are wet T-shirt contests, activities focussing on women's sexuality, showing pornographic movies as fundraisers—that happens at a lot of campuses—or petty hostility toward women, such as throwing things at women, heckling women, pouring drinks over women's heads or inside their clothing. All of these give men and women a message—a message that women don't count except as sexual objects, that friendship with women is not possible, and that women are natural objects of scorn and derision.

29 Now a lot of these activities are seen as fun, and if someone doesn't think so, they are accused as having no sense of humor. That's the worst thing you can say about someone—no sense of humor.

30 Now humor is important, it can be used to relax people and lighten them up. But humor has other functions. It can also be used to enhance group solidarity, to define the outsider, in this case women, and to discuss subjects that are taboo. So rather than discuss gender and sexuality, we find it easier to joke about them instead. And it can also be used to express anxiety and anger and discomfort and resentment, in this case, against women.

31 I've become very interested in humor in recent years, especially when I noticed that all of the so-called locker-room jokes are demeaning to women. So I began to think there must be jokes demeaning to men and I began to seek out these jokes—not because I'm interested in demeaning men—some of my best friends are men—but because I'm curious about the uses of humor. I have been collecting for several years, and I must tell you, jokes demeaning men are quite rare—I have about ten, and some of these are variations on the others. I'm not talking about jokes which demean some men, such as Scotsmen and hillbilly men, but jokes which demean men as a group.

32 And there is a difference between the jokes that demean men and the ones that demean women. The jokes that demean women demean them in all sorts of roles, activities, and behaviors. The jokes that demean men are very limited. They deal with sexual performance and size of the reproductive organ. I'm not sure what these differences mean, but they are interesting, and I also have to tell you that I can't yet tell these jokes in public. If you know of any and want to tell them to me, I'll be glad to add them to my collection.

33 A few years ago the first of my daughters got married, and I was very happy about the forthcoming marriage, I like the young man, etc. But as the time for the wedding approached, I found myself becoming more and more uncomfortable. I finally realized what it was. I, who had been a fairly likeable person, was about to become a mother-in-law, the kind of person who is often ridiculed in jokes. I could see that I was entering a dangerous stage of my life. And again I said, there are a lot of mother-in-law jokes ridiculing women, so where are the father-in-law jokes. I'm even offering a reward of $25 for a father-in-law joke, because I don't think there are any.

34 Now what do these jokes about women tell us? They tell us that there is anger against women, anxiety, and perhaps even fear. I don't understand all of the dynamics about mother-in-law jokes, but probably the mother-in-law is a stand-in for anger against one's own mother, one's spouse, or all women.

35 Similarly racist humor, ethnic humor, jokes about JAPS (the Jewish American Princess), jokes about Black women or other ethnic women are not simple fun, for too often what passes for humor is humor at the expense of someone else. What the men see as friendly fun is often viewed by the women as harassment, even though they may not use that term to define it. The men are having a good time with each other. This is how they build solidarity with each other, by being nasty to women.

36 Now since most men are nice guys, what is going on here? People who might not heckle people of another race may have no difficulty in engaging in the same behavior if the object of their disrespect is female. Well, there are a lot of reasons why, and here are some of them.

37 At a very early age, boys learn to use girls as what the sociologists call a "negative reference group." In other words, the boys define themselves by comparing themselves favorably to girls, the lesser group, the females. After all, what is the worst thing you can call a little boy? A sissy—which says he is acting like a girl. By teasing girls a boy begins to feel good about himself—he is "better" than they are, and teasing them makes him feel like a "real boy." Moreover, by putting down girls and females he can get closer to his buddies. They can all put down the girls, and feel better and bigger than the girls. Harassment, and even sexual assault, can be, for many men, the way in which they show other men how "manly" they really are. We see this in its extreme in the case of gang rape, where psychologists have noted that the men are not raping for sexual reasons, but are really raping for each other. This is how they show their friends how strong, how virile, how manly, how wonderful they are. This is how they strengthen the bond with their brothers. They need to be one of the boys and they find it difficult to go against the group. Harassment, whether it is gang rape or heckling women, is used by some men as a way to bond with their brothers.

38 For some men, harassment and sexual abuse expresses their need to show power over women. In that sense it is something like the bully syndrome—the men feel better and stronger by picking on someone they perceive as weaker than themselves, the women. Some men think primarily in stereotypes, so that they may be uncomfortable with women who have minds of their own. Some men may be angry at feminism, or angry at a particular woman, or at all women in general. Harassment, after all, is simply a milder form of assault. It tells women that men can intimidate them at will.

39 Alcohol and drugs can play a role by lowering people's inhibitions and creating an atmosphere where hurtful and even violent behavior, even a gang rape, can be seen as amusing. Pornography, easily available on most campuses, often portrays situations in which women are weak and treated badly, where women enjoy rape, pain, and humiliation, where violence against women is often an integral part of the scenario. Violence toward women, whether in pornography, movies, music videos and TV, promotes a perception of women as outsiders, as people who are less than human, as people who are objects for men to exploit, manipulate, and harm. Additionally, men in groups are often more prone to bad behavior—in a group, such as a fraternity, or as part of an athletic team, a man may do things that he might not otherwise do, because he is afraid of the hostility of the other men. The peer pressure is very strong. One of the things we need to do is to teach men how to stand up to other men when they are behaving badly, and to say "don't do that." I myself know of several attempted gang rapes that were stopped, simply because one man was strong enough to say something like "Hey guys, cut it out. Let her alone."

40 Moreover, peer harassment sets the stage for rape. Rape is merely the extreme form of peer harassment. The men who intimidate women are most likely to commit assault on women. Remember earlier I told you that 70–90% of women experience some form of peer harassment. I want to give you the figures for acquaintance rape, when one person forces or intimidates another to have intercourse and where both parties know each other. If you ask the men "Have you ever raped a woman?", most will say "No." But if you ask the question, "Have you ever forced or intimidated a woman to have sexual intercourse with you," between 10–15% will say "Yes." For women, the figures are more striking. Somewhere between 15 and 25% of undergraduate women have been raped by someone they know. They don't all call it rape, but if you ask them if anyone has ever forced or intimidated them to have sexual intercourse when they did not want to, that is when you get these 15–25% figures. How many is 15–25% of the women on this campus? That is a lot of women. Peer harassment makes it possible.

41 Other factors: Men are generally socialized in our society to be dominant, and that plays a role in peer harassment. Women have been socialized to play a secondary role, so that men are trained to talk, and women are trained to listen. Who has the most power in our society? Who has the most money? The best jobs? Look at our Supreme Court, our Congress, your own institution. Who holds most of the administrative posts? If you do not believe that men have more power, think of the following. You are walking alone on a dark street—it doesn't matter what sex you are. You see six women on the corner. Are you frightened? Same scenario, next night. You are walking alone on a dark street, and you see six men on the corner. Are you frightened? Who has more power in our society—men or women?

42 There are many stereotypes about women being weaker and passive, although these stereotypes interfere with our view of women as equals. We like to think of men and women, at least intellectually, as equals. But in reality, sexual relations—especially those that occur in a context of sexual harassment, sexual teasing and joking to show power, sexual bullying, and sexual assault—these occur within an implicit power relationship where one person, usually the male, has the power to intimidate and cause harm to the other—usually a woman—through physical and social means. Most men are not conscious of their power to intimidate women, although they may use that power often. In contrast women often recognize the power of men. Men and women have very different perceptions of the relationship between the sexes. Just the other day I read a chilling quotation by the author, Margaret Atwood. I found the quotation in some materials put out by a Wisconsin group called Men Stopping Rape. This is the quotation that the men chose to include in their materials. "Why are you afraid of women?" I asked a group of men. "We're afraid they will laugh at us," replied the men. "Why are you afraid of men?" I asked a group of women. "We're afraid they'll kill us," replied the women." End of quote. The quote shows how men and women view each other very differently and that men are not aware of the power that they hold and how they use that power.

43 It makes it difficult for women to say "Stop that, it bothers me." It makes it difficult for women to report harassment and sexual intimidation. Some women are frightened of retaliation. Some may believe that nothing is going to happen, so why bother? Some women begin to believe that this is the way men are, and nothing can change them. Others don't know about or trust their institution's grievance procedure. And sad to say, some women collude in the harassment and intimidation. They have accepted the ideology that any kind of sexual attention is flattery. They may be angry about feminism in part because they have implicitly accepted the myths of men's domination and power—the myths, the beliefs, and the attitudes that support sexual harassment and intimidation that make women believe that they caused the harassment. They may have seen films like "Animal House" and other media which make them believe that this is the way you have a good time. They may not want to antagonize men because they want to be liked and they are fearful of men being angry at them.

44 Peer harassment makes women feel less than equal. They may feel uncomfortable and annoyed. They may feel embarrassed, humiliated or degraded. They may feel disgusted, they may feel helpless, angry, unsure of how to respond. They may feel insulted, and they may be fearful of violence. They may also feel guilty and blame themselves, as if they did something that caused the men to act so badly. The cumulative effect of repeated harassment can be devastating. It reinforces self-doubt, and affects a woman's self-esteem, and even her academic experience. It makes coeducation less equal for women. It makes some women angry at men, and it may make it more difficult for some women to trust men.

45 Peer harassment also affects men. Peer harassment teaches men that relationships based on power are better than those based on intimacy and friendship. It makes it difficult for a man to form a healthy and satisfying relationship with a woman because it is hard to be committed to someone for whom he and others have so little respect. When men view women as objects to be demeaned and scorned, men find it difficult to relate to women as equal human beings—much less as friends or potential romantic partners or as co-workers. Even a man's friendship with other men will be shallow if the way to friendship with his brothers is to ridicule women rather than [build] a friendship based on shared feelings.

46 Let me end with some questions and then we can have some discussion. You are at the beginning of your adulthood. How do you want to relate to members of the other sex while you are in college? How do you want to relate both personally and professionally when you finish college? Do you want to be able to be friends and colleagues? Can you respect someone who is different from you? Can you have a relationship of equality or must it be based on power? Do you want a relationship where sex exists for its own sake and is not for intimacy or caring or sharing? Do we want men to continue to believe that the way to get points with their peers and the way to feel good about themselves and their sexuality is to dominate, to use and exploit women? Do we want men and women to believe that relationships with the other sex that are based on power are better than relationships based on mutual respect and intimacy?

47 The world is changing. The relationships between men and women are changing. Increasingly women are labeling forced sexual activity as rape, and calling peer harassment by name. The days of "boys will be boys" are fast disappearing as young men and young women are learning that the new world is a world in which men and women recognize that whatever their differences, they are equal, and that they must share a world in which they can work together, a world in which men and women are no longer adversarial, a world in which women and men can be friends.

48 Let me close with something that is characteristic of the new mood of women. It is "a newly discovered Biblical revelation," which was discovered in the Middle East by a woman archeologist, of course, assisted by women staff. You'll probably recognize the paraphrase, and it goes like this:

> And they shall beat their pots and pans into printing presses and weave their cloth in protest banners. Nations of women shall lift up their voices with nations of other women, neither shall they suffer discrimination anymore. [By Mary Chagnon]

49 That may sound apocryphal, but I suspect it may yet prove to come from the book of Prophets, for what women are learning is the politics of power and the politics of change, and the campus and the nation, and the world shall never again be the same.

Address to the United Nations Fourth World Conference on Women

──────────────── ◆ *Hillary Rodham Clinton* ◆ ────────────────

Beijing, China, was the site of the United Nations Fourth World Conference on Women, September 4–15, 1995. A parallel meeting approved by the U.N., the Nongovernmental Organizations (NGOs) Forum on Women, was held August 30–September 8 in the town of Huairou about an hour from Beijing. The main issues at the U.N. conference were the stopping of worldwide violence against women, the economic and political empowerment of women, the granting of sexual rights to women, and the funding and implementation of programs to accomplish

◆ The text of this speech was obtained from the office of Hillary Rodham Clinton through its World Wide Web home page.

these goals. Delegates to the conference represented about 185 nations. Among the speakers were Benazir Bhutto, the prime minister of Pakistan, and Winnie Mandela of South Africa.

On September 5, 1995, in a speech interrupted repeatedly by applause, Hillary Rodham Clinton addressed the conference plenary session and attempted to create a common concern for problems facing women worldwide. She stresses commonalties rather than differences (3–6). Throughout the speech, she provides encouragement for necessary efforts by providing examples of the accomplishments of women (13,18–23, 47–49, 53).

Her central assumption is that abuse of women's rights involves abuse of human rights (35–40). Early in the speech she provides a summary forecast of prominent concerns (7) and places them among "the world's most pressing problems" (10). She emphasizes the vast array of "deeply-rooted problems that continue to diminish the potential of half the world's population" (50).

Hillary Rodham Clinton argues a cause-effect connection. Where the situations of women do not flourish, the result is that families do not flourish; if women flourish then families flourish (14–15, 52). Using the tests for cause-effect reasoning described earlier in the chapter on Propositions of Fact, evaluate the reasonableness of her argument.

She contends that another problem is that women's work, experience, and problems typically are unnoticed, unheard, and devalued (24, 26). She urges women to give voice to the voiceless and to speak for those not heard; to remain silent is to contribute to the problem (29–32, 41).

In an indirect manner, she criticizes practices in China that harm women and children (42) and denounces Chinese efforts to hinder participation in the NGOs Forum (44–45). Such comments showed courage at a time when U.S.-Chinese diplomatic relations were strained.

Frequently she underscores and illustrates the problems facing women by using brief lists of examples (25, 28, 30, 32, 39, 44, 45, 52). On one occasion she employs a lengthy itemization of problems presented in parallel structure (42). Clearly factual examples are her primary type of evidence. Evaluate her use of examples and specific instances by applying the standard tests for reasonableness: (1) Was a sufficient number of instances presented? (2) Were the instances presented typical/representative ones? (3) Were there any negative of counter-instances that were omitted? But also consider how the use of examples (miniature stories) dramatizes the problems and relates them to the audience's experiences.

Hillary Rodham Clinton effectively employs several language resources to sharpen and strengthen the impact of her arguments. Through alliteration she links together a series of either positive or negative items to make her point more memorable (28, 49, 53). She makes extensive use of parallel phrasing and parallel structure to imbed ideas in the audience's memory and to pile example upon example to reinforce significance (8–9, 18–23, 42, 45).

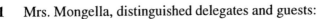

1   Mrs. Mongella, distinguished delegates and guests:

2   I would like to thank the Secretary General of the United Nations for inviting me to be part of the United Nations Fourth World Conference on Women. This is truly a celebration—a celebration of the contributions women make in every aspect of life: in the home, on the job, in their communities, as mothers, wives, sisters, daughters, learners, workers, citizens and leaders.

3   It is also a coming together, much the way women come together every day in every country.

4   We come together in fields and in factories. In village markets and supermarkets. In living rooms and board rooms.

5   Whether it is while playing with our children in the park, or washing clothes in a river, or taking a break at the office water cooler, we come together and talk about our aspirations and concerns. And time and again, our talk turns to our children and our families.

6 However different we may be, there is far more that unites us than divides us. We share a common future. And we are here to find common ground so that we may help bring new dignity and respect to women and girls all over the world—and in so doing, bring new strength and stability to families as well.

7 By gathering in Beijing, we are focusing world attention on issues that matter most in the lives of women and their families: access to education, health care, jobs, and credit, the chance to enjoy basic legal and human rights and participate fully in the political life of their countries.

8 There are some who question the reason for this conference. Let them listen to the voices of women in their homes, neighborhoods, and workplaces.

9 There are some who wonder whether the lives of women and girls matter to economic and political progress around the globe. Let them look at the women gathered here and at Huairou . . . the homemakers, nurses, teachers, lawyers, policymakers, and women who run their own businesses.

10 It is conferences like this that compel governments and peoples everywhere to listen, look and face the world's most pressing problems.

11 Wasn't it after the women's conference in Nairobi ten years ago that the world focused for the first time on the crisis of domestic violence?

12 Earlier today, I participated in a World Health Organization forum, where government officials, NGOs, and individual citizens are working on ways to address the health problems of women and girls.

13 Tomorrow, I will attend a gathering of the United Nations Development Fund for Women. There, the discussion will focus on local—and highly successful—programs that give hard-working women access to credit so they can improve their own lives and the lives of their families.

14 What we are learning around the world is that, if women are healthy and educated, their families will flourish. If women are free from violence, their families will flourish. If women have a chance to work and earn as full and equal partners in society, their families will flourish.

15 And when families flourish, communities and nations will flourish.

16 That is why every women, every man, every child, every family, and every nation on our planet has a stake in the discussion that takes place here.

17 Over the past 25 years, I have worked persistently on issues relating to women, children and families. Over the past two-and-a-half years, I have had the opportunity to learn more about the challenges facing women in my own country and around the world.

Hillary Rodham Clinton (Photo provided courtesy of the Library of Congress)

18   I have met new mothers in Jojakarta, Indonesia, who come together regularly in their village to discuss nutrition, family planning, and baby care.

19   I have met working parents in Denmark who talk about the comfort they feel in knowing that their children can be cared for in creative, safe, and nurturing after-school centers.

20   I have met women in South Africa who helped lead the struggle to end apartheid and are now helping build a new democracy.

21   I have met with the leading women of the Western Hemisphere who are working every day to promote literacy and better health care for the children of their countries.

22   I have met women in India and Bangladesh who are taking out small loans to buy milk cows, rickshaws, thread, and other materials to create a livelihood for themselves and their families.

23   I have met doctors and nurses in Belarus and Ukraine who are trying to keep children alive in the aftermath of Chernobyl.

24   The great challenge of this conference is to give voice to women everywhere whose experiences go unnoticed, whose words go unheard.

25   Women comprise more than half the world's population. Women are 70 percent of the world's poor, and two-thirds of those who are not taught to read and write.

26   Women are the primary caretakers for most of the world's children and elderly. Yet much of the work we do is not valued—not by economists, not by historians, not by popular culture, not by government leaders.

27   At this very moment, as we sit here, women around the world are giving birth, raising children, cooking meals, washing clothes, cleaning houses, planting crops, working on assembly lines, running companies, and running countries.

28   Women also are dying from a disease that should have been prevented or treated; they are watching their children succumb to malnutrition caused by poverty and economic deprivation; they are being denied the right to go to school by their own fathers and brothers; they are being forced into prostitution, and they are being barred from the ballot box and the bank lending office.

29   Those of us who have the opportunity to be here have the responsibility to speak for those who could not.

30   As an American, I want to speak up for women in my own country—women who are raising children on the minimum wage, women who can't afford health care or child care, women whose lives are threatened by violence, including violence in their own homes.

31   I want to speak up for mothers who are fighting for good schools, safe neighborhoods, clean air and clean airwaves . . . for older women, some of them widows, who have raised their families and now find that their skills and life experiences are not valued in the workplace . . . for women who are working all night as nurses, hotel clerks, and fast food chefs so that they can be at home during the day with their kids . . . and for women everywhere who simply don't have time to do everything they are called upon to do each day.

32   Speaking to you today, I speak for them, just as each of us speaks for women around the world who are denied the chance to go to school, or see a doctor, or own property, or have a say about the direction of their lives, simply because they are women.

33   The truth is that most women around the world work both inside and outside the home, usually by necessity.

34   We need to understand that there is no formula for how women should lead their lives. That is why we must respect the choices that each woman makes for herself and her family. Every woman deserves the chance to realize her God-given potential.

35 We also must recognize that women will never gain full dignity until their human rights are respected and protected.

36 Our goals for this conference, to strengthen families and societies by empowering women to take greater control over their own destinies, cannot be fully achieved unless all governments—here and around the world—accept their responsibility to protect and promote internationally recognized human rights.

37 The international community has long acknowledged—and recently affirmed at Vienna—that both women and men are entitled to a range of protections and personal freedoms, from the right of personal security to the right to determine freely the number and spacing of the children they bear.

38 No one should be forced to remain silent for fear of religious or political persecution, arrest, abuse or torture.

39 Tragically, women are most often the ones whose human rights are violated. Even in the late 20th century, the rape of women continues to be used as an instrument of armed conflict. Women and children make up a large majority of the world's refugees. And when women are excluded from the political process, they become even more vulnerable to abuse.

40 I believe that, on the eve of a new millennium, it is time to break our silence. It is time for us to say here in Beijing, and the world to hear, that it is no longer acceptable to discuss women's rights as separate from human rights.

41 These abuses have continued because, for too long, the history of women has been a history of silence. Even today, there are those who are trying to silence our words.

42 The voices of this conference and of the women at Huairou must be heard loud and clear:

- It is a violation of human rights when babies are denied food, or drowned, or suffocated, or their spines broken, simply because they are born girls.
- It is a violation of human rights when women and girls are sold into the slavery of prostitution.
- It is a violation of human rights when women are doused with gasoline, set on fire and burned to death because their marriage dowries are deemed too small.
- It is a violation of human rights when individual women are raped in their own communities and when thousands of women are subjected to rape as a tactic or prize of war.
- It is a violation of human rights when a leading cause of death worldwide among women ages 14 to 44 is the violence they are subjected to in their own homes.
- It is a violation of human rights when young girls are brutalized by the painful and degrading practice of genital mutilation.
- It is a violation of human rights when women are denied the right to plan their own families, and that includes being forced to have abortions or being sterilized against their will.
- If there is one message that echoes forth from this conference, it is that human rights are women's rights . . . And women's rights are human rights.
- Let us not forget that among those rights are the right to speak freely. And the right to be heard.

43 Women must enjoy the right to participate fully in the social and political lives of their countries if we want freedom and democracy to thrive and endure.

44 It is indefensible that many women in non-governmental organizations who wished to participate in this conference have not been able to attend—or have been prohibited from fully taking part.

45 Let me be clear. Freedom means the right of people to assemble, organize, and debate openly. It means respecting the views of those who may disagree with the views of their governments. It means not taking citizens away from their loved ones and jailing them, mistreating them, or denying them their freedom or dignity because of the peaceful expression of their ideas and opinions.

46   In my country, we recently celebrated the 75th anniversary of women's suffrage. It took 150 years after the signing of our Declaration of Independence for women to win the right to vote. It took 72 years of organized struggle on the part of many courageous women and men.

47   It was one of America's most divisive philosophical wars. But it was also a bloodless war. Suffrage was achieved without a shot fired.

48   We have also been reminded, in V-J Day observances last weekend, of the good that comes when men and women join together to combat the forces of tyranny and build a better world.

49   We have seen peace prevail in most places for a half century. We have avoided another world war.

50   But we have not solved other, deeply-rooted problems that continue to diminish the potential of half the world's population.

51   Now it is time to act on behalf of women everywhere.

52   If we take bold steps to better the lives of women, we will be taking bold steps to better the lives of children and families too. Families rely on mothers and wives for emotional support and care; families rely on women for labor in the home; and increasingly, families rely on women for income needed to raise healthy children and care for their relatives.

53   As long as discrimination and inequities remain so commonplace around the world—as long as girls and women are valued less, fed less, fed last, overworked, underpaid, not schooled and subjected to violence in and out of their homes—the potential of the human family to create a peaceful, prosperous world will not be realized.

54   Let this conference be our—and the world's—call to action.

55   And let us heed the call so that we can create a world in which every woman is treated with respect and dignity, every boy and girl is loved and cared for equally, and every family has the hope of a strong and stable future.

56   Thank you very much.

57   God's blessings on you, your work and all who will benefit from it.

Crisis of Community:
Make America Work for Americans

◆ *William K. Raspberry* ◆

The Landon Lecture Series at Kansas State University, Manhattan, is one of the most distinguished lecture series in the country. Endowed by the Alf M. Landon Foundation, the university has been able to bring many of America's most distinguished speakers to campus. On April 13,

◆ William K. Raspberry, "Crisis of Community: Make America Work for Americans," June 1, 1995, pp. 493–496. Reprinted by permission of *Vital Speeches of the Day* and the author.

1995, William Raspberry, columnist for the *Washington Post,* delivered this lecture on the crisis of community.

Raspberry was born in Okolona, Mississippi, October 12, 1935. He attended Indiana Central College, receiving a B.S. in history in 1958, and an L.H.D. in 1973. He was a reporter for the *Indianapolis Recorder* from 1956–1960. He moved to the *Washington Post* as reporter-editor, and received the designation of urban affairs columnist in 1966, a position he still holds. Raspberry has a special interest in race relations and public education. He taught journalism for two years, 1971–1973, at Howard University, and was a TV commentator on station WTTG in Washington from 1973–1975. He received a Pulitzer Prize for commentary in 1994. His editorial column today appears regularly in many of the nation's most prestigious newspapers.

In this address, he moves directly to the subject he plans to deal with. He distinguishes between "the crisis in the community" and the "crisis of community." His argument will be that we

are in danger of national fragmentation rather than focusing on an entity called "American." What does Raspberry say this fragmentation is stemming from? Also, how does he use analogy with the Soviet Union to demonstrate his point? He stresses that we lack honest communication and fail to focus on our problems, but instead look for enemies whom we can blame for our problems. Do you think he develops this idea effectively? Raspberry relies heavily upon the use of example in developing his argument. See for example paragraphs 8, 19, 29 and 46. Discuss how he uses example in these instances.

Relate what Raspberry says about inclusion and cultural isolation with what Molefi Asante is suggesting about education in his address found in this book. Raspberry says that we need national healing rather focusing upon the "politics of difference." We need to focus upon being "Americans." Analyze how he develops this thesis throughout his speech and how his reasoning and use of supporting materials establishes credibility for the idea.

1   I've been writing a good deal of late about the violence in our streets, the apathy in our schools, and the hopelessness among our young people—the crisis in our community.

2   America has a crisis of community that is as deep and wide as it is unnoticed. And it threatens to destroy our solidarity as a nation, in much the same fashion as a similar crisis in community has ripped apart the former Soviet Union and what used to be Yugoslavia.

3   I refer, of course, to the gender wars newly resurrected by the latest battles in the Clarence Thomas/Anita Hill holy wars; to the ethnic battles over university canons and multi-culturalism, to the political warfare that makes party advantage more important than the success of the nation, and to the racial animosities and suspicions fueled by everything from the rantings of Khalid Abdul Muhammed to the O. J. Simpson trial to Charles Murray's pseudo-intellectual call for racial abandonment.

4   But when I express my fear that we are coming unglued, I'm thinking about far more than these things.

5   I'm talking about more even than the normal give and take among the various sectors and ideologies of the society. I am talking about our growing inability to act—even to *think*—in the interest of the nation.

6   It's almost as though there IS no national interest, apart from the aggregate interests of the various components. The whole society seems to be disintegrating into special interests.

7   And not just in politics. College campuses are being ripped apart by the insistence of one group after another on proving their victimization at the hands of white males, and therefore their right to special exemptions and privileges.

8   One example of what I'm talking about: A few years ago, the Federal Aviation Administration adopted a rule that would bar emergency exit row seating to passengers who are blind, deaf, obese,

frail or otherwise likely to inhibit movement during an emergency evacuation. Common sense? Only if you think of the common interests of all the passengers.

9   Surely it is reasonable to have those emergency seats occupied by people who can hear the instructions of the crew, read the directions for operating the emergency doors and assist other passengers in their escape.

10   But some organizations representing the deaf, blind and otherwise disabled reacted to the regulation only as a form of discrimination against their clients who, they insist, have a "right" to the emergency seats.

11   It is true that the majority must never be allowed to run roughshod over the rights of minorities. That is one of the tenets of the American system. But the notion of fairness to particular groups as an element of fairness to the whole has been perverted into a wholesale jockeying for group advantage.

12   Mutual fairness, with regard to both rights and responsibilities, can be the glue that bonds this polyglot society into a nation. Single-minded pursuit of group advantage threatens to rip us apart at the seams. The struggle for group advantage has us so preoccupied with one another's ethnicity that we are losing our ability to deal with each other as fellow humans.

13   What are we to make of this dismaying evidence that the relationships among us are getting worse—even among our college students? I believe two things are happening, and that they reinforce one another. The first is the racism and bigotry that never went away, even though it was relatively quiet for a time.

14   The second is what has been called the politics of difference. There is a pattern I have seen repeated on campuses across America. A black group, perhaps motivated by some combination of discomfort and rejection, goes looking (always successfully) for demonstrable evidence of racism.

15   I used to marvel at this search. Of course there was racism on campus, but what was the point of PROSPECTING for it, as though panning for gold?

16   I mean, where was the assay office to which one took these nuggets of racism and traded them in for something of value?

17   Well, it turns out that there IS such an assay office. It's called the Administration Building. Turn in enough nuggets and you get your reward: a Black Student Union, a special course offering, an African American wing in a preferred dormitory—whatever. All it takes is proof that you are a victim.

18   But despite the reports one hears these days, college students aren't exactly stupid. They are bright enough to see that there are rewards in the politics of difference, in demonstrated victimism. So the victories won by black students become models for similar prizes for gay students or Hispanic students or female students, all of whom gather up their nuggets of victimism and take them to the administration building for redemption.

19   Cornell University, one of the finest institutions in America, has a dormitory called Ujamaa College, a residence for black students; Akwe:kon, a dorm for Native Americans, and also the Latin Living Center.

20   That's the trend when the accent is on difference. And finally, it turns out that everybody gets something out of the politics of difference except white males, who start to feel sorry for themselves.

21   And if they can't find anyone to reward them for their sense of being slighted, they may turn to behavior that was once unthinkable—the "acting out" that manifests itself in incivility, reactionary politics, open bigotry and, on occasion, violence.

22   Every gain by minority groups justifies the sense of victimism on the part of white males, and every repugnant act of white males becomes a new nugget for a minority to take to the assay office.

23   Two things get lost in this sad ritual. The first is that the administration seldom gives up any of its own power: the gains of one group of students are extracted from other groups of students, who then must play up their own disadvantage to wrest some small advantage from another group. The administration's power remains intact.

24 The second overlooked aspect is that the process turns the campus into warring factions—each, no doubt, imagining itself as the moral successor to the heroes of the Civil Rights Movement. There's a difference, though. Dr. King's constantly repeated goal was not special advantage but unity. His dream was not of a time when blacks would finally overcome whites; his dream was that we should overcome, black and white together.

25 His hope was not that we should celebrate our differences but that we should recognize the relative unimportance of these differences. The differences do not *seem* unimportant, of course. Sometimes we seem to notice ONLY our differences.

26 That's why I find it helpful to look at what used to be the Soviet Union and what used to be Yugoslavia. From this distance, it seems clear that the similarities between the Serbs and Croats and other ethnic neighbors in Bosnia-Herzegovinia should outweigh their differences.

27 They share the history of a place and indeed many were intermarried. But now that Yugoslavia has broken up, even the marriages have been ripped apart.

28 I find myself wishing these erstwhile Yugoslavs could see for themselves what distance makes clear to us. And I wish we could learn to appreciate how great our similarities and how trivial our differences, and get OUR act together.

29 A "Star Trek" episode of some years ago makes my point. Capt. Kirk and his crew rescue a humanoid who, on his left side, is completely black. His right side, it turns out, is altogether white.

30 They are in the process of trying to learn the origins of this stranger—Lokai, he is called—when they are confronted by a similar humanoid named Bele—this one black on his right side and white on the left. The Enterprise crew, of course, can hardly tell them apart. But the humanoids can see themselves only as complete opposites—which, of course in one sense they are. And not just opposites. Though they are from the same planet, they are also sworn enemies.

31 I won't try to tell you the whole episode, but let me recall this much. Lokai is thought to be a political traitor, and Bele, an official of their home planet's Commission on Political Traitors, has been chasing him throughout the galaxy for a thousand years.

32 Lokai tries to convince the Enterprise crew that Bele and his kind are murderous oppressors. Bele counters that Lokai and his kind are ungrateful savages. The Enterprise crew decides to travel near the strangers' planet.

33 When they come within sensor range they are surprised to learn there is no sapient life there. The cities are intact, vegetation and lower animals abound, but the people are dead. They have annihilated each other. These two have survived only because they happened to be in the business of chasing each other down.

34 And what do they do when they learn what has happened to their planet? They lunge at each other in furious battle. Though the Enterprise crew is appalled, Kirk is unable to convince the two enemies of the futility of their war.

35 "To expect sense from two mentalities of such extreme viewpoints is not logical," says Spock. "They are playing out the drama of which they have become the captives, just as their compatriots did."

36 "But their people are dead," Sulu says slowly. "How can it matter to them now which one is right?"

37 "It does to them," says Spock. "And at the same time, in a sense, it doesn't. A thousand years of hating and running have become all of life."

38   We don't learn from this "Star Trek" episode the nature of the original problem between these warring humanoids, though we can be certain each felt fully justified in continuing the war. They had made a mistake that too many of us make in real life: They had forgotten the difference between problems and enemies.

39   And so have we. Virtually every issue that strikes us as urgent or important is made more intractable by our insistence on seeing it as a matter of us against them.

40   Give us a problem, and we'll find an enemy. Is the U.S. economy in trouble? Make the Japanese the enemy. Are we concerned about the discouraged and dangerous underclass? Blame white racists.

41   Members of my own profession seem unable to tell a story, no matter how significant, unless they can transform it into a case of one person, or one group, against another—unless they can make it a matter of enemies.

42   It is not so much that the enemies we identify are innocent as that identifying and pursuing them takes time and attention away from the search for solutions.

43   It was no trouble at all to come up with evidence that the Japanese were hurting the American economy through predatory pricing, product dumping and nonreciprocity, and certainly all these things merited attention.

44   But the U.S. auto industry improved its position relative to Japan's auto industry not when we all became expert at bashing our Japanese enemy but when Detroit started making better cars.

45   And that's the point. The failure to distinguish between the enemy and the problem has us looking balefully at one another instead of jointly attacking the problem which, in most cases, is as much a problem for us as for those we attack.

46   Take the current fight over affirmative action, for instance. Politicians who lack the imagination to address the *problem* settle for giving us each other to attack. White men—particularly those with a high school education or less—are not imagining things when they feel less secure economically than their fathers were. But they make a mistake when they suppose that their jobs have somehow been handed over to black people in the name of affirmative action. More likely those jobs are in Taiwan or Singapore or have gone up in the smoke of corporate mergers and downsizing. We've got a problem, and we waste our time assaulting enemies.

47   Honest communication about the problem might lead us to look for ways to restore our industrial base, expand our economy, improve the quality of our products and put our people to work. Focusing on enemies produces stirring speeches and little else.

48   You've heard the speeches. You've watched as communities have been ripped apart by those who deliver these speeches. There's how Teresa Heinz, widow of the late Pennsylvania senator, described them in a recent speech:

> . . . critical of everything, impossible to please, indifferent to nuance, incapable of compromise. They laud perfection but oddly never see it in anybody but themselves. They are right all the time, eager to say I told you so, and relentlessly unforgiving. They occasionally may mean well, but the effect of even their good intentions is to destroy. They corrode self-confidence and good will; they cultivate guilt; they rule by fear and ridicule.

> They are creatures of opportunity as much as of principles, extremists of the left and the right who feed on our fear and promote it, who dress up their opponents in ugly costumes, who drive a bitter wedge between us and the Other, the one not like us, the one who sees the world just a shade differently. . . . They demonize us by our parts and tear our country to pieces.

49 My own formulation is less eloquent; they focus on enemies rather than on problems. They forget that, at the end of the day, when we've all taken our unfair shots at one another, this simple truth remains: The *problem* is the problem.

50 Our politicians and our factional leaders never miss an opportunity to list the atrocities the *enemy* has committed against us. But nothing changes.

51 Sometimes we're not even sure what we want to change, or what we want the people we call enemies to do. We say we want things to get better, when sometimes I think we only want to score points.

52 We say we want a society in which all of us can live together as brothers and sisters, and the whole time we are saying it we are busy creating another group of barriers to place between us.

53 It's a strange sort of progress we have made since the death of Dr. King. We have "progressed" to the point where we are embarrassed to speak of brotherhood, of black and white together, of our shared status as Americans.

54 That's not an accusation; it's a confession. All of us are capable of getting so caught up in the distance that remains to be run that we forget to give ourselves full credit for the distance we've come.

55 Yet, every now and then, we manage to overcome our embarrassment and see things as from a distance. In that spirit, I'd like to share something I wrote a while back—something I still believe but something I may have trouble saying again.

56 Here it is: The immigration applications, the legal and illegal dodges for getting into this country, the longings you hear in virtually every other part of the world all attest to two astounding facts.

57 The first, widely accepted though not always with good grace, is that "everybody" wants to be an American. The second, of which we take almost no notice, is that virtually anybody can *become* an American.

58 To see just how extraordinary a fact that is, imagine hearing anyone— black, white or Asian— saying he wants to "become Japanese." It sounds like a joke. One can live in Japan (or Ghana or Sweden or Mexico)—can live there permanently, and prosper. But it's essentially impossible to imagine anyone born anywhere else becoming anything else—except American.

59 It's a thought that crosses my mind whenever I hear demands that the government protect the ethnic or language heritage of particular groups: when African Americans demand that the *public* schools adopt an Afrocentric curriculum, for instance, or when immigrants from Latin America are sworn in as American citizens—in Spanish.

60 It crossed my mind again when I came across Jim Sleeper's essay, "In Defense of Civic Culture."

61 I won't try to characterize Sleeper's piece or to summarize its recommendations [the Washington-based Progressive Foundation]. I won't even tell you I agree with everything Sleeper has to say on the subject of race and ethnicity.

62 But he says some things that echo my own feelings, especially when I ponder the extraordinary possibility of becoming American.

63 He acknowledges the obvious: that the America that counted my great-great-grandfather as only three-fifths of a human being has never been free of ethnic and racial bigotry, and that that bigotry has sometimes achieved the status of law, of philosophy—even of religion.

64 But he notes something else: that America is one of the few places on the globe where accusation of such bigotry is a serious indictment. Even when America has been at its ugliest in fact—slavery, the slaughter of Native Americans, the internment of the Japanese and the full range of private and public atrocities, "yet always America held out the promise that, as Ralph Waldo Emerson put it, 'in this asylum of all nations, the energy of . . . all the European tribes [and] of the Africans, and of the Polynesians will construct a new race.'"

65 The civic culture Sleeper writes about includes this notion of Americans as a new and different race, but it also entails what he describes as characteristic American virtues: tolerance, optimism, self-restraint, self-reliance, reason, public-mindedness—virtues that are "taught and caught in the daily life of local institutions and in the examples set by neighbors, co-workers and public leaders."

66 It is, he suggests, the internalizing of these virtues that defines "becoming American."

67 But the transformation works both ways. If people from an awesome range of colors, cultures and ethnicities have become Americans, so has America become what it is (and continues to become) by absorbing and embracing these myriad influences.

68 Some of us are angry, and ought to be, that our academic texts and teachings still disregard or underestimate our part of these influences.

69 Some of us are disappointed that what we bring to the smorgasbord is often undervalued, even brutally rejected.

70 But surely the cure is in working for greater inclusion, not cultural isolation. That's what observers as different as Sleeper, Arthur Schlesinger and John Gardner have been saying. That's what Gary Trudeau was saying in that hilarious (and sobering) series of "Doonesbury" strips that ended with black students—already having attained their separate courses and dormitories—demanding, at last, separate drinking fountains. Sleeper's insight is that there is nothing "natural" or automatic about those values and attitudes that used to be called "the American way." Educators must teach them, he says, and also "teach that self-esteem is enhanced not simply through pride in one's own cultural origins but, more importantly, by taking pride in one's mastery of civic virtues and graces that all Americans share and admire in building our society."

71 Critics of this view will argue that Sleeper's virtuous and graceful American is a figment, that America is a deeply—perhaps irredeemably—racist society.

72 I prefer to think that Americans are still becoming Americans, just as America is still becoming America.

73 How can we accelerate that becoming? By recognizing its importance, by understanding that hating and running must not become all of life, and by working to grasp the difference between problems and enemies.

74 Confront a difficulty as a problem and you have taken the first steps toward creating the climate for change.

75 Confront it as the work of enemies and you create the necessity for DEFEATING someone, of intimidating someone, of browbeating someone into doing something against his will.

76 Enemies have to be sought out, branded and punished. Which, naturally, gives them one more reason to find an opportunity to strike back at us. And the beat goes on.

77 Problems, on the other hand, admit of cooperative solutions that can help build community.

78 Searching for enemies is most often a pessimist's game, calculated less to resolve difficulties than to establish that the difficulties are someone else's fault. Identifying *problems* is by its very nature optimistic and healing. The whole point of delineating problems is to fashion solutions.

79 Maybe that's what President Clinton had in mind when he called on America to bring back "the old spirit of partnership, of optimism, of renewed dedication to common efforts."

80 "We need," he said, "an array of devoted, visionary, healing leaders throughout this nation, willing to work in their communities to end the long years of denial and neglect and divisiveness and blame, to give the American people their country back."

81 And that is precisely what we need. America has had enough of the politics of difference, the marketing of disadvantage, the search for enemies. It's about time we started to work on what may be the most important problem we face:

82 How to heal our crisis of community and make America work—not for blacks or whites or women or gays; not for ethnics; not for Christians, Moslems or Jews—but for Americans.

Address on AIDS to the 1992 Republican Convention

◆ *Mary Fisher* ◆

The third night of the 1992 Republican Convention in Houston, Texas, was dubbed "Family Night." On that evening, August 19, the delegates heard speeches from First Lady Barbara Bush, Marilyn Quayle, the Vice-President's wife, and the Rev. Pat Robertson. The emotional highlight, however, of the convention speeches delivered in the Astrodome that evening was the short address by Mary Fisher. Fisher, 44 years old, was the daughter of Max Fisher, a wealthy Republican fund-raiser and former advisor to President Gerald Ford. One year before her speech, Fisher learned that she had tested positive for the human immunodeficiency virus that causes AIDS.

In her 15-minute speech, broadcast live by the major news networks, Fisher used the rhetorical technique of "enactment" to dramatize the problem of AIDS in America. By presenting herself as an example of the point she was trying to prove, Fisher sought a greater national sensitivity to the plight of AIDS victims (1, 2, 5, 15, 19).

At the beginning of the speech, she used compelling statistics to demonstrate the significance of the growing AIDS epidemic (3, 6). Fisher's central thesis was to awaken her immediate convention audience and suggest that the disease was "not a political creature" (4). Since the causes of the AIDS problem are found in ignorance, prejudice and silence (7), she seems to be indirectly attacking the Republican Party's stance on this issue. How well does Fisher establish her case for the true nature of AIDS? Was a national political convention the appropriate forum for this particular message?

Through personal testimony, revealed in balanced antithetical phrasing (12), Fisher issues a national "plea" for greater public awareness of AIDS (12–14). Is Fisher's use of her father's warnings against another Jewish Holocaust an appropriate historical analogy for the current AIDS problem (13)? How can the "shroud of silence" on AIDS (17–18) that she speaks of be finally lifted?

The most compelling part of Fisher's speech came in the closing paragraphs (19–23) designed as a public "letter" to her two young sons, Max and Zachary. Does the emotional power of this conclusion add to or detract from a "reasonable" understanding of the AIDS crisis? How do you finally judge Fisher's role as an enacted "messenger" (20) on this topic?

◆ The text of this speech was obtained from the *Chicago Tribune*, August 23, 1992, section 4, p. 1 & 4.

For a personal account of the events leading up to the composition and delivery of this speech, see Mary Fisher, *My Name is Mary: A Memoir* (New York: Scribner, 1996), pp. 221–244. For a brief analysis of the responses to Fisher's address, see Victoria L. DeFrancisco and Marvin D. Jensen, eds., *Women's Voices in Our Time: Statements by American Leaders* (Prospect Heights, Illinois: Waveland Press, 1994), 267–269.

1   Less than three months ago, at platform hearings in Salt Lake City, I asked the Republican Party to lift the shroud of silence which has been draped over the issue of HIV/AIDS. I have come tonight to bring our silence to an end.

2   I bear a message of challenge, not self-congratulation. I want your attention, not your applause. I would never have asked to be HIV-positive. But I believe that in all things there is a purpose, and I stand before you, and before the nation, gladly.

3   The reality of AIDS is brutally clear. Two hundred thousand Americans are dead or dying; a million more are infected. World-wide, 40 million, 60 million, or a 100 million infections will be counted in the coming few years. But despite science and research, White House meetings and congressional hearings; despite good intentions and bold initiatives, campaign slogans and hopeful promises, it is, despite it all, the epidemic which is winning tonight.

4   In the context of an election year, I ask you—here, in this great hall, or listening in the quiet of your home—to recognize that the AIDS virus is not a political creature. It does not care whether you are Democrat or Republican. It does not ask whether you are black or white, male or female, gay or straight, young or old.

5   Tonight, I represent an AIDS community whose members have been reluctantly drafted from every segment of American society. Though I am white, and a mother, I am one with a black infant struggling with tubes in a Philadelphia hospital. Though I am female, and contracted this disease in marriage, and enjoy the warm support of my family, I am one with the lonely gay man sheltering a flickering candle from the cold wind of his family's rejection.

6   This is not a distant threat; it is a present danger. The rate of infection is increasing fastest among women and children. Largely unknown a decade ago, AIDS is the third leading killer of young-adult Americans today—but it won't be third for long. Because, unlike other diseases, this one travels.

7   Adolescents don't give each other cancer or heart disease because they are in love. But HIV is different. And we have helped it along—we have killed each other—with our ignorance, our prejudice and our silence. We may take refuge in our stereotypes, but we cannot hide there long. Because HIV asks only one thing of those it attacks: Are you human? And this is the right question: Are you human?

8   Because people with HIV have not entered some alien state of being. They are human. They have not earned cruelty and they do not deserve meanness. They don't benefit from being isolated or treated as outcasts. Each of them is exactly what God made: a person. Not evil, deserving of our judgment; not victims, longing for our pity. People, ready for support and worthy of compassion.

9   My call to you, my party, is to take a public stand no less compassionate than that of the President and Mrs. Bush. They have embraced me and my family in memorable ways. In the place of judgment, they have shown affection. In difficult moments, they have raised our spirits. In the darkest hours, I have seen them reaching not only to me, but also to my parents, armed with that stunning grief and special grace that comes only to parents who have themselves leaned too long over the bedside of a dying child.

10 With the President's leadership, much good has been done; much of the good has gone unheralded, and as the President has insisted, "Much remains to be done." But we do the President's cause no good if we praise the American family but ignore a virus that destroys it.

11 We must be consistent if we are to be believed. We cannot love justice and ignore prejudice, love our children and fear to teach them. Whatever our role, as parent or policymaker, we must act as eloquently as we speak—else we have no integrity.

12 My call to the nation is a plea for awareness. If you believe you are safe, you are in danger. Because I was not a hemophiliac, I was not at risk. Because I was not gay, I was not at risk. Because I did not inject drugs, I was not at risk.

13 My father has devoted much of his lifetime guarding against another holocaust. He is part of the generation who heard Pastor Niemoeller come out of the Nazi death camps to say, "They came after the Jews and I was not a Jew, so I did not protest. They came after the trade unionists, and I was not a trade unionist, so I did not protest. They came after the Roman Catholics, and I was not a Roman Catholic, so I did not protest. Then they came after me, and there was no one left to protest."

14 The lesson history teaches is this: If you believe you are safe, you are at risk. If you do not see this killer stalking your children, look again. There is no family or community, no race or religion, no place left in America that is safe. Until we genuinely embrace this message, we are a nation at risk.

15 Tonight, HIV marches resolutely toward AIDS in more than a million American homes, littering its pathway with the bodies of the young. Young men, young women, young parents, young children. One of the families is mine. If it is true that HIV inevitably turns to AIDS, then my children will inevitably turn to orphans.

16 My family has been a rock of support. My 84-year-old father who has pursued the healing of the nations, will not accept the premise that he cannot heal his daughter. My mother refuses to be broken; she still calls at midnight to tell wonderful jokes that make me laugh. Sisters and friends, and my brother, Phillip, whose birthday is today, all have helped carry me over the hardest places. I am blessed, richly and deeply blessed, to have such a family.

17 But not all of you have been so blessed. You are HIV-positive but dare not say it. You have lost loved ones, but you dared not whisper the word AIDS. You weep silently; you grieve alone.

18 I have a message for you: It is not you who should feel shame, it is we. We who tolerate ignorance and practice prejudice, we who have taught you to fear. We must lift our shroud of silence, making it safe for you to reach out for compassion. It is our task to seek safety for our children, not in quiet denial but in effective action.

19 Some day our children will be grown. My son Max, now 4, will take the measure of his mother; my son Zachary, now 2, will sort through his memories. I may not be here to hear their judgments, but I know already what I hope they are.

20 I want my children to know that their mother was not a victim. She was a messenger. I do not want them to think, as I once did, that courage is the absence of fear; I want them to know that courage is the strength to act wisely when most we are afraid. I want them to have the courage to step forward when called by their nation, or their party, and give leadership—no matter what the personal cost. I ask no more of you than I ask of myself, or of my children.

21 To the millions of you who are grieving, who are frightened, who have suffered the ravages of AIDS firsthand: have courage and you will find support. To the millions who are strong, I issue the plea: Set aside prejudice and politics to make room for compassion and sound policy.

22 To my children, I make this pledge: I will not give in, Zachary, because I draw my courage from you. Your silly giggle gives me hope. Your gentle prayers give me strength. And you, my child, give me reason to say to America, "You are at risk." And I will not rest, Max, until I have done all I can to make your world safe. I will seek a place where intimacy is not the prelude to suffering.

23 I will not hurry to leave you, my children. But when I go, I pray that you will not suffer shame on my account. To all within the sound of my voice, I appeal: Learn with me the lessons of history and of grace, so my children will not be afraid to say the word AIDS when I am gone. Then their children, and yours may not need to whisper it at all. God bless the children, and God bless us all. Good night.

The Pretending Press

◆ *Charlton Heston* ◆

A famous actor, better known for playing prophets and warriors, Charlton Heston surprised many Americans when he was elected President of the National Rifle Association (NRA) in 1998. Heston, however, has had a long personal history of political activism. Once a moderate Democrat, Heston, as President of the Screen Actors Guild, attended Martin Luther King, Jr.'s March on Washington in August 1963. Like fellow actor Ronald Reagan, Heston switched parties to become a conservative Republican and now heads Arena PAC, a political action committee dedicated to protecting and promoting the Bill of Rights to the U.S. Constitution. After assuming the presidency of the NRA, Heston told *Time* magazine that he "vowed to continue waging a 'cultural war' in which gun control is only the first line of skirmish." (See *Time,* July 6, 1998, p. 45.) Over the last two decades, Heston has crusaded against such issues as homosexual rights, feminism, and multiculturalism.

On March 2, 1999, Heston spoke to the Inland Press Association convention in Tucson, Ari-

zona. The Inland Press Association, founded in 1885, is a not-for-profit organization owned by its member newspapers and operated by a volunteer board. Inland has more than 720 daily and weekly newspaper members in 48 states, Bermuda, and Barbados.

Heston's presentation is a clear example of a speech designed primarily to create concern for several problems confronting American society in the late twentieth century. The speech could be evaluated according to what the American educator John Dewey termed his "reflective thinking" approach. One of the most recent interpretations of Dewey's approach is outlined by Michael and Suzanne Osborn in *Public Speaking* (5th ed., Boston, Houghton Mifflin: 2000, p. 450). According to Osborn and Osborn, defining a problem that may face society should involve five steps: 1) a specific description of the problem; 2) an exploration of the causes of the problem; 3) a consideration of the history of the problem; 4) a determination of who is affected by the problem; and 5) a decision

◆ The text of this speech was provided by the National Rifle Association in behalf of Charlton Heston and is reprinted with his permission.

whether adequate information is available to understand the problem. If adequate information is not available, obtain the information.

Heston begins his speech with a touch of humor (1–2). Does he effectively establish a sense of credibility with the audience by using this joke? How well does Heston make the transition (3–6) from his opening comments to his thesis (7)? Who does Heston "blame" for the "pretending" (8–9) problem? How might the members of this specific audience react to being partially blamed for this problem? What are the forces that Heston believes have caused a real threat to free speech (10–11)?

Central to Heston's "pretending press" claim is the statement that few seem to care for the truth (13). How well does he support his claim for this aspect of the problem? What caused the problem with current news coverage of Clinton and earlier with Ronald Reagan (14–16)? Who are the people harmed when the "press pretends" (17–18)? Why does Heston believe that the "anti-gun" issue has been incorrectly analyzed by present news coverage (19–21)? What is the real problem, according to Heston, about the Second Amendment (22–25)? What are the consequences of the "dishonesty" (26–28) that Heston seems to blame directly on members of his audience? How appropriate is it for this speaker to be attacking part of his audience regarding this problem on this occasion?

As Heston concludes his speech, he briefly suggests some potential solutions to the "pretending press" problem. Do his proposals (30–34) seem useful and appropriate? How do you think his audience might respond to the implied tone of these suggestions? Is his use of the phrase "co-conspirators" (36) too harsh for the conclusion of this presentation?

◆ ◆ ◆

1   I remember my son when he was five, explaining to his kindergarten class what his father did for a living. "My Daddy," he said, "pretends to be people."

2   There have been quite a few of them. Prophets from the Old and New Testaments, a couple of Christian saints, generals of various nationalities and different centuries, several kings, three American presidents, a French cardinal and two geniuses, including Michelangelo. If you want the ceiling repainted I'll do my best; somehow there always seem to be a lot of different fellows up here. I'm never sure which one of them gets to talk. Right now, I guess I'm the guy.

3   Like all actors I love that explosion of applause when I stir your emotions. But tonight I know I may not get it. That's okay. Because tonight I want to stir your minds instead.

4   I think of myself as an honest man. I think you're honest people, too. You preside over an honorable profession.

5   But when I undertake my beloved profession, I am by definition something less than honest. When I act, I pretend. I'm not really dishonest . . . just participating in a mutually consenting deception. It's an understood covenant with my audience. I agree to deceive them . . . temporarily . . . and they agree to believe me . . . temporarily. When it works, it can be awesome. Audiences laugh, cry, think. For just a while, they believe.

6   Tonight I submit that you are much like me. You too are actors, pretending. I say this because of the remarkable sameness of your script on national news stories. Every day, coast to coast, from paper to paper, newspapers read in surprising sync. Put down one paper and pick up another, and you think "Oh, yes, this is where I came in." The staging is the same, the action is blocked, and the plots unfold so audiences everywhere can play along.

7   I submit that your profession, like mine, is pretending. You manipulate your audience with the experience they seek and an outcome you can predict. In that sense, I've worked with people like you all of my life.

8   Don't get me wrong—I'm not blaming you. Performers must be sensitive to their audiences to gain their approval and to pay the bills. I see the topics on your agenda reflect this. "How to Overcome News Department Resistance to Marketing Change" . . . "How to Link Market Research to News Department Changes." The pressure to pretend, and pretend well, is intense.

9   But as the Twentieth Century closes, we must assess the injury of dishonesty upon the First Amendment freedom of speech and press . . . because they alone lead us to Truth and thus to Freedom.

10   If 50 years ago, you set out to destroy free speech, you'd invent television and the Internet . . . to indoctrinate a drowsy and cynical society into that dumbed-down cult called "couldn't-care-less" whose mantra is "whatever."

11   We're almost there. Political correctness tells us what to think, so the polls tell the press what to say in order to reflect what we think, so we'll feel normal when we're watching TV because we believe what we're being told because it's what we asked them to tell us. This is Clinton's legacy to American culture. Leadership by looking in mirrors. Poll-plug-'n-play pretending. Closed-circuit confirmation of self-affirming, self-gratifying, self-delusion. And an audience that plays along.

12   This makes your duty far more difficult, but infinitely more important. When there is so little respect for the written word, and so much aversion to free thought, causes cannot be championed and truth cannot be revered. As more Americans reject depth to gulp down fast-food journalism, drive-thru thought passes itself off as a self-governing democracy. But it's not. It's bankrupt brain fodder that's all about taste, not health. It offers stimulation, not nutrition. And I fear you're going along with the crowd, converting events into bite-size bits, more factoid and less fact. You're acting the part, just like me in Macbeth . . . pretending.

13   Deception, lying, dishonesty and cheating are now epidemic in America. Whether it's a 9th-grade geography test, or a driver's exam, or SATs, job tests, honors classes at Harvard, term papers or recruitment exams—or before a grand jury—cheating is rampant. Three out of four college students now admit to cheating on tests. Why isn't this a big story? Doesn't anyone here think it's news that deception—the assassin of truth—is now America's great expectation?

14   NBC has been pretending. As you know they sat on a taped interview with a woman who alleges then-Arkansas-attorney-general Bill Clinton brutally raped her in 1978. Her story was thoroughly corroborated. It broke in the *Wall Street Journal* last week, sort of. But NBC sat on it until last Wednesday night, when it was a handy 20-minute diversion in its ratings fight against the Grammies.

15   Imagine—if NBC had a credible woman on tape alleging that then-attorney-general George Bush had smashed the lips and torn the panties of a woman during a sexual assault in 1978—or any year. You'd leave this banquet now to file that story. And tomorrow morning's front pages would ignite like gunpowder. But you pretend not to notice, and the audience plays along.

16   None of you pretended not to notice in 1987 when Ronald Reagan sold arms to freedom fighters. Every paper covered the Iran/Contra scandal daily for weeks. But a weapons technology transfer to the Red Chinese by this President is virtually ignored. We're talking about missile weapons technology that gives the Red Chinese potential for making global war—that dwarfs the small arms of Iran/Contra. But you pretend not to notice, and the audience plays along.

17   Before you call me partisan . . . it's not that the Democrats get a free ride while the Republicans don't. It's that the Red Chinese get a free ride while our allies don't. Imagine if weapons technology were sold by our President to the Germans or the Japanese. There'd be a flood of stories about holocaust reparations and unchecked imperialism. But when it comes to the Red Chinese, the press pretends, and the audience plays along.

18   I don't care what you think about guns. But you hardly miss a chance to report criminal gun violence as evidence of need for gun control. That's dishonest enough. But when lawfully armed citizens defend themselves or thwart crime a million times a year . . . silence. When millions of concealed-carry license-holders commit not a single crime but, by their presence, prevent countless crimes . . . silence. You pretend there are no positive social benefits of firearm ownership, and your audience plays along.

19 Your anti-gun enthusiasm is relishing the new industry litigation. With thinly veiled jubilation, the press reports that growing ranks of big-city mayors are filing lawsuits against firearm manufacturers. They want to make a legitimate industry pay for the acts of criminals their own governments have failed to control.

20 Shifting blame from two-bit criminals to lawful manufacturers is absurd on its face. But there is almost no deployment of investigative reporting to pursue this story to its inevitable endpoint—destruction of the Second Amendment. The absence of critical analysis even leads your audience to the conclusion that it's a good idea.

21 But if a firearm company in Connecticut is financially responsible for the crimes of an armed ex-con in New Orleans, what's next? What about a legitimate pharmaceutical product wrongly used to commit date rape? What about a highpower muscle car wrongly used in a bank robbery getaway? What about your newspaper's coverage of a visiting diplomat's itinerary wrongfully used by a sniper to assassinate him?

22 If you follow the logic of this miasma of misplaced responsibility, as you should, any industry could be litigated to its knees. And if gun makers are forced out of business, there is no Second Amendment freedom. Now *that's* a story. Yet you pretend it's not there, and the audience plays along.

23 Whether it's pandemic cheating, or alleged rape, or weapons technology transfer, or litigation against the Bill of Rights, it seems these stories aren't news by your standards. Instead it seems there's a coordinated effort to ignore them.

24 I know . . . you're thinking, "Hey, pal, we reported that in our paper." But I don't mean an occasional mention. I mean that steady drumbeat of critical daily coverage that sets the agenda of national discourse for all other media . . . I mean taking your leading role to alert the common consciousness about uncommon threats. And as long as you pretend, as long as you abide the dishonesty, you are by your grandfather's standards, cowards.

25 If you say it pays the bills, I say it buys disaster. Because survival by dishonesty is a life not worth living. It's a hollow and counterfeit existence. Ask Bill Clinton. It's the dry residue of spin slung onto the walls—all talk, all coifed hair, all salesmanship, all marketing, all sizzle and no steak.

26 The consequence of all this dishonesty is that we lose our watchdog, which means we lose personal freedoms. Pretending has a price measured in sagging scholastic scores, homogenized thinking, *suffocating* political correctness, repressed ideas, simmering anger, increased divorce rates, more reliance on government, more regulation, exploding litigation, the willingness to voluntarily surrender privacy in return for government security . . . all because the press is no longer warning us about what that submission really means. And an audience that plays along cannot muster that eternal vigilance which is the price of freedom.

27 I believe this dishonesty has become so routinely expected of the press that the daily distribution of real information—the news—is no longer happening.

28 For example, I am weary of the non-story that Hillary Clinton does not live in New York and has not proclaimed that she has not announced that she is not yet a Senate candidate. It's not news, it's not certain, it's not possible for 18 months, it's not relevant, it's not even very interesting. But it gets lots of favorable press . . . they're already running Hillary-versus-Rudy polls. Meanwhile, Elizabeth Dole's speculation about running for President—a far more newsworthy prospect—gets a fraction of the space Hillary gets . . . and the band plays on.

29   So what do I want?

30   I'm asking you to leave the acting to guys like me. That's what I do, and it takes one to know one. Leave the hackneyed scripts and contrived staging to the thespians.

31   Abandon the pretending, deception and play-along-to-get-along dishonesty. Do the job you're supposed to do.

32   Do the job you tell each other and the public you do. Your duty is to debunk the dishonesty, not perpetuate it.

33   Don't report the irrelevant as relevant, don't serve up manufactured thought as news.

34   And please, don't give spin *any more turns*.

35   You will increase your circulation and revitalize your industry—and preserve our precious liberties—by driving out the actors and screenwriters who pose in your newsrooms as journalists.

36   Until you do, you are just co-conspirators, just bit players in predictable daily dramas with outcomes that have immense consequences for personal freedoms in our country.

37   That denouement is the precise opposite of what the Founding Fathers intended when they penned the Amendment which creates you, protects you, and gives you guardianship of the noble and peerless weapon which defends our Republic: the Truth.

38   Please . . . do not pretend there is anything less.

39   Thank you.

Chapter Seven

Speeches That Affirm Propositions of Policy

The Nature and Importance of Speeches That Affirm Propositions of Policy

Whenever people have been free to choose their personal or collective destinies, speakers have arisen to advocate courses of action. When a legislator stands at the rostrum of a state senate to recommend adoption of a new taxation program, he or she is advocating a policy. When a social reformer urges the abolition of capital punishment, a union official the rejection of a contract, a theologian an end to doctrinal conflict, or politicians a vote in their behalf, they all are engaged in the affirmation of policies.

Listeners and speakers would benefit from holding a *process view,* rather than a static view, of life. Such a view assumes that change, process, and coping with change are normal rather than exceptional phenomena. There is no "status quo," no static existing state of affairs, to defend. Present policies and programs always evolve, modify, and change to some degree. The choice is not between change and nonchange. Choices center on how to manage the speed, degree, and direction of inevitable change. Solutions and policies are never entirely permanent. No sooner has a program been instituted than the conditions which necessitated it have altered somewhat and new conditions have arisen, thus at least partly rendering the program obsolete.

Although a society's problems have been clearly illuminated, that society will not grow and prosper unless effective courses of action are advocated and undertaken. Some critics of contemporary American society argue that advocates too seldom conceive and present effective policies. The blunt evaluation in 1951 by William G. Carleton, a professor of political science, still seems remarkably applicable to much public discourse today:

> American speeches . . . for the most part have ceased seriously to examine fundamental policy, to discuss first principles, to isolate and analyze all the possibilities and alternative courses with respect to a given policy. . . . The result is that speeches today are rarely intellectually comprehensive or cogently analytical.

One reason for this shortcoming is the complexity of propositions of policy. The call to take action or change policy is made up of a number of intermediate claims involving all of the intellectual and rhetorical operations identified in the preceding chapters. For example, a speaker who is trying to demonstrate that "It is necessary for the federal government to subsidize the higher education of superior students" might first affirm the proposition of fact that "Many qualified high school graduates are unable to attend college for financial reasons," the proposition of value that "The development of the nation's intellectual resources is socially desirable," and the problem-centered claim that "The loss of intellectual resources constitutes a significant contemporary social and economic problem."

Speakers try to win acceptance of facts and values and create concern for problems on the basis that they are *true, good,* or *significant.* Speakers advocate policies in the belief that they are *necessary* and/or *desirable.* You might note that in the phrasing of propositions of policy, the term *should* (meaning it is necessary or desirable that) appears with great frequency.

Although many persuaders urge *adoption* of a new policy or course of action, in *Perspectives on Persuasion,* Wallace Fotheringham suggests other important categories of action that speakers may seek. In addition to adoption, speakers may defend *continuance* of an existing policy, urge *discontinuance* of an existing policy, or seek *deterrence* by arguing against adoption of a proposed policy. Sometimes speakers urge retention of the basic principles or structure of an existing policy along with *revision* of means and mechanisms of implementing that policy.

All of the following assertions may be classified as propositions of policy:

Proposition A: State sales taxes on internet commerce should be levied.

Proposition B: The United States should continue its support of the United Nations.

Proposition C: The use of marijuana should be decriminalized.

Proposition D: Financial support for Pima County's Sonoran Desert Conservation Plan must be strengthened.

If speakers have been intellectually shallow in affirming propositions of policy, at least a portion of the blame must rest with audiences who place too few demands on the speakers' rhetorical behaviors.

Criteria for Evaluating Speeches That Affirm Propositions of Policy

Although propositions of policy may call for continuance, discontinuance, deterrence, and revision in addition to adoption, the criteria that follow are written for the speech seeking adoption. The criteria can be made applicable to the other kinds of propositions of policy through modest rephrasing.

1. Has the speaker demonstrated or is it readily apparent that a need exists for a fundamental change in policy?

Because programs for action are responses to problems, the critic first should consider whether a legitimate problem exists. Among the subquestions the evaluator will wish to consider are the following:

- Are there circumstances that may legitimately be viewed as a problem?
- Is the present policy to blame for such problems?

- Is the problem sufficiently severe to require a change in policy, or may it be met through repairs, adjustments, or improvements in the present program?

In establishing a need for a fundamental change in policy, the speaker may affirm a series of propositions related to facts, values, and problems, each of which may be tested by the listener against criteria developed in earlier chapters.

2. Has the speaker provided a sufficient view of the nature of the new policy or program?

If a speech affirming a proposition of policy is to have maximum impact, the audience must know exactly what is to be done and how to do it. A sound, well-rounded policy usually encompasses not only the basic principles to guide the course of action but also the specific steps, procedures, or machinery for implementing that policy.

When the speaker describes the nature of a policy, he or she seeks increased understanding and should be assessed by the same criteria outlined in Chapter 3: Has the speaker made the policy meaningful to the audience? Has the speaker explained the policy in a sufficiently interesting way? Has the speaker shown the audience that the information is important?

3. Has the speaker demonstrated that the new policy will remedy the problem?

If the speaker is to be successful, the audience must believe that the policy will solve the problem and that it realistically can be put into operation. Among the questions that the listener should raise are the following:

- Can the policy be put into effect?
- Is the policy enforceable once it has been instituted?
- Will the policy alleviate the specific problem or problems described by the speaker (by removing the basic causes, or by speedily treating symptoms of a problem the causes of which are unknown)?

In response to such questions, a speaker will affirm one or more propositions of fact by advancing varied arguments. Speakers may argue that the proposed course of action has worked effectively elsewhere in similar situations; that analogous policies have succeeded in remedying similar problems; that experts attest to its ability to solve the problem. The best expert testimony is that which supports the specific program advocated, not just the general principle of the policy. Through word pictures and descriptions the audience should be made to vividly visualize the desirable consequences that will follow if the solution is adopted, and the undesirable consequences that will occur if it is not adopted.

4. Has the speaker demonstrated that the new policy is advantageous?

In addition to showing that the policy will alleviate the problem, the speaker should demonstrate that the policy will produce significant additional benefits and should indicate clearly how the advantages will outweigh any possible disadvantages. A speaker who advocates federal economic aid for public education could show that this policy would not only ease the immediate shortages of facilities and equipment but also would have the additional benefit of helping to equalize educational opportunity throughout the nation. The speaker might stress that the possible remote defect of federal interference in local educational matters is far outweighed by definite immediate advantages and benefits. To demonstrate such benefits, the speaker should employ appropriate examples, statistics, analogies, and expert testimony.

Because people characteristically resist new courses of action in favor of traditional policies, the speaker often will find it wise to recognize in advance and discredit relevant major policies and arguments that run counter to the proposed policy. Beyond providing adequate reasons for adopting the proposed policy, the speaker frequently must refute alternative programs and opposing arguments. An advocate might directly refute opposing arguments with evidence and reasoning; or show that the arguments, while true in general, really are irrelevant to the specific proposal at hand; or show that the arguments have only minimal validity and are outweighed by other considerations.

People also judge the advantageousness of policies on the basis of personal values and goals. An audience of business people may judge a program partly by the effect it will have on corporate profits. An audience of clergy may judge a policy by its consistency with spiritual values. An audience of minority group members may judge a proposal by the contribution it will make to equality of opportunity. An audience of laborers may judge a program by its effect on their wages. No matter who composes the audience, the speaker advancing propositions of policy must recognize that the values, wants, and goals of listeners influence their evaluation of courses of action. An advantageous policy not only removes the causes of a problem but also harmonizes with such values as efficiency, speed, economy, fairness, humaneness, and legality.

In evaluating speeches affirming propositions of policy, the listener could ask such questions as these:

- Does the policy have significant additional benefits?
- Do the advantages of the policy outweigh its disadvantages?
- Does the policy have greater comparative advantages than other relevant policies?
- Can the policy be experimented with on a limited basis before full-scale adoption is undertaken?
- Is the policy consistent with relevant personal and societal values?

In responding to these questions, the capable speaker will affirm a cluster of evaluative and factual propositions. Such propositions may, in turn, be evaluated in terms of the criteria proposed in earlier chapters.

Although the advocate may sometimes find it wise to fulfill each of the four major criteria in detail, at other times he or she may deem it unnecessary to meet all of them. Speakers may neglect to elaborate on the need or problem because they know the audience already shares their concern for it. A detailed statement of policy may be avoided because the speaker believes it sufficient to show that a general course of action is in some ways superior to one currently pursued. A persuader may avoid mentioning the negative effects of a proposal because its defects are not major. An arguer may pose a theoretical ideal and demonstrate the superiority of the proposal in light of that ideal. Concerning the appropriateness and ethicality of such choices of emphasis as just described, a critical listener may reach judgments differing from the speaker's. But whatever the constraints imposed by audience, setting, and subject, the speaker affirming a proposition of policy must demonstrate to the audience that the proposed course of action is necessary, desirable, and beneficial.

Conclusion

In a free society people often assemble to consider courses of future action. In evaluating such speeches, the listener/critic may raise numerous questions that cluster around the following four criteria. *Has the speaker demonstrated, or is it readily apparent, that a need exists for a fundamental change in policy? Has the speaker provided a sufficient view of the nature of the new policy or program? Has the speaker demonstrated that the new policy will remedy the problem? Has the speaker demonstrated that the new policy is advantageous?*

FOR FURTHER READING

Carleton, William G. "Effective Speech in a Democracy." *Vital Speeches of the Day,* June 15, 1951, pp. 540–44.

Gronbeck, Bruce E., et al. *Principles and Types of Speech Communication.* 13th ed. Longman, 1997. Chapter 7 explains the nature and uses of the "motivated sequence" structure (attention, need, satisfaction, visualization, action) that is especially useful in speeches advocating policies.

Fotheringham, Wallace C. *Perspectives on Persuasion.* Allyn and Bacon, 1966. Chapters 3 and 11 examine the major goals of persuasive discourse and some undesirable action responses by audiences.

Inch, Edward S., and Warnick, Barbara. *Critical Thinking and Communication: The Use of Reason in Argument.* 3rd ed. Allyn and Bacon, 1998. Chapter 11 discusses advocating and opposing policy propositions.

Jensen, J. Vernon. *Argumentation: Reasoning in Communication.* Van Nostrand, 1981. Chapter 5 explains potential lines of argument basic to presenting solutions, policies, and programs.

Walter, Otis M., and Scott, Robert L. *Thinking and Speaking.* 5th ed. Macmillan, 1984. Chapter 8 presents suggestions for persuading about solutions to problems.

Walter, Otis M. *Speaking Intelligently.* Macmillan, 1976. Chapters 1 and 5 and pp. 222–24. The author stresses the necessity of high-quality problem-solving for societal survival and growth and suggests strategies for persuading about solutions and policies.

Multiculturalism in the Public Schools

◆ *Diane Ravitch* ◆

At a meeting of the New Jersey School Boards Association on November 2, 1990, Diane Ravitch spoke on multiculturalism as an issue and policy for the public schools. She was then an adjunct professor of history and education in the Teachers College of Columbia University

◆ The text of this speech was provided by Diane Ravitch.

in New York City. Diane Ravitch is author of several books, including *The Troubled Crusade: American Education, 1945–1980,* and the California State Board of Education called upon her to structure the state's K–12 history curriculum. Although a Democrat, Ravitch served in the Bush Administration as an Assistant Secretary in the U.S. Department of Education.

What persuasive function might be served by her introductory massing of examples of contemporary European racial, ethnic, and religious conflict and her reassurance that, unlike some European nations, America will not disintegrate (1–4)? Ravitch advocates the general policy of multiculturalism for public school curricula and she specifically advocates adoption of a "pluralist" program to implement that concept (5, 12). She spends little time proving that a need for multiculturalism exists—that there has been a problem requiring a solution (6–11). She seems to assume that her audience of school board members from throughout New Jersey already acknowledge such a need and that they recognize precedents already in place for such a general policy.

Ravitch's major argumentative strategy is to contrast the defining elements of a pluralist and an ethnocentric program of multiculturalism—the former desirable and the latter dangerous (13–15, 26–27)—and also to present the advantages of pluralism and the disadvantages of ethnocentrism (16–22). How clearly and reasonably does she explain and justify the basic components of the pluralist policy? What types of evidence does she use and how soundly does she use them? What values are embodied in pluralism and violated by an ethnocentric approach? Antithesis is a major language resource used to

contrast the desirable and undesirable features of the two policies (17–19, 27). How effectively and fairly do you believe that she uses this resource?

At one point Ravitch mentions a "common American culture" embodied in "music, food, clothing, sports, holidays, and customs" that reflects multicultural influences (14). How clearly and adequately is the nature of this common culture demonstrated here and elsewhere in the speech? At another point she poses an either-or choice with only one of the choices pictured as desirable (22). Must we be forced to choose as she describes? Cannot schools foster *both* pride in heritage *and* knowledge, creativity, and cooperation? Consider her massive accumulation of historical examples of hatred and violence stemming from extreme ethnocentrism (23–25). Does pride in and knowledge about ethnic heritage necessarily result in such barbarism?

Almost in passing, Diane Ravitch mentions Afrocentrism as a type of ethnocentrism and makes an analogy between Afrocentrism and earlier "whites-only" curricula (16). Does she develop this analogy fully and clearly enough to be reasonable? For example, what are the "flaws" and "wild inaccuracies"? Are they simply to be inferred from the following paragraphs? You will want to compare Ravitch's speech with the following speech by Molefi Asante on Afrocentrism. Is Afrocentrism ethnocentric in the major negative ways that Ravitch contends? For a much more complete and detailed defense of the pluralist approach and a more specific attack on the Afrocentric approach, see Diane Ravitch, "Multiculturalism: E Pluribus Plures," *The American Scholar,* 59 (Summer 1990): 337–354.

1   I recently returned from Eastern Europe, where nationalism and ethnicity are on the rise, in ominous ways. Czechoslovakia may split into two nations, the Czechs and the Slovaks. Armenians and Azerbaijanis are killing each other. The Romanians are unresolved about how to deal with their Hungarian minority; the Hungarians are unresolved about how to deal with their Romanian minority. Yugoslavia may disintegrate if Serbs, Croats, Albanians, Slovenians, Slavonians, and Montenegrens find it impossible to get along together.

2   And of course religious tension is also on the rise. The Poles are reintroducing religious education in their public schools. And ugly manifestations of anti-Semitism are again in the air. Throughout Eastern Europe there is the occasional and amazing phenomenon of anti-Semitism without Jews.

3   Here in the United States, we too are preoccupied with tensions about race, ethnicity, and language. This is inevitable, because we are a multiracial, multiethnic society, and we have people in America who speak the languages of every other nation in the world.

4   And, unlike Yugoslavia, Czechoslovakia, and the Soviet Union, we are not going to disintegrate. First, because we have no territorial basis to our racial-ethnic differences; and second, because racial and ethnic and linguistic issues have been part and parcel of American history from our earliest days.

5   The issue that today confronts the schools is multiculturalism. It is the buzzword of the 1990s. What is it? Why has it become a major controversy? How should the schools respond? Why do some people find it threatening? How can it become a positive force in our schools and society?

6   Due to demographic changes and new immigration of the past generation, there is today widespread cultural diversity in our schools and in our society. Children in American classrooms represent all of the world's races, religions, and ethnic groups.

7   Our greatest concern as educators must be to educate all of these children so that they can enjoy productive lives as American citizens. All of our children must be equipped for the demands of the 21st century. In the past few years, demands have been made to change the curriculum to reflect the changing realities of American society.

8   These are not new issues in American education. Twenty years ago, black educators complained about the lily-white textbooks used in the schools. Their complaints were well-founded. The literature textbooks never included a black poet or writer. The history textbooks included slavery as a cause of the Civil War, but otherwise neglected the lives and experiences of black Americans and ignored the grim realities of racial segregation and discrimination.

9   A generation ago, the city of Detroit inaugurated the first multi-ethnic teaching materials, and other big-city districts began to demand changes in the textbooks. In higher education, scholars advanced the frontiers of knowledge, recovering the long-neglected history of blacks, women, Indians, and immigrants. The work of black leaders like W. E. B. Du Bois, Frederick Douglass, Harriet Tubman, James Weldon Johnson, and Ida B. Wells began to receive new attention. Based on years of solid research, the textbooks in our schools began to reflect a far more interesting America.

10   As a result, the textbooks in our schools today are dramatically different from the textbooks that I read as a child. The most widely used history textbook, Todd and Curti's *Triumph of the American Nation,* presents a picture of a pluralistic America, a nation that is multiracial and multiethnic, a nation built by men and women and people of all different origins.

11   And this approach has become commonplace among today's textbooks. Today our textbooks routinely illustrate children and adults of all races engaged in a variety of occupations, and routinely pay attention to the achievements of people from different backgrounds. Children's reading books include the writings of a wide variety of people, of diverse origins.

12   Given the rapid changes of the past generation, why is multiculturalism a controversial issue today? The controversy arises because the word multiculturalism means different things to different people, and it is being used to describe very different educational approaches. The two basic approaches are either pluralist or ethnocentric. One has the potential to strengthen public education, the other has the potential to harm it.

13   The pluralist approach recognizes that one of the purposes of public education is to create a democratic community and to expand children's knowledge beyond their own home and neighborhood to a larger world. In doing so, education must prepare children to live in a world of competing ideas and values, to be able to live and work with people from different backgrounds, and to learn to examine their own beliefs.

14 The pluralist approach to American culture recognizes that we have a common American culture that was shaped by the contributions of all of many different groups—by American Indians, by Africans, by immigrants from all over the world, and by their descendants. Consider American music, food, clothing, sports, holidays, and customs—all of them demonstrate the commingling of diverse cultures in one nation. We are many peoples, but we are one nation. Paradoxically, we have a common culture that is multicultural. It was shaped by all of us, and we reshape it in every generation.

15 The ethnocentric approach to American culture insists that there is no common culture, and that each of us must trace our origins to the land of our ancestors and identify only with people who have the same skin color or ethnicity. Each of us, by this definition, is defined by who our grandparents were. We must look only to people of the same group for inspiration, for it is they—and they alone—who can offer us role models of achievement. By this approach, I cannot be inspired by Harriet Tubman's bravery or by Zora Neale Hurston's moving prose or by Octavio Paz's eloquence because I am not from their racial/ethnic group. And black children, in turn, cannot be moved by the words of Abraham Lincoln or Elizabeth Cady Stanton or Robert Kennedy because they are of a different race. Ethnocentrism insists that each of us is defined by our race or ethnicity.

16 Some of our schools today have adopted the ethnocentric approach. Sometimes it is called Afrocentrism, and it is modeled on the whites-only curriculum that prevailed in American schools until a generation ago. It contains the same flaws and is equally subject to wild inaccuracies and pervasive bias.

17 What I would suggest to you is that these two approaches—pluralism and ethnocentrism—cannot both be multicultural, because they are completely opposite in purpose. One teaches children that they are part of a multiracial, multiethnic world, the other immerses them in a prideful version of their own race or ethnicity.

18 Pluralism teaches us that we are all part of the great American mosaic and provides us with the glue of civic knowledge that holds the mosaic together. Ethnocentrism teaches children to regard with respect only those of their own particular group.

19 Pluralism teaches that despite our surface differences, we are all human. Ethnocentrism teaches that our differences define us.

20 There is a significant difference in the methods by which these two very different approaches are taught. In the pluralist classroom, the teacher should stress critical thinking. Students should learn about every subject with a critical eye. They should be taught to ask questions, to wonder "How do we know what we know?" "What is the evidence for what we believe?" This is the very opposite of indoctrination. By this approach, it is possible to study the history of religion in a public school classroom, because the object is to learn about it, not to become a member of the faith.

21 By contrast, in the ethnocentric classroom, students are taught to believe in certain truths about their race or ethnic group. They are expected to believe what the teacher and the textbook believes, not to raise doubts or look for alternative explanations. The teacher offers up a pantheon of heroes and stories about the struggles of the faithful, and students are not supposed to disagree. The message of the ethnocentric classroom is, believe what you are told; do not question or doubt. In the same sense, the ethnocentric classroom resembles a sectarian approach to teaching.

22 Based on method alone, public education must reject ethnocentrism. The public schools do not exist to indoctrinate students into the faith of their ancestors or to instill ethnocentric pride—not for whites, or blacks, or Hispanics, or Asians, or American Indians. The public schools must prepare the younger generation to live in the world of the 21st century, a world of global interdependence, a world of differences—where what will count is what we know, what we can do, and our ability to think creatively and work with others.

23 The history curriculum should not become a tool to build self-esteem or ethnic pride. It is a subject in which to learn about our society and the world, and sometimes the truth can be unpleasant. All of the peoples in the world have been guilty of terrible misdeeds: the Aztecs and Mayans practiced human slavery and human sacrifice; Germans and other Europeans committed genocide against millions of Jews and other Europeans during the Second World War; in Soviet Russia, millions of landowners and political dissidents were killed by their own government; the regime of Idi Amin slaughtered hundreds of thousands of Ugandans; in Nigeria, a million or more Biafrans were murdered by other Africans; in Cambodia, the Pol Pot regime killed more than a million of their fellow Cambodians; the Turks slaughtered hundreds of thousands of Armenians at the time of the First World War; the Chinese Communists murdered millions of Chinese during the 1950s and 1960s; the Iraqis killed thousands of Iraqi Kurds with poison gas in 1982; the Burmese military gunned down thousands of students in 1988.

24 The record of death and genocide and slavery and human suffering is truly universal. The more we learn about history, the more humble we should all become. Human beings, it seems, have always found plenty of reasons to hate and kill other human beings. Differences in the way we look, the way we dress, the god we worship, the language we speak—almost anything has provided grounds for hatred. And if you pick up the daily paper and read the news, you will see that the beat goes on, all over the world—in India, Pakistan, Armenia, Romania, Liberia, Ireland, Burma, China, South Africa, and Lebanon.

25 Given the dismal record of humankind, particularly during the 20th century, it would seem that we as educators should do whatever we can to discourage ethnocentrism and to promote a sense of respect for our common humanity. Ethnocentrism does not belong in public education. It undermines the very purpose of public education, which is to create a community to which we all belong.

26 How can you tell whether a curriculum is pluralist or ethnocentric? It requires thought—it requires intelligence. How can you tell the difference between objective reporting and propaganda? You have to think about it. How can you tell the difference between science and creation science? You have to think about it.

27 Here are some parameters: The pluralist curriculum stresses learning about a subject, while the ethnocentric curriculum indoctrinates students into the tribe or the ways of the elders. The pluralist curriculum promotes mutual respect among people from culturally different backgrounds, while the ethnocentric curriculum promotes feelings of anger, vengeance, bitterness, and hatred. The pluralist curriculum promotes a sense of mutuality and interdependence, while the ethnocentric curriculum promotes racial and ethnic separatism. The pluralist curriculum promotes the building of a community that crosses ethnic/racial/religious lines, while the ethnocentric curriculum builds separate communities based on race or ethnicity or religion.

28 My parents were immigrants, yet I feel that I too inherited Thomas Jefferson's claim that "All men are created equal." I am a woman, yet I feel that I too share Abraham Lincoln's call to rededicate ourselves to the proposition "that government of the people, by the people, for the people, shall not perish from the earth." I am white, yet I celebrate Martin Luther King, Jr. as a role model of brevity, profundity, and eloquence.

29 We were not born knowing how to hate those who are different. As the song in *South Pacific* says, you have to be taught to hate, "you have to be carefully taught." It should be our goal as educators to teach respect and mutuality.

30 Culture is not skin color. Culture is history, tradition, and experience. Just as we need to know those experiences that make us different, we need to know the ideas and experiences that hold us together in community. We are all of us—black and white, Hispanic and Asian, American Indian and recent immigrant—in a common project. Education is the means that we have chosen to make it work. It is the spirit of interdependence, the spirit of mutuality, the spirit of respect for our many heritages, and the spirit of common purpose that we must build and cultivate in our schools.

Imperatives of an Afrocentric Curriculum

◆ *Molefi Kete Asante* ◆

"When a lot of people, especially white people, hear the word 'Afrocentricity,' they feel threatened, nervous, or both. They shouldn't." This is the reassuring view developed at length in a guest editorial in the *Washington Post National Weekly Edition* (November 26–December 2, 1990, p. 28) by Franklyn G. Jenifer, president of the historically black Howard University in Washington, D.C. In contrast, David Nicholson argues in a commentary essay on multicultural curricula in the *Washington Post National Weekly Edition* (October 8–14, 1990, pp. 23–24): "The question, though, is not whether the curriculum needs to be changed, but whose vision will prevail—that of the nationalists and the zealots, or that of more reasonable people who still believe in a common American culture and shared national values."

When Molefi Kete Asante addressed over two thousand listeners at the Detroit Public Schools Annual Teachers Conference in Cobo Hall in Detroit on February 4, 1991, clearly he was at the center of a national controversy. Asante, then chair of the Department of African American Studies at Temple University in Philadelphia, has been a Fulbright professor at the

Zimbabwe Institute of Mass Communications, and is chief consultant for the Baltimore public school system's Afrocentric Curriculum Project.

Asante intertwines his presentation of the problem and the proposed solution. The problem—the need to change from a Eurocentric to a truly multicultural curriculum—is described and explained at length (7, 9, 12, 16–17). Asante heightens concern for the problem through examples (10–11) and through an analogy that encourages whites to perceive the issue from an African American viewpoint (4–5). In analyzing this analogy, you are encouraged to apply the relevant standards for soundness of literal analogy discussed in the theory section of Chapter 4 on propositions of fact.

Asante advocates adoption of a multicultural public school curriculum based on the model of an Afrocentric curriculum. In describing the basic assumptions and components of the program, how clear are some of the key concepts (8, 19, 21). For example, what does he mean by hegemony (3), or by the subject-object distinction (6)? As another method of defending the components of an Afrocentric curriculum, Asante refutes criticisms by his opponents (4, 12, 18,

◆ The text of this speech was provided by Molefi Kete Asante.

22–24). What arguments and evidence does he use in refutation and how reasonably does he use them? Again, consider the clarity of his key concepts. How well would his audience probably understand his criticism of the pluralist-particularist distinction (19)?

Although in this speech Asante does not mention Diane Ravitch by name, in other speeches he does so in refuting his opponents. On some occasions, Ravitch has distinguished her pluralist multicultural program from what she terms Asante's particularist multiculturalism. Without naming them in this speech, Asante characterizes the criticisms by his opponents as hysterical, strident, screaming, and mis-readings (perhaps intentional). Consider in what ways, if any, Ravitch's arguments in the previous speech warrant such labels. Note that like Ravitch, Asante, too, depicts for his audience a stark either-or choice. Here it is between "true multiculturalism" based on the Afrocentric model and "maintenance of the white hegemony" through Ravitch's "pluralist" approach (20). To what degree would you accept this either-or choice as reasonable? Why?

Does an Afrocentric approach to multiculturalism as proposed by Asante seem dangerously ethnocentric in the ways contended by Ravitch in the previous speech? What concrete evidence from Asante's speech would you cite to support your judgment? For example, what is Asante's view on pride and self-esteem, on devaluation of European-heritage contributions to culture, and on a pluralism of respect for all different cultures?

In response to Ravitch's initial article in *The American Scholar,* 59 (Summer 1990), Asante and Ravitch engage in a very heated and more detailed exchange in the same journal (Vol. 60, Spring 1991, pp. 267–276). You are urged to read this exchange with their speeches. Advocates of policies to solve societal problems often argue their cases through varied channels as part of a continuous persuasive campaign: speeches; articles in scholarly journals or popular magazines; books; television talk-show or news program interviews; guest editorials or letters to the editor in newspapers.

◆ ◆ ◆

1   Since the publication of my first book on centering the educational experience in the child's reality, *Afrocentricity* in 1980 and subsequent works such as *The Afrocentric Idea* (1987) and more recently *Kemet, Afrocentricity, and Knowledge* (1990), there has been quite a lot of controversy about its relationship to the revitalization of curricula at every level of American education. Quite frankly, some of the more hysterical and strident voices against Afrocentricity seem to confirm what Alexander Thomas and Samuel Sillen wrote in their wonderful book, *Racism and Psychiatry,* about the interrelatedness of the idea of African American inferiority and African American pathology in the mainstream thinking.

2   The imperatives of an Afrocentric curriculum are found in three important propositions about education:

1. **Education is fundamentally a social phenomenon.**
2. **Schools prepare children for society.**
3. **Societies develop schools suitable to the societies.**

3   I have argued for an Afrocentric curriculum as a way to systematically augment the teaching of African American children and as a method of centering children in their own historical experiences. Since the primary mode of instruction and the basic design of curriculum are Eurocentric, we have never been in danger of losing the centeredness of white children. An Afrocentric curriculum has to be developed before a general multicultural curriculum can be implemented. If there is no organic presentation of scope and sequence information about the African American, then there can be no

multicultural project because most Americans, including African Americans, are woefully ignorant of the African American experience. Educated in the same system of white hegemony as other students, the African American comes out of the experience of school knowing next to nothing about Africa or African Americans. White students, without the benefit of cultural hearsay, know even less.

4 Opposition to the idea of teaching children from the standpoint of their centeredness rather than marginality has reached screaming levels. Those who oppose a centric education for African American children seem to say that content does not matter, yet the same opponents would find it unthinkable to teach white children a curriculum that is not centered in their experiences. For the most part, what we have right this moment in American education is a self-esteem curriculum for white children. It would be interesting to test the theory that self-esteem does not matter in the curriculum by simply eliminating the Eurocentric basis of the present curriculum and replacing it with, say, an Asio-centric one. Would some white children master such a curriculum? Of course they would. But a larger number would simply find the information, accurate as it might be, about the Vedic Period, varuna, Mokska, Bodhisattva, and the Ulama, a rather dislocating experience for them.

5 Accustomed as they would be to their parents stories about King Henry VIII, Shakespeare, Goethe, Joan of Arc, and Homer, white children in an Asiocentric classroom would find it extremely troubling. Can one expect any less of children of African descent who are fed only Eurocentric information?

6 Across this dynamic nation there is a renewed sense of the possible in education. The reason for the excitement lies in a very simple proposition about education: children will learn with a greater sense of integrity if they view themselves as subjects rather than as objects. When a teacher places a child in the context of the information being taught the child gains a greater sense of self and more enthusiasm for learning. There are enough studies, including those of Dr. Faheem Ashanti of the North Carolina Central University, to demonstrate the value of this proposition.

7 Stated particularly, African American or Latino children should be taught in such a way that they are not alienated from the material they are supposed to be learning. Children of European ancestry do not have to be reinforced in this way because the manner of teaching and the curriculum itself perpetuate a Eurocentric hegemony in education. Furthermore, this view is promoted as a universal truth.

8 Education should reinforce students in their history and heritage as a matter of choice. This does not mean that students should only be taught information that is comfortable and accessible but rather that the teacher should be sensitive to the historical perspectives of the students in the classroom. Any good communicator seeks to know his or her audience.

9 When teachers teach information centered only on the European experience they do not have to make a case about the teaching of European dominance and supremacy; the structure of the curriculum is itself the message of Eurocentric hegemony. What we teach is normally considered what is important and since most schools teach Europe instead of Africa or Asia, students assume that Europe is not only significant but that it is more significant than it ought to be in a multicultural society.

10 When one teaches about Marco Polo, or William of Normandy, or Goethe, or Joan of Arc, one is essentially engaging in the process of transmitting information about a cultural heritage and legacy. The names of the Africans, Ibn Battuta, or King Sundiata of Mali, or Ahmed Baba, or Yenenga, are never spoken in high school classes, and under the current curricular structure, if they were heard, would lack credibility even though they are by world standards certainly the equal of the Europeans I have mentioned in contrast.

11 The African American child whose parents speak of Sojourner Truth or James Weldon Johnson will most likely never hear those names spoken in any respectable way in a classroom from kindergarten to 12th grade. Instead of being reinforced in cultural heritage, African American children are being placed in crisis. Those who remain in school often have to put up with the total disregard of their own history and heritage. This is not so for white children and should not be so for any children.

12   Our society is multicultural and multi-ethnic and the idea of teaching as if the African American has no historical legacy or to force the discussion of our history to the Enslavement is to teach incorrectly and inadequately. More than this, it reinforces the false notion of white superiority and the equally false notion of black inferiority. We cannot afford to continue to promote the idea that African Americans who demand that an Afrocentric curriculum be infused into the general curriculum are asking amiss. It is the path of folly not just for African Americans but for all of the children of this society who are depending upon us to transmit to them the proper tools for living in this global village.

13   Another point should be made about this project. It is a project about accuracy and fullness in education. The aim of Afrocentric education is not merely to raise self-esteem of African American children. Indeed we have found that few African American children have problems with self-esteem; the real problem is with self-confidence. One can have a good feeling about one's personal attributes but feel a deep lack of confidence brought on by a lack of knowledge. Thus, while self-esteem may be a by-product of the central objective of the Afrocentric method, which is to provide a wholistic, accurate interpretation of the world, self-confidence will certainly be improved by this method.

14   Such an approach will have an impact on white students as well as African American, Latino, and Asian students. For some students it will be the first time that they will have heard the ancient Egyptians discussed as Africans or discovered that Africans played a significant role in the Revolutionary War. It is a fact that we African Americans were here before the United States government and many of our families have lived on this land longer than the families of many presidents of this country.

15   Of course, none of these ideas will have a full impact on education until there are big changes in schools of education throughout the nation. I am not aware of any school of education that has grappled with this problem in any serious manner. In some of the training institutions for teachers it is still possible for a teacher who will eventually teach in an urban setting to complete a degree without ever having taken a course in African American studies! This is truly unbelievable, but it is at the heart of the matter. Certainly the Afrocentric idea ought to be among the perspectives taught in institutions of teacher training.

16   A few months ago I asked fifty principals to identify the names of five African ethnic groups from West Africa. I explained to them that there were no African Americans three hundred and seventy-two years ago. Africans who were brought to America against their will came from particular ethnic groups often with long and important histories. Who are the African Americans you see in your schools? What are some of the names of the groups that combined in the Americas to produce the present African American population?

17   Sadly, almost no one knew the name of an African ethnic group that had become a contributor to the African American gene pool. Names like Yoruba, Hausa, Fulani, Ibo, Baule, Congo, Angola, Serere, Wolof, Mandinka did bring something to mind for a few of the principals when I began to mention them. These are the names of the people, who along with Native Americans and some Europeans, contributed to the present day gene pool of African Americans.

18   Afrocentricity is not an ethnocentric view. While Eurocentric views are often promulgated as universal views, e.g., classical music as European concert music or classical dance as European ballet, etc., the Afrocentric view seeks no valorization of African-centeredness above any other perspective on reality. It is human-centered in the sense that no one should be divested of his or her heritage or background. Normally, the only people asked to do so are those who do not hold physical or psycho-

logical power. Ethnocentric views valorize themselves and degrade others. Afrocentricity promotes pluralism without hierarchy.

19   To say that we are a multicultural and multi-ethnic society must not mean that we promote a view of these cultures only through the eyes of whites. A true multiculturalism presupposes that we know something about the cultures. Few of those who have spoken or written about multiculturalism seem to understand that the road to a true multiculturalism leads by the way of Afrocentricity. The development of a systematic, organic, wholistic portrayal of the African culture as opposed to a detached, episodic, personality-based version is necessary for a real multicultural project.

20   The idea of a pluralist multiculturalism and a particularist multiculturalism is a non-starter. This first idea is a redundancy and the second is an oxymoron. You either believe in a true multiculturalism or you believe in the maintenance of the white hegemony in education. As a nation we must choose between these positions, there is no other choice.

21   I have made my choice for multiculturalism which means that I need to know all I can about the cultures of the nation. Does it mean that we will now have to know more about Native Americans, Latinos, Asians? Yes, it does and we will be a better nation because of it. Does it mean that the enforcement of a white hegemony on information and process in education is over? Probably not. However, we will never be able to exercise the full potential of this nation until we realize the incredible beauty and value of the collective cultures of America.

22   Finally, Afrocentricity does not negate all Eurocentric views. It should, however, modify those views that are pejorative and stereotypical. By pointing to other perspectives including Native American, Asian, and Latino as well, Afrocentricity suggests a new compact among American peoples. Of course, this means that the Eurocentric idea will not control the structure of knowledge but become, as it should have been all along, one perspective besides many.

23   This should be welcomed in a society such as ours where we will have in fifty years a largely non-European population needing to be educated but needing to be turned on to education by having the same advantage European Americans have had all along, education which centers them in the experience being taught. No one has suggested that this cease being the case with European Americans. However, we have said that where the Eurocentric perspective has turned racist, ethnocentric, or sexist, it should eliminate those attitudes. Pejoratives and racist language should be removed and the curriculum infused with an Afrocentric curriculum. This step is absolutely necessary, otherwise there are those who say that they want multiculturalism without knowing anything about the African American culture. They say they favor multiculturalism and still want to retain the negative expressions about Native Americans or Latinos. The path to multiculturalism goes by the way of cultural respect. This is as true in the United States as it should be in Israel and South Africa, and any other nation where human beings of different heritages live together.

24   It is certainly a misreading, perhaps even a deliberate misreading, of the concept of Afrocentricity to say that it means a blacks-only curriculum. No one that I know has proposed we replace Shakespeare with Ahmed Baba or James Baldwin. We say let us share in the great diversity of everyone. Why not teach Maimonides alongside Frederick Douglass and Wendell Phillips? Why not discuss the contributions of Yenenga, or Yaa Asantewaa, or Nzingha, alongside those of Joan of Arc? If we learn about Marco Polo, what is wrong with learning about the African, Ibn Battuta who travelled farther than Marco Polo and was considered the greatest traveller of the medieval period? Why not alert students to the story of Abubakari II who is reported to have travelled to Mexico from his empire in West Africa in 1312? We must recognize that this nation is an incomplete project whose present is not its past and whose future will not be what we know now. Let us prepare all of our children for the multicultural future that is surely around the turn of the century.

Sacred Rights:
Preserving Reproductive Freedom

◆ *Faye Wattleton* ◆

Legalized abortion—whether to allow it and, if so, under what restrictions, if any—continues to be a major political and moral issue at the national, state, and local levels. In this continuing debate, advocates of differing positions and policies struggle over fundamental distinctions and concepts: the competing values of life and of freedom of choice; the tension between legal rights and moral responsibilities; the definition of when "life" begins; the constitutional separation of church and state—of religious doctrine and public policy.

In 1973 in *Roe v. Wade,* the U.S. Supreme Court in a 7–2 decision held that a fetus is not a person in a legal sense of the term and that laws restricting women's access to legal abortion violate her constitutional right to privacy. The Court held that a woman had the right to terminate her pregnancy until the final three months of the pregnancy. In July, 1989, in *Webster v. Reproductive Health Services,* a 5–4 decision by the U.S. Supreme Court agreed that Missouri had the right to prohibit use of public facilities and personnel to aid abortions that are not necessary to save the mother's life. Without overturning *Roe v. Wade,* the Court opened the option for states to consider more restrictive laws on abortion.

On June 25, 1990, Faye Wattleton accepted the "Ministry to Women Award" of the Unitarian Universalist Women's Federation at their meeting in Milwaukee, Wisconsin. Wattleton holds both Bachelor of Science and Master of Science degrees in nursing and since 1978 she has been President of the Planned Parenthood Federation of America. Planned Parenthood advocates contraception, abortion, sterilization, and infertility services as means of voluntary fertility regulation. In an analysis of Faye Wattleton as "Ms. Family Planning," Paula Span (*Washington Post National Weekly Edition,* November 2, 1987, pp. 8–9) observes: "Both supporters and foes go on at length about her articulateness, her presence, and her forcefulness." Indeed Faye Wattleton may be one of the most prominent and influential black women in America.

The Unitarian Universalist Women's Federation supports human rights for all, especially rights of women. The Federation supports the *Roe v. Wade* decision, quality in child care centers, concern for the family, and work for and with the aging. In accepting her award from this favorably disposed audience, Wattleton identifies points of commonality between herself, Planned Parenthood, and the Federation (1–4, 29, 33–34).

The policy that Faye Wattleton advocates and defends is legal protection for reproductive choice and for women's right to privacy (5). She advocates continuation of the *Roe* decision, constitutional protection of fundamental freedoms, and privacy from governmental intrusion (14, 28). She also advocates continued separation of church and state (9–10) and believes that morality should not be legislated (25). The *Webster* decision and the orientation of the cur-

◆ The text of this speech was provided by the national office of the Planned Parenthood Federation of America. After 14 years as President of Planned Parenthood, Faye Wattleton resigned on January 8, 1992.

rent Supreme Court are problems that threaten the *Roe* constitutionally protected policy (6, 8). Through antithetical phrasing, she alludes to other policies advocated by Planned Parenthood: sex education in public schools; adequate adoption and child care; improved birth control methods (27).

Wattleton argues against opposing positions by reducing them to absurdities—by extending them to their logical but ridiculous extremes (11–12)—and by exposing contradictions (18). Evaluate how fairly and reasonably she develops these arguments. What persuasive function might be served by her references to positive political changes in Eastern Europe (15, 23)? She employs statistics to argue that the shepherd has inappropriately strayed from the flock (32). Within a religious context, what objections might there be to the logic of this argument?

Finally, consider some of the distinctive language resources that Wattleton employs. Frequently she uses alliteration to associate a series of positive items (4, 5, 31). Parallel structure is utilized effectively to reinforce a point through a series of examples (13, 14, 21, 25). Note the vivid negative images that Wattleton creates to characterize some of her opponents: under siege (5); zealots (6, 22); fanatics (21); obscene (25); oppressive tyrant, vicious and violent (30). How reasonable and appropriate are these labels for the people she describes? What is your evidence to support your judgment?

◆ ◆ ◆

1 As some of you know, I am a minister's daughter, so addressing a religious gathering always feels like coming home. I'm *especially* comfortable in a Unitarian setting: I've had the honor of speaking from the pulpit of All Souls Church in New York; I've joined Forrest Church in his "All Souls World of Ideas" discussion programs; and last fall I took part in a sunrise Unitarian service in Kennebunk, Maine.

2 I can honestly say that some of my *best friends* are Unitarian Universalists!—including Planned Parenthood's executive vice president David Andrews. David and I were chatting recently with one of our affiliate presidents, whose husband is the Episcopal bishop of New Mexico. She was telling David that she feels very warmly toward Unitarians. When she and her husband first moved to Albuquerque, their new Episcopal church wasn't ready for use. Since Unitarians don't have summer services, the Unitarian church facility was made available to them. At that point I asked David, "Why don't Unitarians go to church in the summer?" David said, "I don't know, I guess it's just too hot." To which the bishop's wife replied, "Not as hot as it's *gonna* be!"

3 Planned Parenthood's founder Margaret Sanger was herself a Unitarian. In fact, the Brooklyn Unitarian Church gave her both spiritual and financial support back in 1916, when she opened the nation's first birth control clinic—the tiny storefront that grew to become the nation's foremost public health movement.

4 Since that first auspicious alliance, Planned Parenthood has enjoyed a warm partnership with generations of Unitarians the world over. As individuals and as a church, you've shown your commitment to tolerance and compassion—to civil rights and civil liberties—to the free exercise of any religion or *no* religion. Your faith has been a *clarion call to conscience* for women and men in all walks of life.

5 And your uplifted voices have never mattered more than *now*. For one of our most precious, most personal freedoms is imperilled as never before. Reproductive choice—the right that makes all our *other* rights possible—is under siege. Last July—16 years after *Roe v. Wade* recognized women's constitutional right to abortion—the Supreme Court retreated from that historic ruling. In *Webster v. Reproductive Health Services,* the Court severely curbed women's access to abortion—and invited an all-out attack on our cherished right to *privacy.*

6   Plainly put, *Webster* allows state governments to put *fetuses* first. And zealots in *every state* are trying to do just that. More than *450* anti-choice bills have been introduced in the past year in *44* state legislatures. Re-energized pro-choice forces have defeated most such efforts. But in Pennsylvania, Guam, and now Louisiana, legislatures have advanced bills that would virtually eliminate legal abortion.

7   When *Roe v. Wade* was decided in 1973, who could have *imagined* that Americans would be fighting this battle in *1990*? As Yogi Berra said, "It's like *deja vu* all over again!"

8   Historically, we have counted on the courts to *expand* rights that were not explicit in the Constitution—rights for women, minorities, children, the disabled. But *today's* Court interprets the Constitution the way fundamentalists interpret the Bible—with a stubborn literalism. If a right wasn't *spelled out* by that first quill pen, it doesn't exist! In other words, "If you don't see it on the shelf, we don't carry it—and we won't order it!"

9   One of the *most* troubling aspects of the *Webster* decision is the least-discussed. It concerns the preamble to the Missouri Constitution, which defines *human life* as *beginning at conception.* The Supreme Court refused to rule on this matter—and thus allowed Missouri to make a narrow, *religious* belief *the law of the land!*

10   Preferential treatment for *one* religion over *others* is blatantly unconstitutional. It's like that old bumper sticker from the '60s—"*Your kar*ma ran over *my dog*ma!" Since when is Roman Catholicism our national faith? The view of the Catholic Church—or any other denomination, for that matter—is valid for those who adhere to it. But Americans must *never* be *governed* by it—or by *any religious doctrine!*

11   We've already seen some *bizarre* legal outcomes of this religious definition of human life. Lawsuits have cropped up claiming fetuses as dependents for tax purposes—or charging "illegal imprisonment" of the fetuses of pregnant inmates—or seeking to reclassify juvenile offenders as adults by tacking an extra nine months onto their age!

12   What's *bizarre* today may turn *grim* by tomorrow. Compulsory pregnancy, forced Caesareans, surveillance and detention of pregnant women—these are the chilling, *logical* outcomes of laws that reduce women to *instruments of the state.*

13   We are *not* instruments of the state! We are *persons,* with human needs and human rights. It is nothing less than *evil* to deny our reproductive autonomy. Without it, our other rights are meaningless. Without it, our dignity is destroyed. And the first victims will be those among us who are already most vulnerable—those whose rights are *already* precarious—those whose access to health care is *already* limited—the young, the poor, and usually that means minorities.

14   But reproductive freedom is an issue that goes *beyond* the disadvantaged, *beyond* state boundaries, *far beyond* abortion itself. It goes to the heart of what this country stands for—to the principles embodied in our *Bill of Rights.* Our Constitution established powers of government and majority rule—and the purpose of the Bill of Rights was to set clear *limits* on those powers. The authors of that great document knew that certain fundamental freedoms must be *guaranteed*—*insulated* from public debate, *immune* to partisan politics.

15   For over 200 years, America has been "a light unto the nations." How disgraceful, that in *1989,* the year the Berlin Wall came down and the Iron Curtain parted, the only barricade that started to crumble in *this* country was the precious wall protecting our private freedoms!

16   The crack in that wall may soon go even further—this time disenfranchising *teenagers.* Supreme Court rulings are pending in two cases involving mandatory parental notification for minors' abortions.

17 Most of us think parents *should* be involved in such a serious decision. And most pregnant teens *do* tell their parents. But laws that *force a family chat* can be *deadly*—not only for teens in unstable or violent homes—but also for teens with *loving* families. In Indiana, where parental notice is required, one teenager risked an illegal abortion rather than disappoint her parents—and it killed her.

18 It's true that parental involvement laws provide something called a judicial bypass. Minors who feel they *can't* confide in their parents may appear before a judge instead. But the judge is in a hopeless bind: by ruling that a minor is *too immature* to choose an abortion, the judge rules by implication that she is somehow *mature enough to become a mother!* Such a paradox would try the *wisdom of Solomon!*

19 The fact is, judges simply have *no business* making this decision for teens *or* adult women. Any female capable of *becoming* pregnant must have the ability to *prevent* or *end* a pregnancy. That right must never depend on age, race, state residence, wealth—*or* the vagaries of partisan politics. That right is as basic and as precious as our right to assemble here today.

20 Such fundamental freedoms are the proudest heritage of our nation. But our heritage of *Puritanism* also remains deeply rooted. My favorite description of the Puritans is this one, by a 19th century humorist: "The Puritans nobly fled from a land of despotism to a land of freedom—where they could not only enjoy their *own* religion, but where they could prevent everybody *else* from enjoying *theirs!*"

21 The flames of intolerance still burn brightly in this nation. And, like all religious fanatics, *today's* Puritans subscribe to their own moral code—a code that embraces far more *brutality* than *morality.* To "save lives," they burn clinics. To "defend womanhood," they taunt and threaten pregnant women. To "strengthen the family," they invade our privacy. Blinded by their disregard for the *neediest* of women, they insist that making abortion *harder to get* will make it *go away.*

22 Haven't these zealots learned *anything* from history? Throughout time, women with unwanted pregnancies have *always ended them,* regardless of the law, regardless of the risk to our lives! Throughout the world, women and men equate *freedom* and *democracy* with the right to make private reproductive decisions, *free from government intrusion!*

23 The recent history of Romania is a perfect example. When Ceaucescu was overthrown, two of the *first acts* of the *new* government were to decriminalize abortion—and to deregulate the private ownership of *typewriters.* The new regime clearly recognized that *reproductive choice* is as *fundamental* as *freedom of speech!*

24 If only *our own* government were so wise. On the contrary, our president has taken a *jackhammer* to the bedrock of our basic rights. He has repeatedly asked the Supreme Court to overturn *Roe v. Wade.* He has attacked the federal family planning program, which helps *prevent* half a million abortions each year. And in a recent Supreme Court brief, his administration attacked not only the right to *abortion,* but the very *concept of privacy* that underlies our right to *contraception!*

25 It's nothing short of *obscene* that women are forced to *expose ourselves* to politicians—to submit our *private* matters, our *private* decisions, and our *private* parts to *public* debate! Morality should be taught in the home—it should be preached from the pulpit—it should be practiced in our individual lives—but it must *never* be legislated by lawmakers.

26 *Surely,* America's politicians have more *important* things to do. Like house the homeless, feed the hungry, and educate the ignorant. Like tackle the *root cause* of the abortion issue: *unintended pregnancy.*

27 Instead of compulsory ignorance, we need comprehensive sexuality education—in every home and in every school, from grades K–12. Instead of laws that punish pregnant women, we need our government's commitment to develop better birth control. Instead of pontifications about the *un*born, we need proper care for the children *already* born.

28 Finally, instead of sermons on the stump, we need to be *left alone by the government.* We need to remove the abortion debate *forever* from the legislative arena. We need a universal recognition that our civil liberties are *off limits to partisan politics!* They are *fundamental* rights! *Indivisible* rights! *Non-negotiable* rights!

29 *Your* advocacy is essential to making these goals a reality. I learned a lot about organized religion from my minister mother. So I know that congregational life can have a profoundly positive impact—not only on our daily lives as individuals—but on the formation of our values and principles as a nation. The best possible wielding of that impact is exemplified by all of you today. You are ever aware that *your* right to freely practice your faith is only as secure as *other* people's right to believe differently. You are eternally *intolerant of intolerance.*

30 When the mechanism of religion goes awry, it is an *oppressive tyrant.* Some fanatics are merely self-righteous. Others are vicious and violent. For *all* those who seek to browbeat the rest of us, I have *these* words, by the folklorist Zora Neale Hurston: "I'll bet you, when you get down on them rusty knees and get to worrying God, He goes in His privy-house and slams the door. *That's what He thinks about *you* and *your* prayers!"

31 Those of us who lead spiritual lives have a special responsibility to combat fanaticism. We must remind Americans that *true* morality lies in the freedom to *make* choices—not in *prohibiting* them. We must lift up our voices for liberty—among our families and friends, our colleagues and communities, our pundits and politicians. We must preach from our pulpits that we hold our privacy *sacred!*

32 Happily, the "gospel" *we* are spreading *already* has millions of adherents. The Roman Catholic Church, however, is less fortunate. As I'm sure you've heard, the Church has launched a *$5 million* P.R. campaign to promote its anti-choice message. Questionable priorities aside, this is clearly an act of *desperation.* Has the Church examined its membership lately? Lay Catholics are overwhelmingly *pro-choice!* Three out of four use contraception—77% favor legal abortion in some or all situations— and 85% say a woman can have an abortion and still be a "good Catholic." Clearly, the *shepherd* has strayed from the *flock!*

33 In *this* flock, though, I sense great unity and strength. Maybe that's because you can support reproductive rights and still be a *good Unitarian!* In fact, from what I understand, to be a good Unitarian *by definition* is to support liberty, justice, equality, and a plurality of opinions—and *that's* what *pro-choice really means.*

34 Margaret Sanger, the good Unitarian, once said: "I have always known that it is not enough just to know one great truth. Truth must be *lived*—not merely passively accepted." I know all of you share that courage and that commitment. I am proud to count you among my friends. Thank you for your prestigious award—but much more, for your partnership in our shared faith.

Address on Abortion

◆ *Jerry Falwell* ◆

As a television evangelist, Jerry Falwell's "Old Time Gospel Hour" reached over 500,000 homes during the mid-1980s. His Moral Majority conservative political organization claimed four million members. Falwell is founder and pastor of the Thomas Road Baptist Church in Lynchburg, Virginia, with over 20,000 members. Also he is founder and chancellor of Liberty University in Lynchburg. In late 1987 Falwell stepped down as head of the Moral Majority to devote more time to his ministry. In the summer of 1989, Falwell announced that the Moral Majority was being dissolved although the key policies that it had advocated would continue on the public agenda for national debate.

At the Unity '90 Conference in Chicago on June 28, 1990, Falwell addressed a wide range of groups and individuals associated to one degree or another with the pro-life or anti-abortion movement. At such a conference, one natural goal of the speech was to promote social cohesion (8–10). He warns that conflict and bickering among pro-life groups only weakens the effort to reverse *Roe* and to make abortion illegal (4–7). Also he urges cooperation and compromise among the diverse groups in the service of the larger goal (52–54). And of the four "challenges" he describes facing them, the first two stress the social cohesion theme (10–11). Falwell's early massive accumulation of diverse statistics vividly reminds his listeners of the difficulties they still face (3).

But the bulk of Falwell's speech advocates instrumental courses of action that should be adopted to promote significantly the achievement of the ultimate policy—reversal of *Roe* and making abortion illegal. One major action urged by Falwell is opposition to development and distribution of RU 486, the so-called abortion pill (14–15).

Clearly, however, Falwell's primary focus is advocacy of reframing the public debate on the abortion issue and overcoming confusing and misapplied labels (12–13). He offers an extensive plan of argumentation to retake the initiative through refuting ten "myths and misconceptions" that have been "perpetuated for so long by our opponents and the media" (17–50).

Consider, now, the array of rhetorical choices that characterize his speech. Bear in mind that the unspoken definitional assumption that "life" (humanness) begins at conception undergirds his statistics on the "killing" of "innocent and defenseless children" (1, 3). For some of the statistics he uses, he specifies their sources (36, 39–41) while for other statistics he does not specify sources (3, 43). Why should he or should he not have supplied more information on the sources and methods from which the statistics stem? Note also the specifics on several research studies are lacking (18, 19).

You are urged to apply the relevant standard tests for soundness of use of testimony (discussed in Chapter 4 on propositions of fact) to his extensive reliance on various kinds of testimony. Falwell quotes respected religious figures (9, 14, 37, 55), medical experts (35), opponents to use their own words to convict them (15), and

◆ The text of this speech was provided by Rev. Falwell's office at Liberty University.

journalistic sources that combine judgments with examples (11, 30, 33, 45–46, 49). Especially evaluate the reasonableness of his pervasive use of "reluctant" testimony from persons normally identified with the opposition and normally not expected to say anything favorable to the pro-life cause (20–22, 29, 31–32, 46).

For example, no source is provided for the quotation from Tietze and Henshaw so that a listener might check its accuracy and context (20). The quotation from Dr. Hern's medical textbook (21) should be understood in the context of the chapter in which it appears, where he laments the inadequate training in safe abortion procedures of many surgeons, not that abortion procedures in themselves are unsafe. The quotation by Dr. Calderone (22) represents her personal position and understanding of psychiatric evidence as of 1959, is not an official position of the Planned Parenthood Federation, is part of a speech on the dangers of *illegal* abortion, and is in a context where Calderone advocates reduced need for abortion through increased sex education and contraception availability. (See Calderone, "Illegal Abortion as a Public Health Problem," *American Journal of Public Health,* July 1960, pp. 948–954; Paul K. B. Dagg, "The Psychological Sequelae of Therapeutic Abortion—Denied and Completed," *American Journal of Psychiatry,* May 1991, pp. 578–585.)

Assess, also, the responsibilities of Falwell's interpretation of public opinion poll evidence (24–28) and the soundness of his use of examples (6–7, 37, 42, 44, 48). He argues that morality and religion take precedence over law and human opinion (23, 28). To what extent should this be the case for public policy as well as for private morality? Falwell sometimes uses comparison, analogy, and simile to undercut an opposing argument (15, 21, 50). How fair, accurate, and well-founded are these comparisons?

Among the many books on the abortion controversy, one with special relevance for the rhetorical critic is Celeste Condit, *Decoding Abortion Rhetoric: Communicating Social Change* (University of Illinois Press, 1990).

◆ ◆ ◆

1   January 22, 1973 stands out in my mind as if it were yesterday. I was just 39 years old on the day the United States Supreme Court, by a vote of 7 to 2, struck down state bans on abortion. What has happened "legally" in this country in the 17 years since that infamous decision is almost incomprehensible. The lives of nearly 25 million innocent and defenseless children have been needlessly and selfishly snuffed out.

2   During these 17 years, the debate on abortion has been raging. Dozens, perhaps hundreds of groups and organizations have been formed to fight this issue from both sides. Countless pieces of legislation have been drafted. Some have been passed, some have been defeated, and virtually all have been challenged. Hundreds of thousands of people have marched and picketed both in opposition to and support of abortion. Thousands have even spent time in jail in defense of their position on this volatile issue.

3   With the exception of preaching the Gospel of Jesus Christ, no single issue has captivated my attention for so long a period of time as has the issue of abortion. This is a good time to stop and take a careful look at this issue and to ask ourselves, "Are we winning or losing the abortion struggle?" Well, let us consider some statistics.

1.   **Since 1973, nearly 25 million unborn children have been killed in America by legalized abortion—that is 1.5 million annually and 4,100 daily.**

2.   **There were 1,160,389 American casualties from the Revolutionary War, Civil War, World War I, World War II, Korean War and Vietnam War combined. We will kill that many unborn children legally in the next 283 days.**

3. **Nearly 30 percent of all pregnancies end in induced abortion. 81 percent of abortion patients are unmarried. 43 percent of women having abortions have already had one or more abortions.**

4. **Our national bird enjoys better protection than does an unborn child. To damage an eagle's nest or shoot a bird is a crime that carries a maximum penalty of one year in prison and a $250,000 fine.**

5. **13,000 dolphins died in 1989 at the hands of tuna fishermen, prompting a successful consumer boycott of the three major tuna canners. While this issue received tremendous national media coverage, we will kill nearly that many unborn children in this country by the time we wake up on Monday morning.**

6. **While 1.5 million babies are aborted in this country every year, *50 million* are aborted worldwide every year.**

7. **According to the Allan Guttmacher Institute, *46 percent* of American women over the age of 45 have had an abortion.**

4   While I believe we are making progress on many fronts, I must admit that it is difficult to claim that we are "winning" in the "fight for life." That is why I am excited about UNITY '90. I am proud to join with like-minded people from across the country for this unified strategy session.

5   Unfortunately, it was the call to unity that this conference sent forth which brought to mind the lack of unity within the pro-life ranks which so often besets us. I am ashamed to say that our opponents are publicly far more unified than we are.

6   For example, during debate in the Idaho legislature earlier this year on a bill that would have restricted abortions in that state, a nationally known pro-life organization actually sent a representative to the legislature to testify *against* that bill. That same group later claimed partial credit when Gov. Cecil Andrus vetoed the bill that the legislature had passed. That kind of self-defeating behavior can only drag us down. Whether or not you think that particular bill was the best possible legislation, the fact is that it would have saved lives.

7   Let me give another example. Recently the National Conference of Catholic Bishops announced a $5 million nationwide anti-abortion campaign. *Newsweek* magazine, April 23, 1990 reported the following about this news, "But surprising criticism came from the non-Catholic anti-abortion activist groups the Bishops hoped to reach." One of our nationally recognized pro-life brothers was quoted as saying, "Christ was in the trenches. The Bishops are not committed to fighting abortion in the most effective way, which is confrontation." That kind of public bickering is at best, counterproductive. There is no room or time for that kind of in-fighting. Unfortunately, our opponents are wise enough to speak with one voice.

8   Let me pause for a few moments to thank many people and organizations who are working faithfully to make a difference in the fight for human life. These people could comprise a Human Life Hall of Fame.

[*Editor's Note:* At this point Falwell at length praises numerous anti-abortion organizations, their leaders, and other individuals. American Life Lobby; Americans United for Life; Focus on the Family; National Conference of Catholic Bishops; Annual March for Life; Operation Rescue; and Bethany Christian Services. Dr. Bernard Nathanson, producer of the films "Silent Scream" and "Eclipse of Reason." U.S. Senators Jesse Helms, Orin Hatch, Bill Armstrong, and Gordon Humphrey. U.S. Representatives Henry Hyde, Christ Smith, and Bob Doran. Vice-President Dan Quayle and President George Bush.]

9 As far as I am concerned, this is what UNITY '90 is all about—bringing together different people with different strategies for *one* purpose—bringing an end to this holocaust which we call abortion. We may not agree with every person here on every aspect of the abortion debate but we can and *must* agree *on one* thing—that we must use our collective energies and resources to discontinue this national sin. We should also pledge never to publicly disagree with each other. Dr. Bob Jones, Sr., now in heaven, used to say, "I'd cheer for a hound dog if he came through Greenville barking for Jesus." I feel that way about the abortion issue. I applaud *anyone* who is doing *something* to chip away at this abomination. I appreciate what **Cardinal O'Connor** of New York said last year in an open letter.

> I continue to respect and admire every individual who participates in the Pro-Life Movement in any way—through quiet prayer, through discouraging others through quiet personal persuasion from having abortions, through joining the March for Life in Washington, or in whatever way seems best suited to their own conscience, way of life, or other responsibilities. There is room for all in the Pro-Life Movement. No one need follow the way of others nor should any of us criticize the way of others. United we stand; divided, babies die.

10 Well, what are the challenges that lie before us today? *First* of all, we must develop a unified strategy on every front of the abortion issue. Hopefully, we will begin to put aside our differences and work together with one heart, one mind, and one voice.

11 *Secondly,* we must realize that the Webster decision handed down by the Supreme Court last July and the Minnesota and Ohio decisions handed down Monday did not create an atmosphere in which we could relax but, rather, one in which we must work harder than ever. *U.S. News & World Report* in its April 2, 1990 edition analyzed abortion in this country since the Webster ruling. They reported that "at the time the Court announced its decision in Webster, both pro-life and pro-choice advocates predicted the ruling would mark the denouement of abortion." They went on to quote several prominent leaders on both sides of the issue before drawing this conclusion: "Notwithstanding the hyperbole, the fact is that the right to abortion is just as unencumbered today as it was before the Webster ruling." I say this, not to discourage you, but to challenge all of us to more fervent and diligent work in the months ahead.

12 *Thirdly,* we must re-frame public debate on this issue. We have allowed the debate on abortion to be sidetracked and hijacked from the real issues. Admittedly, we have been virtually helpless on much of this because we do not control the media, but we can do better. For example, we have watched the most basic terminology change before our very eyes. While we were once called "pro-life," we are now routinely referred to as "*anti*-abortion." Likewise, our opponents, rather than being called "pro-abortion," are conveniently referred to as "pro-*choice*." Now, rather than being in *favor* of life, we are "*opposed* to a woman's right to choose." And our opponents, rather than being in favor of abortion are merely in favor of "a woman's right to choose." Let's re-focus the debate—let's debate what abortion *is,* rather than who is for it and who is not. Let's focus on the number of lives that have been lost rather than the number of people who march at our respective rallies.

13 Two months ago, I was proud to be an observer at the "Rally for Life" in Washington, D.C. For over three hours one speaker after another delivered an important message on this issue. Yet throughout the day and in the days that followed, the overriding news story was the running debate over the number of people in attendance. As important as it is to have a strong and public show of support for our cause, it is not nearly as important as spreading the message that abortion is wrong and we have a "better way."

14 *Fourth,* and perhaps our greatest challenge ever, is the development of RU 486—the abortion pill, and its inevitable distribution in this country. As Chuck Colson recently wrote,

> What RU 486 will eventually mean, I fear, is a dramatic shift in the rules of the abortion battle. It will mean that our fight against abortion will no longer focus on the clinic, the dumpster, the Supreme Court steps. It will be relational and educational: Christians persuasively pressing the point among their peers that a life conceived is precious to God and must not be poisoned by a pill. The struggle will no longer be focused on legislatures and suction machines, but on people and the individual values they hold, the values that create their choices. What it means is changing the hearts and minds of a self-centered, callous generation.

15 I recently read, in *People* magazine, an interview with the French medical researcher, Dr. Baulieu who has developed this abortion pill. He talks about abortion as if he were talking about a cure for the common cold, saying, "There is no reason to make a moral debate out of it. If something works, there's no reason to stop it." He goes on to say "there is no reason to be against us. We didn't invent abortion." That is about as logical as a politician supporting the legislation of cocaine and marijuana because he didn't invent the drugs. Some say that Dr. Baulieu may eventually win the Nobel Prize. God help us. If the Nobel Prize is awarded to this Doctor, they might as well award one posthumously to Adolf Hitler.

16 I think you will agree that the task that lies before us is a difficult one. Let's put our heads and hearts together and be heard with one loud voice.

17 How then, can we capture and reframe public debate on the abortion issue? There are many myths and misconceptions about abortion that must be dispelled or corrected. Many of these myths have been perpetrated for so long by our opponents and the media that many people automatically assume them to be accurate. Let me briefly discuss ten of these myths and how we can respond to them.

18 **Myth 1: Making abortion illegal will mean a return to "back alley" abortions.** The fact is that legalized abortion has merely brought "back alley" abortionists to Main Street. In-depth study shows that maternal deaths resulting from legal abortions are replacing those due to illegal abortions almost one-for-one.

19 Another study comparing the year after Medicaid funding was cut off to the year before showed that the number of abortions decreased dramatically and the number of child births decreased slightly. Instead of abortion, many were exercising greater responsibility in avoiding pregnancy.

20 Abortions may have been safer *prior* to *Roe* than they are now. According to Tietze and Henshaw of the Guttmacher Institute, "it is entirely possible that the death-to-case ratio following illegal abortion in the United States is *higher,* not lower, than it was 15 to 20 years ago."

21 **Myth 2: If abortion is legal, it is safe and uncomplicated.** Dr. Warren M. Hern, an abortionist and author of a leading text on abortion procedures, has stated that "in medical practice there are few surgical procedures given so little attention and so underrated in its potential hazards as abortion." Abortions can be performed virtually any place someone chooses to perform the procedure. Over three-fourths of abortions are performed in non-hospital facilities.

22 In 1959, Dr. Mary Calderone, Medical Director of Planned Parenthood, made a speech before the American Public Health Association in which she said:

> I ask you not to assume that I am indiscriminately for abortion. Believe me, I am not, for, aside from the fact that abortion is the taking of life, I am mindful of what was brought out by our psychiatrists, that in

almost every case, abortion, whether legal or illegal, is a traumatic experience that may have severe kickbacks later on.

23   Also, don't forget that just because something is legal does not mean it is a desirable thing to do. A woman has the legal right to smoke and drink heavily during pregnancy, but no one, including the doctors who perform abortions would recommend such irresponsibility.

24   Myth 3: Americans favor abortion on demand. The most important thing to consider when looking at public opinion polls is the wording of the questions. Simply changing two or three words can dramatically change the results. When worded in a fair and objective way, polls, in fact, reveal that an overwhelming majority of the American people oppose abortion in at least 95% of the cases in which abortion is obtained today. All the controversy we hear about maternal health, rape, and incest amount for less than 5% of the 1.5 million abortions performed annually in this country.

25   A January, 1990 Wirthlin Survey asked under which circumstances abortion should be legal. *Only 11%* of Americans said abortion should be legal **"always,"** which is the current solution under Roe. A June 1989 CBS poll asked the question, "What if your state could pass a law that would only permit abortions in the cases of rape, incest, and to save the life of the mother. Would you favor or oppose that law?" 66% said they would favor such a law while only 29% would oppose that law.

26   In March, 1989, a *Boston Globe*/WBZ survey on abortion was released. Due to fairly worded questions, this poll showed that abortion for the reasons given by most women seeking abortions is opposed by an overwhelming majority of Americans. This poll listed common reasons for abortion with the percentage of people who opposed abortion in these cases.

Wrong time in life to have a child	82%
Fetus not desired sex	93%
Woman cannot afford a child	75%
As a means of birth control	89%
Pregnancy would cause too much emotional strain	64%
Father unwilling to help raise child	83%
Father absent	81%
Mother wants abortion father wants baby	72%
Father wants abortion mother wants baby	75%

27   It is also interesting to note how few people even know under what conditions abortion is legal today. Most people are surprised to learn that in all 50 states abortion is legal for *any* reason at *any* time including the ninth month of pregnancy.

28   I would be remiss if I did not go a step further and say that even if a majority of Americans favored or supported abortion for any reason, that would not make it right. Let us not lose sight of the fact that regardless of how abortion is considered in the hearts and minds of men, it is murder in the heart of God.

29   Myth 4: Abortion is a feminist issue—a question of women's rights. Modern day feminists either do not realize or simply ignore the fact that abortion is contrary to the original goals of the feminist movement. Early feminists such as Sarah F. Norton, Mattie Brinkerhoff, Susan B. Anthony, Mother Jones, Emma Goldman and Victoria Woodhull all denounced abortion as oppressive to women.

30 Syndicated columnist Steven Chapman said in an April, 1989 column,

Most pro-choice people are libertarian only when it's personally convenient. Women's groups, while adamantly in favor of barring the Government from any role in abortion decisions, are equally insistent that the Government take a *bigger* role in just about everything else. One demonstrator [in a pro-choice march] carried a sign saying, "My Body, My Baby, My Business." That's the pro-choice view of abortion. But when a woman chooses to *have* a baby, the cherub suddenly becomes society's concern.

Women's groups endlessly lobby to force taxpayers and employers to bear part of the cost of parenthood. Government subsidies for child care, laws requiring businesses to grant time off to new parents, programs to improve health and welfare of mothers and babies—you name it, they're for it.

31 Juli Loesch, the anti-nuclear activist at Three Mile Island, and now a member of "Feminists for Life," commented in the April, 1989 edition of the *Washington Monthly,* on her reconsideration of protests against the Vietnam War. She said she found herself being "inconsistent to the point of incoherence. We are saying that killing was not an acceptable solution to conflict situations, yet when we had our own conflict situation, we were willing to go straight to killing as a technical fix."

32 I think we let men off the hook too easily on the abortion issue. Abortion provides a climate that encourages men to abdicate their responsibility to their born, as well as pre-born children. Juli Loesch suggests that the acceptance of abortion actually encourages exploitation of women by men. She says "The idea is that a man can use a woman, vacuum her out, and she is ready to be used again." Men can help make the pro-choice position a responsible one by contributing to a process where the choice is made prior to conception.

33 Jo McGowan is a writer living in India where nearly all abortion cases involve a female fetus. McGowan discusses this in a 1989 *Newsweek* column where she says:

Feminists are speaking out of both sides of their mouths. When the issue is sex determination and the "selective" abortion of girls, they call it female feticide. But when the issue is reproductive freedom and the abortion of male and female fetuses, they call it a "woman's right to choose." It won't work. They can't have it both ways. Either they accept abortion or they don't.

She concludes by saying: Perhaps from the undeniable truth that it is wrong to kill a baby simply because she is a girl will emerge the larger truth that it is wrong to kill a baby at all.

34 **Myth 5: Forcing women to carry pregnancies to term will only result in unwanted, abused children.** Legalized abortion has not reduced child abuse problems in this country—in fact, such cases have skyrocketed. According to the U.S. Bureau of the Census, in its 1988 *Statistical Abstract of the United States,* between 1978 and 1985, reported cases of child abuse and neglect rose from 607,000 to 1.3 million annually.

35 There is a lack of statistical research to prove any correlation between child abuse and unwanted pregnancies. Several years ago, Dr. Vincent Fontana, a professor of Clinical Pediatrics and a chairman of the Mayor's Task Force on Child Abuse and Neglect of the city of New York, stated that:

Abortion is a "sweeping and simplistic" solution that fails because the assumption that every battered child is an unwanted child, or that most or even a large proportion of abused children are unwanted children is totally false.

36 Myth 6: Pro-lifers care only about the baby and aren't extending any help to the pregnant women. The fact is, there are more crisis pregnancy centers than there are abortion clinics in the United States. The February, 1990 *National Catholic Register* estimates there are over 3,400 pro-life centers in this country, and that 400 new centers are being established each year.

37 I believe that the church of Christ has a better way. I remember 30 years ago, Bishop Fulton Sheen said that the church has no right to preach against abortion unless it is willing to say to that pregnant girl, we have a better way. It was that philosophy that led us through the Thomas Road Baptist Church to start the Liberty Godparent Home in Lynchburg, Virginia eight years ago. This ministry provides housing, medical care counselling, a licensed adoption agency, and an opportunity to continue education, all free of charge to unwed mothers. Through the residence program and the toll-free counselling service, over 3,000 abortions have been prevented since this ministry began in 1982.

38 While much is happening nationwide, much remains to be done. We must establish enough crisis pregnancy homes, adoption agencies, and counselling centers to accommodate the 1.5 million girls and women who, each year, face a traumatic dilemma.

39 Myth 7: If all the women who are currently seeking abortions were forced to carry their pregnancies to term, there would not be enough adoptive parents to care for these children. According to the National Committee for Adoption, there have been approximately 50,000 adoptions per year since 1974. However, there are also 2 million childless couples on agency waiting lists or at fertility clinics who would like to adopt. That means 40 couples are waiting to adopt every available baby. Most people wishing to adopt wait anywhere from three to seven years before a baby is available.

40 We need to begin to promote adoption as a viable alternative to abortion. An editorial in *The Wall Street Journal* last year referred to a study conducted by the U.S. Department of Health and Human Services which indicated that 40% of the time, pregnancy counsellors did not even *mention* adoption as an option during discussions with pregnant women.

41 The National Committee for Adoption cites the "legalization of abortion" as a factor that reduces the potential number of adopted children. For example, in 1972, the year before *Roe v. Wade,* there were 403,000 out-of-wedlock births and 65,000 unrelated adoptions; but, in 1982 there were 715,000 out-of-wedlock births and only *50,000* unrelated adoptions.

42 I believe there is enough love and care in this country to provide a good home for every baby brought into this world. Even the Spina-Bifida Association of America and the National Down's Syndrome Adoption Exchange report waiting lists for babies they are able to place for adoption.

43 Myth 8: What we really need is better education about birth control and safe sex. Rather than teaching young people how to have safe sex, we ought to teach them how to **save** sex for marriage. 81% of all abortion patients are unmarried. This is not how God intended for us to live.

44 There has been much debate in recent years about placing sex clinics in our public schools to make condoms and birth control pills readily available. As far as I am concerned, passing out birth control pills in a public school is like distributing cook books at a fat farm.

45 The April 30 issue of *Insight* magazine recounted an assignment that a *Washington Post* reporter named Leon Dash was given in 1984 to write about teenage pregnancy. He assumed that ignorance about reproduction was the main cause of teenage pregnancy and spent a year living in a neighborhood that had one of the highest numbers of teenage parents. During that year he interviewed his subjects more than 30 hours apiece and reported the following:

> They were all very well-versed in sex education, and those who didn't want children, didn't have them. These girls became mothers to be affirmed as women.

Sixteen-year-old Tauscha Vaughn said "Mr. Dash, will you please stop asking me about birth control? Girls out here know all about birth control. There's too many birth control pills out here. All of them know about it. Even when they're 12, they know what it is."

46 The magazine went on to say that even the Guttmacher Institute, a leading proponent of education and contraception has been rethinking this issue. Jeannie Rosoff, the institute's president, says "Most of the programs we have had have been preaching sex education. We now know that increasing knowledge does *not* necessarily affect behavior." Finally, this article discussed morality.

Young people are supposed to find the very idea of morality laughable. But the best indicator these days for not getting pregnant as a teenager is membership in a fundamentalist Protestant church that teaches in no-nonsense fashion that sex outside of marriage is a sin. A study by Sandra Hofferth, an Urban Institute researcher, shows the direct correlation between weekly attendance at religious services and delayed sexual activity.

47 We need *less* sex education and *more* parents, pastors and teachers serving as role models and providing moral education.

48 Myth 9: You cannot be openly pro-life and win public office in this country. Contrary to popular opinion, certain pro-life candidates have not lost recent elections because they were pro-life, but rather because they handled the issue poorly. Jim Courter, the GOP gubernatorial candidate in New Jersey last year, did not lose because he was pro-life. He lost because he waffled on his pro-life position and record and eventually abandoned it altogether. Frankly, there really was no pro-life candidate in the New Jersey governor's race. In the Virginia governor's race, Republican Marshall Coleman attempted to hide from the abortion issue by not responding to the media campaign that Wilder and pro-abortion groups launched against him. He too, lost in what turned out to be the narrowest margin in Virginia gubernatorial history.

49 In the January issue of the *American Spectator,* columnist Fred Barnes explains why ducking this issue won't work. He says, "Pro-choice Democrats are unwilling to vote for pro-choice Republicans over pro-life Democrats. But pro-life Republicans will jump ship in a hurry. Better to stick with the pro-life stand." This is why I have so much respect for men like Ronald Reagan and Jesse Helms. These men and others like them, stand firmly in defense of the unborn without regard for public opinion polls. May God raise up more men and women who are more concerned with the next generation than with the next election.

50 Myth 10: It's OK to say "I am personally opposed to abortion *but,* I would never force my views on someone else." That rationale would be like saying in 1860, "I am personally opposed to slavery, but if my neighbor wants to own a few, that's OK." The fact is if abortion is wrong and if abortion is murder, we ought to have the guts to stand up and say so. Imagine the backlash if George Bush one day said during a Press Conference that he was personally opposed to Apartheid but if South Africa wanted to practice it, that was OK. He would be run out of office instantly. Yet, we continue to let politicians off the hook who use this warped logic on the abortion issue. Let's not let them get away with it any longer.

51 Where do we go from here? Perhaps more important than *where* we go is that we go *together.* If anything is obvious from our 17-year struggle, it is that there is no quick or easy solution to this problem.

52 Let's win this fight by changing one heart at a time—saving one baby at a time. Let's agree that preventing *some* abortions is better than preventing none. An "all or nothing" mentality will never succeed in this real world in which we live.

53 I remember appearing on ABC's *20/20* program in 1985 to discuss abortion. On that program I said that I would support *legislation* which would outlaw abortions except in the cases of rape, incest, or when the life of the mother is endangered. Judging from the mail and phone calls we received, you would have thought that I had opened an abortion clinic. I was accused of "selling out" and giving in too easily on this issue. My remarks did not mean that I approve of abortion in some cases and not in others but rather, for the purpose of achieving *some* legislative progress, I would support legislation that would legally prevent over 95% of all abortions. *Any* number of abortions we can prevent legally will be more than we are currently preventing.

54 Let's not argue with each other over anything that would save lives. As each day passes, over 4,000 precious babies are snatched away. Let's covenant together to use every available means—legal, political, and most importantly, spiritual—to reverse this terrible tide.

55 Chuck Colson in a recent column, eloquently articulates the challenge before us. Even if we were to win in the battleground states, that will not be the end of the pro-life struggle. True, we will have brought human law into conformity to God's law—a good end, but not enough. While the law is a moral teacher, law alone cannot change peoples' moral choices. Women will still seek out illegal abortions. So we must work on a more fundamental level than legislation alone, painting a fresh moral vision on our dingy national canvas, a vision of hope and human dignity. We must woo peoples' hearts towards righteousness. But we cannot woo unless we love. It is more than the battle against abortion that suffers when Christians conduct themselves with anger and hate. We wound our witness of the truth and the Gospel and the love of Jesus Christ.

56 In my heart, I question how long God can continue to bless a nation that places as little value on human life as we do in America. It is my prayer that the 1990s will be the decade in which the unborn are emancipated. Let us all pray and work to that end.

U.S. and NATO Policy Toward the Crisis in Kosovo

◆ *Madeleine Albright* ◆

On March 24, 1999, President Bill Clinton delivered a nationally televised address to the nation announcing that: ". . . our Armed Forces joined our NATO allies in air strikes against Serbian forces responsible for the brutality in Kosovo." Clinton explained to his live audience that "ending this tragedy is a moral imperative" and that "it is also important to America's na-

◆ The text of this speech was obtained from the Department of State Internet web site for Secretary Madeleine Albright.

tional interest." During this brief fifteen minute speech, Clinton attempted to justify why the 18 member nations of the North Atlantic Treaty Organization were engaged in military actions for the first time in the 50-year history of the organization. In both stated goals, "we will limit his (Milosevic's) ability to make war," and methods, "I do not intend to put our troops in Kosovo to fight a war," the President's announced policy for the nation was as controversial as it was historic.

Less than a month into the air war against Serbia, Secretary of State Madeleine K. Albright delivered the following formal statement as part of her testimony before the Foreign Relations Committee of the U.S. Senate on April 20, 1999. The first woman to ever head the State Department, Albright forcefully defended American policy at this important juncture in the Kosovo crisis.

Albright was born Maria Jana Korbelova on May 15, 1937 in Prague, Czechoslovakia. At the age of two, the Korbels fled to England just ahead of Hitler's invading army. In 1948, her family finally immigrated to the United States after a communist coup engulfed the Czech Republic. The future Secretary attended Wellesley College, where she met Joseph Albright, a publishing heir whom she married in 1959. Albright later earned her Ph.D. in Political Science, International Law and Relations from Columbia University in 1976.

Madeleine Albright's skill as a public speaker has helped to propel her rise to national prominence. The *Washington Post Weekly Edition* noted "that Albright's communications [sic] skills were a pivotal factor in her selection" from a lengthy list of potential candidates for Secretary of State (December 16–22, 1996, p. 32). *Newsweek*'s appraisal of her abilities as a speaker is even more telling: "the best way to understand Madam Secretary is as a Great Communicator" who "vows to take her foreign-policy message not just to Berlin and Beijing, but to Saginaw and San Diego." *Newsweek* concluded its assessment of Albright's talents by noting that: "for her Foggy Bottom is a bully pulpit—a podium for convincing Americans that foreign policy matters" (February 10, 1997, pp. 24–25).

As you read the text of Albright's presentation, it becomes clear that the Senate Foreign Relations Committee is a very specialized audience for this speech. The Secretary frequently uses a variety of acronyms (6, 7, 21, 22, 23, 27) that she assumes the Senate Committee members will understand. Does this assumption seem appropriate? Are her references clear in context? Here are the meanings of some of Albright's key acronyms: OSCE = Organization for Security and Cooperation in Europe; UNHCR = United Nations High Commissioner for Refugees; NGO = Nongovernmental Organization; WHO = World Health Organization; UNICEF = United Nations Children's Fund; USAID = United States Agency for International Development; and FRY = Federal Republic of Yugoslavia.

After previewing her presentation very concisely (2), Albright provides a detailed historical narrative of the events that lead to the present crisis (4–8). Does the accounting of Solbodan Milosevic's actions provide an appropriate basis for argumentative claims made by Albright? How well does Albright demonstrate the need (10–16) for NATO action against Milosevic?

How clearly does Albright explain the nature of NATO's policy against Belgrade (17–18)? Does the Secretary adequately describe what would be an "acceptable outcome" (19) of NATO's military action against Milosevic? Is the evidence used to dramatize the "humanitarian disaster" (21–23) compelling?

The references by Albright to "war crimes," "crimes against humanity," and the "just following orders" defense (26) date back to the post-World War Two era trials (1945–1948) of the German and Japanese leaders conducted by the Allied Powers. The trials of the Nazi leaders were held in Nuremberg, Germany and established many principles of international law still in effect today. For additional information, see Eugene Davidson, ed., *The Trial of the Germans* (Columbia: University of Missouri Press, 1997). By what criteria should the evidence against Milosevic presented by Albright (24–28) be evaluated? Would this type of evidence be appropriate for a domestic criminal trial?

Does the Secretary clearly explain American diplomatic policy in support of NATO's military campaign (29–38)? Are the advantages of pursuing these policy objectives effectively argued? Has Albright effectively responded to the counter-arguments presented by Milosevic (39–42)? Can NATO and the United States confront the underlying causes of the various historic conflicts in the Balkans (43–48)? How well does Albright summarize her presentation in defense of the NATO policy (51–58)?

For a preliminary assessment of the foreign policy rhetoric of the Clinton Administration, see Mary E. Stuckey, "Competing Foreign Policy Visions: Rhetorical Hybrids After the Cold War," *Western Journal of Communication,* 59 (Summer 1995), 214–227. Additional biographical information on Madeleine Albright is in Ann Blackman, *Seasons of Her Life: A Biography of Madeleine Korbel Albright* (New York: Scribner, 1998); and Michael Dobbs, *Madeleine Albright: A Twentieth-Century Odyssey* (New York: Henry Holt and Company, 1999).

1   Good afternoon, Mr. Chairman, and Senators, I am pleased to appear before you concerning U.S. and NATO policy towards the crisis in Kosovo.

2   My intention is to lay out concisely America's stake in the outcome of this crisis; the events that brought us to this point; the status of our military, diplomatic and humanitarian efforts; and our vision for the future.

3   As you know, Mr. Chairman, the potential dangers of the situation in Kosovo have been recognized throughout this decade. Slobodan Milosevic first vaulted to prominence by exploiting the fears of ethnic Serbs in this province. A decade ago, he catered to those fears by robbing Kosovo Albanians of their cherished autonomy. For years thereafter, the Kosovo Albanians sought to recover their rights by peaceful means. And in 1992, after fighting had broken out elsewhere in the Balkans, President Bush issued a warning against Serb military repression in Kosovo.

4   Meanwhile, President Milosevic was the primary instigator in three wars, attacking first Slovenia, then Croatia, and finally triggering a devastating and prolonged conflict in Bosnia.

5   Early last year, he initiated a more extensive and violent campaign of repression against ethnic Albanians in Kosovo. One result was a humanitarian crisis, as tens of thousands of people fled their homes. A second consequence—unforeseen by him—was the strengthening of the Kosovar Liberation Army (KLA), which contributed to the unrest by committing provocative acts of its own.

6   With our allies and partners, including Russia, the United States sought to end this cycle of violence by diplomatic means. Last October, President Milosevic agreed to a ceasefire, to the withdrawal of most of his security forces, and to the entry of a verification mission from the OSCE.

7   It soon became clear, however, that Milosevic never had any intention of living up to this agreement. Instead of withdrawing, his security forces positioned themselves for a new offensive. Early this year, they perpetrated a massacre in the village of Racak. And at Rambouillet, Belgrade rejected a plan for peace that had been accepted by the Kosovo Albanians, and that included provisions for disarming the KLA, and safeguarding the rights of all Kosovars, including ethnic Serbs.

8   Even while blocking our diplomatic efforts, Milosevic was preparing a barbaric plan for expelling or forcing the total submission of the Kosovo Albanian community. First, his security forces threatened and then forced the withdrawal of the OSCE mission. Then, a new rampage of terror began.

9   We have all seen the resulting images of families uprooted and put on trains, children crying for parents they cannot find, refugees recounting how loved ones were separated and led away, and ominous aerial photos of freshly-upturned earth.

10 Behind these images is a reality of people no different in their fundamental rights or humanity than you or me—of children no different than yours or mine—cut off from their homes, deprived of their families, robbed of their dreams. And make no mistake, this campaign of terror was the cause, not the result, of NATO action. It is a Milosevic production.

11 Today, our values and principles, our perseverance and our strength, are being tested. We must be united at home and with our Allies overseas. The stakes are high. To understand why that is, we need, as President Clinton has repeatedly urged, to consult the map. Kosovo is a small part of a region with large historic importance and a vital role to play in Europe's future.

12 The region is a crossroads where the Western and Orthodox branches of Christianity and the Islamic world meet. It is where World War I began, major battles of World War II were fought, and the worst fighting in Europe since Hitler's surrender occurred in this decade.

13 Its stability directly affects the security of our Greek and Turkish allies to the south, and our new allies Hungary, Poland and the Czech Republic to the north. Kosovo itself is surrounded by small and struggling democracies that are being overwhelmed by the flood of refugees Milosevic's ruthless policies are creating.

14 Today, this region is the critical missing piece in the puzzle of a Europe whole and free. That vision of a united and democratic Europe is critical to our own security. And it cannot be fulfilled if this part of the continent remains wracked by conflict.

15 Further, Belgrade's actions constitute a critical test of NATO, whose strength and credibility have defended freedom and ensured our security for five decades. To paraphrase Senator Chuck Hagel, today, there is a butcher in NATO's backyard, and we have committed ourselves to stopping him. History will judge us harshly if we fail.

16 For all of these reasons, NATO's decision to use force against the Milosevic regime was necessary and right. And the conditions the Alliance has set for ending its campaign are clear, just and firm.

17 There must be a verifiable stop to Serb military action against the people of Kosovo. Belgrade's military, police and paramilitary forces must leave so that refugees can return. An international military presence must be permitted. And the people of Kosovo must be given the democratic self-government they have long deserved.

18 As President Clinton has said, as long as Milosevic refuses to accept these conditions, NATO's air campaign will continue, and we will seek to destroy as much of Belgrade's military capabilities as we can. Each day, Milosevic's capacity to conduct repression will diminish.

19 It is evident that the efforts of our courageous military forces are having a significant impact on Milosevic's options and abilities. But that impact is not yet sufficient. We must maintain the pressure until an acceptable outcome is achieved.

20 At the same time, we will continue to help those in the region cope with the humanitarian disaster Milosevic has created.

21 We do not know with any certainty how many people are now homeless inside Kosovo, but officials estimate as many as 800,000. Belgrade has made a terrible situation worse by interfering with efforts to provide food and other basic necessities. We are exploring every possible option for helping these people before it is too late. And we welcome efforts by Greek NGOs and the International Committee of the Red Cross to open up a relief lifeline, which we hope will move desperately needed supplies to the population at risk.

22 In addition to the internally displaced, more than half a million Kosovars have fled the region since the latest violence began. Of these, the vast majority are now in Albania and Macedonia, where the terrain is rugged, the weather harsh and the infrastructure limited. Feverish efforts are underway to build camps and provide services. With local officials, the UNHCR, WHO, UNICEF, our allies and partners, and nongovernmental organizations, we are struggling to save lives, maintain health and restore hope.

23 Thus far, we have contributed $150 million to this effort. Yesterday, the President submitted an emergency supplemental request that includes $386 million in additional State Department and USAID humanitarian assistance funds, and $335 million in Defense Department humanitarian assistance. Last week, NATO approved Operation Allied Harbor, under which 8,000 troops will work with relief agencies in Albania to establish camps, deliver aid and ensure security. The U.S. Information Agency is participating in an effort to provide internal communications facilities at refugee camps in order to help reunify families.

24 Many of the refugees streaming out of Kosovo have reported Serb war crimes and crimes against humanity. These reported abuses include the widespread and systematic destruction of entire settlements, the burning of homes, the seizure of civilians for use as human shields and human blood banks, the rape of ethnic Albanian women and girls, and the systematic separation and execution of military-aged men.

25 For example, there have been reports of the killing of 60 men in Kacanik; and of the burial of 24 people at Glavnik, 30 in Lapastica, 150 in Drenica, 34 in Malisevo, 100 in Pristina; and other suspected mass burials at Pusto Selo and Izbica, where refugees reported that victims were first tortured and then burned to death.

26 There should be no misunderstanding. When it comes to the commission of war crimes or crimes against humanity, "just following orders" is no defense. In the prosecution of such crimes, there is no statute of limitations. And the international war crimes tribunal has rightly indicated that it will follow the evidence no matter where it leads.

27 The tribunal has already put Milosevic and 12 other FRY or Serbian officials on notice that forces under their command have committed war crimes, and that failure to prosecute those responsible can give rise to criminal charges against them. The United States has publicly identified nine military commanders whose forces may have been involved in the commission of such crimes.

28 By helping to document refugee accounts, and by compiling and sharing other evidence, we are and will continue to assist the tribunal in its effort to hold perpetrators accountable.

29 Mr. Chairman, in dealing with Kosovo prior to the last week of March, we were engaged in diplomacy backed by the threat of force. Since that time, we have used diplomacy to back NATO's military campaign.

30 Our diplomacy has several objectives. The first is to ensure that NATO remains united and firm. To this end, I met with Alliance foreign ministers in Brussels last week. And the President will meet with his counterparts here in Washington at the NATO Summit on Friday and Saturday. To date, we have been heartened by the broad participation and strong support the military campaign has received. In one way or another, every Ally is contributing.

31 Our unity has been strengthened by the knowledge that Milosevic refused a diplomatic settlement and by revulsion at his campaign of ethnic cleansing. No country in NATO wanted to have to use force against Serbia. But no country in NATO is willing to stand by and accept in Europe the expulsion of an entire ethnic community from its home.

32 Our second diplomatic objective has been to help leaders in the countries directly affected to cope with the humanitarian crisis, and to prevent a wider conflict. To this end, I have been in regular contact with my counterparts from the region. Their leaders will participate as partners in the NATO

Summit. And the President's supplemental request includes $150 million in emergency and project assistance to these nations and to democratic Montenegro.

33 Our third objective is to work constructively with Russia. We want to continue to make progress in other areas of our relationship, and to bring Russia back into the mainstream of international opinion on Kosovo.

34 When I met with Foreign Minister Ivanov last week, he was clear about Russia's opposition to the NATO air campaign. But we did agree on the need for an end to the violence and repression in Kosovo; the withdrawal of Serb forces; the return of refugees and internally displaced persons; and unimpeded access for humanitarian aid.

35 Where we continue to have differences is over the kind of international presence required to achieve these objectives. As I told Foreign Minister Ivanov, after Milosevic's depredations in Kosovo, refugees will not be able to return home unless the protective force is credible, which requires that its core must come from NATO. As in Bosnia, however, we think that Russia could and should play an important role in that force, and we would welcome the participation of NATO's other partner countries, as well.

36 Our fourth diplomatic objective has been to ensure that NATO's message is understood around the world. We are engaged in a vigorous program of public diplomacy, and have provided information on a regular basis to nations everywhere.

37 We have been encouraged by strong statements from the European Union and UN Secretary General Kofi Annan, and by the participation in relief efforts of diverse countries such as Egypt, Jordan and Ukraine.

38 Moreover, last week, the UN Human Rights Commission in Geneva voted 44 to 1 to condemn Belgrade's campaign of ethnic cleansing in Kosovo and called upon Serb authorities to accept a peace agreement. Supporters of this Resolution came from every continent.

39 We have also tried to pierce the veil of propaganda and ignorance with which Milosevic has tried to shroud the people of former Yugoslavia. Radio Free Europe, Radio Liberty and other broadcasts are reaching the country 24 hours a day. As President Clinton and other NATO leaders have made clear, our actions are directed against Belgrade's policies, not against the region's people. And our effort to broadcast the truth is designed to counteract Belgrade's Big Lie that the refugees from Kosovo are fleeing NATO and not the Serb forces.

40 In the days and weeks to come, we will press ahead with our military, diplomatic and humanitarian strategies. Our purpose will be to steadily bring home to Milosevic the reality that this confrontation must end on the terms we have stated.

41 Our desire is to begin as soon as possible the vital work of returning, reuniting and rebuilding in Kosovo. But we are not interested in a phony settlement based on unverifiable assumptions or Milosevic's worthless word. The only settlement we can accept is one we have the ability to verify and the capability to enforce.

42 Even as we respond to the crisis in Kosovo, we must also concern ourselves more broadly with the future of the region. The peaceful integration of Europe's north, west and center is well advanced or on track. But, as I said earlier, the continent cannot be whole and free until its southeast corner is also stable.

43 Some say violence is endemic to this region, and that its people have never and will never get along. Others say that stability is only possible under the crushing weight of a dominant empire such as the Ottoman, Hapsburg and Communist regimes that once held sway.

44 I am no prophet. Certainly, the scars of the past are still visible. Certainly, the wounds opened by the current devastation will take much time to heal. But the evidence is there in the testimony of average people whether in Zagreb or Tirana, Sarajevo or Skopje, that they are far more interested in plugging into the world economy than in slugging it out with former adversaries.

45 If you look at the region today, you will see Greeks and Turks operating side by side as NATO Allies; you will see Macedonians and Albanians and Montenegrins answering the humanitarian call. You will see Christians and Muslims and Jews united in their condemnation of the atrocities being committed.

46 In Bosnia, NATO and its partners are working with ethnic Serbs, Croats and Bosniaks to implement the Dayton Accords. And through our own Southeast European Cooperative Initiative, you will see leaders and citizens from throughout the region engaged in joint efforts and cooperative planning.

47 The problems that have plagued the Balkans—of competition for resources, ethnic rivalry and religious intolerance—are by no means restricted to that part of the world. Nor does the region lack the potential to rise above them.

48 During the NATO Summit, the President and our partners will discuss the need for a coordinated effort to consolidate democracy in Southeast Europe, promote economic integration and provide moral and material support to those striving to build societies based on law and respect for the rights and dignity of all.

49 Our explicit goal should be to transform the Balkans from the continent's primary source of instability into an integral part of the European mainstream. We do not want the current conflict to be the prelude to others; we want to build a solid foundation for a new generation of peace—so that future wars are prevented, economies grow, democratic institutions are strengthened and the rights of all are preserved.

50 This will require a commitment from us. It will require the involvement of the European Union and the international financial institutions. It will require a continued willingness on the part of local leaders to work together on behalf of the common good. And it will require, ultimately, a change in leadership in Belgrade so the democratic aspirations of the Serb people may be fulfilled and the isolation of the former Yugoslavia can come to an end.

51 Finally, Mr. Chairman, I would like to add just a few words about the crisis in Kosovo and the future of NATO. For the challenge we currently face has dramatized the need for precisely the kind of adaptations the Alliance has already initiated, and which we will take to a new level at the Summit here in Washington later this week.

52 In Kosovo, we are responding to a post-Cold War threat to Alliance interests and values. We are seeing the need for military forces that are mobile, flexible, precise and inter-operable. We are seeing the value to the Alliance of its new members and partners. And we are reaffirming the unshakable strength of the trans-Atlantic bond.

53 Having said that, I want to emphasize that although we are focused now on Kosovo, the future of NATO is a much larger issue. The current fighting notwithstanding, NATO's core mission remains collective self-defense. NATO's relationship to Russia is a key to Europe's future security and will be determined by many factors in addition to Kosovo. The Alliance must be ready to respond to the full spectrum of missions it may face, including the perils posed by weapons of mass destruction. And the United States will continue to welcome efforts to strengthen the European pillar of our Alliance in a way that bolsters overall effectiveness and unity.

54 I know that your Subcommittee on Europe will be conducting a hearing on these and related issues tomorrow, Mr. Chairman, and I am sure that Assistant Secretary Grossman and his counterpart from the Department of Defense will discuss them in greater depth than I have had the opportunity to do in my remarks this afternoon.

55 I also understand that the Congressional leadership will host a reception this week for our visitors from NATO countries. I hope that you will thank them for their efforts and stress to them the importance of standing together and standing tall until the current confrontation is settled.

56 As the President and our military leaders have made clear, this struggle may be long. We can expect days of tragedy for us as well as for the people of the region. But we must not falter and we cannot fail.

57 By opposing Solobodan Milosevic's murderous rampage, NATO is playing its rightful role as a defender of freedom and security within the Euro-Atlantic region. Because our cause is just, we are united. And because we are united, we are confident that in this confrontation between barbaric killing and necessary force; between vicious intolerance and respect for human rights; between tyranny and democracy; we will prevail. To that essential objective, I pledge the full measure of my own efforts, and respectfully solicit both your wise counsel and support.

58 Thank you very much, and now I would be pleased to respond to any questions you might have.

The Second Amendment: America's First Freedom

◆ *Charlton Heston* ◆

One of the hottest political debates of our time stems from attempts at gun control legislation. Violence and crime of all kinds, especially the recent school shootings, have led concerned people to question if our nation has too many guns and if too many people own them. The topic has mostly divided itself along party lines and between conservatives and liberals. The Littleton, Colorado, shootings brought "the right to bear arms," which advocates say stems from the Second Amendment, like never before, into our public dialogue. Postured on the political right of this issue is the National Rifle Association and one of the most impassioned spokespersons the NRA has ever had, its current president, Charlton Heston, the renowned Hollywood actor.

Charlton Heston grew up in the north woods of Michigan as a hunting and fishing enthusiast. From this outdoors tradition, he developed an affinity for guns and gun collecting that has remained a lifelong hobby. He served for three

◆ The text of this speech was provided by the National Rifle Association in behalf of Charlton Heston and is reprinted with his permission.

years in the Army Air Corps during World War II, and then moved to an acting career that led to stardom in more than 70 motion pictures and almost as many theatrical productions. After struggling to get into the acting field in New York, Heston made it to Hollywood to play the lead in the picture *Dark City.* After that, he performed in *The Greatest Show on Earth,* a film that won the Academy Award for Best Picture of the Year. This exposure propelled Heston to numerous leading rolls, including *Ben Hur* in 1959, which won him an Academy Award for Best Actor. A few of the other films in which Heston starred were *Pony Express, The Ten Commandments, The Greatest Story Ever Told, Julius Caesar, Antony and Cleopatra, Mountain Men* and *Midway.*

Heston has been a political activist throughout his life. Starting in 1961, he worked for the Civil Rights Movement and was involved in a number of demonstrations. As President of the Screen Actors Guild, he worked with Martin Luther King in an effort to gain African Americans entry into Hollywood technical unions. He also has served the government in world relief and as narrator of documentary films of a political/economic nature. More recently, he has campaigned for political candidates, most of whom have won their races. Heston was a Democrat until after the Kennedy administration when he switched to the Republican Party.

Heston ties his "right to bear arms" argument into the Second Amendment of the Constitution, which reads, "A well regulated militia being necessary to the security of a free state, the right of the people to keep and bear arms shall not be infringed." In his speech delivered to the National Press Club, September, 1997, Heston argues that the "right to bear arms" protects all the other rights concerning religion, speech, press, peaceable assembly, and petitioning for redress of grievance spelled out in the First Amendment, and, in that sense, "the Second Amendment is, in order of importance, the first amendment" (10). Here he is dealing with the "need step" of a defense of policy speech. He is arguing that we need to continue the policy as it is constituted. Plainly, Heston takes an aggressive stance in arguing his case. Journalists may well feel that freedom of speech and of the press are the most

basic freedoms. As classroom critics, you may wish to discuss the wisdom of Heston taking such a strong stance with this audience. In paragraph 13, Heston tries to give historical authenticity to the importance of weapons to freedom of the press. As a citizen judge, does Heston convince you that the right to bear arms is our most basic freedom? Why or why not?

Whether the speaker is successful depends, firstly, upon his ability to convince his listeners that the right to sell and own guns is indeed a "right" guaranteed by the Constitution, and, secondly, that "right," as he interprets it, is necessary and desirable. The speaker assumes that every law abiding citizen is guaranteed the right to bear arms by the Second Amendment. Making the correct assumptions about the knowledge and views of the audience about the subject is essential to persuasion. Do you think that Heston correctly assumed that his audience accepted the proposition that all citizens have the constitutional right to bear arms?

The speaker uses no statistics about gun ownership to support the thought that no new laws should be passed curbing gun ownership; rather he asserts that journalists swallow "manufactured statistics and fabricated technical support from anti-gun organizations" (21 and 22). Do you think he is alienating his listeners at this point, or is he effectively challenging them and calling them to task?

Heston uses the analogy of the paparazzi (19–22) to show journalists that they don't tend to stand up for the rights of others, not even when it involves their own kind. Once again Heston is hitting at the audience. Why, in your judgment, is he doing this? He even tells journalists that they abuse the First Amendment rights of National Rifle Association members by frequently denying them advertising time or space (22–24). Certainly this speech is a good case study of the question of how strongly a speaker can scold his audience and still be effective with them and get them to accept his argument.

Heston begins the speech bluntly and directly, using no introduction in the usual sense. He simply tells the audience that he is going to talk about guns and what the issues of discussion are going to be (1). Would the speech be stronger if Heston had used a conventional introduction or does his direct approach get sufficient attention and interest? The speech ends with a personal declaration (36–38) and a challenge to the listeners to "go forth and tell the truth" (40). Do these thoughts bring the speech to an uplifting and powerful ending?

1 Today I want to talk to you about guns: Why we have them, why the Bill of Rights guarantees that we can have them, and why my right to have a gun is more important than your right to rail against it in the press.

2 I believe every good journalist needs to know why the Second Amendment must be considered more essential than the First Amendment. This may be a bitter pill to swallow, but the right to keep and bear arms is not archaic. It's not an outdated, dusty idea some old dead white guys dreamed up in fear of the Redcoats. No, it is just as essential to liberty today as it was in 1776. These words may not play well at the Press Club, but it's still the gospel down at the corner bar and grill.

3 And your efforts to undermine the Second Amendment, to deride it and degrade it, to readily accept diluting it and eagerly promote redefining it, threaten not only the physical well-being of millions of Americans but also the core concept of individual liberty our founding fathers struggled to perfect and protect.

4 So now you know what doubtless does not surprise you. I believe strongly in the right of every law-abiding citizen to keep and bear arms, for what I think are good reasons.

5 The original amendments we refer to as the Bill of Rights contain ten of what the constitutional framers termed unalienable rights. These rights are ranked in random order and are linked by their essential equality. The Bill of Rights came to us with blinders on. It doesn't recognize color, or class, or wealth. It protects not just the rights of actors, or editors, or reporters, but extends even to those we love to hate.

6 That's why the most heinous criminals have rights until they are convicted of a crime. The beauty of the Constitution can be found in the way it takes human nature into consideration. We are not a docile species capable of co-existing within a perfect society under everlasting benevolent rule.

7 We are what we are. Egotistical, corruptible, vengeful, sometimes even a bit power mad. The Bill of Rights recognizes this and builds the barricades that need to be in place to protect the individual.

8 You, of course, remain zealous in your belief that a free nation must have a free press and free speech to battle injustice, unmask corruption and provide a voice for those in need of a fair and impartial forum.

9 I agree wholeheartedly . . . a free press is vital to a free society. But I wonder: How many of you will agree with me that the right to keep and bear arms is not just equally vital, but the most vital to protect all the other rights we enjoy?

10 I say that the Second Amendment is, in order of importance, the first amendment. It is America's First Freedom, the one right that protects all the others. Among freedom of speech, of the press, of religion, of assembly, of redress of grievances, it is the first among equals. It alone offers the absolute capacity to live without fear. The right to keep and bear arms is the one right that allows "rights" to exist at all.

11 Either you believe that, or you don't, and you must decide.

12 Because there is no such thing as a free nation where police and military are allowed the force of arms but individual citizens are not. That's a "big brother knows best" theater of the absurd that has never boded well for the peasant class, the working class, or even for reporters.

13   Yes, our Constitution provides the doorway for your news and commentary to pass through free and unfettered. But that doorway to freedom is framed by the muskets that stood between a vision of liberty and absolute anarchy at a place called Concord Bridge. Our revolution began when the British sent Redcoats door to door to confiscate the people's guns. They didn't succeed: The muskets went out the back door with their owners.

14   Emerson said it best:

> By the rude bridge that arched the flood,
> Their flag to April's breeze unfurled,
> Here once the embattled farmers stood,
> And fired the shot heard round the world.

15   King George called us "rabble in arms." But with God's grace, George Washington and many brave men gave us our country. Soon after, God's grace and a few great men gave us our Constitution. It's been said that the creation of the United States is the greatest political act in history. I'll sign that.

16   In the next two centuries, though, freedom did not flourish. The next revolution, the French, collapsed in the bloody terror, then Napoleon's tyranny. There's been no shortage of dictators since, in many countries. Hitler, Mussolini, Stalin, Mao, Idi Amin, Castro, Pol Pot. All these monsters began by confiscating private arms, then literally soaking the earth with the blood of tens and tens of millions of their people. Ah, the joys of gun control.

17   Now, I doubt any of you would prefer a rolled up newspaper as a weapon against a dictator or a criminal intruder. Yet in essence that is what you have asked our loved ones to do, through an ill-contrived and totally naive campaign against the Second Amendment.

18   Besides, how can we entrust to you the Second Amendment, when you are so stingy with your own First Amendment?

19   I say this because of the way, in recent days, you have treated your own—those journalists you consider the least among you. How quick you've been to finger the paparazzi with blame and to eye the tabloids with disdain. How eager you've been to draw a line where there is none, to demand some distinction within the First Amendment that sneers "they are not one of us." How readily you let your lesser brethren take the fall, as if their rights were not as worthy, and their purpose not as pure, and their freedom not as sacred as yours.

20   So now, as politicians consider new laws to shackle and gag paparazzi, who among you will speak up? Who here will stand and defend them? If you won't, I will. Because you do not define the First Amendment. It defines you. And it is bigger than you—big enough to embrace all of you, plus all those you would exclude. That's how freedom works.

Charlton Heston (Photo provided courtesy of the National Rifle Association)

21 It also demands you do your homework. Again and again I hear gun owners say, how can we believe anything the anti-gun media says when they can't even get the facts right? For too long you have swallowed manufactured statistics and fabricated technical support from anti-gun organizations that wouldn't know a semiauto from a sharp stick. And it shows. You fall for it every time.

22 That's why you have very little credibility among 70 million gun owners and 20 million hunters and millions of veterans who learned the hard way which end the bullet comes out. And while you attacked the amendment that defends your homes and protects your spouses and children, you have denied those of us who defend all the Bill of Rights a fair hearing or the courtesy of an honest debate.

23 If the NRA attempts to challenge your assertions, we are ignored. And if we try to buy advertising time or space to answer your charges, more often than not we are denied. How's that for First Amendment freedom?

24 Clearly, too many have used freedom of the press as a weapon not only to strangle our free speech, but to erode and ultimately destroy the right to keep and bear arms as well. In doing so you promoted your profession to that of constitutional judge and jury, more powerful even than our Supreme Court, more prejudiced than the Inquisition's tribunals. It is a frightening misuse of constitutional privilege, and I pray that you will come to your senses and see that these abuses are curbed.

25 As a veteran of World War II, as a freedom marcher who stood with Dr. Martin Luther King long before it was fashionable, and as a grandfather who wants the coming century to be free and full of promise for my grandchildren, I am . . . troubled.

26 The right to keep and bear arms is threatened by political theatrics, piecemeal lawmaking, talk show psychology, extreme bad taste in the entertainment industry, an ever-widening educational chasm in our schools and a conniving media, that all add up to cultural warfare against the idea that guns ever had, or should now have, an honorable and proud place in our society.

27 But all of our rights must be delivered into the 21st century as pure and complete as they came to us at the beginning of this century. Traditionally the passing of that torch is from a gnarled old hand down to an eager young one. So now, at 72, I offer my gnarled old hand.

28 I have accepted a call from the National Rifle Association of America to help protect the Second Amendment. I feel it is my duty to do that. My mission and vision can be summarized in three simple parts.

29 First, before we enter the next century, I expect to see a pro-Second Amendment president in the White House.

30 Secondly, I expect to build an NRA with the political muscle and clout to keep a pro-Second Amendment Congress in place.

31 Third, is a promise to the next generation of free Americans. I hope to help raise a hundred million dollars for NRA programs and education before the year 2000. At least half of that sum will go to teach American kids what the right to keep and bear arms really means to their culture and country.

32 We have raised a generation of young people who think that the Bill of Rights comes with their cable TV. Leave them to their channel surfing and they'll remain oblivious to history and heritage that truly matter.

33 Think about it—what else must young Americans think when the White House proclaims, as it did, that "a firearm in the hands of youth is a crime or an accident waiting to happen?" No—it is time they learned that firearm ownership is constitutional, not criminal. In fact, few pursuits can teach a young person more about responsibility, safety, conservation, their history and their heritage, all at once.

34 It is time they found out that the politically correct doctrine of today has misled them. And that when they reach legal age, if they do not break our laws, they have a right to choose to own a gun—a handgun, a long gun, a small gun, a large gun, a black gun, a purple gun, a pretty gun, an ugly gun—and to use that gun to defend themselves and their loved ones or to engage in any lawful purpose they desire without apology or explanation to anyone, ever.

35   This is their first freedom. If you say it's outdated, then you haven't read your own headlines. If you say guns create only carnage, I would answer that you know better. Declining morals, disintegrating families, vacillating political leadership, an eroding criminal justice system and social mores that blur right and wrong are more to blame—certainly more than any legally owned firearm.

36   I want to rescue the Second Amendment from an opportunistic president, and from a press that apparently can't comprehend that attacks on the Second Amendment set the stage for assaults on the First.

37   I want to save the Second Amendment from all these nitpicking little wars of attrition—fights over alleged Saturday night specials, plastic guns, cop killer bullets and so many other made-for-prime-time non-issues invented by some press agent over at gun control headquarters that you guys buy time and again.

38   I simply cannot stand by and watch a right guaranteed by the Constitution of the United States come under attack from those who either can't understand it, don't like the sound of it, or find themselves too philosophically squeamish to see why it remains the first among equals: Because it is the right we turn to when all else fails.

39   That's why the Second Amendment is America's first freedom.

40   Please, go forth and tell the truth. There can be no free speech, no freedom of the press, no freedom to protest, no freedom to worship your god, no freedom to speak your mind, no freedom from fear, no freedom for your children and for theirs, for anybody, anywhere, without the Second Amendment freedom to fight for it.

41   If you don't believe me, just turn on the news tonight. Civilization's veneer is wearing thinner all the time.

42   Thank you.

Against Gun Violence in America

◆ *Bill Bradley* ◆

Born the son of a small-town banker in Crystal City, Missouri, a blue-collar town thirty-six miles south of St. Louis, Bill Bradley, as a youngster, was kept active by his mother who enrolled him in piano, trumpet, French, swimming, basketball, boxing and French horn. In the summer, Bill played American Legion baseball and learned about racial prejudice when his team

◆ The text of this speech was obtained from the Internet web site of Bill Bradley for President, Inc.

traveled with two black players and was refused service at a New Madrid restaurant. At Joplin, they were housed in a second-rate, run-down hotel because the good places turned them away. Bradley carried these memories with him to adulthood. From his father, he inherited a strong sense of ethics and a strict code of conduct. His father's bank never foreclosed on a single homeowner throughout the Great Depression. From this, young Bill learned to respect those who were less fortunate than he.

Bill was an excellent student and, upon graduation from high school, was accepted into Princeton University, a school that did not give out athletic scholarships, but had a great record for producing Rhodes scholars. He was an outstanding student, but he retained his love for sports. Nature determined what sport he was ultimately to play since Bill grew to be somewhat tall for baseball but just right for basketball. He practiced hard, trying to perfect his shooting. He decided that if he failed at basketball it wouldn't be for a lack of effort. He became a three-time All-American.

Upon graduation from Princeton, he was drafted by the New York Knicks of the National Basketball Association. But Bradley put his basketball career on hold, and opted for a Rhodes Scholarship to study at Oxford. He spent his semester breaks traveling throughout Europe. These experiences supplemented the master's degree he received from Oxford in politics, philosophy and economics. He knew that he ultimately wanted a political career.

But his love for basketball remained and he turned professional when he returned from his study abroad. In the NBA, despite being short for his position and slower than most other players, he was quick to exploit the weaknesses of the opposition and proved to be a clutch player. Bradley helped the Knicks to the world championship in 1969–1970, and again in 1972–1973. He was elected into the Basketball Hall of Fame in his first year of eligibility.

Politically, young Bill Bradley assumed that he was at least a nominal Republican, since that is what his parents were. But in June 1964, Bill sat in the gallery of the United States Senate as they passed the Civil Rights Act, which, to him,

was a momentous event. From this he learned that he was sympathetic to the Democratic Party and its leadership on civil rights. Thoughts of a career in politics began shaping in his mind.

In the spring of 1977, Bradley retired from professional basketball; and late in the year, he began running for the U.S. Senate. In the June 1978 primary, he defeated two main opponents for the nomination; and then in the general election, he won the Senate seat against strong Republican opposition. At age 35, Bradley was the youngest member of the Senate.

His first-time Senate performance was good enough so that in 1984 he was reelected with the largest plurality ever achieved by a New Jersey Democrat. In 1990, he won a third term as U.S. Senator from New Jersey. Helping American children was always in the forefront of his thinking in the Senate. He sought to reform and enforce child support. He spearheaded the passage of legislation addressing children's health problems caused by lead. He also was an advocate in the Senate of the Earned Income Tax Credit which reduces taxes for Americans of modest means. In the 1980's, Bradley made reducing the federal budget deficit a priority. Bradley also was a constant advocate of campaign finance reform.

In August, 1995, Bradley announced his retirement from the Senate at the end of his third term. Out of office, he continued to address key issues. He spoke on the economy, social problems, and the country's role in the world. One of the issues that has attracted his attention is the matter of gun control. Violence and guns were important issues in the 2000 presidential election, and Bradley was a candidate for the Democratic nomination against Vice President Al Gore.

Bradley spoke on the question of gun violence in America at the Legal Community Against Violence Dinner in San Francisco, June 18, 1999. The speech he gave was a classic problem-solution speech. Paragraphs 4 through 21 set forth the problem and paragraphs 22 through 34 present Bradley's solution. In paragraph 6, Bradley begins to lay out the gun problem by referring to the large number of Americans that have been murdered, which he blames upon the narrow way in which we have allowed the gun issue to be defined, i.e., you either uphold the Second Amendment literally or else you seek to undermine the Second Amendment entirely (7–8). Bradley says that "like two lumbering warriors" (9) the two sides have squared off on "the same sacred ground of liberty" while "the haunting hail of gun fire goes on" (9). What rhetorical value do you see in this bifurcation of sides? How does this strengthen Bradley's position in the speech? Whenever a peculiarly tragic incident occurs such as the Oklahoma City bombing (11), Bradley contends, the dialogue heats up and we think that we need to do something. He says that "now is such a time" and then reviews the sorry situation our society is in. Analyze his use of supporting materials in paragraphs 12 through 21. Do his materials make the problem seem compelling?

To Bradley, the first dimension of the solution to the problem is leadership. What kind of leadership do we need, according to Bradley? Generally explore how he develops the leadership theme to good advantage (21–23). In paragraph 24, he discusses how we might "end the thirteen gun deaths a day." Closely outline the recommendations of this section of the speech and then explore the techniques Bradley uses to make them effective. What role does Bradley's reference to his own boyhood play in giving impetus to the solution (27)? How does Bradley make use of comparison in this section of the speech (e.g., see 36)? At the end of the solution phase of the speech, Bradley returns to the "debate of extremes" with which he started and says that we have a choice either to continue that debate and allow the carnage to go on or to "seek the common ground" (34). This paragraph is designed to tie up his argument. His strategy here is return the focus of the speech to the thesis he is presenting, a common rhetorical principle.

Although Bradley's manner of speaking tends to lack dynamism, his linguistic style is impressive. Consider, for example, his use of parallelisms. Note that paragraphs 12, 13 and 14 all begin with the kind of a society "we see." Do you find other such parallelisms in the speech? What do you consider to be the special effect of such parallelisms? Paragraph 34 is a good example of the "either-or" approach. What is the special rhetorical power of such an "either-or"?

The first six paragraphs of the speech constitute its introduction. Identify what you consider to be the basic strategy of the introduction. The greatest strength of the introduction perhaps lies in how it discloses and leads into the topic Bradley wishes to discuss. Observe how he uses information to develop paragraph 6. The introduction does not have a strong attention step; but does it need one? To start the listener thinking about gun violence, Bradley provides a general statement of his speech topic in the first paragraph. Later, in paragraphs 7–9, he gives his specific slant on the topic.

Paragraph 34, as noted earlier, is the transition to the conclusion. Then Bradley begins his conclusion with the blunt statement, "Let me end my conversation with two stories." Do you think that his use of the word "conversation" is strategic here? If so, how?

In paragraphs 41 and 42, Bradley uses two examples that are designed to give impact to his message for his immediate audience. What is peculiarly powerful about these examples?

In his ending note, Bradley returns to the idea that we Americans are a caring people. Why do you think he does this?

◆ ◆ ◆

1   Two days ago, I talked about the four freedoms I believe we must commit ourselves to guaranteeing for our children: freedom from want, freedom from illness, freedom from ignorance, and freedom from fear. Tonight, I want to talk about fear and the violence that has produced it.

2   If you've read the newspapers, watched television, talked with parents, had a casual conversation with colleagues, or lived in America over the last two months, you know about the fear of violence that has left a trail of tears, along with broken dreams, broken promises, and broken hearts in communities all across America.

3   The fear is real. But what you don't hear as much about is the fact that a graduating senior today is less likely to have tried drugs and alcohol than twenty years ago. Today's senior is less likely to get pregnant while still a teen and more likely to believe in God. Our children are basically good children. Our parents are good parents, trying to raise good children. The American people are a good people.

4   So why is it so difficult in this country to have a rational dialogue about reducing gun violence, built around the commonsense notion that it is in the interests of our children and families to do so? Why are our conversations based on what polls, focus groups, or political calculation tell us is the least likely to offend any voters? Why should our leaders self-censor their proposals on gun violence to what they think Congress might be willing to pass, as opposed to what might work?

5   I believe a president has to trust the American people enough to be honest about the issues facing our nation. And, let's be honest—any conversation about reducing violence has to begin with talking about guns.

6   Despite the assassinations of our political leaders and heroes over the last four decades, despite the fact that the number of Americans murdered in the last ten years is double the number killed in the Vietnam War, despite the fact that thirteen children every day are killed by guns—we have allowed the terms of the discussion to be defined within a narrow context that often has little to do with the realities of life in America. Often, it seems as though the only voices heard are the small numbers at either end of the spectrum—those who believe in no guns, and those who believe in no regulation of guns. We end up with a shrill and stale debate that offers false choices and little hope of reducing the carnage in America.

7   The source of this frustrating and, ultimately, tragic debate is the Second Amendment. The NRA and its allies take the view that the Second Amendment is absolute—that any regulation of any gun, regardless of how deadly or destructive, infringes on their individual right to "bear arms." As a result, they have tenaciously and effectively fought all attempts to regulate the manufacture, distribution, registration, and licensing of guns. They have gone so far as to oppose the banning of assault weapons and cop killer bullets—all weapons that have no sporting or hunting purpose and exist for only one purpose: to destroy human life. They have resorted to slandering the ATF as "jack-booted government thugs" and falsely accused them of wearing "Nazi bucket helmets and black storm trooper uniforms." And just two weeks after the last funeral for the victims of the shootings in Littleton, Colorado, the NRA sent letters to its 2.6 million members warning that President Clinton would "demand that you pay the price for the insanity of the killers."

8   On the other side, there are some in the gun control community who also have an absolutist view of the Second Amendment. They believe that the government has the right to regulate all guns out of existence. They sometimes seem to demonize all gun owners as an extreme faction aligned with the most radical elements of the NRA, when the truth is actually quite different.

9   So like two lumbering warriors, both sides have been fighting over the same sacred ground of liberty—brandishing the arguments of no guns versus no regulation of guns. The effect of this unproductive debate has produced policy choices that don't reflect the complexity of our jurisprudence or the texture of where we live our lives—in real communities with real people whose lives are shattered every day by the haunting hail of gun fire. And it has produced a thirty-year legislative roadblock that has prevented almost every effective and meaningful reform that would reduce gun violence from being adopted.

10   This I know for sure: In America, no individual or group can claim to have a monopoly on freedom. We have fought and struggled too long in our own country and around the world to preserve our basic freedom to allow it to be hijacked by any group who seeks to manipulate it for their own political gain at the expense of the public good.

11 Every now and then, a tragedy occurs like the school shootings and the bombing in Oklahoma City where we react collectively as one nation and one family. Where the event touches a deep chord in the American soul, and we begin to look inward at who we are and what we have become.

12 Now is such a time and here is what we see. We live in a society with over 200 million guns where thirteen children a day are killed by them in homicides, suicides, or unintentional shootings. In 1996 alone, 4,643 children and teenagers were killed by guns. According to a 1997 Centers for Disease Control report, the rate of children up to fourteen years old killed by guns is nearly twelve times higher in the United States than in twenty-five other industrialized countries combined.

13 We see a society where, until recently, there were more gun dealers than gas stations and grocery stores. Where there are roughly seven gun dealers for every McDonald's. These dealers sell an estimated 7.5 million guns every year—of which 3.5 million are handguns. In 1996, handguns were used to murder two people in New Zealand, fifteen in Japan, thirty in Great Britain, 106 in Canada, 213 in Germany, and 9,390 in the United States.

14 Furthermore, we see a society where hamburgers and children's cribs have more regulations than guns. There are no federal manufacturing or safety standards that govern how guns are made or marketed. The TEC DC-9 semi-automatic pistol, one of the weapons that was used in the Columbine High School massacre, is made by a Miami-based company. Their ads bragged that the gun's finish is "resistant to fingerprints," a marketing campaign clearly targeted to those who engage in criminal activity.

15 By contrast, think about this: The Consumer Products Safety Commission requires that the slats on cribs be no more than two and three-eighths of an inch apart, to reduce the possibility of children getting stuck between them. The National Highway Transportation and Safety Administration recalls children's car seats that are found to be unsafe, or even just unreliable. And the Consumer Products Safety Commission mandates that safety caps be put on medicine bottles to prevent children from accidentally poisoning themselves.

16 We are willing to regulate to protect our children in many areas—food, toys, clothing, and equipment. But not guns.

17 We have become a culture where in neighborhoods children once played in the streets, police now draw chalk silhouettes on the sidewalks.

18 Where businesses once thrived, storeowners now speak to customers through grilles and bulletproof glass.

19 Where neighbors once left their doors unlocked, private security guards now patrol walled-in communities, protecting those who can afford it in gated citadels of illusory security.

20 The fear of violence stops people from going to a PTA or church meeting at night. It stops us from reaching out to our neighbor. It robs us of our liberty. It destroys the world of trust.

21 The effort to find a framework for what makes sense, what will work, what will save lives is lost on a Republican Congress consumed by partisan passions and special interest politics, more interested in issues to use in the next election than solutions that would make a difference today. The roar of the Columbine tragedy still echoes across the land. But the Congress, at a time of momentous opportunity, stumbles all over each other to weaken an already watered down background check for guns sold at gun shows. The gridlock persists, and reasonable people are left to wonder: What will it take to save our children's lives?

22 It's going to take leadership—leadership at every level of our society. Leaders in every community. Leadership that seeks to do big things, rather than nibble at the edges of a crisis. Leadership that gives people a reason to believe that we can begin to extinguish the epidemic of violence if we have the will to confront it honestly. And we need leaders who believe that, if politics is the art of the possible, it is the role of a leader to expand the possibilities.

23 It's going to take people like you here tonight and in communities all across the country to realize the power we possess if we work together toward a common goal. We are a strong and vibrant country, and we have fought the right fights before and won. State-sanctioned racism began to fall when we objected to its moral depravity and we furthered the cause of justice. Today, we have the power to save our children's lives and further the cause of liberty.

24 So let's talk about what makes sense for our children. Let's talk about how we might end the thirteen gun deaths a day—a daily Columbine, 365 days a year.

25 Every amendment of our Constitution is open to interpretation. Our most cherished amendment, our First Amendment guaranteeing freedom of speech, has restrictions. You can't yell fire in a crowded theater. You cannot commit perjury. You cannot slander or libel an individual.

26 There is no doubt in my mind that the Second Amendment confers rights on individuals to own guns. My reasons for supporting the rights of an individual to own a gun is based more on personal experience, and less on legal doctrine.

27 When I was a boy, I used to take my 22 and shoot targets along the Mississippi River with my grandfather. Millions of sportsmen and hunters use guns responsibly, and I see no reason why their passionate pursuit should not continue. Many sportsmen and sportswomen are concerned about government intrusion in their lives. But most of them would agree that there is no need for the junk handguns and assault weapons that are causing carnage in our communities.

28 A commonsense approach to what kind of gun regulation is needed must be built on the shoulders of the Second Amendment—by applying the same restrictions to it that are applied to other amendments. In our constitutional system, we must always balance the public safety of the people—especially children—against the rights of the individual. And in a society with over 200 million guns and thirteen children a day killed by them, I believe that the government has a legitimate interest in regulating guns.

29 That means we can decide who is safe to entrust with a gun, what kinds of guns may be manufactured or sold, and how those guns can be distributed. It means that we can pursue a goal of making our country safer from gun violence by applying principles like making guns safer, regulating the distribution of them more carefully, making owners more responsible, and giving police greater abilities to stop gun violence.

30 But it also means that if you use your gun responsibly, store it safely and use it lawfully—then your rights under the Second Amendment will continue to be protected.

31 This is the model I used in my attempt to grapple with these issues during my eighteen years in the Senate.

32 I sponsored the effort to limit the purchase of a handgun by any one person to one gun a month. The flood of illegal guns in our streets begins with middlemen known as straw purchasers who make legal buys of thousands of guns—which they turn around and sell illegally to street criminals. When Virginia passed a one gun a month law, the effect was felt in Philadelphia, New Jersey, and New York—because that's where the guns were going.

33 Then there is the question of handgun registration. There are some words that are so emotionally charged that they inhibit discussion of an issue, and this is one of them. Some gun owners hear this word, and fear unfair government intrusion in their lives. But most Americans would agree that those who own handguns should have to pass a basic safety course on instruction before they can operate them. Most Americans would agree that it is in our interests to know who owns handguns, and to be able to track where those handguns go. And I have supported efforts that would let us do just that.

34 I led an effort to eliminate junk handguns completely and permanently. Saturday Night Specials are 81% of the ten most used guns which are traced by the BATF. Many of these junk handguns are manufactured here in California by gun manufacturers known as the "Ring of Fire." The evidence is clear and convincing that these guns lack any sporting use and pose a significant threat to the safety of the American public. They are a menace to society and they should be outlawed.

35 I also led an effort to make it illegal for any person to possess a handgun if they have been convicted of domestic violence. We must do everything we can to offer better protections for fearful women and innocent children against the brutality of batterers. No country—especially ours—should be more worried about protecting the right to bear arms than protecting the arms that carry our children.

36 Finally, with seven times more gun dealers than McDonald's Restaurants, I supported an effort to increase substantially the license fees on gun dealers and require them to have pictures and fingerprints taken with their application. Between this effort and work on the local level, we've reduced the number of gun dealers from 287,000 to 80,000. But we can go farther, and we can get that number much, much lower. With a simple change in our current law, we can do nationwide what you are doing community by community here in California. By simply restricting federal firearm licenses to businesses located in commercial zones and eliminating "FFLs" in residential areas, we can get the gun dealers out of our neighborhoods and into commercial areas with the legitimate dealers who respect the law. Most businesses cannot be located in residential neighborhoods—gun dealing shouldn't be the exception. In addition to trigger locks and mandatory background checks at gun shows, these are sensible measures that should be taken now.

37 I know the blaze of violence has many fires. We won't end violence by reducing gun violence. There are many reasons and many causes. But think how much more effectively we can deal with the other root causes if we find common ground on reducing gun violence. Then, the discussion about prevention, and education, and collaboration between parents, teachers, the private sector, and government becomes a constructive discussion.

38 We can discuss violent and lethal influences on our children. We can talk about the responsibility each of us has in how our children get the idea that violence is somehow glamorous. But we can't have an honest discussion until we confront the fact that, while our children may be exposed to lethal special effects in movies and videogames, we are doing very little about their access to lethal weapons.

39 It seems to me that we have a choice. We can continue to participate in a debate of extremes that offers false and hopeless choices. A debate that has allowed the carnage in our culture to become so deeply imbedded that it has become a fact and a way of life. Or we can seek the common ground—a place that offers fewer guns, less violence, and fewer tears. The commonsense approach to discussing violence is only a beginning, not an end. And all proposals that will save the lives of our children and fellow citizens should be considered.

40 Let me end my conversation with two stories.

41 A few years ago, the *Washington Post* ran a story about violence—and in it, they told of an eight-year-old girl who wrote a letter to her parents saying which of her dresses she wanted to be buried in. She wrote the letter because she didn't think she would live to see her twelfth birthday.

42 And then there are the people in this room. When senseless gun violence left eight people killed and six injured at 101 California six years ago, you responded to tragedy with a purpose. From a small group of lawyers and volunteers mobilized to prevent gun violence, you have grown and persevered over the years. You know the result—today, over seventy cities and counties here in California have enacted nearly 200 local firearms regulations, ranging from junk gun prohibitions to trigger lock requirements. You're doing at the local level what few are even willing to discuss at the national level—and you've made a difference in the lives of hundreds of thousands of people.

43 When I look around this room and think about the hard work you have done in the name of protecting children and families, I know there is hope and reason to be optimistic about the future. I know that we can look at you and your accomplishments and take that same model of hard work, perseverance, dedication, and will to a national level, and to every community in this country. Because we are a good people and a caring people, who want the best for our children, who want to raise good children, and who believe in the enormous power of working together for the common good. And working together for the common good is what it will take to make a difference in the fear our children—and our parents—live with.

The Duty of Hope

◆ *George W. Bush* ◆

On July 22, 1999, Republican presidential candidate George W. Bush delivered a major policy address to a racially mixed, non-denominational church audience in Indianapolis. The speech was a featured part of a celebration of the Front Porch Alliance, an initiative led by Indianapolis Mayor Stephen Goldsmith, designed to encourage cooperation between churches, charitable organizations, and government agencies in effecting welfare reform.

The speech was significant in that it was Bush's first major policy address since he became the presidential front-runner of the Republican party. Furthermore, it sought to flesh out his "compassionate conservatism" theme by providing details of his plan to expand and encourage the role of charitable and faith-based groups in helping the needy. The speech has been credited with being a "double-barrel hit" by embracing "two of the most cherished ideas of the right and the left: religious faith and helping the poor" (*Chicago Tribune,* July 25, 1999, Sec. 1, p. 17).

The speech begins with a strong statement of praise for the audience (1). It is probable that the speaker is sincere in his praise since one would be hard pressed to assemble an audience more sympathetic to the speaker's policy proposition than the one facing Bush in Indianapolis. In fact, the Front Porch Alliance may be seen as a living example of the type of cooperation between public and private agencies that Bush urges in this speech.

Having credited the Front Porch Alliance with setting an example of innovative, compassionate government, Bush proceeds by articulating some of the dimensions of compassion that should be reflected in American life: prosperity that leaves no one behind; material wealth that

◆ Copyright © 1999 by Bush for President, Inc. Reprinted by permission.

is matched by richness in justice, family love, and moral courage; and a commitment to serving those living in hardship.

Bush then moves, with broad strokes, to paint a portrait of his "bold new approach" to the role of government. Beginning with faith-based organizations, Bush envisions government as a means of providing assistance to these agencies. His narrative is punctuated by examples of successful faith-based programs in action "that have shown their ability to save and change lives" (17). He condemns the failed compassion of towering, distant bureaucracies while praising individuals and groups who are serving their neighbors in inspired and effective manners.

One may legitimately question whether Bush has offered sufficient evidence in support of his factual claim that private and faith-based efforts work. Do you find that the examples provided constitute sufficient justification for the claim? If not, how much confidence should be placed in a new policy that depends on the workability of these voluntary programs?

Paragraphs 27 and 28 provide a major transition from existing voluntary programs to Bush's "bold new approach." The basic principles that undergird this approach are then revealed (29–

33). The burden of describing the new policy falls upon twelve paragraphs (34–45). To what extent are the provisions of this new approach identified in a clear manner? How would you summarize the major provisions of the new approach?

Speakers sometimes sense the objections or reservations that their listeners may have toward what they are proposing. In such cases, speakers often identify and refute or discredit such concerns. To what extent does Governor Bush seem to anticipate and refute such objections or reservations in paragraphs 46 through 52? Does this strategy help to defuse the objections implicit in the two mindsets identified by Bush?

The term "compassionate conservatism" has been labeled contradiction in terms by detractors who believe that Republicans care more about cutting budgets than about helping the poor. To what extent and through what means does Bush thwart such cynicism, particularly in paragraphs 53 through 55?

What reservations do you have concerning the workability of a partnership between faith-based/charitable organizations and the government? If the government's role is largely reactive, how may central planning and coordination be assured?

◆ ◆ ◆

1   It is a pleasure to be with you—among people transforming this city with good will and good works. The Front Porch Alliance is the way things ought to be. People on the front lines of community renewal should work together. And government should take your side. Mayor Goldsmith, my thanks to you. You have set an example of innovative, compassionate government. And that example has become a model for the nation.

2   Everywhere I've gone in this campaign—from farms in Iowa to Latino communities in California—I've carried one message. Our country must be prosperous. But prosperity must have a purpose. The purpose of prosperity is to make sure the American dream touches every willing heart. The purpose of prosperity is to leave no one out . . . to leave no one behind.

3   We are a wealthy nation. But we must also be rich in ideals—rich in justice and compassion and family love and moral courage.

4   I am an economic conservative. I believe we should cut taxes to stimulate economic growth. Yet I know that economic growth is not the solution to every problem. A rising tide lifts many boats—but not all. Many prosper in a bull market—but not everyone. The invisible hand works many miracles. But it cannot touch the human heart.

5   The American Dream is so vivid—but too many feel: The dream is not meant for me. Children abandoned by fathers. Children captured by addiction and condemned to schools that do not teach and

will not change. Young mothers without self-respect or education or the supporting love of a husband. These needs are found everywhere, in cities and suburbs and small towns. But the places where these problems are concentrated—from North Central Philadelphia to South Central Los Angeles—have become the ruins of communities. Places where despair is the easy path, and hope the narrow gate.

6   For many people, this other society of addiction and abandonment and stolen childhood is a distant land, another world. But it is America. And these are not strangers, they are citizens, Americans, our brothers and sisters.

7   In their hopes, we find our duties. In their hardship, we must find our calling—to serve others, relying on the goodness of America and the boundless grace of God.

8   The reality here is simple. Often when a life is broken, it can only be rebuilt by another caring, concerned human being. Someone whose actions say, "I love you, I believe in you, I'm in your corner." This is compassion with a human face and a human voice. It is not an isolated act—it is a personal relationship. And it works. The mentors in Big Brothers/Big Sisters—spending only a few hours a week with a child—cut first-time drug use by 50 percent and violent behavior by a third. The success of this fine program proves the obvious: in solving the problems of our day, there is no substitute for unconditional love and personal contact.

9   I was struck by the story of a gang initiation in Michigan. A 15-year-old boy was forced to stand and take two minutes of vicious beating from other members without fighting back. At the end, he was required to stand up and embrace his attackers. When asked why he submitted to this torture, he answered, "I knew this was going to hurt really bad, but I felt that if I could take it for just a couple of minutes, I'd be surrounded by people who loved me."

10   Imagine a young life that empty, so desperately in need of real love. And multiply it by millions. This crisis of the spirit creates an expanding circle of responsibility. Individuals are responsible to love our neighbors as we want to be loved ourselves.

11   Parents must understand that being a good mom or dad becomes their highest goal in life.

12   Congregations and community groups must fight for children and neighborhoods, creating what Pope John Paul II calls, "a hospitable society, a welcoming culture."

13   A president has responsibilities as well. A president can speak without apology for the values that defeat violence and help overcome poverty. A president can speak for abstinence and accountability and the power of faith.

14   In the past, presidents have declared wars on poverty and promised to create a great society. But these grand gestures and honorable aims were frustrated. They have become a warning, not an example. We found that government can spend money, but it can't put hope in our hearts or a sense of purpose in our lives. This is done by churches and synagogues and mosques and charities that warm the cold of life. A quiet river of goodness and kindness that cuts through stone.

15   Real change in our culture comes from the bottom up, not the top down. It gathers the momentum of a million committed hearts.

16   So today I want to propose a different role for government. A fresh start. A bold new approach.

17   In every instance where my administration sees a responsibility to help people, we will look first to faith-based organizations, charities and community groups that have shown their ability to save and change lives. We will make a determined attack on need, by promoting the compassionate acts of others. We will rally the armies of compassion in our communities to fight a very different war against poverty and hopelessness, a daily battle waged house to house and heart by heart.

18   This will not be the failed compassion of towering, distant bureaucracies. On the contrary, it will be government that serves those who are serving their neighbors. It will be government that directs help to the inspired and the effective. It will be government that both knows its limits, and shows its heart. And it will be government truly by the people and for the people.

19 We will take this path, first and foremost, because private and religious groups are effective. Because they have clear advantages over government.

20 Sometimes the idea of compassion is dismissed as soft or sentimental. But those who believe this have not visited these programs. Compassion is not one of the easy virtues.

21 At InnerChange—a faith-based program run by Prison Fellowship inside a Texas prison—inmates are up at 5 am and fill their days with work and study rather than soap operas. At Teen Challenge—a national drug treatment program—one official says, "We have a rule: If you don't work, you don't eat." This is demanding love—at times, a severe mercy. These institutions, at their best, treat people as moral individuals, with responsibilities and duties, not as wards or clients or dependents or numbers.

22 Self-control and character and goal-setting give direction and dignity to all our lives. We must renew these values to restore our country.

23 Many of these organizations share something else in common: A belief in the transforming power of faith. A belief that no one is finally a failure or a victim, because everyone is the child of a loving and merciful God—a God who counts our tears and lifts our head. The goal of these faith-based groups is not just to provide services, it is to change lives. And lives are changed. Addicts become examples. Reckless men become loving fathers. Prisoners become spiritual leaders—sometimes more mature and inspiring than many of us can ever hope to be.

24 In Texas, there is a young man named James Peterson, who'd embezzled his way into a prison term. But when he was offered parole, he turned it down, to finish the InnerChange course, which teaches inmates to rely on faith to transform their lives. As James put it, "There is nothing I want more than to be back in the outside world with my daughter Lucy, [but] I realized that this was an opportunity to . . . become a living [witness] . . . for my brothers [in prison] and to the world. I want to stay in prison to complete the transformation [God] has begun in me."

25 One example, but a miracle that is common. Sometimes our greatest need is *not* for more laws. It is for more conscience. Sometimes our greatest hope is *not* found in reform. It is found in redemption.

26 We should promote these private and faith-based efforts because they work. But we should also promote them because their challenges are often greater than their resources. Sometimes the armies of compassion are outnumbered and outflanked and outgunned. Visit Mission Arlington in Texas on a day they offer free dentistry, and people are often lined up at 3 or 4 in the morning. Or consider that only 3 percent of America's 13.6 million at-risk children now have mentors. These groups are widespread, but their scale, in some cases, is not sufficient.

27 It is not enough for conservatives like me to praise these efforts. It is not enough to call for volunteerism. Without more support and resources—both private and public—we are asking them to make bricks without straw.

28 So today I am announcing a series of proposals. And they are guided by some basic principles.

29 Resources should be devolved, not just to states, but to charities and neighborhood healers.

30 We will never ask an organization to compromise its core values and spiritual mission to get the help it needs.

31 We will keep a commitment to pluralism—not discriminating for or against Methodists or Mormons or Muslims, or good people of no faith at all.

32   We will ensure that participation in faith-based programs is truly voluntary—that there are secular alternatives.

33   And we will recognize there are some things the government *should* be doing—like Medicaid for poor children. Government cannot be replaced by charities—but it can welcome them as partners, not resent them as rivals.

34   Where do we start? Our nation is so prosperous that we can meet our current priorities and still take on new battles. We will strengthen Social Security and Medicare. We will fortify the military. We will cut taxes in a way that creates high-paying jobs. Yet there is another priority. In my first year in office, we will dedicate about $8 billion—an amount equal to 10 percent of the non-Social Security surplus—to provide new tax incentives for giving, and to support charities and other private institutions that save and change lives. We will prove, in word and deed, that our prosperity has a purpose.

35   My administration will act in three broad areas:

36   First, we will encourage an outpouring of giving in America. Americans are generous with their time and money. But we can foster that generosity even further—creating fertile ground for the growth of charities.

37   Right now approximately 70 percent of all tax filers cannot claim the charitable tax deduction, because they do not itemize. We will give people who don't itemize the same treatment and incentive as people who do, rewarding and encouraging giving by everyone in our society, not just the wealthy.

38   We will provide for charity tax credits—credits which will allow individuals to give a part of what they owe in state taxes directly to private and religious institutions fighting poverty in their own communities. Individuals will choose who conducts this war on poverty—and their support won't be filtered through layers of government officials.

39   Second, we will involve the armies of compassion in some specific areas of need, to demonstrate how our new approach will work.

40   Here is an example. America has tripled its prison population in the last 15 years. That is a necessary and effective role of government—protecting our communities from predators. But it has left a problem—an estimated 1.3 million children who have one or both parents in prison. These are forgotten children—almost six times more likely to go to prison themselves—and they should not be punished for the sins of their fathers. It is not only appropriate, it is urgent, to give grants to ministries and mentoring programs targeting these children and their families for help and support. My administration will start bringing help and hope to these other, innocent victims of crime.

41   As well, we will encourage and expand the role of charities in after-school programs. Everyone agrees there is a problem in these empty, unsupervised hours after school. But those hours should not only be filled with sports and play, they should include lessons in responsibility and character. So we will invite the Boys and Girls Clubs, the YMCA and local churches and synagogues to be a central part of after-school programs.

42   We will encourage private and religious charities to be more involved in drug treatment and maternity group homes. We will bring programs like InnerChange to four federal prisons, to test if its early promise is fulfilled. And we will set up a compassion capital fund, to identify good ideas transforming neighborhoods and lives and provide seed money to support them—helping to expand the scale of effective programs.

43   Third, we will change the laws and regulations that hamper the cooperation of government and private institutions. In 1997, Texas officials tried to close down faith-based drug treatment programs because they didn't fit the regulations. When challenged that these programs were effective, one official responded, "We're not interested in results, we're interested in complying with the law." We solved that problem in Texas. If I am president, federal workers in every department of my administration will know that we value effectiveness above red tape and regulation.

44 We will allow private and religious groups to compete to provide services in every federal, state and local social program. We will promote alternative licensing procedures, so effective efforts won't be buried by regulation. And we will create an advocate position—reporting directly to the president—to ensure that charities are not secularized or slighted.

45 I visit churches and charities serving their neighbors nearly everywhere I go in this country. And nothing is more exciting or encouraging. Every day they prove that our worst problems are not hopeless or endless. Every day they perform miracles of renewal. Wherever we can, we must expand their role and reach, without changing them or corrupting them. It is the next, bold step of welfare reform.

46 To take that step, our nation must get beyond two narrow mindsets. The first is that government provides the only *real* compassion. A belief that what is done by caring people through church and charity is secondary and marginal. Some Washington politicians call these efforts "crumbs of compassion." These aren't "crumbs" to people whose lives are changed, they are the hope of renewal and salvation. These are not the "crumbs of compassion," they are the bread of life. And they are the strength and soul of America.

47 There is another destructive mindset: the idea that if government would only get out of our way, all our problems would be solved. An approach with no higher goal, no nobler purpose, than "Leave us alone."

48 Yet this is not who we are as Americans. We have always found our better selves in sympathy and generosity—both in our lives and in our laws. Americans will never write the epitaph of idealism. It emerges from our nature as a people, with a vision of the common good beyond profit and loss. Our national character shines in our compassion.

49 We are a nation of rugged individuals. But we are also the country of the second chance—tied together by bonds of friendship and community and solidarity.

50 We are a nation of high purpose and restless reform—of child labor laws and emancipation and suffrage and civil rights.

51 We are a nation that defeated fascism, elevated millions of the elderly out of poverty and humbled an evil empire.

52 I know the reputation of our government has been tainted by scandal and cynicism. But the American government is not the enemy of the American people. At times it is wasteful and grasping. But we must correct it, not disdain it. Government must be carefully limited—but strong and active and respected within those bounds. It must act in the common good—and that good is not common until it is shared by those in need.

53 In this campaign, I bring a message to my own party. We must apply our conservative and free-market ideas to the job of helping real human beings—because any ideology, no matter how right in theory, is sterile and empty without that goal. There must be a kindness in our justice. There must be a mercy in our judgment. There must be a love behind our zeal.

54 This is where my campaign is headed. We will carry a message of hope and renewal to every community in this country. We will tell every American, "The dream is for you." Tell forgotten children in failed schools, "The dream is for you." Tell families, from the barrios of LA to the Rio Grande Valley: "El sueno americano es para ti." Tell men and women in our decaying cities, "The dream is for you." Tell confused young people, starved of ideals, "The dream is for you."

55   As Americans, this is our creed and our calling. We stumble and splinter when we forget that goal. We unite and prosper when we remember it. No great calling is ever easy, and no work of man is ever perfect. But we can, in our imperfect way, rise now and again to the example of St. Francis—where there is hatred, sowing love; where there is darkness, shedding light; where there is despair, bringing hope.

Challenges for Technology and the Economy

◆ *Elizabeth Dole* ◆

Born and raised in North Carolina, Elizabeth Dole graduated with distinction from Duke University in 1958 and was accepted into Phi Beta Kappa. She took a degree from Harvard Law School in 1965 and a master's degree in education and government from Harvard as well.

Dole has served several United States Presidents. Her first presidential appointment was by President Nixon as Deputy Assistant for Consumer Affairs. From 1981–1983, Dole was Assistant to President Reagan for Public Liaison, and in February of 1983, she joined President Reagan's Cabinet as Secretary of Transportation. President Bush named Elizabeth Dole Secretary of Labor in January of 1988. In 1991, Dole became president of the American Red Cross, and, under her leadership, the Red Cross prospered. *Money* magazine named it the nation's Top-Rated Charity for its great efficiency over a three-year period. Dole resigned her position with the Red Cross in January 1999, contemplating a run for the presidency in the year 2000.

Dole made many important contributions in her various roles. For her vital endeavors, she has received numerous awards, ranging from public service, to government initiatives, to women issues. For example, she received the National Safety Council's Distinguished Service Award; the Peter Parker Medal from the Yale University School of Medicine; the Humanitarian Award from the National Commission Against Drunk Driving; the North Carolina Award; the Lifetime Achievement Award from Women Executives in State Government; and numerous others. In January, 1998, *Good Housekeeping* named Dole as one of the 10 Most Admired Women, her third appearance in the magazine's Top 10.

Elizabeth took a 14-month unpaid leave from the Red Cross to accompany her husband Bob on his presidential campaign in 1996, albeit a losing effort.

On March 10, 1999, Elizabeth Dole announced that she was creating an exploratory committee to determine whether she should run for the Republican presidential nomination in 2000. Although she is not the first woman to ever announce her candidacy for the presidency—Belva Lockwood was a candidate in the nineteenth century—she, nevertheless, in recent times, is engaging in a ground breaking move. She made the announcement in Des Moines.

◆ The text of this speech was obtained from the Elizabeth Dole for President Exploratory Committee.

As a viable candidate in a major political party, Dole has moved the cause of women in politics forward.

Dole has spoken on a number of vital political topics. She gave one such speech on June 16, 1999, at the Rotary Club of San Jose, California. Since San Jose is in the Silicon Valley, she took the opportunity to talk about the challenges of technology and the economy. Dole is a very dynamic, energetic speaker, and on this occasion, as she frequently does, wandered about the audience as she addressed her listeners.

Since she spoke at a luncheon, as is common, Dole began her speech with numerous references to members of the audience, and she expressed heartfelt appreciation for their inviting her (1, 2). Since the task of a political candidate is personal ingratiation, she tactfully engages in ethos-building tactics from the beginning. Dole praises Rotary International for their funding of scholarships and for their contributions to the victims of the Balkan crisis (3). Dole also makes two positive references to herself; first, by pointing to her relationship with the Red Cross, and then, by calling attention to her recent visit to the Balkans, where she observed things first hand (3). In paragraph 5, she praises the San Jose Rotary Club that she is addressing, and she further praises the program chair who has introduced her. She uses her introduction as a lead-in to a narrative about her first court case as a lawyer. This narrative has its humorous aspects—after all, a person is not so often tried for annoying a lion—and she points out that she won the case. Try to identify the humorous elements of the story and discuss how this would help her gain good will with the audience.

Dole ends her introduction ingeniously. She tells the audience that she "never understood what could possess a person to crawl into a lion's den," and follows that with the abrupt statement, "Then I announced I was thinking about running for President," which she obviously considers akin to crawling into a lion's den!

Dole's speech has strong transitions: paragraph 24, for example. Try to identify others. At the same time, the speech lacks a strong organizational structure. Paragraph 24 is an internal summary of things the government in Washington can provide for the technology community. It consists of a statement of policy goals. Then she attacks Washington for having expanded more than ever and that there is more government regulation than before. Examine Dole's use of evidence in developing these ideas.

Do you see Dole's speech as principally an attack on the Clinton administration or is it mostly a construction of policy goals? Note that she is pointing forward to the next election and mentions Al Gore, the likely Democratic candidate and noted for his expertise on technology, as often as she can.

Persuasion, to a great extent, is a matter of appealing to audience values. What values do you find Dole utilizing that she thinks will appeal to her immediate audience? Basic to Dole's economic values is that of market economies (60). How effectively does she support that value in paragraph 60? Why, or why not, would the immediate audience most likely be sympathetic to this value?

Politicians are fond of generating labels and catch phrases. In paragraph 27, Dole speaks of "courageous conservatism." What do you think she means by that expression? Might it be an intentional contrast to her rival Republican candidate, George W. Bush, and his concept of "compassionate conservatism"?

Paragraph 61 is a transition to her very short conclusion. Paragraph 62 is fundamentally a summary of her speech. In the next paragraph (63), she tries to end with an uplifting note. Do you find her conclusion effective? Could she profitably have referred back to her introduction, about the annoyed lion, or was it mostly extraneous to her speech?

◆ ◆ ◆

1   Thank you, for that wonderful, warm welcome, and thank you, Bernie (Vogel) for those very kind words of introduction and for your invitation for me to be part of this wonderful luncheon. The San Jose Rotary is fortunate, indeed, to have your service as chairman of the program committee. With your business and legal background and knowledge of the community, you certainly provide invaluable insights and leadership to a number of organizations—including YMCA, the local Chamber and Catholic Charities.

2   Heartfelt thanks to Mary Ann Diridon [DEER.don] for this opportunity to be with you today and to meet your fellow Rotarians. I understand you are the first woman President of the San Jose Rotary, and you know, I admire any woman who is the first in her field!

3   As the largest service club between San Francisco and Los Angeles your members provide humanitarian service, encourage high ethical standards, and help build goodwill in the Silicon Valley and beyond. I was interested to learn that Rotary International boasts the largest privately funded scholarship program in the world. You are truly shaping the future of our country and our world. And, Rotary recently established an account with the International Committee of the Red Cross—an organization very dear to my heart—to provide assistance to the victims of the crisis and conflict in the Balkans, an area I visited recently. I commend you on your efforts to help these innocent victims and your dedication to promoting peace around the world.

4   I am sorry my good friend and esteemed Congressman, Tom Campbell, could not be here today. As most of you know, Tom is back in Washington "fighting the good fight" for the 15th district! I am truly delighted that he has endorsed my candidacy for President and am grateful to have his advice and support.

5   What a distinguished gathering of community, business, government and education leaders from across the Silicon Valley! I am delighted to be with you all today.

6   You know, Bernie, I first came to appreciate the value of a good introduction the very first time I ever practiced law in a courtroom. Because that's when I discovered what can happen if there's any mistake about just who you are!

7   It was when I was just out of Harvard Law School . . . and went down to work in Washington, D.C. I passed the bar, and I thought I might do a little pro-bono work. Well, I hadn't taken trial practice at Harvard. And you may have heard, I hate to be unprepared. So I decided I'd go to D.C. night court and observe for a while . . . just to learn my way around.

8   Presiding over the proceedings was a big, black-robed judge known as Edward "Buddy" Beard. Believe me, no young lawyer ever called him Buddy.

9   Well, one night Judge Beard spotted me sitting in the back and pointed his finger in my direction and said, "Who are *you?*"

10   I explained that I was just looking on.

11   "Are you a member of the D.C. bar?" he asked. I said, "Yes." He said, "Come up here. I have a case for you."

12   I tried to tell him that he was making a mistake, I was just an observer—but I couldn't talk my way out of it. I didn't even have the *case* yet and I couldn't persuade the judge! I thought that was a bad sign.

13   Well, I *reluctantly* approached the bench and Judge Beard handed me the information slip. It turns out my client was a visitor to Washington who'd tried to crawl into a cage to pet the lion at the National Zoo. He was accused of "annoying" the lion.

14   When I went down to the cells where they were holding my new client, I found out he was determined to skip town the minute he got out. I knew I couldn't ask the judge for bail, and I didn't want to leave this hopeless fellow in the hoosegow . . . I knew I'd have to go to trial that night. Worse—

when I got back to the courtroom, I discovered who my adversary from the U.S. Attorney's Office was. It was my former classmate Lee Freeman, editor of the *Harvard Law Review*! Lee is now vice president of a major Chicago firm . . . and a *very* able attorney.

15 I won't go through the whole story of what followed. But by the grace of God, I won that case! I argued—I'm not making this up—that unless the lion was brought into court as a witness . . . there was no way to know he was really annoyed!

16 The next day, Judge Beard passed me in the hallway and said, "Not bad for the first time out of the box."

17 You know, it was wonderful to win my first case. But I'm going to confess to you—until this year, I never understood what could *possess* a person to crawl into a lion's den.

18 Then I announced I was thinking about running for President.

19 This afternoon I'd like to talk briefly about an important subject . . . what government should—and shouldn't—do, to keep the technology sector and our nation's economy strong and growing.

20 We are living in a period of tremendous global change, change which brings exciting possibilities—and worrisome challenges, as well. The end of the Cold War, and the recognition that free markets *work,* brought an explosion in world output and trade. New information technologies . . . along with rapid advances in engineering, materials, design and electronics . . . have driven a fast-changing economic environment. These developments are *transforming* existing businesses and building new ones for the 21st century.

21 Last year in this country, the Internet accounted for 1.3 million jobs and $300 billion in economic activity. From 1995 to 1998, the annual compounded growth of the U.S. Internet economy topped 170 percent. Today, if the Internet sector of the U.S. economy were a country to itself, it would be among the twenty largest economies.

22 The Internet revolution reaches beyond the business world. When I was head of the Red Cross, our team used the latest technologies and business methods to transform the way this nation's blood supply is collected, tested and distributed. And as I saw on my recent trip to Macedonia, the computers and logistics that are helping *industry* move faster to meet consumer demand, are also helping *disaster-relief* organizations meet humanitarian tragedies like Kosovo.

23 Among the Kosovar refugees, relief agencies are using the Internet to reunite families scattered in different camps. The Internet is a mighty tool.

24 Well, this is certainly an appropriate place to talk about that mighty tool and to reflect on America's part in the global economy and technological revolution. Because in many ways, Silicon Valley's experiences are *America's* experiences. And Silicon Valley's *achievements* are the achievements of the American free market system.

25 The free market has made possible the greatest burst of human intellectual creativity since Gutenberg invented moveable type. And because technology is driven by human imagination along with market demands, it can add more to our lives than government can fathom.

26 Washington's biggest technology challenge is to stay out of your way.

27 As a former Department of Transportation Secretary, I recognize that Washington is too big and it spends too much money. I have led the way in several successful privatization efforts. I sold Conrail, the nation's great railroad and I moved Dulles and Reagan National airports out of the hands of the Federal Government and into the private sector. That's what leadership is all about—recognizing that the private sector can do things better. That's why I led the way to privatize things that are better left to the private sector. I call it "courageous conservatism"—it's knowing who you are and what you believe and being willing to take a stand.

28 In some areas the federal government can help your industry and in a few areas such as encryption and export controls, the government must act. Making the R&D tax credit permanent, fostering Y2K solutions by providing a liability shield, and opening our doors to more highly skilled immigrants are just a few ways Washington can help Silicon Valley.

29 Encryption is a priority issue. Adequate levels of encryption are necessary to maintain the integrity of electronic commerce and to preserve consumer confidence. But Congress should pass legislation which allows the use of U.S. encryption technology both domestically and to all but rogue nations. We must maintain our dominance of this field.

30 The new millennium provides tremendous opportunities—but it also provides a huge challenge. We must be prepared for Y2K. There should be no barriers to industry doing all it can to ensure our people are protected. For that reason I support Y2K legislation pending in Congress that would provide a cooling off period to fix problems; a cap on liability; and limiting liability to damages actually caused by a company.

31 Maintaining our technology edge after New Year's Day includes making the R&D tax credit permanent. Since 1981, the R&D credit has been extended nine times. In some years, Washington didn't get around to the job until long after the law expired. We can't expect you to maximize research efforts with that kind of uncertainty. You should be able to plan and invest for the new century in confidence that the R&D credit is here to stay.

32 To maintain technological advances—you must have a skilled work force. Congress should continue to increase the number of visas for immigrant technology experts. While the cap on skilled immigrants was raised this year, we've already hit this cap. We need to ensure that our industries have the skilled work force to maintain our dominance in the world economy. But this is only a remedy—not a solution.

33 The real solution is to improve our educational system—we must restore our public schools to greatness and we must ensure that our students graduate with the necessary skills.

34 The challenge for Washington and the technology community in the new century will be to keep a good thing going by providing skilled workers, adopting sensible tax policies and—most importantly—preserving the free market approach which brought us so far, so fast.

35 The New Digital Economy seems to have arrived only yesterday but it is creating economic and social progress across the nation. We can sustain this growth and share it with the world only by ensuring freedom for the technology sector while crafting regulatory policies to guarantee competition and creativity.

36 Some of you may be as old as 35. Since you were born, computer power has increased by a factor of 1 million while the price of a basic home PC has decreased by a factor of 1000. The analogy that many of you have come to know is astounding: if the automobile industry had matched that record, this year's models would be cruising comfortably at 1 million miles per hour—getting a half million miles per gallon—and selling for about $2.40.

37 The information technology revolution has spurred growth in all sectors of the economy and has made a direct contribution to our global dominance. Jobs created in the tech sector and in other industries by the New Digital Economy have helped to bring record low unemployment and high wages.

38 Choices made by the next President can build on this success or impede progress. She can set the direction of world affairs, or allow America to trail behind. Choices we make at the federal level can advance economic growth or hold it back. They can set the direction of world affairs, or allow this country to trail behind.

39   We saw that clearly during the 1980s, when the values and vision that Ronald Reagan brought to the White House revitalized America . . . and changed the face of the globe. He was the architect of our low-inflation economy . . . supporting then-Federal Reserve Chairman Paul Volcker in getting inflation rates down from double-digit levels. Reagan's determination to *free up* the power of the U.S. economy led to a remarkable expansion that has continued, almost uninterrupted, to this day.

40   President Clinton and Vice President Gore often take credit for economic good news during their term in office. But if you want to see the people most responsible for our economic health, I suggest you look around this room. It is *private* enterprise and investment that has driven today's prosperity.

41   So powerful is the swing to free-market principles that it dominates the political debate. Few politicians will dispute that the big-government, welfare state failed. Sadly, not all politicians who talk the talk, walk the walk.

42   In fact, just last year Vice President Gore vowed to "continue the hard work of reforming and reinventing our government." He spoke about cutting federal employees, eliminating regulations and saving billions of dollars. *Today, the size, cost and impact of Washington have all grown. That's right; the federal government has grown.*

43   The personnel cuts this administration has bragged about? Well, a new Brookings study, published just this year, reports that if you remove *defense* downsizing from the total, the federal workforce is actually *bigger, not smaller* than it was in 1984.

44   Today the full-time, permanent, civilian workforce stands at a hefty 1.9 million. And that's just the *official* total. *Add in* what Brookings calls the "shadow" workforce—people who work under federal contracts and grants, or federal mandates imposed on state and local government—and another 12.7 million *more* employees are on *your* payroll.

45   There's also more *regulation* than ever. According to the General Accounting Office, *every* year since 1996 has brought an *increase* in major federal rules—*and* in total rules. In 1998, the grand total for new regulations was nearly 5,000. You can look them up for yourself in the 1998 Federal Register, if you can get through its *record* 68,571 pages. Picture a stack of paper twice as tall as I am and you'll get some idea how much that is.

46   Then there's the second-hand burden of *mandated* state and local regulation. According to the Competitive Enterprise Institute, nearly 12 percent of municipal revenue is spent meeting unfunded mandates imposed by the federal government. County governments spent more than $16 billion on environmental mandates between 1994 and 1998.

47   The federal government may have passed the buck to somebody else's budget—but it all comes out of *our pockets* in the end. All told, complying with government regulations costs Americans some $700 billion a year—an invisible "tax bill" often concealed in the price of goods and services.

48   But the *visible* tax bills are bad enough. Today's families are paying an average of 40 percent of their hard-earned dollars in taxes. People are working five months a year just to pay their taxes.

49   Washington not only drains family budgets, it continues to drain our economy of dollars that could fuel future growth. Last year, federal receipts—income, social security, excise and other taxes—totaled *20.5 percent* of the gross domestic product. That's *another* historic high. In fact, 1998 taxes were a larger percentage of GDP than at any time since 1944—a year when this nation was fighting a world war with every resource we possessed!

50   What's more, the Administration's budget for fiscal year 2000 would *add* 75 tax hikes, costing up to $172 billion *more*. Under the administration's budget, reports the Tax Foundation, "the share of the nation's resources claimed by the federal government will remain at historic levels."

51 Vice President Gore may call this "reinventing government" but I think that he's just reinvented *big* government.

52 When you look at these realities, it's *clear* that we have been fortunate that the powerful engine of private enterprise has continued to promote growth in our economy.

53 It's a truism that we live in a global world. But history has shown that the *kind* of world it is makes a *world* of difference. An international economic system dominated by closed markets, command economies, trade barriers and mistrust—would cripple our economy. A world of open markets, free enterprise, free trade and the rule of law—helps us and all our friends to thrive.

54 Frankly, there's just no turning back. The global marketplace pervades American industry. Global thinking has created a vast new market for American technology and services—a sector in which we run a positive balance of trade. And global thinking is transforming manufacturing.

55 To uphold our core economic values, this country must take a decisive leadership role in international trade organizations. First and foremost, I believe, is a strong stand for global free trade. And that effort, I believe, requires Congress and the Clinton-Gore team to get going on approval of fast-track—the President's authority, consulting with Congress, to negotiate trade agreements around the world.

56 Fast-track is an essential part of effective American trade policy in today's global economy. While we debate and delay, other countries are moving forward with trade partnerships that put our products at a disadvantage. Fast-track does not diminish Congress's role—it still has the final say, by majority vote, before any agreement would take effect. But fast-track does recognize the vital role of the executive in speaking for our country in world trade forums. This Administration should put its leadership behind moving this issue forward.

57 Frankly, every President from Gerald Ford to George Bush has had fast-track authority. Congress should grant it to President Clinton now—and to his successor, whomever she may be.

58 It's time, under the tough conditions just negotiated, that the United States moves forward toward the entry of China into the World Trade Organization.

59 History teaches that greater economic freedom moves nations down the path to political freedom . . . and that promotes peace. The terms of the agreement recently negotiated contain strong provisions to protect core American interests . . . provisions that commit China to opening its markets on a definite schedule. Let's now resolve our remaining differences. Then, by all means, let's monitor those commitments . . . let's be skeptical and prudent . . . let's watch our defenses . . . but let's not lose this opportunity to promote and participate in China's market economy.

60 What can market economies do for nations? Look at central and eastern Europe. There, support for free enterprise has nourished fragile new markets. Many of these new democracies have made dramatic economic progress. Countries such as Poland, Hungary, and the Czech Republic have emerged almost overnight as Western-style free market democracies. Even Bulgaria, which lagged behind for years after the fall of the Berlin Wall, finally shed its Soviet-style economics . . . and was recently identified as one of the four most promising emerging markets of the world.

61 You in Silicon Valley can be proud of what you've done to set the standard for these countries and many others. America's private companies and entrepreneurs are truly the best in the world.

62 Now it's time for government to stop slowing things down. But for Washington to turn that corner, we need leadership with the vision and values to point the way—and the common sense to sometimes stay out of the way.

63 The road ahead beckons. God willing, and with all of us pulling together, Americans will discover that peaceful world of limitless possibility.

64 Thank you very much.

Speech to NAACP
Detroit Metro Chapter

◆ *Al Gore* ◆

As the son of the late Senator Albert Gore, Senior and Pauline Gore, Al Gore's interest in and concern for American politics began at an early age. Raised in Carthage, Tennessee, and Washington, D.C., his academic interests led him to Harvard University where he earned a degree, with honors, in government in 1969. He subsequently served in the U.S. Army in Vietnam and as an investigative reporter with *The Tennesseean* in Nashville. After additional studies in Law and Divinity at Vanderbilt University, Gore began his career in public service in 1976 when he was elected to represent Tennessee in the U.S. House of Representatives (1977–1985). In 1984 he was elected to the U.S. Senate (1985–1993) where he served until his inauguration as the 45th Vice President of the United States on January 20, 1993.

During his service as Vice President, he and President Clinton have formed an unprecedented partnership by sharing many of the duties of the Executive office. Gore has served as an advisor to the President on a wide range of administrative initiatives. He has provided leadership in a number of significant areas including aviation safety, telecommunication access, government efficiency, job creation, and workforce flexibility. His record on environmental issues is especially noteworthy as one might expect from the author of *Earth in the Balance: Ecology and the Human Spirit* (Boston: Houghton Mifflin, 1992).

The speech that follows was delivered by Vice President Gore to the Detroit Metropolitan

Chapter of the National Association for the Advancement of Colored People on Sunday, April 25, 1999. As representatives of the oldest and largest civil rights organization in the United States, the members of Gore's audience, like the more than 500,000 NAACP members nationwide, share a concern for equality of opportunity for all Americans and a commitment to promoting a society rich in diversity. Members of the NAACP in Detroit as elsewhere also share a strong sense of historical context.

Founded on February 12, 1909, the 100th anniversary of Abraham Lincoln's birthday, the NAACP has for more than ninety years fought for the abolition of segregation, the promotion of civil rights, and the end of racial intolerance. Across the years, the collective voice of the NAACP has been raised in opposition to racial oppression and violence and in support of minority rights and justice. Race relations in the United States has a checkered past, including incidents of lynching, discriminatory employment practices, segregation in educational and military institutions, and the blatant denial of civil rights to members of minority groups. While the popular mind may have a short memory for such appalling circumstances, those gathered to hear Vice President Gore in Detroit on April 25, 1999 would not be so afflicted.

How does Vice President Gore demonstrate historical sensitivity in the introduction to his speech (1–3)? He also demonstrates a personal connection with the NAACP and its struggles in his introduction (4–5). How is this done? Does

◆ The text of this speech was obtained from the Internet web site of Gore 2000, Inc.

the speaker seek to "borrow" credibility from his father (5–9)? Is this an effective thing to do?

As the introduction draws to a conclusion, Gore praises past progress before stressing the urgency and importance of the work yet to be done (11–14). The accomplishments of the Clinton/Gore administration are then itemized (15) before Gore returns to the challenges that lie ahead. Ratios are used to characterize the extent of the problems faced by African American children (18). Do such seemingly cold statistical data succeed in dramatizing the disadvantages faced by black American society?

The policy being advocated in the speech involves four lines of activity, "things we can do right now," to improve the quality of life in America. Create four policy ("we should") statements that identify the central threads of Gore's proposed program. Has the Vice President ignored any significant policy dimensions that should be considered and elaborated?

Vice President Gore employs a recurring plea using the words "stand with me." How many times is this phrase repeated in the speech? What effect do you think Gore was seeking in his use of this device? Do you find this strategy personally effective? Does it invite your sense of involvement and your support for his policy?

Many stylistic devices are evident in this speech. Which device most caught your fancy? What role does figurative language play in policy speeches?

1   As I was preparing to come here tonight, I realized something remarkable. This is the very last time the Detroit chapter will meet in the 1900s. So tonight, let us first pause to look back on a legacy of struggle for justice and righteousness that has truly defined this century. And then let us look forward with commitment and dedication to the work that lies ahead.

2   The history we remember tonight is long. But the cord that connects us to ages past is short. If you close your eyes and listen to Mayor Archer, you can feel the passion of Booker T. Washington. Lean back and listen to Carolyn Cheeks Kilpatrick, and you can feel the leadership of Shirley Chisolm. Listen to John Conyers, and you can hear the justice of Thurgood Marshall. If you wonder what it was like to talk to Fannie Lou Hammer, spend a few minutes talking to Mrs. Bullah Work. If you wonder what Roy Wilkins was like, spend a few minutes with Dr. Lionel Swann. If you wonder about the wisdom of Mother Pollard, you'll get the same good advice from Mrs. Irene Graves.

3   Although she is not here tonight, I know you are proud to have as a member of this chapter a true American legend, not just to African Americans, but to all Americans—Ms. Rosa Parks. Thanks to the leadership of the Michigan Congressional Delegation—with a vote taken just this week—Rosa Parks now joins Nelson Mandela, Mother Teresa, and Robert Kennedy as one of the few Americans to receive our highest civilian honor: the Congressional Gold Medal.

4   I feel a connection to that struggle and to the NAACP in a personal way. You see, I was raised to believe in racial justice and civil rights.

5   My father was a United States Senator from the South who had courage. He fought against the poll tax in the 1940s, and for civil rights in the 1950s. He was one of only two senators to refuse to sign the hateful Southern Manifesto. He voted for the Voting Rights Act of 1965 and he voted against Supreme Court nominees whose commitment was suspect. And those brave stands probably cost him his career.

6   I remember when I was eight years old, we lived in a little house on Fisher Avenue, halfway up a hill. At the top of the hill was a big old mansion. One day, as the property was changing hands, the neighbors were invited to an open house. My father said: "Come, son, I want to show you something." So we walked up the hill and through the front door.

7   But instead of stopping in the parlor, or the ornate dining room, or the grand staircase with all the other guests, my father took me down to the basement and pointed to the dark, dank stone walls—and the cold metal rings lined up in a row.

8   Slave rings.

9   I thank God that my father taught me to love justice. Not everyone was eager to learn. One unreconstructed constituent once said, in reference to African Americans—though that was not the term he used—"I don't want to eat with them, I don't want to live with them, I don't want my kids to go to school with them." To which my father replied gently: "Do you want to go to heaven with them?"

10   After a brief pause came the flustered response: "No, I want to go to hell with you and Estes Kefauver."

11   We need to know that history. We need to recognize just how far we have come in this century—toward that more perfect union we all seek for our children. But now we must take stock of the present—and we must look to the future. The next time you meet, it will be the dawn of not just a new century, but a whole new era in human history.

12   Will we build on the progress of this century toward justice and tolerance and inclusion? Will we make the 21st century the brightest time our nation has ever seen?

13   In the 20th century, we broke down barriers and overcame discrimination in our laws. We learned along the way that sometimes, good laws aren't good enough.

14   Tonight, I pledge to you: if you stand with me, we will lead America into a 21st century where we break down barriers not just in our lawbooks—but also in our workplaces, in our schoolhouses, in our police stations—and in the human heart.

15   We've made a lot of progress these past six years: more African American business owners, homeowners, and CEO's than ever before. African American poverty and unemployment are at their lowest point in recorded history. The doors to college open wider than ever before. We're bringing long-overdue justice to America's black farmers. And over the past six years, our administration has named more African Americans to Cabinet seats, judgeships, and high posts than any administration in history.

16   As the NAACP has taught us for 90 years, we are not successful as a nation in spite of our diversity—we are successful because of it.

17   But let's be honest: we have a lot of unfinished business ahead of us.

18   Today, an African American child is one and a half times more likely to grow up in a family whose head did not finish high school. Two times as likely to be born to a teen mother. Two and a half times more likely to be born at low birthweight. Three times more likely to live in a single parent home. Four times more likely to have a mother who had no prenatal care. And nine times more likely to be a victim of a homicide.

19   I'll tell you: those numbers should weigh on our national consciousness as strongly as the number "three-fifths" did 150 years ago.

20   To borrow from your theme, I want a "level playing field" in America.

21   Tonight, I want to present four ideas—things we can do right now—to make this nation more equal and open for all Americans. I am here tonight to ask you to stand with me, and help me put them into practice.

22   The first thing I want to ask you to do is help me expand economic opportunity and tap the untapped markets of America's cities—because I believe America's inner cities are America's hidden jewel.

23 That begins with a strong, job-creating economy—one that leaves no one behind, keeps interest rates low, and does even more to help African-American-owned businesses invest and grow. I was proud last year to call on the Small Business Administration to guarantee a record $3.5 billion in loans to African American and Hispanic American businesses by the year 2000. But we need to do more.

24 Expanding opportunity also means opening new markets around the world—and saying as loud as we can: yes, trade with Africa is good for America.

25 But let's be clear: some of the greatest untapped markets for our products today aren't halfway around the world, they're halfway down the street, in our inner cities and urban communities.

26 We need to light up our neglected neighborhoods with the spark of private investment. I am proud that I have led our Empowerment Zone initiative, which has brought more than $2 billion of new investment to Detroit.

27 Now I call on Congress to fully fund our second round of Empowerment Zones, which have the potential to create 90,000 jobs and stimulate more than $20 billion in public and private investment. Let's give our cities the hope and opportunity they deserve.

28 We've also proposed a new $15 billion markets initiative to get more start-up capital into the hands of people who need it. This initiative will help create more than just jobs—it will also create more black-owned businesses in America's cities, and I urge Congress to pass it.

29 It will also do one other thing: it will help more minority women smash through the glass ceiling. At a time when African-Americans earn just 62 cents on each dollar that white Americans earn, don't you think it's time for an equal day's pay for an equal day's work?

30 The second thing I want you to help me do is to protect civil rights in America, including affirmative action. I've heard the critics of affirmative action. They're in favor of affirmative action if you can dunk the basketball or sink a three-point shot. But they're not in favor of it if you merely have the potential to be a leader of your community and bring people together, to teach people who are hungry for knowledge, to heal families who need medical care.

31 I have a different view: America still needs affirmative action. And while scientists work to slow down the speed of light, all of us need to work to speed up the speed of justice. People like Martin Luther King died to give us the civil rights laws on the books today. The least we can do is enforce them.

32 Last year, from Dr. King's pulpit at Ebenezer Baptist Church, I was proud to announce the largest increase in civil rights enforcement in nearly two decades. I fought for that increase, and we won it last year. But we're not done: Congress still won't vote to confirm Bill Lann Lee as head of the Civil Rights Division at the Justice Department. We know he's qualified. We know there is work to be done. So I say to Congress: let's give Bill Lann Lee the up-or-down vote he deserves.

33 Civil rights include basic rights, too—and that includes the right to be treated with respect.

34 Now, I am proud of our nation's law enforcement. I'm proud of the 100,000 new community police we are putting on our streets, and the work they are doing to protect all of our families.

35 But I want to be perfectly clear: the strong arm of justice must also respect justice. I am outraged by recent reports of "racial profiling." DWI is a crime in this nation. DWB shouldn't be. It is wrong to pigeon-hole and punish innocent citizens on the basis of race. It is wrong to stereotype somebody as a suspect simply because of the color of their skin.

36 Let me be very clear: I believe we should abolish racial profiling in America. And any police department in America that is using it should stop right now.

37 Right now, our administration is exploring this issue—to see what we can do to help end this hateful practice, once and for all.

38   While we work to protect rights, the third thing I want you to do is to help me give every child in this country a world-class education.

39   Who in this room tonight believes we need revolutionary change in our public schools?

40   Who believes we can do a better job of working with the parents and teachers who want to see real reform—not ten years from now, after their child graduates, but right away?

41   Then stand with me for the change our children deserve.

42   Most of our kids in urban schools are ready to learn and ready to study. But how can we expect them to learn the skills they need for the future if 26 percent of our urban teachers who teach math have never studied math? If 40 percent who teach chemistry have never studied chemistry? And 71 percent who teach physics haven't studied physics?

43   How can we expect them to get the attention they need if there are 35 other students shoe-horned into the classroom? How can we build the experienced, highly-trained teaching corps we need for our future when nearly half the teachers in poor, minority schools leave after only three years?

44   How can we expect them to learn the Internet if in some urban schools, you blow the circuits if you even plug in a computer? African American children are 40 percent less likely to use a computer at home. We didn't tear down the cotton curtain in this country to replace it with a digital divide.

45   I will fight to bring more accountability in our school system. That's why I'm working right now to pass the President's plan to turn around failing schools, and narrow the disparities in our education system. To end the social promotion that is only failing our children. To raise up standards—and give students and teachers more of the tools to meet them. To rebuild crumbling schools, and hire 100,000 new teachers to reduce class sizes in the early grades. To bring more discipline and character education to the classroom.

46   At the beginning of the 21st century, I'll tell you what else I want to do:

47   I want to reduce class sizes not just in the early grades, but in all grades. I want to make pre-school available to every child, in every community in America. I want to cut in half the achievement gap between rich and poor, and between racial and ethnic groups.

48   And at a time when our nation is becoming more diverse, I am deeply committed to the goal of integration. Today, more than one-third of all black and Hispanic students attend schools with greater than 90 percent minority enrollment. A minority student is 16 times more likely than a white student to be in a high-poverty school. I say we should use voluntary tools such as charter schools, magnet schools, and public school choice to seek more diversity, not less, in our schools. Schools are our best hope to break the chains of racial isolation in our nation.

49   Some people say, "Be patient." But it's too late to be patient. Our children will not be young forever, and their future won't wait. We need to fix our schools today. Stand with me, and we will.

50   We need a strong economy. We need revolutionary change in our schools. But our children can't reach for their dreams if they're ducking for cover. The tragedy at Columbine High School in Colorado shows just how much more work we must do—to make our communities safe, to banish violence and hate, and to replace a culture of violence with a culture of values.

51   And this is the fourth thing I want you to help me do. Help me build a safer society and safer schools for all our children.

52   I just came from Littleton, Colorado, where I met with the families of the children who were brutally slain last week at Columbine High School. Included among the dead was a 17-year-old boy named Isaiah, who was killed simply because he was black.

53   Julian Bond likes to say that when he was a child, bad boys fought with knives, not automatic weapons. And crack was something that, if you stepped on it, would break your mother's back.

54 For parents, last Tuesday's tragedy yielded more questions than answers: how do two teenage boys get their hands on TEC-9 assault weapons, sawed off shotguns, and pipe bombs?

55 I want to work with you to change a popular culture that glorifies violence and mayhem. We must cut off our young people's easy access to guns and deadly weapons. We must invest in the programs that prevent our children from turning to a life of crime and drugs in the first place.

56 I call on Congress to pass a new initiative to help schools hire and train 2,000 new community police officers—to work closely with teachers and students to prevent violence. Let's pass it into law.

57 And I believe we need more drug counselors and violence prevention coordinators in our middle schools. I have seen the work that is being done through peer mediation and violence prevention programs—and it is cooling tempers and saving lives. I call on Congress to work with us and hire another 1,300 drug counselors and violence prevention coordinators across the country.

58 And I'll tell you what my wife Tipper would say if she were here. She would say: "Al, don't forget to tell them this: when first-grade teachers see a new class of students the first week of the year, they can tell you at the end of that first week that one, two, or three of those kids are troubled already, even at that age." And we need to have more resources devoted to community mental health centers and mental health treatment and mental health counseling for families that need it.

59 These are some of the things we must do at the national level. But we all know: responsibility begins in the home.

60 Parents, we've got to talk to our children. We've got to know what's going on in our children's lives. If a child is making pipe bombs in the garage, we've got to know about it. We've got to teach them right from wrong. And we must teach them that embracing the right values can transcend a moment's cheap sensation. Or a sudden impulse of hatred and revenge. Or the easy surge of power learned from a violent culture with too few anchors, too little family stability, and a dearth of spiritual nurturing.

61 It's not just the responsibility we have to our children—it's the responsibility we have to each other.

62 We've all got to take a role in our children's lives. Parents, take your child to school. Meet your child's teachers. Trade phone numbers with other parents and teachers. Turn off the television at night. Help them with their homework. Pick up their report cards. Play a role in their lives.

63 Ladies and gentlemen, stand with me, and help me do these four things. For if we can build a nation of opportunity through jobs and education, and a nation of safety and justice through strong values, then we can reach for our highest aspirations. Then we can build that more perfect union our founders envisioned.

64 I believe that God's hand has touched the United States of America—not by accident, but on purpose. He has given us not just a chance, but a mission, to prove to men and women throughout this world that people of different racial and ethnic backgrounds, of all faiths and creeds, cannot only work and live together, but can enrich and ennoble both themselves and our common purpose.

65 We don't need more division in America. We don't need more scapegoats. What we need is more love and understanding and cooperation. We need to work together on solutions, to give our children and our families the future they deserve.

66 Jesus said in the Gospel of Matthew: "Thou shalt love the Lord thy God with all thy heart, and with all thy soul, and with all thy mind. This is the first and greatest commandment. And the second is like unto it, thou shalt love thy neighbor as thyself. On these two commandments hang all the laws and the prophets."

67   So let us not be weary in well-doing as we address the unfinished agenda of NAACP. Let us make His dream our agenda for action. And always remember, in the words of the hymn:

68   "In Christ there is no east or west, In him, no south or north, but one great fellowship of love throughout the whole wide earth.

69   "Join hands, disciples of the faith, whate'er your race may be, who serves my father as a child is surely kin to me."

Chapter Eight

Speeches That Intensify Social Cohesion

The Nature and Importance of Speeches That Intensify Social Cohesion

At the heart of any social order is a set of values that constitutes the basis for all social action. In recognition of the importance of values, Chapter 5 discussed the nature of speeches that seek to establish propositions of value. However, once values have been established, the perpetuation of social order demands that these values periodically be reaffirmed and intensified. A rhetorical critic, Ronald F. Reid, reminds us: "Building and maintaining social cohesion is an ever present need; for although individuals within society are obviously not all alike, they must transcend their differences if they are to function as a viable social unit."

There are numerous occasions in our society on which speeches that intensify social cohesion are given: church services, victory celebrations, award convocations, retirement luncheons, funeral services, nominating conventions, fund-raising rallies, sales promotion meetings, and commencements are such occasions. At moments like these, speakers address audiences about the values that both share as members of a common group. The speeches given in such moments are noncontroversial for a specific audience. They do not urge adoption of new values or rejection of old values. Rather, they seek to reinforce and revitalize existing audience values. Speakers seek unity of spirit or a reenergizing of effort or commitment; they try to inspire, to kindle enthusiasm, or to deepen feelings of awe, respect, and devotion.

Among the types of speeches that intensify social cohesion are the following:

- *Sermons:* A sermon articulates the tenets of a faith. It is designed to inspire stronger commitment to religious beliefs and values.
- *Eulogies:* A eulogy pays tribute to the dead. It identifies, in the life of the departed, qualities which those who remain behind should value and emulate.
- *Dedication Speeches:* A dedication speech marks the completion of a group project. It praises group achievement and stresses the importance of the object being dedicated to future group endeavors.

- *Commemorative Speeches:* A commemorative speech marks the anniversary of an event. It demonstrates the significance of the event in the light of present group values, beliefs, and goals.
- *Commencement Speeches:* A commencement speech signals the completion of a course of study. It praises those being graduated and speaks to the values that should be reflected in their future lives.
- *Keynote Speeches:* A keynote speech serves as a preface to a meeting, conference, or convention. It stresses the social worth and importance of the work to be done by those assembled.
- *Welcoming Speeches:* A speech of welcome extends a greeting to people who are new to a group. It expresses satisfaction with the presence of new members or visitors and relates the values of the group to the values of those joining or visiting the group.
- *Farewell Speeches:* A farewell speech is given by a person who is leaving a group. The speaker usually reflects on the quality of the experiences that were shared with the group and the emotions he or she is experiencing at the moment of departure.
- *Presentation Speeches:* A presentation speech accompanies the presentation of an award to a group member. It specifies the qualities the award is meant to symbolize and justifies the presentation of the award to the person being honored.
- *Nomination Speeches:* A nominating speech places the name of a person before a group of voters as a candidate for an elective office. It describes the requirements of the office (abilities, personal qualities, duties, problems to be faced), praises the virtues, accomplishments, and experiences of the person being nominated, and depicts the success the group will have under the leadership of the nominee if he or she is elected.
- *Acceptance Speeches:* An acceptance speech is given by the recipient of an award or honor. In accepting an award, a speaker is expected to express gratitude and to demonstrate the personal qualities the award is intended to symbolize.
- *Inaugural Addresses:* An inaugural address is given by a person as he or she is about to assume a position of leadership in a group. The speaker normally acknowledges the passing of leadership, praises past group performance and achievements, and identifies the values and goals of future group activities.

Each of these types of speeches serves a different immediate purpose. However, all share the larger social purpose of intensifying social cohesion by paying tribute to the values of the group. By nature, the speech that intensifies social cohesion invites members to reaffirm their commitment to the values, customs, and traditions that are at the heart of group life.

Students often assign less importance to this form than to informative or persuasive communication. Drawing on their past experiences with ceremonial gatherings, they conclude that speeches that intensify social cohesion are often "flowery" and trite—given more to affected *or* artificial flourishes than to substantive issues. However, sociologist Robert Bellah warns against taking this speech form lightly. He observes:

> . . . we know enough about the function of ceremonial and ritual in various societies to make us suspicious of dismissing something as unimportant because it is "only a ritual." What people say on solemn occasions need not be taken at face value, but it is often indicative of deep-seated values and commitments that are not made explicit in the course of everyday life.[1]

1. Cited in Michael Novak, *Choosing Our King: Powerful Symbols in Presidential Politics* (New York: Macmillan, 1974), p. 142.

Careful students will recognize that ceremonial speeches often capture the essence of a social fabric. Such speeches help to illuminate the central values that undergird group traditions, procedures, and goals. In fact, many of the greatest speeches of recorded history have sought to intensify social cohesion.

Criteria for Evaluating Speeches That Intensify Social Cohesion

Although one could devise discrete criteria for the evaluation of each type of speech discussed in the previous section, each type may be meaningfully considered by applying criteria common to them all.

1.   Has the speaker satisfied the ceremonial purpose(s) of the gathering?

Because speeches that intensify social cohesion are usually given at ceremonial gatherings, the first question to be asked is whether the speech has satisfied the ceremonial purpose. For example, when one attends a dedication ceremony, it is expected that the speaker will praise the object being dedicated. When one attends a commencement, it is expected that the graduating seniors will be appropriately honored and advised. A welcoming ceremony calls for a tribute to both the person being welcomed and the institution extending the welcome. A presentation ceremony calls for a speech in praise of the person being awarded a tribute.

Whenever the speaker prepares a speech designed to intensify social cohesion, the audience's expectations at that moment must be considered. The Christian minister who on Easter Sunday ignores the meanings of the resurrection, the commencement speaker who ignores the graduating seniors assembled, and the eulogist who ignores or condemns the life of the departed all err in their omissions by failing to meet the ceremonial demands of the occasion. Whatever their personal reasons for speaking, speakers must conform to the particular expectations of their audiences on specific occasions if their speeches are to succeed.

2.   Has the speaker selected group values worthy of perpetuation?

Although the ceremonial demands of the occasion strongly constrain the speaker's behavior when seeking to intensify social cohesion, the speaker should still be held responsible for the substantive worth of the message. Because speeches that intensify social cohesion attempt to strengthen group values, the speaker should be expected to identify values worthy of esteem and perpetuation by the audience.

In applying this criterion, the enlightened listener or reader will test the values selected by the speaker. Has the eulogist selected the finer values examplified by a person's life? Has the inaugural speaker identified the most significant and worthy values as guides for future group action? Has the commencement speaker identified relevant and meaningful values for his audience of graduates? In evaluating Douglas MacArthur's speech "Farewell to the Cadets," reprinted later in this chapter, the reader should ask, "Are 'duty, honor, country' the finer values to which a soldier should subscribe in a free society?" In evaluating Martin Luther King's speech "I Have a Dream," also reprinted later, the reader should question whether the values of creative suffering and nonviolent resistance were those most relevant and wise for the black minority in a "white" America in 1963.

3. Has the speaker given impelling expression to the values selected?

Many critics have condemned speeches of this type because they tend to reexpress the common-place values of our social order. For example, many critics have condemned the commencement speech as a genre. Such speeches, they claim, are seldom more than dull rearticulations of established truths. Born of truisms, these speeches are infrequently more than trite reexpressions of the public mind. Although such charges are too often justified, they are not inherent indictments of the speech form. Rather, they are criticisms made valid by speakers who are incapable of giving impelling expression and redefinition to the values that bind our society together.

Because speeches that intensify social cohesion must by definition treat shared values, speakers must exercise special skill in giving new meaning and purpose to old values. Speakers have succeeded in accomplishing this difficult task. Through incisive analysis and amplification and through vivid and compelling language, gifted speakers succeed in gaining renewed audience commitment to old values without seeming trite.

Through the process of analysis, speakers must determine the particular relevance of cherished values to contemporary events and problems. Through the process of amplification, speakers must select those anecdotes, comparisons, contrasts, descriptions, examples, restatements, and definitions that make their contemporary analyses come alive. In the process, they must also demonstrate that their analyses are appropriate to the emotions that the nature of the occasion naturally evokes—whether elation, hope, gratitude, affection, pride, sympathy, anger, hate, shame, remorse, or grief. Speakers must also select vivid and compelling language to clothe their ideas. Through such stylistic devices as metaphor, vivid imagery, alliteration, parallelism, antithesis, hyperbole, and personification, gifted speakers can find ways for language to give new excitement and meaning to old values.

Conclusion

Many situations call for speeches that urge audience recommitment to social values. Among the common types of speeches that intensify social cohesion are sermons, eulogies, dedication speeches, commemorative speeches, commencement speeches, keynote speeches, welcoming speeches, fare-well speeches, presentation speeches, acceptance speeches, and inaugural speeches.

In evaluating speeches of this form, the critic must consider *whether the speaker has met the ceremonial purpose of the gathering, whether the speaker has selected group values worthy of perpetuation, and whether the speaker has given impelling expression to the values selected.*

FOR FURTHER READING

Condit, Celeste. "The Function of Epideictic: The Boston Massacre Orations as Exemplar." *Communication Quarterly*, 33 (Fall 1985): 284–298. Describes the functions of epideictic/ceremonial discourse as definition/understanding, shaping/sharing community, and display/entertainment. Suggests "communal definition" as the aim of a "complete" epideictic speech.

Hart, Roderick P. "The Functions of Human Communication in the Maintenance of Public Values." In Carroll Arnold and John Bowers, eds. *Handbook of Rhetorical and Communication Theory*, Allyn and Bacon, 1984, Chapter 12.

Lucas, Stephen. *The Art of Public Speaking.* 6th ed. McGraw-Hill, 1998. Chapter 17 discusses the variety of speeches for special occasions. Pages 445–449 comment on the power of commemorative speeches to inspire an audience.

Osborn, Michael, and Osborn, Suzanne. *Public Speaking.* 5th ed. Houghton Mifflin, 2000. Chapter 15 examines various types of ceremonial speaking and their functions in reinforcing existing values and promoting group and cultural cohesion. Pages 286–288 discuss language techniques that create cohesion.

Perelman, Chaim, and Olbrechts-Tyteca, L. *The New Rhetoric.* Trans. John Wilkinson and Purcell Weaver. University of Notre Dame Press, 1969. Pages 47–54 discuss types of discourse that "establish a sense of communion centered around particular values recognized by the audience."

Reid, Ronald F. *The American Revolution and the Rhetoric of History.* Speech Communication Association, 1978. Chapter 3 analyzes ways in which present societal values are reinforced through appeals to noble Revolutionary forebears and to noble Revolutionary principles.

Rosenfield, Lawrence W. "The Practical Celebration of Epideictic." In Eugene White, ed. *Rhetoric in Transition.* Pennsylvania State University Press, 1980, pages 131–155. A scholarly reinterpretation of the nature and function of speeches in honor of excellence, speeches that acknowledge goodness, grace, and intrinsic excellence rather than merely praise achievements and accomplishments.

Inaugural Address

◆ *John F. Kennedy* ◆

On January 20, 1961, the late John Fitzgerald Kennedy delivered his Presidential inaugural address to a large outdoor audience before the nation's Capitol on a cold, clear day. In contrast to his rapid-fire delivery during the campaign, Kennedy spoke slowly, giving careful emphasis to special phrases and the cadence of his prose.

An inaugural address by an American President typically reflects some now-traditional expectations and characteristics. Multiple audiences are addressed directly or indirectly: the inaugural crowd, Americans everywhere, world heads-of-state, and the people of the world. One major function is to set the general tone of the new administration. On social, economic, and military matters domestically and internationally, the President usually outlines in broad strokes some intended stances. But advocacy of specific, detailed policies and programs is not expected and abstract language may be more acceptable here than in other kinds of political discourse. A second major function is to promote social cohesion. The President seeks to heal the wounds and antagonisms of the recent political campaign, to urge reenergized commitment to central societal values and goals, and to promote a feeling of national unity. In an inaugural address, the President frequently will cite or adapt the words and wisdom of revered past Presidents and leaders. And such a speech may

◆ The text of this speech was taken from a recording of the address.

praise noble elements of America's heritage and applaud America's destiny. Both the introductions and conclusions of inaugural addresses typically call upon the blessings of God.

Kennedy's address demonstrates that effective style is not bombast or artificial ornament. Perhaps the most important stylistic quality of his speech is his sentence construction. Observe that his sentence length varies widely and that he employs many abstract and few concrete words. Is abstractness perhaps a natural quality of an inaugural address? What role do antithesis, parallelism, rhythm, and energy and movement play in this speech? Kennedy utilizes numerous metaphors, some rather hackneyed, but some fresh and subtle. Can you identify metaphors of each type?

The passage most frequently quoted from this speech is "Ask not what your country can do for you—ask what you can do for your country." Examine the context in which this sentence is used. Does it appear to be a natural outgrowth from the flow of ideas in the speech? Notice also phrases that echo passages in speeches by Abraham Lincoln (paragraphs 6 and 22) and by Franklin D. Roosevelt (10 and 25). Kennedy uses Biblical allusions (19 and 23) and images reflecting his Navy days in the South Pacific (20).

For a detailed analysis of the functions and techniques of American Presidential inaugural addresses, see Karyln Kohrs Campbell and Kathleen Hall Jamieson, *Deeds Done In Words: Presidential Rhetoric and the Genres of Governance* (University of Chicago Press, 1990), Ch. 2.

1   *Vice President Johnson, Mr. Speaker, Mr. Chief Justice, President Eisenhower, Vice President Nixon, President Truman, Reverend Clergy, Fellow Citizens:* We observe today not a victory of party but a celebration of freedom—symbolizing an end as well as a beginning—signifying renewal as well as change. For I have sworn before you and Almighty God the same solemn oath our forebears prescribed nearly a century and three quarters ago.

2   The world is very different now. For man holds in his mortal hands the power to abolish all forms of human poverty and all forms of human life. And yet the same revolutionary beliefs for which our forebears fought are still at issue around the globe—the belief that the rights of man come not from the generosity of the state but from the hand of God.

3   We dare not forget today that we are the heirs of that first revolution. Let the word go forth from this time and place, to friend and foe alike, that the torch has been passed to a new generation of Americans—born in this century, tempered by war, disciplined by a hard and bitter peace, proud of our ancient heritage—and unwilling to witness or permit the slow undoing of those human rights to which this nation has always been committed, and to which we are committed today, at home and around the world.

4   Let every nation know, whether it wishes us well or ill, that we shall pay any price, bear any burden, meet any hardship, support any friend, or oppose any foe to assure the survival and the success of liberty.

5   This much we pledge—and more.

6   To those old allies whose cultural and spiritual origins we share, we pledge the loyalty of faithful friends. United, there is little we cannot do in a host of cooperative ventures. Divided, there is little we can do—for we dare not meet a powerful challenge at odds and split asunder.

7   To those new states whom we welcome to the ranks of the free, we pledge our word that one form of colonial control shall not have passed away merely to be replaced by a far more iron tyranny. We shall not always expect to find them supporting our view.

8   But we shall always hope to find them strongly supporting their own freedom—and to remember that, in the past, those who foolishly sought power by riding the back of the tiger ended up inside.

9   To those people in the huts and villages of half the globe struggling to break the bonds of mass misery, we pledge our best efforts to help them help themselves, for whatever period is required—not because the Communists may be doing it, not because we seek their votes, but because it is right. If a free society cannot help the many who are poor, it cannot save the few who are rich.

10   To our sister republics south of our border, we offer a special pledge—to convert our good words into good deeds—in a new alliance for progress—to assist free men and free governments in casting off the chains of poverty. But this peaceful revolution of hope cannot become the prey of hostile powers. Let all our neighbors know that we shall join with them to oppose aggression or subversion anywhere in the Americas. And let every other power know that this hemisphere intends to remain the master of its own house.

11   To that world assembly of sovereign states, the United Nations, our last best hope in an age where the instruments of war have far outpaced the instruments of peace, we renew our pledge of support—to prevent it from becoming merely a forum for invective—to strengthen its shield of the new and the weak—and to enlarge the area in which its writ may run.

12   Finally, to those nations who would make themselves our adversary, we offer not a pledge but a request: That both sides begin anew the quest for peace, before the dark powers of destruction unleashed by science engulf all humanity in planned or accidental self-destruction.

13   We dare not tempt them with weakness. For only when our arms are sufficient beyond doubt can we be certain beyond doubt that they will never be employed.

14   But neither can two great and powerful groups of nations take comfort from our present course—both sides overburdened by the cost of modern weapons, both rightly alarmed by the steady spread of the deadly atom, yet both racing to alter that uncertain balance of terror that stays the hand of mankind's final war.

15   So let us begin anew—remembering on both sides that civility is not a sign of weakness, and sincerity is always subject to proof. Let us never negotiate out of fear. But let us never fear to negotiate.

President John F. Kennedy (Photo No. KNC-20213, John F. Kennedy Library)

16 Let both sides explore what problems unite us instead of belaboring those problems which divide us.

17 Let both sides, for the first time, formulate serious and precise proposals for the inspection and control of arms—and bring the absolute power to destroy other nations under the absolute control of all nations.

18 Let both sides seek to invoke the wonders of science instead of its terrors. Together let us explore the stars, conquer the deserts, eradicate disease, tap the ocean depths, and encourage the arts and commerce.

19 Let both sides unite to heed in all corners of the earth the command of Isaiah—to "undo the heavy burdens . . . [and] let the oppressed go free."

20 And if a beachhead of cooperation may push back the jungle of suspicion, let both sides join in creating a new endeavor: Not a new balance of power, but a new world of law, where the strong are just and the weak secure and the peace preserved.

21 All this will not be finished in the first one hundred days. Nor will it be finished in the first one thousand days, not in the life of this administration, nor even perhaps in our lifetime on this planet. But let us begin.

22 In your hands, my fellow citizens, more than mine, will rest the final success or failure of our course. Since this country was founded, each generation of Americans has been summoned to give testimony to its national loyalty. The graves of young Americans who answered the call to service surround the globe.

23 Now the trumpet summons us again—not as a call to bear arms, though arms we need—not as a call to battle, though embattled we are—but a call to bear the burden of a long twilight struggle, year in and year out, "rejoicing in hope, patient in tribulation"—a struggle against the common enemies of man: Tyranny, poverty, disease and war itself.

24 Can we forge against these enemies a grand and global alliance, North and South, East and West, that can assure a more fruitful life for all mankind? Will you join in that historic effort?

25 In the long history of the world, only a few generations have been granted the role of defending freedom in its hour of maximum danger.

26 I do not shrink from this responsibility—I welcome it. I do not believe that any of us would exchange places with any other people or any other generation. The energy, the faith, the devotion which we bring to this endeavor will light our country and all who serve it—and the glow from that fire can truly light the world.

27 And so, my fellow Americans: Ask not what your country can do for you—ask what you can do for your country.

28 My fellow citizens of the world: Ask not what America will do for you, but what together we can do for the freedom of man.

29 Finally, whether you are citizens of America or citizens of the world, ask of us here the same high standards of strength and sacrifice which we ask of you. With a good conscience our only sure reward, with history the final judge of our deeds, let us go forth to lead the land we love, asking His blessing and His help, but knowing that here on earth God's work must truly be our own.

Inaugural Address

◆ Gary Locke ◆

On January 15, 1997, Gary Locke was sworn in as the new Governor of the state of Washington. This ceremony, held in the capital of Olympia, marked the first time in American history that an Asian was inaugurated as the chief executive of a state in the continental United States. *Time* magazine reflected on the uniqueness of Locke's climb to political prominence when reporting that "despite being the fastest growing, best educated and most affluent minority group in America, Asians have traditionally been somewhat diffident when it comes to politics" (*Time*, October 12, 1998, p. 38). Washington, however, was able to reverse this political trend because Asian-Americans represent six percent of that state's population. (See the *Chicago Tribune*, December 6, 1996, section 1, p. 4.)

Locke, born into an immigrant family on January 21, 1950 in Seattle, spent his first six years in a public housing project for families of World War Two veterans. Locke's father, a D-Day army veteran, owned a restaurant and grocery store. The future governor did not learn to speak English until after his fifth birthday because his parents spoke only Cantonese at home (see the *Washington Post National Weekly Edition*, November 25–December 1, 1996, p. 12). After receiving an undergraduate degree in political science from Yale University in 1972, Locke later earned his law degree from Boston University in 1975. From 1983–1993, Locke served in the Washington House of Representatives and in 1996 he was elected chief executive of King County, the state's largest county.

The inaugural addresses of new chief executives have long attracted the attention of rhetorical scholars especially because of their embodiment of the elements of social cohesion. Bruce Gronbeck suggests that in these moments of cultural and political transition, members of societies assemble to mark the occasion ceremonially. The ceremonies performed at such moments link the past with the present through the use of three symbolic devices. First, "Remembrance": the speaker selectively recites and ideologically interprets the past so that heroes, villains, and cultural myths are effectively employed. Second, "Legitimation": the speaker sanctifies institutional authority, authorizes acts of power, and articulates codes of collective and individual conduct. Three, "Celebration": the speaker emphasizes past triumphs in hopes of future victories with a rehearsal of the previously tested values of orderly transitions. (See Bruce E. Gronbeck, "Ronald Reagan's Enactment of the Presidency in his 1981 Inaugural Address," in Herbert W. Simons and Aram A. Aghazarian, Eds. *Form, Genre, and the Study of Political Discourse*, Columbia: University of South Carolina Press, 1986, pps. 226–245.)

Locke begins his Inaugural by systematically introducing his family and extended family (3). After presenting his family to the audience, Locke next recalls how the past experiences of his ancestors (4–5, and 7–9) helped to establish his "mainstream American values" (6). Are the values (6 and 9) highlighted by Locke appropriate for the occasion? How does he interpret his

◆ The text of this speech was obtained from the State of Washington Internet web site for Governor Gary Locke.

family's past? Who are the heroes and villains of the Locke family?

After citing contributions of additional immigrants to Washington's history (10–13), Locke uses the rhetorical technique of enactment (14) by presenting himself as proof of the point he is trying to make. Does the new governor properly employ Martin Luther King, Jr.'s dream metaphor (14)? Has this figurative comparison (18) been extended in a meaningful way for Locke's audience?

Locke finally moves into an extended discussion of three key principles (19) that he suggests will guide his response to proposals from the legislature. Has Locke selected principles that seem worthy of perpetuation? How are these principles related to the family values introduced earlier in the speech? Are the principles presented appropriately related to Locke's policy initiatives (26–39)? Does Locke establish a sense of legitimacy for his leadership on these issues?

The new governor concludes his speech with emotional references to the impending birth of his first child (44–46). Is his use of amplification and personification effective? Does Locke succeed in giving impelling expression to the values (47–48) he selects?

1   Mr. President, Mr. Speaker, Madam Chief Justice, distinguished justices of the Supreme Court, statewide elected officials, members of the Washington State Legislature, other elected officials, members of the Consular Corps, fellow citizens, and friends of Washington state across America and around the world.

2   I am humbled by the honor of serving as your governor. And I am deeply grateful to all those who have made our American tradition of freedom and democracy possible.

3   I also want to express my gratitude to members of my family, and to introduce them to you. First I'd like you to meet my father, Jimmy Locke, who fought in World War II and participated in the Normandy invasion. I'd like you to meet my mother, Julie, who raised five children, learned English along with me when I started kindergarten, and who returned to school at Seattle Community College when she was nearly 60. And I'd like to introduce my brothers and sisters Marian Monwai, Jannie Chow, Jeffrey Locke and Rita Yoshihara. And finally, it is my greatest pleasure to introduce Washington's new First Lady, Mona Lee Locke. This truly is a wonderful day for the Locke family.

4   One of my ancestors—a distant cousin, actually—was a merchant who immigrated to Olympia in 1874 and became a leader of the Chinese-American community just a few blocks from this state capitol. He acted as a bridge between the Chinese and white communities, and became friends with the other downtown merchants, and with the sheriff, William Billings.

5   In 1886, an anti-immigrant, anti-Chinese mob threatened to burn down the Chinese settlement here. But what happened next is a story that every Washington resident ought to know: Sheriff Billings deputized scores of Olympia's merchants and civic leaders. And those citizen deputies stood between the angry mob and the Chinese neighborhood at Fifth and Water streets. Faced by the sheriff and the leading citizens of Olympia, the mob gradually dispersed. Not a single shot was fired, nor a single Chinese house burned.

6   For the Locke family, that incident helped establish a deep faith in the essential goodness of mainstream American values:

- The values that reject extremism and division, and embrace fairness and moral progress;
- The value of working together as a community; and
- The values of hard work, hope, enterprise and opportunity.

7   Just a few years after that Olympia show of courage, my grandfather came to America to work as a "house boy" for the Yeager family, who lived in a house that's still standing, less than a mile from here.

8   His purpose was to get an education, and so the Yeager family agreed to teach him English in return for his work. Like everyone else in our family, my grandfather studied and worked hard, and he eventually became the head chef at Virginia Mason Hospital in Seattle.

9   So although I may be standing less than a mile from where our family started its life in America, we've come a long way. Our journey was possible because of the courage of Sheriff Billings and the heroes of Olympia history. And our journey was successful because the Locke family embraces three values: Get a good education, work hard and take care of each other.

10   Our family history is more the norm than the exception. There is Governor Rosellini, this state's first Italian-American governor, whose parents migrated to America at the beginning of this century.

11   There is Representative Paul Zellinsky, whose grandfather was a Russian sea captain.

12   There is Senator Dan McDonald, whose ancestors were among the pioneer families of this state.

13   And there is Senator Rosa Franklin, whose family rose from slavery in South Carolina to civic leadership in Tacoma.

14   There are millions of families like mine, and millions of people like me—people whose ancestors dreamed the American Dream and worked hard to make it come true. And today, on Martin Luther King's birthday, we are taking another step toward that dream.

15   In the 108 years since Washington became a state, we have gone from riding horses to flying in jets; from sending telegrams to sending e-mail; and from woodstoves to microwave ovens.

16   Can anyone even guess what the next hundred years will bring? We already know that computers will think, that telephones and television will merge, and that biotechnology will reveal the secrets of our genetic code. Many of our children will produce goods and services that haven't even been invented yet.

17   For us, the challenge is to embrace change rather than to fear it. We have no time to waste.

18   To keep the American Dream alive in a high-tech and unpredictable future, we have to raise our sights, and our standards. We must raise our sights above the partisanship, the prejudice, and the arrogance that keep us from acknowledging our common humanity and our common future. And we must raise our standards of academic achievement, of government productivity and customer service, of the careful preservation of the natural environment we cherish, and of our determination to protect the well-being of Washington's working families.

19   The principles that will guide me in this quest for higher standards—and the principles that will guide my response to legislative proposals—are clear and simple.

- My first principle is that education is the great equalizer that makes hope and opportunity possible. That's why I am passionately committed to developing a world-class system of education.

- In the last century, the drafters of our Constitution made the education of children the "paramount duty" of the state. But learning is not just for kids anymore. For the next century, the paramount duty of this state will be to create an education system for lifelong learning—a system that every person regardless of age can plug into for basic skills, professional advancement or personal enrichment.

- My second principle is to promote civility, mutual respect and unity, and to oppose measures that divide, disrespect, or diminish our humanity. I want our state to build on the mainstream values of equal protection and equal opportunity, and to reject hate, violence and bigotry. And I want our state to be known as a place where elected officials lead by example.
- My third principle is to judge every public policy by whether it helps or hurts Washington's working families. Everyone who works hard and lives responsibly ought to be rewarded with economic security, the opportunity to learn and to advance in their chosen field of work, and the peace of mind that comes from knowing that the essential services their families need—like health care insurance and child care—will be affordable and accessible. And every senior citizen who has spent a lifetime contributing to the freedom and prosperity we enjoy deserves dignity and security.
- My fourth principle is to protect our environment, so that future generations enjoy the same natural beauty and abundance we cherish today.

20 These principles require self-discipline, and a commitment not to settle for quick fixes, Band-Aids, or political expediency. To help us live up to these principles, I intend to set clear, challenging goals, and to measure our progress toward achieving those goals. Everyone in state government will be held accountable for achieving results—not for convening meetings, creating commissions, or following reams of clumsy regulations.

21 I want to liberate the creativity and expertise of every state employee, and to make working for government as prestigious as building airplanes, designing software, or inventing new medical technologies.

22 I call on every state employee to search for new and better ways of doing our work, to strive toward a higher level of customer service to citizens, and to show greater respect for every hard-earned tax dollar that we collect.

23 In fact, let's take a moment to thank both state and local government employees for the truly heroic work they've done during the storms of the past few weeks.

24 They made visible something too many of us often don't see: that we truly can't live without basic government services, and that these services are provided by people—our dedicated public employees. In the storm and its aftermath, those public employees focused on helping citizens and solving problems and they achieved results.

25 Now it's time to harness that same energy and sense of urgency to solve problems and achieve results in our education system. We have to do a better job of making our schools safe, and ensuring that students respect their teachers, and each other.

26 We must hold both schools and students accountable for learning, not just for following all the rules or sitting through the required number of classes. We will not break our promise to raise academic standards. Every third grader must read at the third grade level, and every high school graduate must master basic academic skills and knowledge.

27 To meet these ambitious goals, our schools need a stable base of funding, including the ability to pass school levies with the same simple majority that it takes to pass bond measures to build other public facilities.

28 But money alone is not the whole solution. Greater accountability—coupled with more local control and more flexibility are also essential to school improvement. To meet the growing demand for education in our colleges and universities, my administration will present a proposal to increase enrollments, to improve quality, and to provide more management flexibility while insisting on greater productivity and accountability.

29 To do all this, we will make education the first priority in every budget we write. That will not be easy. Developing a quality education system depends on the soundness of our fiscal and tax policies.

30 That's why it's so important to write budgets that are sustainable beyond the current biennium. And that's why we ought to maintain a prudent reserve, so we'll have funds to see us through a recession without cutting schools or vital services.

31 This year, a balanced approach to budgeting will also include tax relief. In the last biennium, we gave almost a billion dollars in tax breaks to business. Isn't it time to help working families? To me, that means property tax relief for middle-class homeowners.

32 Of course, I also support rolling back the business and occupation tax to pre-1993 levels. We raised that tax in a time of fiscal emergency. That emergency has passed, and it's important that we keep faith with the business community by repealing the increase.

33 We also have a host of other problems that urgently need our attention. We need to agree on a bipartisan, comprehensive plan to invest in our transportation system, on which all our jobs and our economic growth depend.

34 Our farmers need good highways and rail systems to get their crops to market. Our commuters must have transit and carpool lanes, so they can spend more time with their children and less time stuck in traffic. Our ports need a transportation system that supports the growth of our international trade, which generates so many of our new jobs. There is a great deal the state can and must do to secure our competitive position in the world economy. We have an opportunity to improve Washington's international trade climate. I'm committed to establishing strong personal relationships with overseas government and business leaders to help Washington companies expand existing export markets and establish new ones.

35 It's also time to stop procrastinating and make some tough decisions about how to use and protect our water resources, which have been tangled in a web of conflicts and controversies year after year. And it's time to fine-tune our commitments to manage growth, to protect fish and wildlife, and to preserve the vitality of our farms and our forest products industry.

36 As a result of last year's federal welfare reform legislation, we have a once-in-a-lifetime chance to redesign our social safety net, so that it reflects our mainstream values of hard work, hope and opportunity. If we do this right, we can reduce poverty and protect children—and that ought to be our purpose.

37 So I will propose a system that puts work first—a system designed to help people in need build on their strengths rather than be paralyzed by their problems. To make welfare reform succeed, we need to become partners with the business community to find jobs and to improve training programs, so that every entry-level job in Washington is the first step on a career ladder rather than a treadmill that keeps the poor stuck in place. And to make work the solution to poverty, we will make sure that work pays better than public assistance.

38 At the same time, we have a duty to ensure that the ill, elderly and disabled live with dignity, and that legal immigrants are accorded equal treatment and equal protection.

39 And finally, we have already waited too long to fix our juvenile justice system—a system that lets kids get away with too much; that misses too many opportunities to turn kids around; and a system that leaves too many of us vulnerable to violent and dangerous young criminals.

40 To procrastinate on any one of these issues—from education to water to juvenile justice—is to court disaster. The clock is ticking. A new century is coming at us like a bullet train. And it's up to us to either rise to these challenges, or to watch as that train passes by.

41 If we cultivate the habit of genuine partnership—partnership entered with a commitment to solving problems and achieving results—we can accomplish all our goals.

42 Students, parents and teachers can create the best schools in the world. Community leaders, local and state governments can shape a transportation system second to none. And farmers, city-dwellers, tribal governments and developers can, if they work as real partners, untangle the web of water disputes and find ways to protect this precious resource.

43 We must all come together, work together, and stay together until our work is complete. Let's work as hard as our parents and grandparents did. Let's match their record of accomplishment, and their level of responsibility to the next generation.

44 As most of you already know, Mona and I are expecting our first child in March. So in very rapid succession, I will be blessed with two titles that carry immense responsibility and immense honor: Governor and Dad.

45 As the advent of fatherhood gets closer, I am more and more conscious that everything I do as governor—and everything we do together—we do for our children.

46 Our child will be a child of the 21st Century. He or she will come of age in a world that we can scarcely imagine. But it is his or her world that we must now work together to create. For our children and yours, I want to foster a new century of personal responsibility, of community, and of hope and optimism.

47 Please help me carry on the Locke family tradition of focusing on those three crucial values: get a good education, work hard, and take care of each other.

48 With your hand in partnership, and with an abiding faith in the essential goodness of the people of our great state, I want to devote the next four years to making the American Dream come true for children whose faces we have yet to see.

49 Thank you.

I Have a Dream

◆ *Martin Luther King, Jr.* ◆

Late in August, 1963, more than 200,000 people held a peaceful demonstration in the nation's capital to focus attention on Negro demands for equality in jobs and civil rights. The marchers assembled at the Washington Monument on the morning of the 28th and filed in

◆ Reprinted by arrangement with The Heirs to the Estate of Martin Luther King, Jr., c/o Writers House, Inc. as agent for the proprietor. Copyright 1963 by Martin Luther King, Jr., copyright renewed 1991 by Coretta Scott King.

two columns down to the Lincoln Memorial. A little later, 10 civil-rights leaders met with President Kennedy at the White House and subsequently returned to the Lincoln memorial, where each of them addressed the assembled throng. As measured by crowd reaction, this speech by Martin Luther King was the high point of the day. In the months prior to his assassination in April, 1968, King broadened his advocacy to include the rights of poor people of all races and ethnic groups and to condemn continued American involvement in the Vietnam War.

One way to assess this speech would be to apply the criteria suggested at the start of this chapter for evaluating speeches that intensify social cohesion. Has the speech satisfied the ceremonial purpose(s) of the gathering? Has the speaker selected group values worthy of perpetuation? Has the speaker given impelling expression to the values selected? Or this speech might be examined as a particular type of social cohesion speech, namely a *rally speech* that arouses enthusiasm for tasks ahead through uplifting sagging spirits and through deepening of commitments. Rally speeches occur on various occasions, such as keynote addresses at political and professional conventions, sales promotion speeches at meetings of company sales personnel, and speeches to civic action groups. Speakers at rallies typically utilize some combination of the following approaches: (1) Stress the importance, the value, of the work the group has been doing. (2) Promote group self-confidence by praising their past success, dedication, and sacrifice and by praising their basic values, principles, and goals. (3) Outline the tasks, opportunities, and challenges ahead. (4) Use vivid imagery and emotionally stimulating language to paint word pictures of the better future achievable through united, sustained group effort.

In this speech, King urges rededication to the black non-violent civil rights movement and reinforces values central to this view of that movement: courage, faith, hope, freedom, justice, equality, non-violence, sacrifice, dignity, and discipline. He sees these values as rooted in the traditional American Dream. Early in the speech, King balances pleas for non-violence and for cooperation between blacks and whites with a strong sense of urgency to achieve results. Perhaps to blunt the charges of gradualism and overmoderation made by some black leaders such as Malcolm X, King stresses the "fierce urgency of now."

King's audience on this occasion would have attributed to him a very high level of ethos, a very positive degree of speaker credibility. His followers saw him as an expert, trustworthy, dynamic leader of their movement. In the speech and setting themselves, echos of Abraham Lincoln further reinforce his high ethos with this particular audience. As the Lincoln Memorial provides the physical setting, echos of the Gettysburg Address come through the structure of the speech (past, present, future) and in paragraphs two and five.

King utilizes varied language resources to lend power, motivation, and inspiration to his message. Consider where, for what possible functions, and how effectively he uses such stylistic devices as repetition, parallelism, and refrain. Consider especially the "I have a dream" and "Let freedom ring" passages. In the same manner, examine his use of antithetical phrasing, including "meeting physical force with soul force," "heat of oppression . . . oasis of freedom and justice," and "jangling discords . . . beautiful symphony." How appropriate to the occasion and to King as a Southern Baptist minister was his frequent use of imagery, paraphrases, and direct quotations from the Bible? Finally, assess his heavy use of metaphors throughout the speech. Would the audience probably experience them as natural to the topic, as artificial, as fresh and stimulating, as trite and dull, or as familiar and reassuring? What functions might have been served by particular metaphors? Note especially the early extended metaphor (figurative analogy) of cashing a check.

Rhetorical scholar Keith D. Miller has explored the ways in which King in his speeches, as one thoroughly exposed to the heritage of black folk preaching, reflected the tradition of "voice merging." In voice merging, black ministers created their own identities "not through original language but through identifying themselves with a hallowed tradition"—often by "borrowing homiletic material from many sources, including the sermons of their predecessors and peers."

In his speeches King typically both explicitly capitalized on revered biblical and national traditions with which his audiences agreed and "borrowed without acknowledgement from the sermons of both black and white Protestant ministers." In this way much of King's rhetoric had "been tested—often repeatedly tested—with both listeners and readers before King employed it." After extensive analysis, Miller argues that rhetorical critics should reconsider their "unquali-

fied remonstrations against plagiarism and the use of cliches." See Keith D. Miller, "Voice Merging and Self-Making: The Epistemology of 'I Have A Dream'," *Rhetoric Society Quarterly,* 19 (Winter 1989): 23–32; Miller, "Martin Luther King Borrows a Revolution: Argument, Audience, and Implications of a Second Hand Universe," *College English,* 48 (March 1986): 249–265. Also see Richard L. Johannesen, "The Ethics of Plagiarism Reconsidered: The Oratory of Martin Luther King, Jr.," *Southern Communication Journal,* 60 (Spring 1995): 185–194.

1   I am happy to join with you today in what will go down in history as the greatest demonstration for freedom in this history of our nation.

2   Five score years ago, a great American, in whose symbolic shadow we stand today, signed the Emancipation Proclamation. This momentous decree came as a great beacon light of hope to millions of Negro slaves, who had been seared in the flames of withering injustice. It came as a joyous daybreak to end the long night of their captivity.

3   But one hundred years later, the Negro is still not free. One hundred years later, the life of the Negro is still sadly crippled by the manacles of segregation and the chains of discrimination. One hundred years later, the Negro lives on a lonely island of poverty in the midst of a vast ocean of material prosperity. One hundred years later, the Negro is still languished in the corners of American society and finds himself an exile in his own land. So we have come here today to dramatize a shameful condition.

4   In a sense, we've come to our nation's Capitol to cash a check. When the architects of our republic wrote the magnificent words of the Constitution and the Declaration of Independence, they were signing a promissory note to which every American was to fall heir. This note was a promise that all men—yes, black men and well as white men—would be guaranteed the unalienable rights of life, liberty, and the pursuit of happiness.

5   It is obvious today that America has defaulted on this promissory note insofar as her citizens of color are concerned. Instead of honoring this sacred obligation, America has given the Negro people a bad check; a check which has come back marked "insufficient funds." But we refuse to believe that the bank of justice is bankrupt. We refuse to believe that there are insufficient funds in the great vaults of opportunity of this nation. So we've come to cash this check—a check that will give us upon demand the riches of freedom and the security of justice. We have also come to this hallowed spot to remind America of the fierce urgency of *now.* This is no time to engage in the luxury of cooling off to take the tranquilizing drug of gradualism. *Now is the time* to make real the promises of Democracy. *Now is the time* to rise from the dark and desolate valley of segregation to the sunlight of racial justice. *Now is the time* to lift our nation from the quicksands of racial injustice to the solid rock of brotherhood. *Now is the time* to make justice a reality for all of God's children.

6   It would be fatal for the nation to overlook the urgency of the moment. This sweltering summer of the Negro's legitimate discontent will not pass until there is an invigorating autumn of freedom and equality. Nineteen sixty-three is not an end, but a beginning. Those who hope that the Negro needed to blow off steam and will now be content will have a rude awakening if the nation returns to business as usual. There will be neither rest nor tranquility in America until the Negro is granted his citizenship rights. The whirlwinds of revolt will continue to shake the foundations of our nation until the bright day of justice emerges.

7   But there is something that I must say to my people who stand on the warm threshold which leads into the palace of justice. In the process of gaining our rightful place we must not be guilty of wrongful deeds. Let us not seek to satisfy our thirst for freedom by drinking from the cup of bitterness and hatred.

8   We must forever conduct our struggle on the high plane of dignity and discipline. We must not allow our creative protest to degenerate into physical violence. Again and again we must rise to the majestic heights of meeting physical force with soul force. The marvelous new militancy which has engulfed the Negro community must not lead us to a distrust of all white people, for many of our white brothers, as evidenced by their presence here today, have come to realize that their destiny is tied up with our destiny. And they have come to realize that their freedom is inextricably bound to our freedom. We cannot walk alone.

9   And as we walk we must make the pledge that we shall always march ahead. We cannot turn back. There are those who ask the devotees of civil rights, "When will you be satisfied?" We can never be satisfied as long as the Negro is the victim of the unspeakable horrors of police brutality. We can never be satisfied as long as our bodies, heavy with the fatigue of travel, cannot gain lodging in the motels of the highways and the hotels of the cities. We cannot be satisfied as long as the Negro's basic mobility is from a smaller ghetto to a larger one. We can never be satisfied as long as our children are stripped of their selfhood and robbed of their dignity by signs stating "For Whites Only." We cannot be satisfied as long as a Negro in Mississippi cannot vote and a Negro in New York believes he has nothing for which to vote. No, no, we are not satisfied, and we will not be satisfied until justice rolls down like waters and righteousness like a mighty stream.

10   I am not unmindful that some of you have come here out of great trials and tribulations. Some of you have come fresh from narrow jail cells. Some of you have come from areas where your quest for freedom left you battered by the storms of persecution and staggered by the winds of police brutality. You have been the veterans of creative suffering. Continue to work with the faith that unearned suffering is redemptive.

11   Go back to Mississippi, go back to Alabama, go back to South Carolina, go back to Georgia, go back to Louisiana, go back to the slums and ghettos of our Northern cities knowing that somehow this situation can and will be changed. Let us not wallow in the valley of despair.

12   I say to you today, my friends, so even though we face the difficulties of today and tomorrow, I still have a dream. It is a dream deeply rooted in the American dream.

13   I have a dream that one day this nation will rise up and live out the true meaning of its creed: "We hold these truths to be self-evident; that all men are created equal."

14   I have a dream that one day on the red hills of Georgia the sons of former slaves and the sons of former slaveowners will be able to sit down together at the table of brotherhood; I have a dream—

15   That one day even the state of Mississippi, a state sweltering with the heat of injustice, sweltering with the heat of oppression, will be transformed into an oasis of freedom and justice; I have a dream—

16   That my four little children will one day live in a nation where they will not be judged by the color of their skin but by the content of their character; I have a dream today.

17   I have a dream that one day down in Alabama with its vicious racists, with its governor having his lips dripping with the words of interposition and nullification, one day right there in Alabama little black boys and black girls will be able to join hands with little white boys and white girls as sisters and brother; I have a dream today.

18 I have a dream that one day every valley shall be exalted, every hill and mountain shall be made low, and rough places will be made plane and crooked places will be made straight, and the glory of the Lord shall be revealed, and all flesh shall see it together.

19 This is our hope. This is the faith that I go back to the South with. With this faith we will be able to hew out of the mountain of despair a stone of hope. With this faith we will be able to transform the jangling discords of our nation into a beautiful symphony of brotherhood. With this faith we will be able to work together, to pray together, to struggle together, to go to jail together, to stand up for freedom together, knowing that we will be free one day.

20 This will be the day. . . . This will be the day when all of God's children will be able to sing with new meaning. "My country 'tis of thee, sweet land of liberty, of thee I sing. Land where my fathers died, land of the pilgrim's pride, from every mountainside, let freedom ring," and if America is to be a great nation—this must become true.

21 So let freedom ring—from the prodigious hilltops of New Hampshire, let freedom ring; from the mighty mountains of New York, let freedom ring—from the heightening Alleghenies of Pennsylvania!

22 Let freedom ring from the snowcapped Rockies of Colorado!

23 Let freedom ring from the curvaceous slopes of California!

24 But not only that; let freedom ring from Stone Mountain of Georgia!

25 Let freedom ring from Lookout Mountain of Tennessee!

26 Let freedom ring from every hill and molehill of Mississippi. From every mountainside, let freedom ring, and when this happens. . . .

27 When we allow freedom ring, when we let it ring from every village and every hamlet, from every state and every city, we will be able to speed up that day when all of God's children, black men and white men, Jews and Gentiles, protestants and Catholics, will be able to join hands and sing in the words of the old Negro spiritual, "Free at last! free at last! thank God almighty, we are free at last!"

Democratic Convention Keynote Address

◆ *Barbara Jordan* ◆

On July 12, 1976, Barbara Jordan, U.S. Congresswoman from Texas, delivered this nationally televised keynote address to the Democratic National Convention in New York City. A lawyer, Jordan was the first black woman elected to the Texas state senate. She came to national

◆ Reprinted by permission from *Vital Speeches of the Day,* August 15, 1976, pp. 645–46.

public prominence on July 25, 1974, with her eloquent and impassioned defense of the Constitution as a committee speaker during the televised hearings of the U.S. House of Representatives committee on President Nixon's impeachment. Her 21-minute speech at the 1976 Democratic convention followed a comparatively lackluster keynote speech by Sen. John Glenn, the astronaut hero. She was introduced via a film biography of her life and career and was greeted by the convention audience with a three minute standing ovation. In keeping with her reputation as an excellent public speaker, Jordan delivered the speech in a clear, forceful, and dramatic manner. A *New York Times* reporter (July 13, 1976, p. 24) describes the audience reaction: "Time and again, they interrupted her keynote speech with applause. And, after it was all over . . . she was brought back for a final curtain call and for the loudest ovation of all."

Clearly a political convention keynote address seeks to mold social cohesion. Typically the keynote speaker stresses the importance of the convention and the deliberations of the delegates, castigates the opposing party, praises the heritage, values, and policies of their own party, and exhorts the convention delegates and all party members to unite in a vigorous, successful campaign. A keynote speaker attempts to inspire and reenergize members by setting a theme, a tone, a *key note,* for the convention.

Jordan left the Congress in 1978 to become a professor at the University of Texas. After enduring a progressively worsening case of multiple sclerosis, Barbara Jordan died, at age 59, on January 17, 1996. A recent biography that contains significant commentary on her influence as a public speaker is Mary Beth Rogers, *Barbara Jordan: American Hero* (NY: Bantam Books, 1998).

Throughout the speech Jordan develops the central theme of a people in search of a national community, in search of the common good. This note of cohesiveness is reflected in her choice of phrases: one nation; common spirit; common endeavor; common ties; each person do his or her part. Frequently she justifies a position or judgment as harmonious with the will or interests of "the people." She attributes to "the people"

such values as common sense and generosity. (For an analysis of the socially cohesive function served by appeals to "the people" in political discourse, see Michael C. McGee, "In Search of 'The People'," *Quarterly Journal of Speech,* October 1975.)

In a major section of the speech, Jordan utilizes parallel phrasing (we believe, we are, we have) to outline the Democratic Party's concept of governing—its basic beliefs that reflect its view of human nature. She metaphorically ("bedrock") stresses the fundamental nature of these beliefs and claims that they are not negotiable. The beliefs have explicit or implicit values imbedded in them: equality (note the double antithetical phrasing of the first belief); opportunity; government of, by, and for the people; activity; innovativeness; adaptability; sacrifice for a good cause; optimism.

Note that Jordan frequently repeats words, rephrases ideas, and in vocal delivery overenunciates the pronunciation of words (gov-er-ning; hyp-o-crit-i-cal). She may have intentionally used such techniques of redundancy and emphasis to overcome the physical noise and listener inattention typical of political conventions. Some in the audience, most likely the television audience, may have felt that her attitude toward them was one of superiority, as if they were simpleminded folk who needed everything spelled out and overemphasized for comprehension.

In at least two ways, Jordan's address differs slightly from the expectations or traditions associated with political convention keynote speeches. First, she makes virtually no direct attacks on the Republicans. Her apparent attacks are implied. By metaphorically characterizing past Democratic mistakes as those "of the heart," she may be indirectly asserting calculating, devious mistakes by the Nixon Administration. By arguing that no President can veto the decision of the American people to forge a national community, she indirectly may be attacking President Ford's heavy use of the veto to block Congressional legislation.

In a second departure from tradition, she does criticize her own party, but in such a moderate way as to freshen the speech without weakening her praise of party principles or generating negative audience reaction. She admits the Democratic Party has made past mistakes, but they were in behalf of the common good and the Party was willing later to confess them. Metaphorically she underscores the point by saying that Party "deafness" to the will of the people was only temporary. Her warning that the Democratic Party at times has attempted to be "all things to all people" may be indirect criticism of Jimmy Carter who was faulted during the primaries for making that kind of appeal. As a final analytic consideration here, assess whether this warning against being "all things to all people" is to some degree inconsistent with her point earlier in the speech that the Demo-

cratic Party is an inclusive party ("Let everybody come").

Two prominent rhetorical critics have said of Jordan's speech: "Many critics who watched and heard her speak will have recognized a recurrent rhetorical form, a reflexive form, a form called 'enactment' in which the speaker incarnates the argument, *is* the proof of the truth of what is said." (Karlyn Kohrs Campbell and Kathleen Hall Jamieson, *Form and Genre, Shaping Rhetorical Action* (Falls Church, VA: The Speech Communication Association, n.d., p. 9.) Discuss the speech from this perspective of rhetorical enactment by the speaker. Does it help you to understand the power of Jordan's words?

1　One hundred and forty-four years ago, members of the Democratic Party first met in convention to select a Presidential candidate. Since that time, Democrats have continued to convene once every four years and draft a party platform and nominate a Presidential candidate. And our meeting this week is a continuation of that tradition.

2　But there is something different about tonight. There is something special about tonight. What is different? What is special? I, Barbara Jordan, am a keynote speaker.

3　A lot of years passed since 1832, and during that time it would have been most unusual for any national political party to ask that a Barbara Jordan deliver a keynote address . . . but tonight here I am. And I feel that notwithstanding the past that my presence here is one additional bit of evidence that the American Dream need not forever be deferred.

4　Now that I have this grand distinction what in the world am I supposed to say?

5　I could easily spend this time praising the accomplishments of this party and attacking the Republicans, but I don't choose to do that.

6　I could list the many problems which Americans have. I could list the problems which cause people to feel cynical, angry, frustrated: problems which include lack of integrity in government; the feeling that the individual no longer counts; the reality of material and spiritual poverty; the feeling that the grand American experiment is failing or has failed. I could recite these problems and then I could sit down and offer no solutions. But I don't choose to do that either.

7　The citizens of America expect more. They deserve and they want more than a recital of problems.

8　We are a people in a quandary about the present. We are a people in search of our future. We are a people in search of a national community.

9　We are a people trying not to solve the problems of the present—unemployment, inflation—but we are attempting on a larger scale to fulfill the promise of America. We are attempting to fulfill our national purpose: to create and sustain a society in which all of us are equal.

10　Throughout our history, when people have looked for new ways to solve their problems, and to uphold the principles of this nation, many times they have turned to political parties. They have often turned to the Democratic Party.

11   What is it, what is it about the Democratic Party that makes it the instrument that people use when they search for ways to shape their future? Well I believe the answer to that question lies in our concept of governing. Our concept of governing is derived from our view of people. It is a concept deeply rooted in a set of beliefs firmly etched in the national conscience of all of us.

12   Now what are these beliefs?

13   First, we believe in equality for all and privileges for none. This is a belief that each American regardless of background has equal standing in the public forum, all of us. Because we believe this idea so firmly, we are an inclusive rather than an exclusive party. Let everybody come.

14   I think it no accident that most of those emigrating to America in the 19th century identified with the Democratic Party. We are a heterogenous party made up of Americans of diverse backgrounds.

15   We believe that the people are the source of all governmental power; that the authority of the people is to be extended, not restricted. This can be accomplished only by providing each citizen with every opportunity to participate in the management of the government. They must have that.

16   We believe that the government which represents the authority of all the people, not just one interest group, but all the people, has an obligation to actively, underscore actively, seek to remove those obstacles which would block individual achievement . . . obstacles emanating from race, sex, economic condition. The government must seek to remove them.

17   We are a party of innovation. We do not reject our traditions, but we are willing to adapt to changing circumstances, when change we must. We are willing to suffer the discomfort of change in order to achieve a better future.

18   We have a positive vision of the future founded on the belief that the gap between the promise and reality of America can one day be finally closed. We believe that.

19   This my friends, is the bedrock of our concept of governing. This is a part of the reason why Americans have turned to the Democratic Party. These are the foundations upon which a national community can be built.

20   Let's all understand that these guiding principles cannot be discarded for short-term political gains. They represent what this country is all about. They are indigenous to the American idea. And these are principles which are not negotiable.

21   In other times, I could stand here and give this kind of exposition on the beliefs of the Democratic Party and that would be enough. But today that is not enough. People want more. That is not sufficient reason for the majority of the people of this country to vote Democratic. We have made mistakes. In our haste to do all things for all people, we did not foresee the full consequences of our actions. And when the people raised their voices, we didn't hear. But our deafness was only a temporary condition, and not an irreversible condition.

22   Even as I stand here and admit that we have made mistakes I still believe that as the people of America sit in judgment on each party, they will recognize that our mistakes were mistakes of the heart. They'll recognize that.

23   And now we must look to the future. Let us heed the voice of the people and recognize their common sense. If we do not, we not only blaspheme our political heritage, we ignore the common ties that bind all Americans.

24   Many fear the future. Many are distrustful of their leaders, and believe that their voices are never heard. Many seek only to satisfy their private work wants. To satisfy private interests.

25   But this is the great danger America faces. That we will cease to be one nation and become instead a collection of interest groups: city against suburb, region against region, individual against individual. Each seeking to satisfy private wants.

26 If that happens, who then will speak for America?

27 Who then will speak for the common good?

28 This is the question which must be answered in 1976.

29 Are we to be one people bound together by common spirit sharing in a common endeavor or will we become a divided nation?

30 For all of its uncertainty, we cannot flee the future. We must not become the new puritans and reject our society. We must address and master the future together. It can be done if we restore the belief that we share a sense of national community, that we share a common national endeavor. It can be done.

31 There is no executive order: there is no law that can require the American people to form a national community. This we must do as individuals and if we do it as individuals, there is no President of the United States who can veto that decision.

32 As a first step, we must restore our belief in ourselves. We are a generous people so why can't we be generous with each other? We need to take to heart the words spoken by Thomas Jefferson:

33 "Let us restore to social intercourse that harmony and that affection without which liberty and even life are but dreary things."

34 A nation is formed by the willingness of each of us to share in the responsibility for upholding the common good.

35 A government is invigorated when each of us is willing to participate in shaping the future of this nation.

36 In this election year we must define the common good and begin again to shape a common future. Let each person do his or her part. If one citizen is unwilling to participate, all of us are going to suffer. For the American idea, though it is shared by all of us, is realized in each one of us.

37 And now, what are those of us who are elected public officials supposed to do? We call ourselves public servants but I'll tell you this: we as public servants must set an example for the rest of the nation. It is hypocritical for the public official to admonish and exhort the people to uphold the common good if we are derelict in upholding the common good. More is required of public officials than slogans and handshakes and press releases. More is required. We must hold ourselves strictly accountable. We must provide the people with a vision of the future.

38 If we promise as public officials, we must deliver. If we as public officials propose, we must produce. If we say to the American people it is time for you to be sacrificial; sacrifice. If the public official says that, we (public officials) must be the first to give. We must be. And again, if we make mistakes, we must be willing to admit them. We have to do that. What we have to do is strike a balance between the idea that government should do everything and the idea, the belief, that government ought to do nothing. Strike a balance.

39 Let there be no illusions about the difficulty of forming this kind of a national community. It's tough, difficult, not easy. But a spirit of harmony will survive in America only if each of us remembers that we share a common destiny. If each of us remembers, when self-interest and bitterness seem to prevail, that we share a common destiny.

40 I have confidence that we can form this kind of national community.

41 I have confidence that the Democratic Party can lead the way. I have that confidence. We cannot improve on the system of government handed down to us by the founders of the Republic, there is no way to improve upon that. But what we can do is to find new ways to implement that system and realize our destiny.

42 Now, I began this speech by commenting to you on the uniqueness of a Barbara Jordan making the keynote address. Well I am going to close my speech by quoting a Republican President and I ask you that as you listen to these words of Abraham Lincoln, relate them to the concept of a national community in which every last one of us participates: "As I would not be slave, so I would not be master. This expresses my idea of Democracy. Whatever differs from this, to the extent of the difference is no Democracy."

Women's Movement

◆ *Donna E. Shalala* ◆

The inception of the American Women's Movement is dated back to 1848, when a small group of women, headed by Lucretia Mott and Elizabeth Cady Stanton, sponsored a meeting in Seneca Falls, New York, for the purpose of discussing women's issues. Approximately 300 people attended, of which about 40 were men. The convention adopted a Declaration of Sentiments, which Stanton and Mott had modeled after the nation's Declaration of Independence. Seventy years later the United States Congress adopted the Nineteenth Amendment guaranteeing woman suffrage. The amendment was ratified by the states in 1920. Woman's struggle for basic legal and political rights was long and arduous. Certain women, such as Susan B. Anthony and Anna Howard Shaw, devoted their entire adult lives to the cause. One woman, Charlotte Woodward, who at age 18 attended the Seneca Falls convention, at age 88, cast a ballot for the president in 1920.

During July 16–19, 1998, a celebration of the 150th anniversary of the First Women's Rights Convention, was held in Seneca Falls. In part, the celebration honored the Declaration of Sentiments concerning women's rights that had been presented at that convention. On July 16, Hillary Rodham Clinton gave the keynote address as part of the opening ceremonies of the celebration.

On the morning of July 17, just prior to the presentation of a 1998 Declaration of Sentiments, Donna E. Shalala, the Secretary of Health and Human Services in the Clinton administration, delivered this speech on the "Women's Movement." About 400 people heard the speech in the outdoor speaker's pavilion near the Elizabeth Cady Stanton House in the Women's Rights National Historical Park in Seneca Falls.

Shalala was appointed by President Clinton in January 1993 to the cabinet position of Secretary of Health and Human Services. The agency is the federal government's principal effort for protecting the health of all Americans and for providing essential human services. Health and Human Services administers a wide variety of programs, including Medicare, Medicaid, federal welfare, and children's programs. During her term as Secretary, Shalala has guided the welfare reform process and the approval of the Children's Health Insurance Program. She also has fought to increase child immunization rates, to decrease young people's use of tobacco, to eliminate racial and ethnic health disparities,

◆ The text of this speech was obtained from the Department of Health and Human Services Internet web site for Secretary Donna Shalala.

and to eliminate violence against women. She also has founded initiatives to fight breast cancer. She is generally acknowledged as one of the nation's foremost advocates for children and families.

Dr. Shalala's first career was that of a scholar and teacher. She received her Ph.D. from the Maxwell School of Citizenship and Public Affairs at Syracuse University in 1970. She taught political science. Her administrative talents were soon recognized. She served as president of Hunter College in New York for eight years, and was an Assistant Secretary at HUD during the Carter Administration. As Chancellor of the University of Wisconsin–Madison, from 1987–1998, she was the first woman to head a Big Ten University. *Business Week* named her one of the five best managers in higher education.

The speech Shalala delivered at Seneca Falls is epideictic rhetoric. It is a rally speech. It is a pep talk. It is a ceremonial address. It is a speech of celebration. It is a speech to promote social cohesion. It is a speech to reinforce and re-energize audience commitment to values they already hold and, through that renewed commitment, to stimulate them to carry forward the cause that the founding mothers so diligently and so arduously pursued.

Epideictic rhetoric, to a great extent, is a linguistic exercise. A eulogy, for example, has its purpose to linguistically honor the dead and to uplift the living. Thus diction and style become critical attributes of the address. As a critic of speeches, begin your analysis of Shalala's address by carefully looking at stylistic factors. Begin with the second line of the speech: "We are here to honor women who made a difference in all of our lives." The next three lines function much like a small lyric poem (2–4). They each say something about the topic sentence and need be in no particular order, for they are independent statements, exuberant and rhapsodic, that makes the initial statement memorable.

Note in paragraph 6, "a shout heard around the world." What is that statement an imitation of? Why is it a significant statement in the speech? In paragraph 7, Shalala uses a technique that omits coordinating conjunctions. This shorter, choppier style has much greater impact than if coordinating conjunctions would be used. Each new statement beginning with the word "For" builds to a climax. Can you find other such usage in the speech? In paragraph 8, the speaker uses one word sentences that form a list of attributes, again much like a lyric poem.

Parallel structure plays an important role in paragraph 9. Once more, the speaker is ticking off all the things that women are changing. The only things the sentences have in common is that they all relate what women are changing. Paragraph 10 once more uses the listing approach, as do paragraphs 11, 12, 13, and 14.

Paragraph 16 is the dividing point between the first half and the second half of the speech. It reaches a crescendo with the statement, "HELL NO." The second part of the speech essentially points to the future rather than celebrating the past. Discuss the stylistic features Shalala uses in pointing to the future and motivating the women in attendance to go forward to that future. Paragraphs 22 and 23 comment directly upon the purpose of the event. In that sense, they are the culmination of the speech. What does Shalala do to give impact to the celebration of the Declaration of Sentiments?

Shalala's conclusion essentially is a personal anecdote involving her friend Dr. Elizabeth Karlin. Do you think that Dr. Karlin and Shalala's feelings about her embodies a summation of what the Secretary of Health and Human Services has been trying to say in her speech? If so, how and why?

In a sense, this speech lacks the usual kind of evidence. Yet, in another sense, it is chock full of supporting material. What supporting materials do you find in this speech?

◆ ◆ ◆

1   It's a great honor to share this stage with so many extraordinary leaders, legends, and champions for all women, for all people, for all time.

2   We are here to honor women who made a difference in all of our lives.

3   Their voices thunder down the years.

4   Their legacy is alive and thriving today.

5   Their language is part of our lives.

6   Generations have come and gone since Lizzy Stanton added two crucial words to the most hallowed phrase in our history. She said, "All men and women are created equal." As, the First Lady said yesterday, it was a shout heard 'round the world. A newspaper man called the convention at Seneca Falls "the most shocking and unnatural incident ever recorded in the history of womanity."

7   Well, thank the Lord for shocking women. Thank the Lord for women who've shaken up the status quo. For women who've dreamed and dared. Thank the Lord for the rights we've declared. For the fights we've endured. For the dignity we have struggled to win.

8   I saw that dignity in Beijing. Thousands of women from all over the world—women of different colors, wearing different clothing, speaking different languages. Different women—but one clear message: The progress of nations depends on the progress of women. All of us have felt that dignity flowing through the words of our greatest poets and patriots. Through the words of Toni Morrison and her character Sula, who captures the essence of the strong, audacious women who've made a difference in our lives. Women who are tenacious. Inventive. Disruptive. Imaginative. Modern. Uncontained. And uncontainable.

9   Witness the wave of women's dignity surging through every field of American life. We've been called the "everyday revolutionaries." We are changing how businesses are run. How language is heard and used. How families are structured. We're changing how communities are organized. How children are raised and taught. We're changing how goods and services are conceived, marketed, and sold.

10   We've come to Seneca Falls to celebrate women who—quite literally—are changing the course of human events. The world of sports. The exploration of space. The hand of healing. The science of curing. The march of technology.

11   Let us also celebrate women who are shaking up the political world. We have put more women in Congress and the state capitals. More women in the courts. More women in charge.

12   And more women in the President's Cabinet. There's Madeleine Albright, Janet Reno, Alexis Herman, Carol Browner, Aida Alvarez, Janet Yellen, Charlene Barshefsky—and me.

13   What are these women doing? With the leadership of the President and the First Lady; of the Vice President and Mrs. Gore; with the dedication of all women who've advanced the cause of Seneca Falls, we are reordering our national priorities. Reshaping our national agenda. Rewriting the definition of "national security." Recognizing the importance of family issues, from the kitchen table to the national stage. Realizing the real needs of women, children and families.

14   What has the power of women achieved? We've defended every woman's right to reproductive freedom. We've expanded the enforcement of child support. We've defined violence against women as a public health crisis. We've stood fast for affirmative action, keeping the President's promise to "mend it—not end it." We've advanced women's education, training and economic opportunities. We've stopped drive-by childbirth deliveries. We've advanced women's health. We've protected children's health. We've supported the breast cancer action plan. We've advocated for a patient's Bill of Rights. And, we've helped parents relieve their child care headaches. We've helped working families succeed. Not only by raising their incomes. But by raising all incomes—by building a stronger economy. All in the human interest. All in the national interest.

15 But as everyone in this room knows, the road from Seneca Falls has been long and hard. Our feet are sore. Our backs are tired. Our hearts are strained. Sisters—let me tell you—the struggle isn't over yet. We have miles to go before we sleep. Miles to go before our dreams come true. As we celebrate the memory and the meaning of Seneca Falls, we cannot rest or claim victory. Not when we have so much to do. So much to lose.

16 Just look at the cover of *Time* magazine a few weeks ago. It asked—"Is Feminism Dead?" Well, we have a two-word answer for them. HELL NO. Is Feminism Dead? HELL NO. Women have far to go. Our movement will take us there. The women's movement must continue to thrive because men and women are still not created equal everywhere.

17 Just imagine if women controlled 51 percent of Congress. Imagine the sentiments we would declare on Capitol Hill. Sentiments we will declare. Sentiments that embody every American's fondest hopes. And the dreams for their children and their families.

18 Parents want Congress to protect their children from tobacco. Women will declare it. Consumers want Congress to guarantee their rights in the health care system. Women will declare it. Families want Congress to help them get child care they can afford and trust. Women will declare it.

19 Women want Congress to protect their right to reproductive choice and health. We will declare it and defend it. We will never, never go back.

20 As our fight goes on, let me sound a note of caution. As we change the world around us, let us not forget about the world within us. It would be a Pyrrhic victory, to win our human rights, but lose our precious health. We must respect ourselves. Think about ourselves. Take care of our bodies, and ourselves. Sisters—the Declaration of Sentiments must begin from within. Not only in our souls. But in the strength of our hearts, our minds and our muscles, our blood and our bones.

21 Sojourner Truth knew something about the strength of women. She said, "If the first woman God ever made was strong enough to turn the world upside down all alone—women together ought to be able to turn it back—and get it right side up again!" If we're going to turn the world right-side up, we must stay strong.

22 That is the best way to honor the Declaration of Sentiments today. To remember how far we've come. To imagine how far we'll go. The best way to honor the Declaration of Sentiments is to appreciate the women who've shocked and shaken up every generation, everywhere. To keep fighting in their name, in their memory, and to never stop struggling until we win.

23 So, on this 150th anniversary, we must gird ourselves to take our battle into the next century. Our enemies are putting on their armor to end opportunity and decent lives and fairness for waitresses in Topeka and corporate executives in New York. This is not a class war—every American family— rich or poor—will lose if they win. This is a fight for hard-working families. It is a fight for our children—for our daughters and our sons. It is a fight for old and young—strong and weak. It is about race, religion, gender, sexual orientation, and disability. It is about Asian and African, Native American and Hispanic. It is about all of us—Republicans and Democrats.

24 And we will win. We will win in the name of women like Elizabeth Cady Stanton, Lucretia Mott, Alice Paul, Sojourner Truth, Susan B. Anthony, Carrie Chapman Catt, Bella Abzug, Betty Friedan, Gloria Steinem. And the countless others—men and women, Republicans and Democrats—who opened up the steel doors with their sacrifices and courage in factories and offices and homes and clinics. On battlefields and playing fields they stepped up with us—so that all of us could walk right through to the dream—and the opportunity—of this extraordinary country.

25 One of them is my friend, Dr. Elizabeth Karlin. Outside of Madison, Wisconsin today, Liz Karlin lies very ill from cancer. Dr. Elizabeth Karlin is one of this country's most courageous abortion providers. For years—day and night—she and her nurses endured harassment from demonstrators outside their clinic and their homes. She never wavered in her commitment to protect a woman's right to choose.

26 More than anyone I have ever met, Liz Karlin has the courage of her convictions. Like our founding mothers, she is tenacious and brave. A hero of our movement.

27 Last weekend, I flew to Madison to see her. I promised her I would never, never give up—that we would never, ever give up our struggle for equality. I intend to keep that promise—and I know you will too.

28 Thank you, sisters.

The Rainbow Coalition

◆ *Jesse Jackson* ◆

On July 17, 1984, the evening following Mario Cuomo's eloquent keynote speech (see the CD-ROM for a text of Cuomo's speech), candidate Jesse Jackson addressed the Democratic National Convention. Although now it was clear that Walter Mondale would receive the nomination for President, the convention audience was very uncertain what the tone and substance of Rev. Jackson's message might be. His campaign rhetoric often was characterized by the press as confrontative and divisive. During the campaign Jackson won seven presidential primaries, brought some prisoners home after visiting Fidel Castro in Cuba, and secured freedom for an American naval pilot shot down over Syria. Delegates and viewers on national television would recall his early ethnic slur against Jews ("Hymies") and his refusal for much of the campaign to reject the support and views of Louis Farrakhan, the Black Muslim leader.

But Jackson's speech in San Francisco was one of conciliation rather than division. *News-week* (July 30, 1984, p. 23) observed that "without departing from the dictates of his conscience, he said nearly all the things party leaders had hoped for." *Newsweek* also contended that his speech "brought a new music to the mainstream of American oratory, stirring the spirit and wrenching the emotions in a way more reminiscent of the revival tent than the convention hall." Florida's Governor Bob Graham, according to *Newsweek*, declared: "If you are a human being and weren't affected by what you just heard, you may be beyond redemption."

Clearly Jackson's general purpose was social cohesion. He sought to re-energize the commitment of his followers in the Rainbow Coalition, to heal divisive wounds that he and others had inflicted during the campaign, and to unite all Democrats around shared values and against a common enemy, Reaganism. Justifiably his address also could be analyzed as an unofficial keynote speech (see introduction to speech by Barbara Jordan in this chapter) or as a rally

◆ With some corrections added based on a recording of the speech, the text is reprinted with permission from *Vital Speeches of the Day,* November 15, 1984, pp. 77–81.

speech (see introduction to Martin Luther King, Jr. speech in this chapter).

Throughout the speech he stresses the need for unity (6, 12, 14–16, 25–26, 31–33, 39, 76, 84), even to the extent of setting a personal example through apology (20–21). Fundamental values shared by Democrats are emphasized: justice, fairness, humaneness, sharing, conscience, and inclusiveness. Jackson depicts the role of diversity and competition as healthy (12, 25) and describes the inclusiveness of the Rainbow Coalition and of the Democratic Party (27–28, 34–38, 71, 86).

To demonstrate that he has a firm command of political and economic realities, both domestic and foreign, Jackson relies heavily on two forms of support for his contentions. He employs statistics to quantify the seriousness of problems (42, 44–51, 61–67). Often he supports a judgment or defines a concept by itemization of examples or qualities (2, 6, 9, 18, 22, 56, 63, 76). To what extent are his uses of statistics and examples appropriate and reasonable?

In a very real sense, Jackson's speech can be characterized as a political sermon. Much more so than is typical of American political discourse, Jackson overtly preaches. He frequently describes God's nature and role. Allusions are made to the Bible (10, 12, 34, 76, 81) and religious concepts are employed (6, 24, 79, 85), including being called to redemption and to a mission. Search Jackson's address for additional illustrations of these, or other, sermonic features. For purposes of clarity and emphasis, Jackson often structures a series of ideas in parallel sequence (33, 34–38, 44–50, 77). Indeed parallelism in the form of repetition (54, 71, 73) and refrain provide stress on some central themes,

such as the need to "dream" and his view that "our time has come" (78–79, 80–84).

Metaphorical imagery is a stylistic tactic important to the power of Jackson's message. The cumulative metaphorical image, developed in different ways at various points, is of movement upward and into the light (10, 22, 32, 71, 76–77). This movement takes the form of a journey (10, 69), a rising boat (10, 42–43), and progress to higher ground (32–33, 84). In paragraph 26 Jackson vividly captures his theme of unity-in-diversity through the metaphors of the rainbow and the quilt. Alliteration is used to associate in a memorable way clusters of things or ideas, either all positive or all negative (4, 5, 20, 37, 62–63, 72). Antithesis is the phrasing of two opposing or competing items into sharp, terse contrast with one item of the pair given clear preference over the other. Jackson frequently employs antithesis to crystalize value judgements (2, 8, 18, 20–21, 37–38, 52, 54, 69, 73, 77, 79, 84–85). Pervasive antithesis is such a marked feature of the speech that the rhetorical critic cannot ignore assessing the appropriateness, clarity, and persuasive functions of specific usages.

Parts of this analysis of Jackson's speech are indebted to two insightful essays: Martha Cooper and John Makay, "Political Rhetoric and the Gospel According to Jesse Jackson," in Charles W. Kneupper, ed., *Visions of Rhetoric* (Rhetoric Society of America, 1987), pp. 208–218; Leslie A. DiMare, "Functionalizing Conflict: Jesse Jackson's Rhetorical Strategy at the 1984 Democratic National Convention," *Western Journal of Speech Communication*, 51 (Spring 1987): 218–226.

◆ ◆ ◆

1   Tonight we come together bound by our faith in a mighty God, with genuine respect for our country, and inheriting the legacy of a great party—a Democratic Party—which is the best hope for redirecting our nation on a more humane, just, and peaceful course.

2   This is not a perfect party. We are not a perfect people. Yet, we are called to a perfect mission: our mission, to feed the hungry, to clothe the naked, to house the homeless, to teach the illiterate, to provide jobs for the jobless, and to choose the human race over the nuclear race.

3   We are gathered here this week to nominate a candidate and write a platform which will expand, unify, direct, and inspire our party and the nation to fulfill this mission.

4   My constituency is the damned, disinherited, disrespected, and the despised.

5   They are restless and seek relief. They've voted in record numbers. They have invested the faith, hope, and trust that they have in us. The Democratic Party must send them a signal that we care. I pledge my best not to let them down.

6   There is the call of conscience: redemption, expansion, healing, and unity. Leadership must heed the call of conscience, redemption, expansion, healing, and unity, for they are the key to achieving our mission.

7   Time is neutral and does not change things.

8   With courage and initiative leaders change things. No generation can choose the age or circumstances in which it is born, but through leadership it can choose to make the age in which it is born an age of enlightenment—an age of jobs, and peace, and justice.

9   Only leadership—that intangible combination of gifts, discipline, information, circumstance, courage, timing, will, and divine inspiration—can lead us out of the crisis in which we find ourselves.

10   Leadership can mitigate the misery of our nation. Leadership can part the waters and lead our nation in the direction of the Promised Land. Leadership can lift the boats stuck at the bottom.

11   I have had the rare opportunity to watch seven men, and then two, pour out their souls, offer their service, and heed the call of duty to direct the course of our nation.

12   There is a proper season for everything. There is a time to sow and a time to reap. There is a time to compete, and a time to cooperate.

13   I ask for your vote on the ballot as a vote for a new direction for this party and this nation: a vote for conviction, a vote for conscience.

14   But I will be proud to support the nominee of this convention for the President of the United States of America.

15   I have watched the leadership of our party develop and grow. My respect for both Mr. Mondale and Mr. Hart is great.

16   I have watched them struggle with the cross-winds and cross-fires of being public servants, and I believe that they will both continue to try to serve us faithfully. I am elated by the knowledge that for the first time in our history a woman, Geraldine Ferraro, will be recommended to share our ticket.

17   Throughout this campaign, I have tried to offer leadership to the Democratic Party and the nation.

18   If in my high moments, I have done some good, offered some service, shed some light, healed some wounds, rekindled some hope, or stirred someone from apathy and indifference, or in any way along the way helped somebody, then this campaign has not been in vain.

19   For friends who loved and cared for me, and for a God who spared me, and for a family who understood, I am eternally grateful.

20   If in my low moments, in word, deed, or attitude, through some error of temper, taste, or tone, I have caused anyone discomfort, created pain, or revived someone's fears, that was not my truest self.

21   If there were occasions when my grape turned into a raisin and my joy bell lost its resonance, please forgive me. Charge it to my head and not to my heart. My head is so limited in its finitude; my heart is boundless in its love for the human family. I am not a perfect servant. I am a public servant. I'm doing my best against the odds. As I develop and serve, be patient. God is not finished with me yet.

22 This campaign has taught me much: that leaders must be tough enough to fight, tender enough to cry, human enough to make mistakes, humble enough to admit them, strong enough to absorb the pain, and resilient enough to bounce back and keep on moving. For leaders, the pain is often intense. But you must smile through your tears and keep moving with the faith that there is a brighter side somewhere.

23 I went to see Hubert Humphrey three days before he died. He had just called Richard Nixon from his dying bed, and many people wondered why. And, I asked him.

24 He said, "Jesse, from this vantage point, with the sun setting in my life, all of the speeches, the political conventions, the crowds, and the great fights are behind me now. At a time like this you are forced to deal with your irreducible essence, forced to grapple with that which is really important to you. And what I have concluded about life," Hubert Humphrey said, "when all is said and done, we must forgive each other, and redeem each other, and move on."

25 Our party is emerging from one of its most hard-fought battles for the Democratic Party's presidential nomination in our history. But our healthy competition should make us better, not bitter. We must use the insight, wisdom, and experience of the late Hubert Humphrey as a balm for the wounds in our party, this nation, and the world. We must forgive each other, redeem each other, re-group, and move on.

26 Our flag is red, white, and blue, but our nation is rainbow—red, yellow, brown, black, and white—we're all precious in God's sight. America is not like a blanket—one piece of unbroken cloth, the same color, the same texture, the same size. America is more like a quilt—many patches, many pieces, many colors, many sizes, all woven and held together by a common thread.

27 The white, the Hispanic, the black, the Arab, the Jew, the woman, the Native American, the small farmer, the businessperson, the environmentalist, the peace activist, the young, the old, the lesbian, the gay, and the disabled make up the American quilt.

28 Even in our fractured state, all of us count and fit somewhere. We have proven that we can survive without each other. But we have not proven that we can win or make progress without each other. We must come together.

29 From Fannie Lee Hamer in Atlantic City in 1964 to the Rainbow Coalition in San Francisco today; from the Atlantic to the Pacific, we have experienced pain but progress as we ended American apartheid laws; we got public accommodations; we secured voting rights; we obtained open housing; as young people got the right to vote; we lost Malcolm, Martin, Medgar, Bobby and John and Viola.

30 The team that got us here must be expanded, not abandoned. Twenty years ago, tears welled up in our eyes as the bodies of Schwerner, Goodman, and Chaney were dredged from the depths of a river in Mississippi. Twenty years later, our communities, black and Jewish, are in anguish, anger, and pain.

31 Feelings have been hurt on both sides. There is a crisis in communication. Confusion is in the air. We cannot afford to lose our way. We may agree to agree, or agree to disagree on issues; we must bring back civility to these tensions.

32 We are co-partners in a long and rich religious history—the Judeo-Christian traditions. Many blacks and Jews have a shared passion for social justice at home and peace abroad. We must seek a revival of the spirit, inspired by a new vision and new possibilities. We must return to higher ground. We are bound by Moses and Jesus, but also connected to Islam and Mohammed.

33 These three great religions—Judaism, Christianity, and Islam—were all born in the revered and holy city of Jerusalem. We are bound by Dr. Martin Luther King, Jr. and Rabbi Abraham Heschel, crying out from their graves for us to reach common ground. We are bound by shared blood and shared sacrifices. We are much too intelligent; much too bound by our Judeo-Christian heritage; much too victimized by racism, sexism, militarism, and anti-Semitism; much too threatened as historical scape-goats to go on divided one from another. We must turn from finger-pointing to clasped hands. We must share our burdens and our joys with each other once again. We must turn to each other and not on each other and choose higher ground.

34   Twenty years later, we cannot be satisfied by just restoring the old coalition. Old wine skins must make room for new wine. We must heal and expand. The Rainbow Coalition is making room for Arab-Americans. They too know the pain and hurt of racial and religious rejection. They must not continue to be made pariahs. The Rainbow Coalition is making room for Hispanic-Americans who this very night are living under the threat of the Simpson-Mazzoli bill, and farm workers from Ohio who are fighting the Campbell Soup Company with a boycott to achieve legitimate workers rights.

35   The Rainbow is making room for the Native Americans, the most exploited people of all, a people with the greatest moral claim amongst us. We support them as they seek the restoration of their ancient land and claim amongst us. We support them as they seek the restoration of land and water rights, as they seek to preserve their ancestral homelands and the beauty of a land that was once all theirs. They can never receive a fair share for all that they have given us, but they must finally have a fair chance to develop their great resources and to preserve their people and their culture.

36   The Rainbow Coalition includes Asian-Americans, now being killed in our streets—scape-goats for the failures of corporate, industrial, and economic policies. The Rainbow is making room for the young Americans. Twenty years ago, our young people were dying in a war for which they could not even vote. But 20 years later, Young America has the power to stop a war in Central America and the responsibility to vote in great numbers. Young America must be politically active in 1984. The choice is war or peace. We must make room for Young America.

37   The Rainbow includes disabled veterans. The color scheme fits in the Rainbow. The disabled have their handicap revealed and their genius concealed; while the able-bodied have their genius re-vealed and their disability concealed. But ultimately we must judge people by their values and their contribution. Don't leave anybody out. I would rather have Roosevelt in a wheelchair than Reagan on a horse.

38   The Rainbow is making room for small farmers. They have suffered tremendously under the Reagan regime. They will either receive 90 percent parity or 100 percent charity. We must address their concerns and make room for them. The Rainbow includes lesbians and gays. No American citizen ought be denied equal protection under the law.

39   We must be unusually committed and caring as we expand our family to include new mem-bers. All of us must be tolerant and understanding as the fears and anxieties of the rejected and of the party leadership express themselves in many different ways. Too often what we call hate—as if it were deeply rooted in some philosophy or strategy—is simply ignorance, anxiety, paranoia, fear, and inse-curity. To be strong leaders, we must be long-suffering as we seek to right the wrongs of our party and our nation. We must expand our party, heal our party, and unify our party. That is our mission in 1984.

40   We are often reminded that we live in a great nation—and we do. But it can be greater still. The Rainbow is mandating a new definition of greatness. We must not measure greatness from the mansion down, but the manger up.

41   Jesus said that we should not be judged by the bark we wear but by the fruit that we bear. Jesus said that we must measure greatness by how we treat the least of these.

42   President Reagan says the nation is in recovery. Those 90,000 corporations that made a profit last year but paid no federal taxes are recovering. The 37,000 military contractors who have benefited from Reagan's more than doubling the military budget in peacetime, surely they are recovering. The big corporations and rich individuals who received the bulk of the three-year, multibillion tax cut from

Mr. Reagan are recovering. But no such recovery is under way for the least of these. Rising tides don't lift all boats, particularly those stuck on the bottom.

43   For the boats stuck at the bottom there is a misery index. This administration has made life more miserable for the poor. Its attitude has been contemptuous. Its policies and programs have been cruel and unfair to working people. They must be held accountable in November for increasing infant mortality among the poor. In Detroit, one of the great cities of the Western world, babies are dying at the same rate as Honduras, the most underdeveloped nation in our hemisphere.

44   This administration must be held accountable for policies that contribute to the growing poverty in America. Under President Reagan, there are now 34 million people in poverty, 15 percent of our nation. Twenty-three million are white, 11 million black, Hispanic, Asian, and others. Mostly women and children. By the end of this year, there will be 41 million people in poverty. We cannot stand idly by. We must fight for change, now.

45   Under this regime we look at Social Security. The 1981 budget cuts included nine permanent Social Security benefit cuts totaling $20 billion over five years.

46   Small businesses have suffered under Reagan tax cuts. Only 18 percent of total business tax cuts went to them—82 percent to big business.

47   Health care under Mr. Reagan has been sharply cut.

48   Education under Mr. Reagan has been cut 25 percent.

49   Under Mr. Reagan there are now 9.7 million female-head families. They represent 16 percent of all families, half of all of them are poor. Seventy percent of all poor children live in a house headed by a woman, where there is no man.

50   Under Mr. Reagan, the administration has cleaned up only 6 of 546 priority toxic waste dumps.

51   Farmers' real net income was only about half its level in 1979.

52   Many say that the race in November will be decided in the South. President Reagan is depending on the conservative South to return him to office. But the South, I tell you, is unnaturally conservative. The South is the poorest region in our nation and, therefore, has the least to conserve. In his appeal to the South, Mr. Reagan is trying to substitute flags and prayer cloths for food, and clothing, and education, health care, and housing. But President Reagan who asks us to pray, and I believe in prayer— I've come this way by the power of prayer. But, we must watch false prophecy.

53   He cuts energy assistance to the poor, cuts breakfast programs from children, cuts lunch programs from children, cuts job training from children and then says, to an empty table, "let us pray." Apparently he is not familiar with the structure of a prayer. You thank the Lord for the food that you are about to receive, not the food that just left.

54   I think that we should pray. But don't pray for the food that left, pray for the man that took the food to leave. We need a change. We need a change in November.

55   Under President Reagan, the misery index has risen for the poor, but the danger index has risen for everybody.

56   Under this administration we've lost the lives of our boys in Central America, in Honduras, in Granada, in Lebanon.

57   A nuclear standoff in Europe. Under this administration, one-third of our children believe they will die in a nuclear war. The danger index is increasing in this world.

58   With all the talk about defense against Russia, the Russian submarines are closer and their missiles are more accurate. We live in a world tonight more miserable and a world more dangerous.

59   While Reagonomics and Reaganism is talked about often, so often we miss the real meaning. Reaganism is a spirit. Reaganomics represents the real economic facts of life.

60   In 1980, Mr. George Bush, a man with reasonable access to Mr. Reagan, did an analysis of Mr. Reagan's economic plan. Mr. Bush concluded Reagan's plan was "voodoo economics." He was right. Third-party candidate John Anderson said that the combination of military spending, tax cuts, and a balanced budget by '84 could be accomplished with blue smoke and mirrors. They were both right.

61   Mr. Reagan talks about a dynamic recovery. There is some measure of recovery, three and a half years later. Unemployment has inched just below where it was when he took office in 1981. But there are still 8.1 million people officially unemployed, 11 million working only parttime jobs. Inflation has come down, but let's analyze for a moment who has paid the price for this superficial economic recovery.

62   Mr. Reagan curbed inflation by cutting consumer demand. He cut consumer demand with conscious and callous fiscal and monetary policy. He used the federal budget to deliberately induce unemployment and curb social spending. He then waged and supported tight monetary policies of the Federal Reserve Board to deliberately drive up interest rates—again to curb consumer demand created through borrowing.

63   Unemployment reached 10.7 percent; we experienced skyrocketing interest rates; our dollar inflated abroad; there were record bank failures; record farm foreclosures; record business bankruptcies; record budget deficits; record trade deficits. Mr. Reagan brought inflation down by destablizing our economy and disrupting family life.

64   He promised in 1980 a balanced budget, but instead we now have a record $200 billion budget deficit. Under President Reagan, the cumulative budget deficit for his four years is more than the sum total of deficits from George Washington to Jimmy Carter combined. I tell you, we need a change.

65   How is he paying for these short-term jobs? Reagan's economic recovery is being financed by deficit spending—$200 billion a year. Military spending, a major cause of this deficit, is projected over the next five years to be nearly $2 trillion, and will cost about $40,000 for every taxpaying family.

66   When the government borrows $200 billion annually to finance the deficit, this encourages the private sector to make its money off of interest rates as opposed to development and economic growth. Even money abroad—we don't have enough money domestically to finance the debt, so we are now borrowing money abroad, from foreign banks, government, and financial institutions—$40 billion in 1983; $70 to $80 billion in 1984 (40 percent of our total); over $100 billion (50 percent of our total) in 1985.

67   By 1989, it is projected that 50 percent of all individual income taxes will be going to pay just for the interest on that debt. The U.S. used to be the largest exporter of capital, but under Mr. Reagan we will quite likely become the largest debtor nation. About two weeks ago, on July 4, we celebrated our Declaration of Independence. Yet every day, supply-side economics is making our nation more economically dependent and less economically free. Five to six percent of our gross national product is now being eaten up with President Reagan's budget deficit.

68   To depend on foreign military powers to protect our national security would be foolish, making us dependent and less secure. Yet Reaganomics has us increasingly dependent on foreign economic sources. This consumer-led but deficit-financed recovery is unbalanced and artificial.

69   We have a challenge as Democrats: to point a way out. Democracy guarantees opportunity, not success. Democracy guarantees the right to participate, not a license for either the majority or a minority to dominate. The victory for the Rainbow Coalition in the platform debates today was not whether we won or lost; but that we raised the right issues. We can afford to lose the vote; issues are non-negotiable. We cannot afford to avoid raising the right questions. Our self respect and our moral integrity were at stake. Our heads are perhaps bloodied but now bowed. Our backs are straight. We can go home and face our people. Our vision is clear. When we think, on this journey from slaveship to championship, we've gone from the planks of the boardwalk in Atlantic City in 1964 to fighting to have the right planks in the platform in San Francisco in '84. There is a deep and abiding sense of joy in our soul, despite the tears in our eyes. For while there are missing planks, there is a solid foundation upon which to build. Our party can win. But we must provide hope that will inspire people to struggle and achieve; provide a plan to show the way out of our dilemma, and then lead the way.

70 In 1984, my heart is made to feel glad because I know there is a way out. Justice. The requirement for rebuilding America is justice. The linchpin of progressive politics in our nation will not come from the North; they in fact will come from the South. That is why I argue over and over again—from Lynchburg, Va., down to Texas, there is only one black congressperson out of 115. Nineteen years later, we're locked out of the Congress, the Senate, and the governor's mansion. What does this large black vote mean? Why do I fight to end second primaries and fight gerrymandering and annexation and at large. Why do we fight over that? Because I tell you, you cannot hold someone in the ditch unless you linger there with them. If we want a change in this nation, reinforce that Voting Rights Act—we'll get 12 to 20 black, Hispanic, female, and progressive congresspersons from the South. We can save the cotton, but we've got to fight the boll weevil—we've got to make a judgment.

71 It's not enough to hope ERA will pass; how can we pass ERA? If blacks vote in great numbers, progressive whites win. It's the only way progressive whites win. If blacks vote in great numbers, Hispanics win. If blacks, Hispanics, and progressive whites vote, women win. When women win, children win. When women and children win, workers win. We must all come up together. We must come up together.

72 I tell you, with all of our joy and excitement, we must not save the world and lose our souls; we should never short-circuit enforcement of the Voting Rights Act at every level. If one of us rises, all of us must rise. Justice is the way out. Peace is a way out. We should not act as if nuclear weaponry is negotiable and debatable. In this world in which we live, we dropped the bomb on Japan and felt guilty. But in 1984, other folks also got bombs. This time, if we drop the bomb, six minutes later, we, too, will be destroyed. It's not about dropping the bomb on somebody; it's about dropping the bomb on everybody. We must choose developed minds over guided missiles, and think it out and not fight it out. It's time for a change.

73 Our foreign policy must be characterized by mutual respect, not by gunboat diplomacy, big stick diplomacy, and threats. Our nation at its best feeds the hungry. Our nation at its worst will mine the harbors of Nicaragua; at its worst, will try to overthrow that government; at its worst, will cut aid to American education and increase aid to El Salvador; at its worst our nation will have partnership with South Africa. That's a moral disgrace. It's a moral disgrace. It's a moral disgrace.

74 When we look at Africa, we cannot just focus on apartheid in southern Africa. We must fight for trade with Africa, and not just aid to Africa. We cannot stand idly by and say we will not relate to Nicaragua unless they have elections there and then embrace military regimes in Africa, overthrowing Democratic governments in Nigeria and Liberia and Ghana. We must fight for democracy all around the world, and play the game by one set of rules.

75 Peace in this world. Our present formula for peace in the Middle East is inadequate; it will not work. There are 22 nations in the Middle East. Our nation must be able to talk and act and influence all of them. We must build upon Camp David and measure human rights by one yardstick. In that region we have too many interests and too few friends.

76 There is a way out. Jobs. Put Americans back to work. When I was a child growing up in Greenville, S.C. the Rev. Sample who used to preach every so often a sermon linked to Jesus. He said,

"If I be lifted up, I'll draw all men unto me." I didn't quite understand what he meant as a child growing up. But I understand a little better now. If you raise up truth, it's magnetic. It has a way of drawing people. With all this confusion in this convention—the bright lights and parties and big fun—we must raise up the simple proposition: if we lift up a program to feed the hungry, they'll come running. If we lift up a program to study war no more, our youth will come running. If we lift up a program to put America back to work, an alternative to welfare and despair, they will come working. If we cut that military budget without cutting our defense, and use that money to rebuild bridges and put steelworkers back to work, and use that money, and provide jobs for our cities, and use that money to build schools and train teachers and educate our children, and build hospitals and train doctors and train nurses, the whole nation will come running to us.

77   As I leave you now, and we vote in this convention and get ready to go back across this nation in a couple of days, in this campaign, I'll try to be faithful to my promise. I'll live in the old barrios, and ghettos and reservations, and housing projects. I have a message for our youth. I challenge them to put hope in their brains, and not dope in their veins. I told them like Jesus, I, too, was born in a slum, but just because you're born in a slum, does not mean the slum is born in you, and you can rise above it if your mind is made up. I told them in every slum, there are two sides. When I see a broken window, that's the slummy side. Train that youth to be a glazier, that's the sunny side. When I see a missing brick, that's the slummy side. Let that child in the union, and become a brickmason, and build, that's the sunny side. When I see a missing door, that's the slummy side. Train some youth to become a carpenter, that's the sunny side. When I see the vulgar words and hieroglyphics of destitution on the walls, that's the slummy side. Train some youth to be a painter, an artist—that's the sunny side. We need this place looking for the sunny side because there's a brighter side somewhere. I am more convinced than ever that we can win. We'll vault up the rough side of the mountain; we can win. I just want young America to do me one favor. Just one favor.

78   Exercise the right to dream. You must face reality—that which is. But then dream of the reality that ought to be, that must be. Live beyond the pain of reality with the dream of a bright tomorrow. Use hope and imagination as weapons of survival and progress. Use love to motivate you and obligate you to serve the human family.

79   Young America, dream! Choose the human race over the nuclear race. Bury the weapons and don't burn the people. Dream of a new value system. Teachers, who teach for life, and not just for a living, teach because they can't help it. Dream of lawyers more concerned about justice than a judgeship. Dream of doctors more concerned about public health than personal wealth. Dream of preachers and priests who will prophesy and not just profiteer. Preach and dream. Our time has come.

80   Our time has come. Suffering breeds character. Character breeds faith. And in the end, faith will not disappoint.

81   Our time has come. Our faith, hope, and dreams will prevail. Our time has come. Weeping has endured for the night. And, now joy cometh in the morning.

82   Our time has come. No graves can hold our body down.

83   Our time has come. No lie can live forever.

84   Our time has come. We must leave racial battleground and come to economic common ground and moral higher ground. America, our time has come.

85   We've come from disgrace to Amazing Grace, our time has come.

86   Give me your tired, give me your poor, your huddled masses who yearn to breathe free, and come November, there will be a change because our time has come.

87   Thank you and God bless you.

Farewell to the Cadets

◆ *Douglas MacArthur* ◆

General Douglas MacArthur became a national hero during World War II as the Supreme Allied Commander in the Pacific. Perhaps his greatest moment was when he successfully returned to Manila after the Japanese early in the war had driven American forces from the Philippines. Upon leaving Manila, MacArthur had vowed, "I shall return." At the close of the war, he commanded the Allied occupational forces in Japan, and his skillful supervision of the restoration of the Japanese nation was widely acclaimed, even by the Japanese. When President Truman ordered American forces into Korea in 1950 to stop the invasion of the South by the North, General MacArthur was again placed in command of the expedition. However, he became an outspoken critic of the administration's Korean policy, and, as a consequence, President Truman relieved General MacArthur of his command in 1951. MacArthur returned to America to a hero's welcome. He accepted an invitation to address a joint session of Congress, and his concluding remarks on the ballad of the "Old Soldier" captured the imagination of the American people. He died on April 5, 1964.

In leaving formal, active association with a group or position, persons sometimes deliver farewell speeches; at times the farewell is combined with an acceptance of an award from the group for outstanding service. In such a situation a critic could assess the ways in which the speaker satisfies various expectations probably held by audiences on such occasions: (1) Expression of gratitude for the award presented and/or for the cooperation and opportunities provided by the group. (2) Expression of sadness and other emotions on leaving the group or position. (3) Recollection of praiseworthy accomplishments or memorable events shared with the group. (4) Praise for the group's values, principles, and goals, along with urging rededication to their continuation. (5) Discussion of the speaker's reasons for leaving: sometimes this even may mean discussion of disagreements or conflicts with superiors or others that led to the departure. (6) Description of the future in broad, sometimes vivid, terms if the group's values and efforts are perpetuated.

On May 12, 1962, General MacArthur, an honor graduate of the United States Military Academy at West Point, went there to receive the Sylvanus Thayer award for service to his nation. The Old Soldier, then 82, accepted the award and, despite failing health, made a moving and inspirational farewell speech to the cadets of the academy, an institution he had served earlier as superintendent. He sought to reinforce and defend the cadets' commitment to the values of "duty, honor, country," the motto inscribed on the academy coat of arms. Although MacArthur originally was gifted with an exceptionally rich and resonant voice, it was now hoarse and often faint. He spoke slowly and deliberately, gaining intensity with phrases such as "faint bugles blowing reveille" and "the strange, mournful mutter of the battlefield."

◆ This speech was taken from a recording of the address and is printed by permission of the MacArthur Memorial Foundation.

MacArthur had employed many of the key ideas and vivid phrases in this speech repeatedly in varied contexts in earlier speeches throughout his career. And parts of two paragraphs (9, 25) were derived, without acknowledging the sources, from the previously published words of other people.[1] Although his powers of rhetorical invention might be criticized as being limited, an ability to combine rhetorical elements for moving impact nevertheless is reflected in this address.

As you analyze this speech, you should focus upon several important rhetorical factors. The first is credibility of source. MacArthur, a legendary war hero, doubtlessly enjoyed high ethos with the cadets. Moreover, the text of the speech reveals that MacArthur was fully aware of ethos factors. Second, MacArthur was a conscious speech stylist, a fact readily apparent in this address; imagery, metaphor, antithesis, parallelism, and elegance of language are pronounced. Do any of his images seem strained, or are any of his metaphors mixed? Third, note his strategy of linking "duty, honor, country" with desirable consequences (paragraphs 7–10) and with valiant men (11–18). And in paragraph 6 he promotes these values by asserting that blameworthy men consistently downgrade them. Finally, to what higher values does MacArthur relate "duty, honor, country" in order to defend the worth of the cadets' motto?

1   As I was leaving the hotel this morning, a doorman asked me, "Where are you bound for, General?" And when I replied, "West Point," he remarked, "Beautiful place. Have you ever been there before?"

2   No human being could fail to be deeply moved by such a tribute as this, coming from a profession I have served so long and a people I have loved so well.

3   It fills me with an emotion I cannot express. But this award is not intended primarily to honor a personality, but to symbolize a great moral code—the code of conduct and chivalry of those who guard this beloved land of culture and ancient descent. That is the animation of this medallion. For all eyes and for all time it is an expression of the ethics of the American soldier. That I should be integrated in this way with so noble an ideal arouses a sense of pride and yet of humility, which will be with me always.

4   Duty, honor, country: those three hallowed words reverently dictate what you want to be, what you can be, what you will be. They are your rallying points to build courage when courage seems to fail, to regain faith when there seems to be little cause for faith, to create hope when hope becomes forlorn.

5   Unhappily, I possess neither that eloquence of diction, that poetry of imagination, nor that brilliance of metaphor to tell you all that they mean.

6   The unbelievers will say they are but words, but a slogan, but a flamboyant phrase. Every pedant, every demogogue, every cynic, every hypocrite, every troublemaker, and, I am sorry to say, some others of an entirely different character, will try to downgrade them even to the extent of mockery and ridicule.

7   But these are some of the things they do. They build your basic character. They mold you for your future roles as the custodians of the nation's defense. They make you strong enough to know when you are weak and brave enough to face yourself when you are afraid.

---

1. Stephen Robb, "Pre-Inventional Criticism: The Speaking of Douglas MacArthur," in G. P. Mohrmann et al., eds., *Explorations in Rhetorical Criticism* (University Park: Pennsylvania State University Press, 1973), pp. 178–90.

8   They teach you to be proud and unbending in honest failure, but humble and gentle in success; not to substitute words for action; not to seek the path of comfort, but to face the stress and spur of difficulty and challenge; to learn to stand up in the storm, but to have compassion on those who fall; to master yourself before you seek to master others; to have a heart that is clean, a goal that is high; to learn to laugh, yet never forget how to weep; to reach into the future, yet never neglect the past; to be serious, yet never take yourself too seriously; to be modest so that you will remember the simplicity of true greatness, the open mind of true wisdom, the meekness of true strength.

9   They give you a temper of the will, a quality of the imagination, a vigor of the emotions, a freshness of the deep springs of life, a temperamental predominance of courage over timidity, of an appetite for adventure over love of ease.

10   They create in your heart the sense of wonder, the unfailing hope of what next, and the joy and inspiration of life. They teach you this way to be an officer and a gentleman.

11   And what sort of soldiers are those you are to lead? Are they reliable? Are they brave? Are they capable of victory? Their story is known to all of you. It is the story of the American man-at-arms. My estimate of him was formed on the battlefields many, many years ago, and has never changed. I regarded him then, as I regard him now, as one of the world's noblest figures—not only as one of the finest military characters but also as one of the most stainless.

12   His name and fame are the birthright of every American citizen. In his youth and strength, his love and loyalty, he gave all that mortality can give. He needs no eulogy from me or from any other man. He has written his own history and written it in red on his enemy's breast.

13   But when I think of his patience under adversity, of his courage under fire, and his modesty in victory, I am filled with an emotion of admiration I cannot put into words. He belongs to history as furnishing one of the greatest examples of successful patriotism. He belongs to posterity as the instructor of future generations in the principles of liberty and freedom. He belongs to the present—to us—by his virtues and by his achievements.

14   In twenty campaigns, on a hundred battlefields, around a thousand campfires, I have witnessed that enduring fortitude, that patriotic self-abnegation, and that invincible determination which have carved his statue in the hearts of his people.

15   From one end of the world to the other, he has drained deep the chalice of courage. As I listened to those songs, in memory's eye I could see those staggering columns of the First World War, bending under soggy packs on many a weary march, from dripping dusk to drizzling dawn, slogging ankle-deep through the mire of shell-shocked roads; to form grimly for the attack, blue-lipped, covered with sludge and mud, chilled by the wind and rain, driving home to their objective, and, for many, to the judgment seat of God.

16   I do not know the dignity of their birth, but I do know the glory of their death. They died unquestioning, uncomplaining, with faith in their hearts, and on their lips the hope that we would go on to victory.

17   Always for them: duty, honor, country. Always their blood, and sweat, and tears, as we sought the way and the light and the truth. And 20 years after, on the other side of the globe, again the filth of murky foxholes, the stench of ghostly trenches, the slime of dripping dugouts, those boiling suns of relentless heat, those torrential rains of devastating storms, the loneliness and utter desolation of jungle trails, the bitterness of long separation from those they loved and cherished, the deadly pestilence of tropical disease, the horror of stricken areas of war.

18   Their resolute and determined defense, their swift and sure attack, their indomitable purpose, their complete and decisive victory—always victory, always through the bloody haze of their last reverberating shot, the vision of gaunt, ghastly men, reverently following your password of duty, honor, country.

19 The code which those words perpetuate embraces the highest moral law and will stand the test of any ethics or philosophies ever promulgated for the uplift of mankind. Its requirements are for the things that are right and its restraints are from the things that are wrong. The soldier, above all other men, is required to practice the greatest act of religious training—sacrifice. In battle and in the face of danger and death he discloses those divine attributes which his Maker gave when he created man in his own image. No physical courage and no brute instinct can take the place of the divine help, which alone can sustain him. However horrible the incidents of war may be, the soldier who is called upon to offer and to give his life for his country is the noblest development of mankind.

20 You now face a new world, a world of change. The thrust into outer space of the satellite spheres and missiles marks a beginning of another epoch in the long story of mankind. In the five-or-more billions of years the scientists tell us it has taken to form the earth, in the three-or-more billion years of development of the human race, there has never been a more abrupt or staggering evolution.

21 We deal now, not with things of this world alone, but with the illimitable distances and as yet unfathomed distances of the universe. We are reaching out for a new and boundless frontier. We speak in strange terms of harnessing the cosmic energy; of making winds and tides work for us; of creating synthetic materials to supplement or even replace our old standard basics; to purify sea water for our drink; of mining ocean floors for new fields of wealth and food; of disease preventatives to expand life into the hundreds of years; of controlling the weather for a more equitable distribution of heat and cold, of rain and shine; of space ships to the moon; of the primary target in war no longer limited to the armed forces of an enemy, but instead to include his civil populations; of ultimate conflict between a united human race and the sinister forces of some other planetary galaxy; of such dreams and fantasies as to make life the most exciting of all times.

22 And though all this welter of change and development your mission remains fixed, determined, inviolable. It is to win our wars. Everything else in your professional career is but corollary to this vital dedication. All other public purposes, all other public projects, all other public needs, great or small, will find others for their accomplishments; but you are the ones who are trained to fight.

23 Yours is the profession of arms, the will to win, the sure knowledge that in war there is no substitute for victory, that if you lose the nation will be destroyed, that the very obsession of your public service must be duty, honor, country.

24 Others will debate the controversial issues, national and international, which divide men's minds. But serene, calm, aloof, you stand as the nation's war guardians, as its lifeguard from the raging tides of international conflict, as its gladiator in the arena of battle. For a century-and-a-half you have defended, guarded, and protected its hallowed traditions of liberty and freedom, of right and justice.

25 Let civilian voices argue the merits or demerits of our processes of government: whether our strength is being sapped by deficit financing indulged in too long; by federal paternalism grown too mighty; by power groups grown too arrogant; by politics grown too corrupt; by crime grown too rampant; by morals grown too low; by taxes grown too high; by extremists grown too violent; whether our personal liberties are as firm and complete as they should be.

26 These great national problems are not for your professional participation or military solution. Your guidepost stands out like a tenfold beacon in the night: duty, honor, country.

27 You are the leaven which binds together the entire fabric of our national system of defense. From your ranks come the great captains who hold the nation's destiny in their hands the moment the war tocsin sounds.

28 The long, gray line has never failed us. Were you to do so, a million ghosts in olive drab, in brown khaki, in blue and gray, would rise from their white crosses, thundering those magic words: duty, honor, country.

29 This does not mean that you are warmongers. On the contrary, the soldier above all other people prays for peace, for he must suffer and bear the deepest wounds and scars of war. But always in our ears ring the ominous words of Plato, that wisest of all philosophers: "Only the dead have seen the end of war."

30 The shadows are lengthening for me. The twilight is here. My days of old have vanished—tone and tints. They have gone glimmering through the dreams of things that were. Their memory is one of wondrous beauty watered by tears and coaxed and caressed by the smiles of yesterday. I listen vainly, but with thirsty ear, for the witching melody of faint bugles blowing reveille, of far drums beating the long roll.

31 In my dreams I hear again the crash of guns, the rattle of musketry, the strange, mournful mutter of the battlefield. But in the evening of my memory always I come back to West Point. Always there echoes and reechoes: duty, honor, country.

32 Today marks my final roll call with you. But I want you to know that when I cross the river, my last conscious thoughts will be of the Corps, and the Corps, and the Corps.

33 I bid you farewell.

Eulogies for the *Challenger* Astronauts

◆ *Ronald Reagan* ◆

On January 28, 1986, at 11:39 A.M. EST, only 70 seconds after lift-off from Cape Canaveral, Florida, flying at almost 2000 miles per hour, the space shuttle, *Challenger*, exploded and all seven crew members were killed. The flight was being shown live on national television and the tragedy stunned the nation. President Ronald Reagan delivered two eulogies in response to the disaster.

Speeches of tribute, such as testimonials for living persons and eulogies for the dead, typi-cally reflect rather traditional rhetorical resources to praise accomplishments and acknowledge virtues. The speaker may remind us that the person being paid tribute possesses various qualities of character, such as courage, justice, wisdom, temperance, concern for others, faith, charity, generosity, courtesy, dedication, honesty, industriousness, or humility. The speaker could describe qualities of the person's accomplishments: bravery; extreme difficulty; acknowledgement of excellence by others; personal

◆ These eulogies are reprinted from *Weekly Compilation of Presidential Documents*, 22 (February 3, 1986), pp. 104–105, 117–119.

harm incurred; a "first"; the "best"; the unexpected; the "only"; frequency of achievement; a "last" time ever. Immediate and long-term influences could be stressed, perhaps by describing the "debts" that society owes the person and how we can continue to "repay" that indebtedness through our attitudes and actions, how we can carry on the person's values and commitments. Speakers frequently emphasize the praiseworthy values, ideals, motives, and life goals held by the person. Among the kinds of rhetorical supporting materials typically used in speeches of tribute are factual examples, testimony from notables, experts, or literary sources, narration of incidents, comparison to other persons, Biblical quotations or allusions, and quotations or paraphrases of the person's own words.

By summarizing and slightly modifying the extensive research of Kathleen Jamieson, we can describe four characteristic functions of eulogies in European-American cultures.[1] First, by publicly confirming the person's death, the eulogy helps us overcome our temporary denial of the reality of the death; we overcome our initial reaction of "I just don't believe it." Second, the uneasy realization of our own eventual death is lessened by descriptions of ways in which the deceased "lives on" in history, in heaven, through good works, through followers, or through the person's family. Third, a recounting of the life and virtues of the person *in the past tense* allows us to reorient our own relationship with the deceased from present to past and from physical encounter to memory. Finally, by expressing community solidarity and social cohesion, the eulogy reassures us that our community or group will survive the death. To promote such social cohesion, audiences expect that the eulogist will not "speak ill of the dead," although some eulogists may mention modest "faults" in order to "humanize" the person. Sometimes the eulogist provides a rationale for the death so that we do not feel the death was in vain or due to pure chance. Such reasons might include God's will, fulfillment of destiny, evil conditions in society,

or even a conspiratorial plot. Another study of eulogies describes three major purposes of the eulogistic form: (1) to express appropriate personal and audience grief; (2) to deepen appreciaton and respect for the deceased; and (3) to give the audience strength for the present and inspiration for the future.[2]

At 5:00 P.M. on the same day of the *Challenger* tragedy, the day on which he was scheduled to present his annual State of the Union address, President Ronald Reagan offered a brief eulogy nationally televised from the Oval Office at the White House. At the outset he expresses appropriate personal grief (1–2) and grief on behalf of the audience (3–4). He deepens respect and appreciation for the dead by praising their courage (3–4) and by depicting them as pioneers (5) and explorers (6). He promotes solidarity in the "community" of space program employees by expressing faith and respect for the program (7) and by praising their dedication and professionalism (9). Reagan reassures American citizens that in a sense the astronauts' example and efforts will "live on" through the continuation of a vigorous manned space program; they will not have died in vain (8).

Reagan mentions two coincidences, one directly (10) and one indirectly (3). They place the tragedy in a larger historical context of exploration. They may even imply that fate or destiny was at work. The conclusion (11) is a moving and poetic confirmation of the astronauts' death. The quotation is paraphrased from "High Flight," a sonnet by John Gillespie Magee, Jr., a World War II American airman who died in the service of the Royal Canadian Air Force.

Peggy Noonan, a member of Reagan's speechwriting staff, wrote most of the January 28 eulogy. For her account, see Peggy Noonan, *What I Saw at the Revolution* (Random House, 1990), pp. 252–259. For an extensive analysis of the January 28 eulogy, see Steven M. Minter, "Reagan's Challenger Tribute: Combing Generic Constraints and Situational Demands," *Central States Speech Journal*, 37 (Fall 1986): 158–165.

---

1. Kathleen M. Jamieson, *Critical Anthology of Public Speech* (Chicago: Science Research Associates, 1978), pp. 40–41.
2. Paul C. Brownlow and Beth Davis, "'A Certainty of Honor': The Eulogies of Adlai Stevenson," *Central States Speech Journal*, 25 (Fall 1974), 217–24.

Shortly before noon on January 31, 1986, President Reagan delivered a second and longer eulogy (10 minutes) at the formal memorial service for the *Challenger* astronauts. The scene was the mall in front of the Avionics Building at the Johnson Space Center in Houston, Texas, and the audience was estimated at 10,000, including 2000 space program employees, 90 members of the House and Senate, and 200 relatives of the astronauts. The memorial service was nationally televised.

Reagan's introductory sentence succinctly reflects two purposes of any eulogy: to express personal and collective grief and to give the audience strength for the present and hope for the future. Use of the parallel structure, "we re-member" (6–12), forcefully confirms the reality of their deaths, a reality made more emotionally moving through the personal details provided about each of their lives. The President praises values and virtues exemplified in the way "they led . . . and lost their lives" (3), especially perseverance (10, 12) and heroism (7–8, 13, 15). As in the first eulogy, he honors the astronauts' achievement by comparison to the explorations of American pioneers (16). Again Reagan reassures Americans that the astronauts will continue to live in several ways: in heaven (21); through our following their example of courage and character (17); and through continuation of the space shuttle program (10, 18–20).

◆ ◆ ◆

Address to the Nation. January 28, 1986

1   Ladies and gentlemen, I'd planned to speak to you tonight to report on the state of the Union, but the events of earlier today have led me to change those plans. Today is a day for mourning and remembering.

2   Nancy and I are pained to the core by the tragedy of the shuttle *Challenger*. We know we share this pain with all of the people of our country. This is truly a national loss.

3   Nineteen years ago, almost to the day, we lost three astronauts in a terrible accident on the ground. But we've never lost an astronaut in flight; we've never had a tragedy like this. And perhaps we've forgotten the courage it took for the crew of the shuttle; but they, the *Challenger* Seven, were aware of the dangers, but overcame them and did their jobs brilliantly. We mourn seven heroes: Michael Smith, Dick Scobee, Judith Resnik, Ronald McNair, Ellison Onizuka, Gregory Jarvis, and Christa McAuliffe. We mourn their loss as a nation together.

4   For the family of the seven, we cannot bear, as you do, the full impact of this tragedy. But we feel the loss, and we're thinking about you so very much. Your loved ones were daring and brave, and they had that special grace, that special spirit that says, "Give me a challenge and I'll meet it with joy." They had a hunger to explore the universe and discover its truths. They wished to serve, and they did. They served all of us.

5   We've grown used to wonders in this century. It's hard to dazzle us. But for 25 years the United States space program has been doing just that. We've grown used to the idea of space, and perhaps we forget that we've only just begun. We're still pioneers. They, the members of the *Challenger* crew, were pioneers.

6   And I want to say something to the school children of America who were watching the live coverage of the shuttle's takeoff. I know it is hard to understand, but sometimes painful things like this happen. It's all part of the process of exploration and discovery. It's all part of taking a chance and expanding man's horizons. The future doesn't belong to the fainthearted; it belongs to the brave. The *Challenger* crew was pulling us into the future, and we'll continue to follow them.

7   I've always had great faith in and respect for our space program, and what happened today does nothing to diminish it. We don't hide our space program. We don't keep secrets and cover things up. We do it all up front and in public. That's the way freedom is, and we wouldn't change it for a minute.

8   We'll continue our quest in space. There will be more shuttle flights and more shuttle crews, and yes, more volunteers, more civilians, more teachers in space. Nothing ends here; our hopes and our journeys continue.

9   I want to add that I wish I could talk to every man and woman who works for NASA or who worked on this mission and tell them: "Your dedication and professionalism have moved and impressed us for decades. And we know of your anguish. We share it."

10   There's a coincidence today. On this day 390 years ago, the great explorer Sir Francis Drake died aboard ship off the coast of Panama. In his lifetime the great frontiers were the oceans, and an historian later said, "He lived by the sea, died on it, and was buried in it." Well, today we can say of the *Challenger* crew: Their dedication was, like Drake's, complete.

11   The crew of the space shuttle *Challenger* honored us by the manner in which they lived their lives. We will never forget them, nor the last time we saw them, this morning, as they prepared for their journey and waved goodbye and "slipped the surly bonds of earth" to "touch the face of God."

Remarks at the Johnson Space Center in Houston, Texas. January 31, 1986

1   We come together today to mourn the loss of seven brave Americans, to share the grief that we all feel, and perhaps in that sharing, to find the strength to bear our sorrow and the courage to look for the seeds of hope.

2   Our nation's loss is first a profound personal loss to the family and the friends and the loved ones of our shuttle astronauts. To those they left behind—the mothers, the fathers, the husbands and wives, brothers and sisters, yes, and especially the children—all of America stands beside you in your time of sorrow.

3   What we say today is only an inadequate expression of what we carry in our hearts. Words pale in the shadow of grief; they seem insufficient even to measure the brave sacrifice of those you loved and we so admired. Their truest testimony will not be in the words we speak, but in the way they led their lives and in the way they lost their lives—with dedication, honor, and an unquenchable desire to explore this mysterious and beautiful universe.

4   The best we can do is remember our seven astronauts, our *Challenger* Seven, remember them as they lived, bringing life and love and joy to those who knew them and pride to a nation.

5   They came from all parts of this great country—from South Carolina to Washing-

President Ronald Reagan (Photo provided courtesy of the Library of Congress)

ton State; Ohio to Mohawk, New York; Hawaii to North Carolina to Concord, New Hampshire. They were so different; yet in their mission, their quest, they held so much in common.

6   We remember Dick Scobee, the commander who spoke the last words we heard from the space shuttle *Challenger.* He served as a fighter pilot in Vietnam earning many medals for bravery and later as a test pilot of advanced aircraft before joining the space program. Danger was a familiar companion to Commander Scobee.

7   We remember Michael Smith, who earned enough medals as a combat pilot to cover his chest, including the Navy Distinguished Flying Cross, three Air Medals, and the Vietnamese Cross of Gallantry with Silver Star in gratitude from a nation he fought to keep free.

8   We remember Judith Resnik, known as J. R. to her friends, always smiling, always eager to make a contribution, finding beauty in the music she played on her piano in her off-hours.

9   We remember Ellison Onizuka, who as a child running barefoot through the coffee fields and macadamia groves of Hawaii dreamed of someday traveling to the Moon. Being an Eagle Scout, he said, had helped him soar to the impressive achievements of his career.

10   We remember Ronald McNair, who said that he learned perseverance in the cottonfields of South Carolina. His dream was to live aboard the space station, performing experiments and playing his saxophone in the weightlessness of space. Well, Ron, we will miss your saxophone, and we *will* build your space station.

11   We remember Gregory Jarvis. On that ill-fated flight he was carrying with him a flag of his university in Buffalo, New York—a small token, he said, to the people who unlocked his future.

12   We remember Christa McAuliffe, who captured the imagination of the entire nation; inspiring us with her pluck, her restless spirit of discovery; a teacher, not just to her students, but to an entire people, instilling us all with the excitement of this journey we ride into the future.

13   We will always remember them, these skilled professionals, scientists, and adventurers, these artists and teachers and family men and women; and we will cherish each of their stories, stories of triumph and bravery, stories of true American heroes.

14   On the day of the disaster, our nation held a vigil by our televison sets. In one cruel moment our exhilaration turned to horror; we waited and watched and tried to make sense of what we had seen. That night I listened to a call-in program on the radio; people of every age spoke of their sadness and the pride they felt in our astronauts. Across America we are reaching out, holding hands, and finding comfort in one another.

15   The sacrifice of your loved ones has stirred the soul of our nation and through the pain our hearts have been opened to a profound truth. The future is not free; the story of all human progress is one of a struggle against all odds. We learned again that this America, which Abraham Lincoln called the last, best hope of man on Earth, was built on heroism and noble sacrifice. It was built by men and women like our seven star voyagers, who answered a call beyond duty, who gave more than was expected or required, and who gave it little thought of worldly reward.

16   We think back to the pioneers of an earlier century, the sturdy souls who took their families and their belongings and set out into the frontier of the American West. Often they met with terrible hardship. Along the Oregon Trail, you could still see the gravemarkers of those who fell on the way. But grief only steeled them to the journey ahead.

17   Today the frontier is space and the boundaries of human knowledge. Sometimes when we reach for the stars, we fall short. But we must pick ourselves up again and press on despite the pain. Our nation is indeed fortunate that we can still draw on immense reservoirs of courage, character, and fortitude—that we're still blessed with heroes like those in the space shuttle *Challenger.*

18   Dick Scobee knew that every launching of a space shuttle is a technological miracle. And he said, "If something ever does go wrong, I hope that doesn't mean the end to the space shuttle program." Every family member I talked to asked specifically that we continue the program, that that is what their departed loved one would want above all else. We will not disappoint them.

19   Today we promise Dick Scobee and his crew that their dream lives on, that the future they worked so hard to build will become reality. The dedicated men and women of NASA have lost seven members of their family. Still, they, too, must forge ahead with a space program that is effective, safe, and efficient, but bold and committed.

20   Man will continue his conquest of space. To reach out for new goals and ever greater achievements—that is the way we shall commemorate our seven *Challenger* heroes.

21   Dick, Mike, Judy, El, Ron, Greg, and Christa—your families and your country mourn your passing. We bid you goodbye; we will never forget you. For those who knew you well and loved you, the pain will be deep and enduring. A nation, too, will long feel the loss of her seven sons and daughters, her seven good friends. We can find consolation only in faith, for we know in our hearts that you who flew so high and so proud now make your home beyond the stars, safe in God's promise of eternal life.

22   May God bless you all and give you comfort in this difficult time.

Memorial on the Death of Matthew Shepard

◆ *James Darsey* ◆

Although violence motivated by hatred of others always has been a part of human history, the 1990s saw growing public concern about so-called "hate crimes." These are crimes of violence against a person because of that person's race, ethnicity, sex, religion, or sexual orientation. On the night of October 6–7, 1998, Matthew Shepard, an openly homosexual University of Wyoming student, was tied to a ranch fence for eighteen hours until he was found. He died on October 12, having suffered burns, a severe beating, and a fatal blow to his skull. The two men charged with his first-degree murder were believed to have been motivated primarily by hatred of Shepard's sexual orientation.

On the night of October 14, across the nation numerous candlelight vigils were held to commemorate Shepard's death. On the west steps of the Capitol Building in Washington, D.C., thousands of participants gathered for such a vigil. Among the speakers was U.S. Senator John F. Kerry of Massachusetts. He opened his speech with a passionate condemnation: "We come here this evening—straight and gay—Americans all—to express our passionate conviction and knowledge that there is no room in our country

◆ The text of this speech was provided by James Darsey and is printed with his permission.

for the kind of vicious, terrible, pathetic, ignorant hate that took the life of Matthew Shepard."

On that same night, in DeKalb, Illinois, on the campus of Northern Illinois University, a candlelight vigil for Shepard was held. Students, faculty, administrators, and townspeople gathered on the Martin Luther King Commons between the student center and the library. King Commons is the traditional place on the campus for the exercise of free speech, for protest rallies, and for memorial ceremonies. Among the various speakers that night was the president of the university. Another speaker was James Darsey, an Associate Professor of Communication and a member of the President's Commission on Sexual Orientation. According to the student newspaper, the *Northern Star* (October 15, 1998, pp. 3, 6), "As weeping, saddened mourners finished singing the last song, 'We Shall Overcome'," they placed their candles on a circular bench surrounding the King memorial sculpture with an inscription around it that reads: "Hatred paralyzes life; love releases it. Hatred confuses life; love harmonizes it. Hatred darkens life; love illuminates it."

James Darsey's brief remarks are not a eulogy in the sense of praise of the deceased's accomplishments and character but in the sense of a memorial that asks us to remember the symbolic significance of the person (1, 8). Shepard as a remembered symbol will live on through audience commitment to fight intolerance and to promote tolerance of difference (7, 8). How does Darsey use the language resources of alliteration and antithesis to reinforce these points?

Darsey's compact and vivid description of Shepard's death (2) powerfully recognizes and certifies the necessary eulogistic transition from present to past, from life to death. Darsey does not have first-hand knowledge about Shepard (as a eulogist often would), but he uses second-hand knowledge to paint a moving portrait of him (3), a description reinforced through alliteration. To what degree would the audience, or do you, understand the historical examples he uses of the "four little black girls in a Birmingham church," of "Lennard Clark in Chicago," and of "James Byrd in Texas" (6)?

A major theme developed by Darsey throughout the speech centers on the fragility the existence of persons viewed as different, persons on the fringes of society (4, 6, 8). He contends that the fragile existence of such persons demands of most of them a special kind of courage every day. Other than variations on the word *fragile*, what other choices of words or phrases help him to strengthen this sense of fragility?

Think of the discussion of eloquence and excellence in public speaking in Chapter One. To what degree would you judge this speech to be eloquent or to possess excellence? Why or why not?

◆ ◆ ◆

1 A human life should never be reduced to mere symbol, but there are times when the life is stolen, and we must salvage what we can. Sadly, this is what we must now do in the case of Matthew Shepard.

2 Five days after he was found where he had been left tied to a fence post for eighteen hours, badly beaten, skull fractured with the butt of a pistol, burned, Matthew Shepard died.

3 I did not know Matthew Shepard, did not even know of him until this past weekend. From accounts I've read, this is not surprising. Matthew Shepard was apparently small and shy and smart and charming, a world traveler, fluent in Arabic, and a recent transfer to the University of Wyoming. And Matthew Shepard was gay. Not in-your-face, militantly gay—as if it should matter—but quietly, perhaps fearfully gay.

4 Described as slight, effeminate, maybe a bit fey, Matthew Shepard knew that he lived in a world in which all that he was, all his lovely qualities and learning could, in an instant, be reduced to nothing with the ugly epithet "fag," or "homo," or "queer," or "fairy." It is a fragile existence to be always vulnerable this way.

5   Every great cause in our history has its martyrs. Some freely and bravely offer themselves, as did the signers of the Declaration of Independence who pledged their lives, their fortunes, and their collective sacred honor to the cause of liberty. The commons where we stand this evening bears the name of another who sacrificed himself, Dr. Martin Luther King, Jr., who said in his last speech in Memphis something that he had always known, that he might not be able to join his people in the promised land. Within hours of that speech, his dark prophecy had been fulfilled.

6   We admire the courage of those who commit themselves to a cause in this way. Others, though, have no choice. By accidents of birth and history, they must be courageous every day simply to live their lives as who they are, subject at any moment and without provocation to be the victims of nameless, unreasoning hate and fear. I think of four little black girls in a Birmingham church, of every woman who has feared to walk alone at night. I think of Lenard Clark in Chicago, of James Byrd in Texas, and now I think of Matthew Shepard, lashed to that fence post in Wyoming.

7   The painful truth is, sickening as such events may be, such brutality takes place in communities that will tolerate it, whether by smiling slyly at the denigrating joke, or by saying nothing to the hateful boast. Our presence here this evening is intended to signal that our community will not be complicit in these ways, that hate and bigotry have no place here and should not anywhere.

8   The lighted candle has long served as a symbol of knowledge over ignorance, of the warmth and security of the home over the wilderness outside the door. Tonight we light these candles to stand against unreasoning fear and to offer comfort, especially in this Coming Out Week to all those who are struggling to balance personal honesty with personal safety. And the fragility of these flames, like the fragility of our memories of Matthew Shepard, should remind us of the great effort and commitment required—every day—to keep our community free of intolerance.

Appendix

How to Use the CD-ROM

SYSTEM REQUIREMENTS

The recommended requirements for PC or Macintosh users:

- Minimum 16 megabytes of RAM
- CD-ROM drive
- 20 megabytes of hard drive space
- Ink jet or laser printer (optional)

INSTALLATION INSTRUCTIONS

Installation for PC Users

- Place the *Contemporary American Speeches* CD in your CD-ROM drive, print side up.
- Double-click on "My Computer."
- Double-click on the CD-ROM drive; it should be labeled *Contemporary American Speeches*.
- Double-click on "Win95" if you have Windows 95, or "Win98" for Windows 98.
- Double-click on "Setup.exe" (the computer icon, not the telephone icon).
- Follow the directions on the screen and DO INSTALL ACROBAT READER even if you already have it.
- After the installation is finished, close out of all application windows.

To access *Contemporary American Speeches*:

- Keep the CD in your CD-ROM drive.
- Double-click on "My Computer" to access your CD-ROM drive.
- Double-click on your CD-ROM drive; it should be labeled *Contemporary American Speeches*.
- Double-click on "Welcome."

Installation for Macintosh Users

- Place the *Contemporary American Speeches* CD in your CD-ROM drive, print side up.
- Double-click the *Contemporary American Speeches* icon.
- Double-click on "Reader."

- Double-click on "Install Acrobat Reader 4.0."
- Follow the directions on your screen and DO INSTALL READER even if you already have it.
- After the installation is finished, restart your computer.
- Close the Acrobat window.

To access *Contemporary American Speeches*:

- Keep the CD in your CD-ROM drive.
- Double-click on the *Contemporary American Speeches* icon.
- Double-click on "Welcome."
- If you have followed the installation instructions, you should be on the "Welcome Page."

INSTRUCTIONS FOR USE

To use, the CD must remain in your CD-ROM drive.

- Once the software has been opened, simply click on the yellow starburst in the lower righthand side that says, "Click here to start" to move through the CD. Clicking on the yellow starburst will take you to the Table of Contents.
- To go to a specific speech, find the speech in the Table of Contents and click. The first page of that speech will appear.
- To move up or down within a single page, use the "Page Up" and "Page Down" keys on your keyboard or click on the arrows along the right margin of each page.
- All of the speeches will have several pages. To move back and forth within a speech, use the "Back" and "Next" links at the top of the page.
- To adjust the viewing size of a page, click on "View" in the toolbar at the top of the page. This will give you a drop down menu that will allow you to adjust the size of the view from "actual size" to a zoom.
- To print the entire speech for hardcopy viewing, open the first page of the speech. Then select your print command.

How to Access the Web Site of Current Speeches

A web site provides selected current speeches along with comments from the authors. For access to this site, go to *www.kendallhunt.com* and click on College Division Catalog→Johannesen→ *Contemporary American Speeches*.